Leadership and Organization in the Aviation Industry

MARC-PHILIPPE LUMPÉ
Air Berlin, Germany

ASHGATE

© Marc-Philippe Lumpé 2008

Published by
Ashgate Publishing Limited
Gower House
Croft Road
Aldershot
Hampshire GU11 3HR
England

Ashgate Publishing Company
Suite 420
101 Cherry Street
Burlington, VT 05401-4405
USA

Ashgate website: http://www.ashgate.com

British Library Cataloguing in Publication Data
Lumpé, Marc-Philippe
    Leadership and organization in the aviation industry
    1. Aeronautics, Commercial - Employees 2. Leadership
    3. Corporate culture
    I. Title
    387.7'068

Library of Congress Cataloging-in-Publication Data
Lumpé, Marc-Philippe.
  Leadership and organization in the aviation industry / by Marc-Philippe Lumpé.
      p. cm.
  Includes bibliographical references and index.
  ISBN 978-0-7546-7144-2
  1. Airlines--Management. 2. Airlines--Employees. I. Title.
  HE9780.L86 2008
  387.7068--dc22

                                                    2007035364

ISBN 978-0-7546-7144-2

Mixed Sources
Product group from well-managed
forests and other controlled sources
www.fsc.org Cert no. SGS-COC-2482
© 1996 Forest Stewardship Council
FSC

Printed and bound in Great Britain by
TJ International Ltd, Padstow, Cornwall

Contents

About the Author

Dr. Marc-Philippe Lumpé is currently holding the position of Corporate Director Quality and Safety Management and Corporate Process Management for the Air Berlin Group in Germany. Prior to that he was Assistant COO for the same company since May 2006.

Before entering management he was a pilot for Lufthansa German Airlines for more than six years, flying the Airbus A320 family out of Frankfurt. During this time at Lufthansa, Marc-Philippe also achieved a Diplom-Volkswirt (the German equivalent of a 'Master of Economics' qualification), a Diplom-Kaufmann (the German equivalent of 'Master in Business Administration') and served an internship at EADS in Munich and Toulouse. Furthermore he began studying for his Ph.D. in Business Administration from Cranfield University in the UK.

Marc-Philippe left Lufthansa in mid 2005 and completed his doctorate in 2006.

List of Figures

List of Tables

Preface

The idea for the following book surfaced while I was working on a research project regarding the best-suited leadership style for the integration of a transnational organization. After having worked for quite a while on that project, it occurred to me that the empirical base of a majority of leadership and organizational theories is to be found in the upper middle and upper echelons of management.

Considering the fact, that these groups only represent a relatively small portion of all occupations to be found in a company, it seemed reasonable to check whether this limited database would have some impact on the results obtained. While searching for an answer to that question it became clear that virtually no prior research existed concerning possible differences between various occupations. Mostly, prior research concentrated on specific occupations and their characteristics without however putting them into any kind of occupational context.

This conclusion led to two questions.

The first dealt with possible differences between different occupations. Mainly, at this stage, it was important to check if there are objective differences between members of different occupations. Furthermore, it was important to find out whether such differences, if they were to exist, had any kind of relevant consequences for the behaviour of the persons concerned.

The second question was directly linked to the first, as it was only relevant if significant differences between different occupations were to occur. It dealt with the possible consequences of such differences for appropriate leadership and organizational styles.

The main difficulty in the present context was the nearly complete absence of prior research. Therefore, it was necessary to develop completely new tools in order to tackle this rather demanding issue. Despite the obvious complications when performing a project dealing with such fundamental research, the results as described below are highly rewarding. Not only it was possible to identify a variety of different mind sets originating in different occupations but, in addition, corresponding leadership and organizational structures could be developed. In particular, considering the large number of cross-functional work teams in any large organization then knowledge about the differences between various occupations and how to deal with them is of the utmost importance. Furthermore, leadership and organizational development and change can take great advantage of the presented results.

Hence, the present book should not only be interesting to scholars, but also to a large variety of practitioners, such as senior management, Human Resources Experts, Experts in Organizational Development and change, etc. Each group may have a different focus when reading this book and may also just pick the individually interesting parts of it. Nevertheless, reading the book in its entirety is most likely worthwhile to all parties concerned, as it gives a comprehensive overview of the different theoretical constructs in use in leadership and organizational research, and immediately shows how they can be put to use.

PART 1
The Theoretical Bases

Chapter 1

Introduction

1.1   The Aim of this Book

The objective of this book is the development of leadership and organizational structures that can cope with the demands exhibited by different occupational backgrounds. It is argued in the current work that these backgrounds create a genuine cultural system comparable to those of organizational and national culture. The construct introduced to characterize this cultural system will be called *professional culture*.

The question as to how far certain cultures influence professional interaction between people has long since been an area of interest to the scientific community. Two different aspects of the term 'culture' have triggered specific research efforts in the past and are still of major importance today (e.g. Dülfer 1992; Martin 1995; Redding 1995).

The first aspect is represented by the different *national cultures* (e.g. the extensive work of House *et al.* 1999, 2004, see also Chapter 4). This approach has been the focus of a wide variety of interests, both from a theoretical and a practical point of view (e.g. Keller 1995; Redding 1995). The second major aspect can be subsumed under the term *organizational cultures* (e.g. Schein 1992, see also Chapter 4), which has also gained remarkable popularity among scholars and practitioners (Martin 1995; Schreyögg 1992).

Given these various activities around different theoretical constructs concerning the term 'culture', it is quite amazing that one aspect of 'culture' is almost completely absent from academic research. This aspect focuses on the above-mentioned 'professional cultures'. In this context it has to be stated that, up to now, no broad-occupational study exists, which has further complicated the development of the above-mentioned leadership and organizational structures (Hofstede 2001, p. 414).

Hence, two major research problems have arisen that have both theoretical and empirical backgrounds.

First, a definition of what is to be considered a Professional Culture has to be developed. This development will be undertaken in Chapter 4 with an initial definition given below. In order to define the term Professional Culture, we should initially clarify the term Culture.

House *et al.* (1999, p. 184[1]) define 'culture' in general as 'shared motives, values, beliefs, identities and interpretations, or meanings of significant events that result from common experiences of members of collectives and are transmitted across age generations'.

Professional Culture can therefore be understood as a culture that emerges as a consequence of a common occupational background.

The second problem was the absence of both sufficiently usable empirical data and appropriate research tools to collect these data. Hence, it was necessary initially to develop a research tool, followed by the collection and evaluation of substantial empirical data, as will be pointed out further below. This book therefore deals with the above-mentioned knowledge gap and consequently intends to create a thorough understanding of the construct of Professional Culture itself and the way in which leadership and organization have to be adapted to the different 'professional cultures' found in reality.

This undertaking is of great importance, as considerable frictions between people with different professional backgrounds who work on the same projects, departments, etc. can be observed across all hierarchical levels (e.g. Schütz 2003; van Maanen and Barley 1984).

Given this evidence for potential inter-occupational conflicts, it is hard to understand how it could be possible to develop theories that deal with leadership and organization without taking into account employee characteristics that evolve due to their different Professional Cultures. This lack of research is even more striking if one considers the above-mentioned extensive efforts in connection with National and Organizational Cultures.

The empirical data for this book were gathered exclusively from companies in the aviation industry. Although one may argue that by sticking to one industry only the results may have an industry specific bias, the following logic led to the choice.

First, the highly competitive environment of the aviation industry puts enormous demands on all actors in this industry. Therefore, it is crucial that each actor performs excellently, which obviously includes the employees of the different companies. This in turn leads to deficiencies within the leadership and organizational structures surfacing more clearly. This specific trait is especially advantageous under analytical considerations, as it emphasizes the requirements that different Professional Cultures have in respect of leadership and organization, so it is obviously a highly favourable trait for the purpose of this book. Furthermore, these demands render our results highly beneficial for the aviation industry itself. Issues such as safety, labour relations, customer orientation and innovation are of prime importance in that environment. Therefore, motivational factors play a decisive role for a significant portion of the employees present in this industry. This in turn implies that appropriate leadership and organizational structures represent a rather important factor in that industry.

Second, the aviation industry unites a vast variety of different occupations. These occupations include, among others, technical, administrative, innovative and service-

---

1   The following abbreviations will be used: p. *X* = to be found specifically on page *X*; pp. *X*f. = to be found on page *X* and the following one page; pp. *X*ff. = to be found on page *X* and the following pages.

oriented occupations of all hierarchical levels. This trait is specifically important for the generalizability of the results developed, since with the Professional Cultures isolated in the current work most functions of any industry can be fulfilled.

Third, the global nature of the aviation industry is highly advantageous. As will be pointed out further below, this trait was necessary in order to compensate for a systematic bias due to possible peculiarities of one or two National Cultures. In this context, it has to be mentioned that all nationalities present have a western background, which implies the possibility that the study has a 'western bias'. Nevertheless, the inclusion of ten different National Cultures in the sample should greatly reduce the danger of an unwanted systematic bias manifesting itself.

Due to these special traits, the results that could be expected by taking the course of action described led to the restriction to the aviation industry.

In summary it can be stated that the research issue of this book is highly complex and incorporates a significant portion of genuinely new aspects. The various challenges encountered in the course of the collection and the evaluation of the data for this book are a direct reflection of the complexity and novelty of the issue at hand and consequently led to a rather complex layout of the data collection process itself.

1.2   Methodological Aspects

Due to the above-mentioned complexity of the issues dealt with, the methodology used to derive the empirical data gained is based on a multi-method approach including an extensive pilot study.

A pilot study is used to develop and subsequently check empirical research tools for their validity and reliability. Validity in the present context means that the research tool used actually does measure what it is supposed to measure, whereas reliability indicates the accuracy of the measurement itself. Weighing scale(s), for example, are valid if they measure the weight of the person using it and nothing else. They are reliable if the measurement taken is correct, and can be replicated if environmental factors (such as the person's weight) objectively do not change.

The first decision that had to be made in the development phase concerned the method itself. Preference was given to a research procedure, which is referred to as *triangulation*.

This term incorporates the use of qualitative and quantitative research methods to the same degree. The quantitative part uses a standardized questionnaire to determine the interconnection between the characteristics of the people questioned and their preferred style of leadership and organization.

After having collected these data, a slightly structured interview was carried out with a number of employees, to get a better in-depth understanding of the underlying processes, preferences and worries of the employees. This course of action was the most promising for gaining the maximum amount of available data.

The quantitative part of the research program was carried out with 507 employees, from 19 companies/independent subsidiaries. The qualitative part was carried out with 84 employees from six companies.

The results can be found in Chapters 6 and 7, which illustrate the interconnection between occupational characteristics and preferred leadership and organizational styles.

Finally an initial evaluation as to the actual superiority of the developed structures will be undertaken. This evaluation will be based on the quantitative analysis of a set of questions from the standardized questionnaire. Details can be found in Chapter 8.

To sum up, the methodological approach used provides a well-founded database, which in turn assured a well-founded and in-depth analysis of the research topic in question.

1.3   The Structure of the Book

The structure of this book is intended to give the reader a thorough understanding of the various aspects of the different topics treated. Hence, Chapters 2, 3 and 4 are dedicated to introducing the major theoretical constructs that represent the base of the later stages of the survey, whereas the remaining chapters will illustrate the results of this work.

Chapter 2 will give an overview of the different major leadership theories that exist today, and also their development. For this reason, the presentation of these theories will follow a chronological order, ending with the most recent approaches to this research area.

Chapter 3 serves the same purpose as Chapter 2, except for the fact that the focus of this chapter will be organizational theories. Here, a chronological approach will also be pursued, ending with the most recent theories of organizational research.

Chapter 4 introduces the term *Professional Culture*. This chapter is of considerable importance since it guides the reader towards the area of interest that is the main focus of the present book.

Chapter 5 illustrates the methodology used and highlights the need for the chosen course of action.

In Chapters 6 and 7 the different leadership styles and organizational structures will be developed that are in accordance with the expectations of the employees surveyed.

Chapter 8 serves the initial validation of these results through the above-mentioned quantitative analysis.

Hence, Chapters 6, 7 and 8 illustrate the core insights gained with the depicted research project. Their findings will be the result of the link between the theoretical constructs illustrated above and the empirical data gained. They are thus intended to show new, different ways of designing leadership and organizational structures.

Finally, Chapter 9 will deal with the question of whether the developed leadership and organizational structures can be generalized beyond the boundaries of the industry surveyed. Furthermore, the relevance of this research project, from both a practical and an academic point of view, will be highlighted.

Chapter 2

The Major Leadership Theories

In this chapter, an introduction to the major leadership theories and models will be given. Starting points are the two classic branches of leadership research: the *uni-dimensional* (participation-oriented) and *bi-dimensional* (task/employee-oriented) approaches. This introduction will be followed by the description of more recent theories, which in turn will be used to elaborate an adequate leadership and organization structure with respect to the developed Professional Cultures (Weibler 2001, pp. 292ff.)

One theory quite frequently mentioned in leadership literature is the 'Contingency Theory of Leadership', which goes back to Fred Fiedler (1967). This theory can be seen as taking an intermittent position between the two above-mentioned branches.

The problem with this theory is that Fiedler (1967) used rather 'questionable measurement procedures' (Neuberger 1995, p. 181) and that it was impossible to get any kind of independent verification for Fiedler's results (Schreyögg 1995, column 996; Neuberger 1995, p.180f.; Jago 1995a, column 629). To make matters worse, Fiedler (1967) used a variety of different explanations in order to adjust his only empirically-based generalizations to a number of different findings (Neuberger 1995, p. 180; Schreyögg 1995, column 995).

Because of these significant shortcomings, it can be stated that the Contingency Theory of Leadership, according to Fiedler (1967), is restricted to being interesting in only the context of the history of this science (Neuberger, 1995, p. 181). For this reason it will not be treated in more detail below.

2.1   Classical Leadership Theories

As an introduction, the most widespread leadership typologies will be described as follows (see Figure 2.1).

They can be traced back to the work of Kurt Lewin (1948) at the Iowa University Elementary School on the one hand, and to those of Fleishman and Hemphill at the Ohio State University on the other. The former typology characterizes a leadership style with the dimension of 'participation-orientation' whereas the latter characterizes leadership with the two dimensions: 'task-orientation', and 'employee-orientation' (Scherm and Süß 2001, pp. 340f.).

The work of Lewin led, inter alia, to reference the most prominent examples: the leadership continuum of Tannenbaum and Schmidt and the approach of Vroom and Yetton (Weibler 2001, p. 299).

The research at the Ohio State University also led to the development of a variety of approaches. Here, the most recognized ones are the 'Managerial Grid' by Blake, Mouton and McCanse and the 'Life-Cycle Theory of Leadership' by Hersey and Blanchard (Weibler 2001, p. 315).

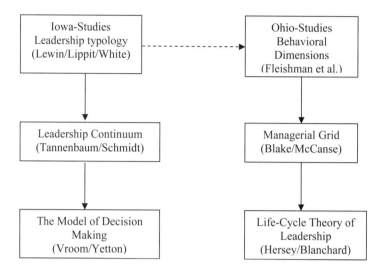

Figure 2.1 The Different Development Stages in Classic Leadership Research

In the following, *leadership* will be defined as the 'influence of others on one's own socially accepted behavior, which indirectly or directly leads to intentional behavior by one's influenced self'[1] (Weibler 2001, p. 128).

2.1.1   *The Degree of Employee Participation as a Reference Point*

The degree of participation is the first dimension that will be described in the following. Despite significant differences in the explicit operationalization of this dimension, all the theoretical approaches take as a reference point the amount of employee participation in the leadership relationship. The presentation of these approaches will be executed in chronological order, ending with the most recent of the classic approaches.

The Approach of Lewin

The historic roots of leadership research can be seen in the work of Kurt Lewin (1948), who examined the consequences of different kinds of leadership on the work of small groups.

The background of this research was that Lewin wanted to prove that it is not certain personal traits of a leader that are responsible for leadership success, but rather, that a certain leadership style, which is completely independent from these personal traits, is the decisive factor. With this approach, Lewin took a definite counter-position to the then prevailing 'Trait theory of leadership', which postulates that certain partly congenital traits of the individual leaders are responsible for their success (Wunderer 2001, pp. 274ff.).

---

1   'andere durch eigenes, sozial akzeptiertes Verhalten so zu beeinflussen, dass dies bei den Beeinflussten mittelbar oder unmittelbar ein intendiertes Verhalten auslöst.'

In his theory, Lewin (1948 pp. 71ff.) distinguished the two 'autocratic' and 'democratic' extremes, to which he later added the 'laissez-faire style' (see Figure 2.2).

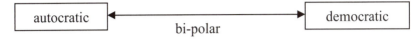

Figure 2.2 The Leadership Typology according to *Lewin*

The autocratic leadership style is characterized by a leader who leads the group tightly, e.g. the leader explicitly commands the individual's goals and actions; whereas the individual does not clearly know the governing goals of the leader.

Democratic leadership, in contrast, is characterized by the fact that the leaders in due time give an overview of the goals to be reached. Their role is much more that of an adviser than a commander.

The laissez-faire style will not be discussed in more detail as it is characterized by the fact that the leader is not exercising any kind of influence upon the group members. Hence, with reference to the above definition of leadership, it can be stated that this 'leadership style' does not really fulfil the criteria for behaviour to be considered as leadership per se.

According to Lewin *et al.* (1939), the key results of this work are as follows. Democratic leadership is, as far as employee satisfaction is concerned, significantly superior to autocratic leadership. However, as far as group efficiency is concerned democratic leadership is only superior when the leader is physically absent.

These results remained controversial as they could only be reproduced with ideologically prejudiced researchers (Seidel *et al.* 1988, p. 117). Furthermore, the significant reduction of possible leadership behaviours, to democratic and autocratic, fuelled lively criticism. The consequence of this criticism was the development of so-called 'leadership continua' characterized by the fact that each leadership style can be localized on a scale limited by the two polar leadership styles (Reber 1995, column 657).

The Approach of Tannenbaum and Schmidt

The most prominent example for a leadership style continuum is the theory of Tannenbaum and Schmidt (Weibler 2001, p. 299).

This approach clearly represents further development compared with the above-described approach, in that it offers a significantly greater number of different leadership styles on the one hand, and a totally different mechanism for choosing one of these leadership styles on the other.

Tannenbaum and Schmidt differentiate between seven leadership styles, which are distinguished by the degree of the employee participation (see Figure 2.3). Furthermore, they postulate that the superior's behaviour has to be adequate to the situation. Hence, they are of the opinion that there is no perpetually correct leadership style. The choice of an adequate leadership style has to take into account three factors (Tannenbaum and Schmidt 1958, pp. 95ff.):

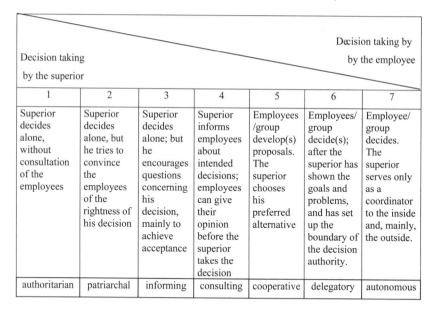

Figure 2.3 The Leadership Continuum of Tannenbaum and Schmidt
Source: Wunderer 2001

1. Characteristics of the superiors,
2. Characteristics of the employees, and
3. Characteristics of the situation.

Characteristics of the superiors include such factors as personal traits of the superiors, their moral concepts and the trust they give their employees. *Characteristics of the employees* refers to their abilities, expectations towards the superior, etc. *Characteristics of the situation* can be seen as the current problem, specifics of the organization, and so on.

Hence, the theory of Tannenbaum and Schmidt can be seen as a decisive step forward, as its progress is twofold. On the one hand it offers a significantly higher number of leadership styles, which permits a more precise description of possible behavioural patterns of leaders. On the other hand – and in the present context that is even more valuable – it introduces the *situation* as an important factor for determining the appropriate amount of employee participation.

However, according to Wunderer (2001, p. 210f.), this approach has a number of shortcomings. First, it is not capable of attributing distinct behavioural effects to the different leadership styles. Furthermore, it is also questionable whether it is possible to create an appropriate leadership model based on a single dimension, i.e. on the degree of participation. The key factor here is that through the sole emphasis of participation it is only possible to examine aspects of power in the leadership relationship, whereas social aspects are not examined at all.

The Approach of Vroom and Yetton

The approach of Vroom and Yetton is intended to give the superiors a tool that permits them to choose an efficient leadership style in every decision situation; efficiency is operationalized through the criteria 'quality of the decision', and 'acceptance of the decision' (Vroom and Yetton 1973, p. 20). Quality is understood to be the objective rightness of a decision (Jago 1995b, column 1062).

The model incorporates:

1. a number of leadership style alternatives,
2. a number of leadership situation determinants, and
3. a number of decision rules.

The leadership style alternatives are AI, AII, CI, CII, GII (see Figure 2.4 for details). The leadership situation determinants are A, B, C, D, E, F, G (see Figure 2.4 for details).

The assignment of the leadership styles to the different situations is performed by the use of seven decision rules (Vroom and Yetton 1973, pp. 32ff.):

1. *Information rule*. If a high quality of the decision is necessary, and the superior does not possess sufficient information; style AI is not to be used.
2. *Trust rule*. If the quality of the decision is to be high, but the employees have diverging goals from those of the organization, GII is not to be used.
3. *Unstructured problem rule*. If the quality of the decision is to be high, and the superior is not in possession of enough information or knowledge to solve the problem, which is furthermore unstructured, AI, AII, and CI are not to be used.
4. *Acceptance rule*. If acceptance of the decision by the employees is important for the implementation of the decided issue, but not assured with an autocratic decision, AI, and AII are not to be used.
5. *Conflict rule*. If acceptance of the decision by the employees is important for the implementation of the decided issue, but not assured by an autocratic decision, and if, furthermore, diverging opinions within the group of employees are to be expected, AI, AII, and CI are not to be used.
6. *Fairness rule*. If the quality of the decision is not important, but its acceptance by the employees is, and which, furthermore, is not assured by an autocratic decision, AI, AII, CI, and CII are not to be used.
7. *Acceptance-priority rule*. If the acceptance of the decision by the employees is important, but not assured through an autocratic decision, and if it is probable that the goals of the employees and the organization are congruent, AI, AII, CI, and CII are not to be used.

As the decision rules indicate only what should not be done, eight out of the 14 solutions permit more than one leadership style. So as to come to an unambiguous decision, Vroom and Yetton (1973 p. 44f.) introduced two more rules, one of which has to be applied. The first is 'speed of decision taking', which implies short-term

A: Is the decision quality important?

B: Do you have sufficient information to take the decision on your own?

C: Is the problem structured?

D: Is the acceptance of the decision by the subordinates necessary for its effective implementation?

E: Is acceptance assured if you take the decision on your own?

F: Do subordinates share the organisational goals, to be attained in solving this problem?

G: Are conflicts to be expected between the employees, concerning the preferred way to proceed?

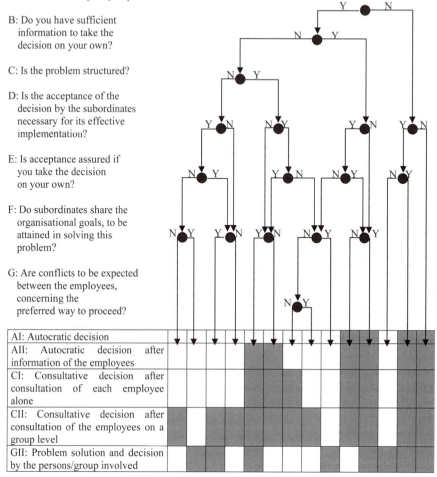

AI: Autocratic decision												
AII: Autocratic decision after information of the employees												
CI: Consultative decision after consultation of each employee alone												
CII: Consultative decision after consultation of the employees on a group level												
GII: Problem solution and decision by the persons/group involved												

Figure 2.4 The Decision Tree

Source: Vroom and Jago 1988

leader orientation. The second one is 'promotion of team-spirit', which is based on a long-term perspective. 'Speed of decision taking' implies the choice of the solution, which is as high as possible in Figure 2.4, 'promotion of team-spirit' implies the choice of the solution, which is as low as possible in Figure 2.4.

It can be stated that Vroom and Yetton continued in the logic of the above-presented model of Tannenbaum and Schmidt. The participation of the employees is once again the decisive variable, which, in conjunction with the situation, serves to choose the appropriate leadership style.

In later studies, the approach of Vroom and Yetton was empirically verified in a number of surveys with different leaders, and found to be valid, both for scientific research and for practical leadership training (Böhnisch 1991; Field and House 1990; Vroom and Jago 1988). These results could not be reproduced in a survey by Field and House (1990), who led a survey among employees. Therefore, the question arises as to how far the positive results of the formerly mentioned surveys were only a consequence of a biased perception of the surveyed leaders.

In summary, it can be stated that this model shows once again the same main weakness of all uni-dimensional approaches in that its sole focus is on the balance of power within the leader–employee relationship. This shortcoming led to the development of the bi-dimensional approaches which, besides the power structure, also model the social relationship between leader and employee (Wunderer 2001, p. 210f).

Furthermore, it seems unlikely that the individual leaders always have time for the necessary performance of situation evaluation, and, even if they had this time, it is even more unlikely that they would be able to switch adequately between the different necessary leadership styles. Nevertheless, in the context of leadership training, this approach is valuable in as far as it clearly emphasizes the importance of the dimension 'employee participation' for the leadership relationship.

2.1.2 The Degree of Task and Employee Orientation as Reference Point

The two main shortcomings of the uni-dimensional theories – the restriction to one leadership dimension and the absence of any explicit link between leadership styles and behavioural effects – led to the development of a number of bi-dimensional theories. Specifically, because of the second characteristic of these approaches, they proved to be especially interesting for leadership development and training.

The three most prominent theories of the bi-dimensional leadership theories will be introduced in the following and, again, the presentation will be in chronological order.

The Ohio/Michigan Studies

The task-/human-oriented approaches had their starting point in the work of Fleishman and Quaintance (1984), who defined, through the recording of different real behavioural patterns of leaders, different leadership styles. These leadership styles were understood in their model to be the independent variable, whereas the effects on employee behaviour were understood to be the dependent variables (Weibler 2001, p. 310).

These research projects, later called the 'Ohio-Studies', led to the isolation of two statistically independent factors that characterize leadership behaviour. This was achieved through a survey in which employees had to rate their superiors on a multi-item scale, which was later the subject of a factor analysis (Fleishman and Quaintance 1984, p. 119). These two factors were called 'consideration', and 'initiating structure' and they represent human and task orientation respectively (see Figures 2.5 and 2.6).

Furthermore, the studies of the so-called Michigan Group, which were pursued at the same time, also supported the insight that it is possible to make a distinction between a human-oriented and a task-oriented leadership style (Ridder 1999, p. 483). The main problem with these approaches is that they are nonetheless incapable

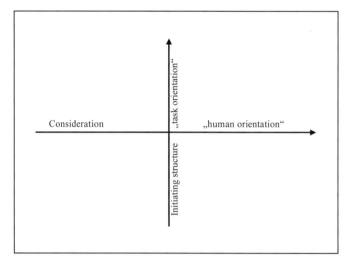

Figure 2.5 The Two Dimensions of the Ohio-Study
Source: Gagné and Fleishman 1959

Consideration (human orientation)	Initiating Structure (task orientation)
• He takes care of his employees • He endeavors to achieve a good relationship with his employees • He treats all of his employees as equal human beings • He supports his employees at whatever they are actually doing, or at what they have to do • He makes it easy for his employees to talk freely and naturally with him • He works hard for his employees	• He reprimands bad work • He urges slowly working employees to make a greater effort • He puts significant emphasis on the quantity of the work done • He reigns with an iron fist • He makes sure that his employees are making full use of their work capacity • He drives his employees through pressure and manipulation to an even greater effort • He demands from weaker employees that they make more out of themselves

Figure 2.6 The Main Contents of the Ohio-Dimensions
Source: Wunderer 2001

of creating a clear link between a certain type of leadership behaviour and its effects. Neuberger (1995 pp. 141ff.) comes to the conclusion that consideration is well correlated with work satisfaction, but that the connection between 'consideration' and 'initiating structure' on the one hand and efficiency on the other is rather vague. Hence, it seems that further factors moderate this connection. For the most part, one can quote the actual effectiveness of the individual superiors, which is a function of their direct superior, and/or the expectations of the employees as far as leadership behaviour is concerned (Kossbiel 1988, pp. 1226ff.).

Furthermore, the validity of the questionnaire used is criticized. This is mainly due to the assumption that the employees have a general picture of their superior to which they then adjust their responses. A high correlation between work satisfaction and consideration would then no longer represent a link between an independent and a dependent variably, but rather one between two interdependent variables (Nachreiner and Müller 1995, column 2121).

Despite these different criticisms, it can be stated that the results of the Ohio-Studies were used for a number of different leadership typologies. The best known are the two described below: the 'Managerial Grid' and the 'Life-Cycle Theory of Leadership'.

The Managerial Grid of Blake, Mouton and McCanse

The Managerial Grid introduces the dimensions of:

- concern for people, and
- concern for production.

Each dimension can occur in nine different strengths, which leads to 81 possible combinations or leadership styles. The graphical representation of these combinations (Figure 2.7), which is in the form of a grid, gave this approach its name (Blake and Mouton 1985, pp. 10ff.).

The five main leadership styles identified by the grid are (Blake and Mouton 1985, pp. 13f.):

- Impoverished Management
- Country Club Management
- Authority-Obedience Management
- Organization-Man Management
- Team Management.

Further, three other leadership styles are mentioned, which are a combination of the main leadership styles. These are:

- *Paternalism*, as a combination of the 'Country Club Management' and 'Authority-Obedience Management'.
- *Opportunism*, which combines the different possible leadership styles to achieve the maximum personal advantage.
- *Facades*, which implies role-playing at 'Team Management' orientation to hide the true motivation.

'Team Management' is perceived as the most positive leadership style (Lux 1995, column 2128).

As this approach is mainly designed for training purposes, its main focus is, in a first step, to determine the individual leadership behaviour by means of a questionnaire. The second step then consists of the development of an individually optimized behavioural pattern, to achieve, as far as possible, the desired 'Team Management'.

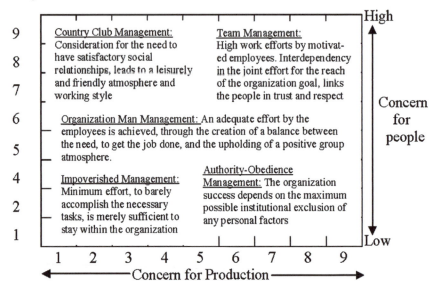

Figure 2.7 The Management Grid
Source: Blake and Mouton 1985

The main problem of this approach is that despite the fact that it was later extended by a third dimension, which was supposed to indicate why the superiors do what they do, it is of highly questionable value from an academic point of view (Neuberger 1995, pp. 189f.). This evaluation is mainly due to the operationalization of the two dimensions, as no instructions are given as to how their measurement should be achieved. The motivation for the specific design of the used questionnaire is therefore not clear. Furthermore, the situational factors that led to the development of the 'Life-Cycle Theory of Leadership' are not taken into consideration.

The Life-Cycle Theory of Leadership

The 'Life-Cycle Theory of Leadership' defines three dimensions (Hersey and Blanchard 1977, pp. 159ff). These three dimensions are:

1. *relationship behaviour*
2. *task behaviour*, thereby taking the situation into account, and
3. the *maturity* of the employee.

Therefore, this approach again utilizes the results of the Ohio-Studies, but augments them by explicitly incorporating the situation into the theory. In this theory, four different levels of maturity of the employees are described, which are to be seen in conjunction with four different leadership styles of the leader. The four levels of maturity, M1 through M4, where 'M' means maturity, are as follows.

- M1 stands for employees who neither want, nor can take responsibility.
- M2 implies employees, who want to take responsibility, but are not able to.
- M3 stands for employees who are able, but not willing to take responsibility.
- M4 finally represents the mature employee who is willing and able to take responsibility.

The corresponding leadership styles (Q), are also numbered from one to four. These different styles are characterized by the shaping of two distinct dimensions: the task and the relationship behaviour. The task behaviour of the superior, for instance, decreases with increasing employee maturity, whereas the relationship behaviour increases initially, reaching its maximum level at an average level of maturity of the employee. After having reached this maximum, it decreases with a further increase of employee maturity.

The bell-curve-like shape of this diagram (Figure 2.8) is the result of the following presumptions. A very immature employee has to be led mostly directly, so that in practice there is neither the need nor the room to give the employee support, respectively an intensive relationship. With increasing maturity, the leadership

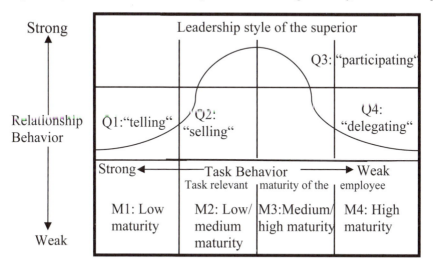

Figure 2.8 The Life-Cycle Theory of Leadership
Source: Hersey and Blanchard 1977

style becomes increasingly cooperative so that the employee, who is still not overly independent, needs a growing amount of supportive behaviour. But with the crossing of a certain level of maturity, the employee needs ever less support so that the supportive behaviour and therefore the intensity of the relationship between the employee and the superior can be reduced gradually, and tasks are therefore increasingly delegated.

This approach claims to be a tool with which a superior is supposed to be able to lead the employees to a state of high maturity. However, a number of aspects of this view are rather problematical. First, there was no survey (not carried out by the authors themselves) that was able to support the central assumptions of this model (Blank *et al.* 1990, pp. 593ff.). In addition, the restriction to one single situational variable, which is furthermore not undisputed because of its content, has to be seen as rather critical. The situation, as it is seen by Hersey and Blanchard, places every problem as the responsibility of the employees, who over and above that are not even able to influence the establishment of their degree of maturity. Finally, it has to be stated that this approach implies a questionable understanding of the harmony between the leader and the employees, as really mature employees supposedly do, with joy and without any objection, what they have to do (Neuberger 1995, p. 196).

Despite these deficits, the Life-Cycle Theory of Leadership gained widespread popularity for leadership training. Furthermore, it can be stated that it is a complete and logical model, although it basically only propounds that a good leader is a leader who chooses a behavioural pattern respectively adjusted to the situation.

The important point of this theory is the emphasis it puts on the dimension 'maturity', which for the first time represented a clear differentiation of leadership behaviour according to the situation. With this special focus on the situation, the Life-Cycle Theory of Leadership goes also well beyond the theory of Tannenbaum and Schmidt (Weibler 2001, p. 328).

2.1.3   *The Different Classical Approaches in Comparison*

As closing remarks concerning the presented approaches, a few aspects have to be kept in mind. Most importantly, it has to be stated that both research branches either neglect the design of the social relationship between leader and employee (participation-oriented approaches), or aspects concerning the balance of power between superior and employee (task-/employee-oriented approaches) (Weibler 2001, pp. 209f.). Furthermore, both assume a given personality structure of the employees, and consider the exercise of influence, although adjusted to the situation, without further analysis, to be normal (Weibler 2001, p. 333).

Concerning the situational component in the approach of Hersey and Blanchard, it is important to remember that, in addition, the restriction to one sole variable and the importance and operationalization of this variable itself led to lively criticism (Wunderer 2001, pp. 310f.) (Table 2.1).

2.2   More Recent Leadership Models

The main branches of recent leadership research can be subdivided into Team-Oriented Leadership as depicted with the example of the SuperLeadership approach,

Table 2.1. The Central Strengths and Weaknesses of the Classic Approaches

Leadership Styles	Main strength	Main weakness
Lewin	For the first time questioning of the conviction that superior leadership is a congenital human trait.	Restriction to only two leadership styles.
Tannenbaum/Schmidt	Enlargement of the bi-polar approach of Lewin, to a continuum and initial incorporation of the situation.	Negligence of social aspects within the leadership relationship.
Vroom/Yetton	Valuable for leadership training to emphasize the importance of employee participation	Same as above, and in addition too complicated to be used in practical leadership situations
Fleishman *et al.*	Integration of social aspects into leadership research.	Link between leadership style and efficiency is not clear. Furthermore, problems with the validity of the questionnaire.
Blake/McCanse	Easily comprehensible realization of the approach according to Fleishman *et al.*	Highly questionable scientific value, as its main focus is leadership training.
Hersey/Blanchard	Explicit consideration of the situation.	The central assumptions could never be independently validated, restriction to one situational variable.

Transformational Leadership, and as a transition from the above described theories, the Leadership-Typology according to Wunderer (Figure 2.9).

2.2.1   The Leadership Typology according to Wunderer

The basis of the Leadership-Typology according to Wunderer (2001, pp. 207ff.) is an integrative approach that joins the participation oriented leadership theories and the human-/task-oriented leadership theories.

Wunderer argues that, in both theories mentioned, either aspects of the social relationship between superior and subordinate or aspects of the balance of power within that relationship are neglected. He therefore proposes illustrating the decision participation of the employees through a first dimension that represents the power distribution in the employee–leader relationship.[2]

The social relationship is illustrated by a second dimension,[3] which is drawn perpendicularly to the first and therefore to be seen as entirely independent.

---

2   Machtdimension der Führung.
3   Prosoziale Dimension der Führung.

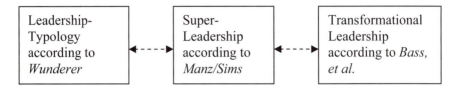

Figure 2.9 More Recent Theories in Leadership Research

Hence, Wunderer explicitly integrates the two aspects of the leadership–employee relationship, which were separately treated in the approaches described above.

The leadership styles themselves are similar to those of Tannenbaum and Schmidt (1958; see also section 2.1.1 for details).

Wunderer (2001, p. 214) focuses on the consultative, the cooperative, and the delegatory leadership style, as he considers these to be of significant relevance (Figure 2.10).

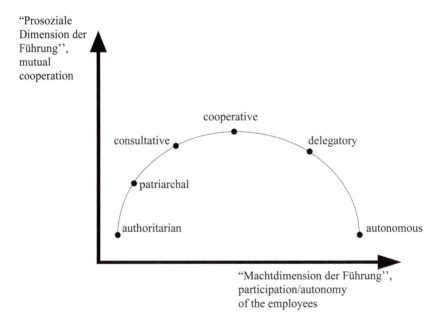

Figure 2.10 The Leadership-Typology According to *Wunderer*
Source: Wunderer 2001

According to the consultative leadership style, the employees act upon the initiative of their superior. They are therefore not merely executing orders, but can participate in the decision process, even though their degree of influence is still rather limited. Consultative leadership seems therefore to be the most promising approach in situations of high stress and/or decision preparation. The main problem with this leadership style is that is does not make full use of the potential of higher qualified and motivated employees. Therefore, it cannot be reasonably used beyond a certain degree of complexity of the task (Wunderer, 2001, p. 219).

The cooperative leadership style is characterized by the enormously high degree of communication between the leader and the subordinates (Wunderer, 2001, pp. 220f.). Furthermore, work-planning and control can be designed in an iterative way, due to the intensive interaction between leader and employees. Hence, this leadership style is the socially most demanding and most time-consuming concept, since conflict solutions have to be reached through negotiations instead of simple orders. Coaching, staff appraisals, etc. are central elements of this kind of leadership. The main problem of this approach is the fact that only an equal emphasis of the so-called 'prosoziale Dimension' and the 'Machtdimension' ensure really cooperative leadership. Especially the 'prosoziale Dimension' will most of the time be the limiting factor, as it requires high levels of social competence from all persons involved, as well as high levels of emotional intelligence. These two qualities are unfortunately hardly learnable, so it is only in special circumstances advisable to use this kind of leadership. Furthermore, self control is used to a limited degree only in this leadership style, and therefore it represents mainly an intermediate stage before reaching delegatory leadership (Wunderer 2001, p. 229).

Delegatory leadership is characterized by the fact that the employees are authorized to take decisions on their own most of the time (Wunderer 2001, p. 229). The direct consequence of this is that there still has to be a positive social relationship between the leader and the employees, but that in comparison with the cooperative leadership style the importance of this relationship is significantly reduced. Therefore, the demands on the leader as far as the above-mentioned social competence and emotional intelligence are concerned, are also significantly reduced, which eases the leadership relationship. A further consequence is that decision activities have to be performed in a more organized manner. Direct leadership is less used and has to be replaced by different alternatives, such as leadership culture, organization, etc.

The main problem of this approach is the high demands on the qualification and the motivation of the employees on the one hand, and the cultural, organizational, and strategic degree of maturity of the company on the other (Wunderer 2001, p. 240). Implementation is therefore difficult and bound to certain conditions, e.g. the quality of the leadership relationship in connection with the prevailing leadership style, since the pace of development must not be too fast. The organization structure needs to be adjusted to this kind of leadership and the employees have to be willing to cooperate, as it requires a high degree of self-responsibility.

According to Wunderer (2001, p. 242), however, delegatory leadership corresponds best to the present developments of the society, and it is therefore to be expected that it will be more often used in the future.

The illustrated approach here represents a very interesting summary of the above-described leadership typologies. Especially when considering it as a transition to the above-described SuperLeadership, the Leadership Typology according to Wunderer is highly valuable. This appraisal is due to the fact that SuperLeadership picks up a number of ideas that are very close to the delegatory leadership introduced by Wunderer. The main problem is that even this rather progressive integration of the two classic approaches is unable to liberate itself from the basic restrictions found therein. Although a number of new ideas are developed by Wunderer, one has to state that this does not lead to a genuinely new theory. In particular, the approach according to Wunderer does not intend to alter the personality structure of the employees. Furthermore, the measures that are taken to influence the employees are not thoroughly analysed, which in turn leads to a leadership relationship in the classic sense (Weibler 2001, p. 333). In the following sections, however, two completely different ways of designing the leadership relationship will be introduced, which propagate a significantly new and highly inventive view of leadership.

2.2.2   Team-Oriented Leadership

The proposal presented here of how to design the leadership relationship represents, in various ways, a significantly different approach in comparison with the others presented in this work. The only theories showing vaguely analogous traits are those of Wunderer and Tannenbaum and Schmidt, since SuperLeadership – as an example of team-oriented leadership – can be seen as being positioned between delegatory and autonomous leadership.

The main idea of this theory is the maximum liberation of the potential of the persons being led. This is to be achieved through a distribution of power that is as equal as possible between the superior and the subordinates (Manz and Sims 2001, p. 45).

The bases of SuperLeadership can be traced back to the Socio-Technical Approach and the Social Cognitive Theory of Learning (Ridder 1999, p. 524). The Social-Technical Approach postulates that it is necessary to focus the leader's attention as much on the accomplishment of the work task as on the individual satisfaction of the employees. This goal is to be achieved via a shift of the decision competence back into the work group. Therefore, it is a plea for the implementation of self-governing work groups (Manz and Sims 1995, column 1876). Departing from this goal, the SuperLeader has to be seen as a leader able to lead the group in such a way as to permit this group and each individual employee eventually to achieve a state of self-leadership (Manz and Sims 1995, column 1877).

The leader has three roles in this phase (Manz and Sims 1995, column 1882):

1. That of a *coach* for the support of the individual professional-learning;
2. That of a *referee* for the support of the individual social-learning;
3. That of an *entertainer* to create a positive group atmosphere.

The Social Cognitive Theory according to Bandura (1986), postulates among other aspects that learning through observation is of significant importance in a learning process. This theory is used within SuperLeadership to illustrate the importance of the leaders as a learning model. The leaders themselves have to demonstrate the kind of behaviour they want their employees to achieve. Through these constant demonstrations of the desired behavioural patterns, the leaders support the reproduction of these patterns by their employees.

Manz and Sims explicitly describe how the leaders can develop the desired self-control in their employees (Ridder 1999, p. 524). The first step for the leaders is to optimize their own behaviour with respect to the set goals. Once this is achieved, the leaders have to make their behaviour clearly understandable for their employees. The people being led have to be supported in the achievement of their self-set goals through the creation of positive thinking patterns. Leadership should be exercised through rewards rather than punishment. These rewards ought to be the result of intrinsic motivation (Ridder 1999, p. 527).

Behaviour is intrinsically motivating if it is in itself rewarding, which means that it is not necessary to use, for example, material motivators to create the desired incentive. Intrinsic motivation is considered to be superior to extrinsic motivation, which could, for example, be the above-mentioned monetary reward (Maslow 1970; Deci 1975; Thomae 1999).

Finally, it is necessary to adjust the organization structure to this leadership style, as teamwork is a necessary prerequisite for its successful implementation. For this process it is vitally important that the top management is actively supporting the implementation of the necessary culture of self-control within the organization.

Even after the accomplishment of this leadership structure, the role of the leaders does not become irrelevant, but the focus of their task shifts. These new tasks imply mainly those of a link to other groups and superior organizations, and the integration of individual contributions into a harmonious whole (Alioth 1995, column 1900). This is again a reference to the above-mentioned roles of a leader as coach, referee, and entertainer. Wunderer (2001 p. 233) spoke in this context about the evolution of the leadership role from that of an author to that of an editor; the editor chooses the authors, motivates them and integrates the different individual contributions into one monograph.

SuperLeadership has a number of interesting consequences. First, a new definition of hierarchy takes place. Command and control are taken as less important and are replaced by strictly team-oriented work. The decision participation is even greater than it is in delegatory leadership according to Wunderer. Especially for the integration of very heterogeneously composed work groups, this kind of leadership is very promising, considering that it becomes increasingly unlikely that a single person can possess the knowledge necessary to competently fill a purely hierarchical leadership position (Yukl 2002, p. 310). Furthermore, it is to be expected that a further positive influence will be exercised upon the employees' motivation, especially with highly motivated and qualified employees.

On the other hand, this feature of the approach places certain restrictions upon the possibility of employing this kind of leadership. Depending on the employee structure, design of the organization, or timely restrictions of the task, it may not always be possible to make successful use of SuperLeadership (Manz and Sims 1995, column 1888). Furthermore, it has to be stated that the SuperLeadership approach is highly demanding for the employees, as it implies that a rational way to solve problems is always possible and is seriously desired by all the employees concerned, which in turn negates the existence of any kind of intra-group concurrence. This implied harmony is in strict contradiction with other highly recognized theories, as for example the Theory of Micro-Politics (Küpper and Ortmann 1986), which leads to certain reservations as to the validity of this assumption.

Despite these reservations, it can be stated that for the further development of the present work, SuperLeadership represents an interesting and, considering its restrictions, also very fruitful theory to lead efficiently, and in an integrative way, work teams.

2.2.3   *Charismatic/Transformational Leadership*

The term 'Transformational Leadership' was used for the first time by the political scientist Burns (1978). Later, Bass undertook some further research and tried for the first time to validate it empirically (Bass and Steyrer 1995, column 2053ff.). The best way to understand this approach is by comparing it with the Transactional Leadership Style.

The Transactional Leadership Style concentrates on the classic interpretation of task- and goal-oriented delegation, which means that the leaders reward employees for following their orders (Wunderer 2001, p. 243). Two different kinds of Transactional Leadership Style can be distinguished. The first is called 'Conditional Reinforcement' and the second is called 'Management by Exception'. The first leadership style, which could also be called leadership through reward, gives rewards always as close as possible to the triggering situation. The latter implies any action by the superior will occur only if there are non-satisfactory results (Bass and Avolio 1993, p. 52). However, the key factor of this approach is that the superiors do not try to change the preferences, values and convictions of their employees. At best, their intention is to reach the optimum for all parties concerned, within their given traits. That in turn means that, in the long run, the achievement of the delegatory leadership style, the most demanding leadership style, is the aim (Wunderer 2001, p. 240).

In comparison, the Transformational Leadership Style has a completely different approach (Figure 2.11). The goal of Transformational Leadership is to modify the values and motives of the employees, to raise them to a higher level defined by the superior (House and Shamir 1993, pp. 89ff.). This transformation can be achieved by the leader through the four behavioural components: charisma, inspiration, mental stimulation and individual consideration (Bass and Avolio 1993, pp. 51f.).

According to Wunderer (2001, p.244), charisma can arise through the conveying of enthusiasm, acting as integrator, behaving with integrity. Inspiration means, for example, motivating through a captivating vision, or increasing the meaning of tasks and goals. Mental stimulation is composed of elements such as changing established thinking patterns and passing on new insights. Finally, individual consideration implies, for example, taking care of employees and supporting employees.

If the superior is able to practise this kind of leadership, a 'performance beyond expectations' can be expected, which implies a level of efficiency that can be achieved with no other leadership style (Bass 1985). Despite this fact, Transactional Leadership does not become useless, but serves to cope with routine tasks, whereas Transformational Leadership is always to be used when there are special, unusual, or especially demanding tasks, to be performed (Weibler 2001, pp. 335f.).

Through a successful combination of these two leadership styles it is therefore possible to have more influence on employees than with traditional kinds of leadership. This assumption goes back to the Augmentation-Theory, which states that Transformational Leadership is a further development of cooperative-delegatory kinds of leadership (Wunderer 2001, p. 245).

The main problem with this approach is the component 'charisma', as the other three can be considered

1. to be employable by significantly more people, and
2. that it is possible to generalize to a certain degree their advantageous effects (Wunderer 2001, p. 247).

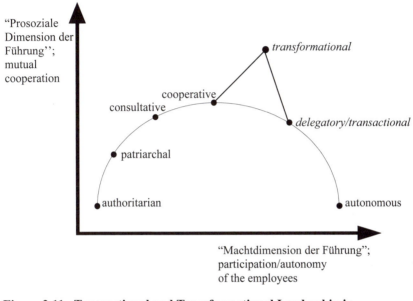

Figure 2.11   Transactional and Transformational Leadership in Comparison
Source: Wunderer 2001

Charisma, in contrast, can be seen as a highly unusual trait. It is only present in very few people and, furthermore, it is learnable only to a very limited degree, if at all. Over and above that, a too great identification with the superior implies seriously dangerous behavioural patterns since following the leader blindly leads, in turn, to the danger of misuse of employees, and there is also the danger of polarizing employees' views, which in turn can lead to serious splits within the group of employees (Wunderer 2001, pp. 278f.).

Furthermore, charisma exists only through its attribution by the employees. This leads to charisma being extremely dependent on success and therefore tending to be unstable over time (Weibler 1997a, pp. 30f.). Finally, Charismatic Leadership is not compatible with other approaches in leadership research, such as for example SuperLeadership in particular, or the cooperative leadership styles in general, as all the activities of the group are focused on the leader (Weibler 1997a, p. 31).

To sum up, it can be said that there have to be three components for a Charismatic Leadership relationship to materialize. These components are (House and Shamir 1995, column 891):

1. the presence of a charismatic person,
2. followers who are willing to attribute charisma to this person,
3. a situation that enhances the emergence of charisma; involving for example a situation of high uncertainty, or situations in which a serious lack of information prevails, etc.

Despite these restrictions, Transformational Leadership is highly relevant for the present work. This is because, on the one hand, three out of its four components can be seen as generally advantageous. On the other hand, in special circumstances, such as for instance in a company crisis, or other highly demanding situations, Transformational Leadership may not only represent the most effective approach, but possibly the only approach capable of coping with that situation at all (Bass 1990, pp. 195f.; Yukl 2002, p. 255).

2.3   Summarizing the Evaluation of the Different Leadership Theories

After the introduction of the different leadership theories, the question arises as to how far they may be useful for the present work.

The first topic to be clarified in this context is whether it is possible for one leadership style, independent of any cultural influences, to be superior to any other leadership style. The proponents of this, who advocate the so called 'culture-free thesis', consider management principles and techniques to be independent of culture and employable always and everywhere in the same way (Scherm and Süß 2001, p. 27).

This branch of research is challenged by the proponents of the so called 'culture bound thesis', who consider management principles and techniques to be bound to culture, which leads them not to be transferable to different cultural environments. This second approach has in recent years gained increasing support, and will therefore be preferred in the following elucidation (Keller 1995, column 1398). Keller (1989, column 238) postulates in this context that certain parts of management, such as planning, production, cost control, or investment calculation, are influenced, by only a relatively small amount, by culture, whereas other parts, especially motivation and leadership, are indeed highly dependent upon culture.

Therefore, it can be stated that the aspects of leadership researched in this work, and in this logic organization design are culture bound, and that it is therefore not possible, for example, to find one leadership style that is superior in all circumstances. Statements such as that of Wunderer, who considered the 'delegatory' leadership style to be superior to any other leadership style, can therefore only be upheld for certain distinct cultures (Keller 1995, column 1402f.).

The main question is, however, whether the cultural influence also extends to the Professional Cultures introduced below, as these have not yet been researched in a sufficiently profound manner. Therefore, the response as to how far the individual leadership theories introduced are relevant for the further pursuit of the present work will have to be postponed until the presentation of the results of the empirical survey.

Chapter 3

The Major Organization Theories

The following chapter is intended to give the reader a thorough understanding of organizational theory and research. In order to achieve this goal, initially a chronological overview of the most important historical organization theories will be given. This course of action is the most promising way to introduce readers to this area of research, and to provide them with the necessary knowledge to understand fully the organizational part of this work (Robbins 1990, p. 30).

Following this introduction, the most important modern organizational theories for the research project will be described. These theories are the *Neo-Human-Relations Approach*, the *Cognitive-Symbolic Approach* and the *Contingency Theory* (Schreyögg 1999, pp. 52ff.). To conclude the chronological description of organizational theory, an introduction to *Complexity Theory* will be given (Stacey *et al.* 2000). This theory represents an example of post-modern organizational theories, which are the most recent developments within this area of research (Weik and Lang 1999).

Finally, a number of approaches are presented, which are intended to pragmatize certain of the theories presented. The course of action will be the same as above, starting with the classical approaches and finishing with the most recent ones. This part serves mainly to give the reader an idea of how theoretical constructs can be transformed into suggestions for the structuring of organizations. This is specifically important with regard to the development of the different adequate organizational structures in Chapter 6 and 7.

In summary, the present section will give the reader a thorough and well-founded knowledge base focusing on the development of the adequate organizational structures described below.

3.1 Classical and Neo-Classical Organizational Theories

In this section, an overview of the historic development of organization theory, as represented by the so called 'Classical' and 'Neo-Classical' theories, will be given. Those two parts are treated together since they trace the historic heredity of this area of research.

3.1.1 Classical Organizational Theories

The very beginnings of organizational research can be traced back to three main basic theories. They evolved in three different countries and from three genuinely different theoretical backgrounds. The first is American (Scientific Management), the second is French (Administrative Management) and the third goes back to the German sociologist Weber (e.g. Mitchell 1982, pp. 17 ff.; Robbins 1990, pp. 34ff.).

Scientific Management

The basis for this approach, which goes back to the American engineer Frederick W. Taylor (1967; initially 1911), is the analysis of specific work routines. The most efficient division and performance of labour was to be developed via this analysis.

According to Taylor, work organization represented a revolution in the way work was performed at that time (Robbins 1990, p. 35). This was due to the fact that, up to then, the prevailing work organization had been oriented on an integral perspective. In this perspective the individual workers were responsible for the whole task, beginning with the work planning, and ending with the quality control of their work (Schreyögg 1999, p. 40).

Taylor's underlying idea was to achieve significant efficiency gains through specialization of the workforce. Furthermore, he wanted to ensure a tighter control over the workforce, as he considered the regular worker to be unwilling to work more than absolutely necessary (Taylor 1967, pp. 13ff.).

Three main principles can be seen in Taylor's (1967) theory. The first is the strict separation of cognitive and manual work. This is to be realized by the implementation of three different functions within a company (Taylor 1967, pp. 35ff).

- The first function is performed by a planning department, which is composed of specialized engineers.
- The second function is the production itself, which is performed by highly specialized workers in a highly standardized manner
- The third function is quality control, which is again performed by highly specialized employees.

The first task, which has to be performed in order to implement Taylor's theory, is therefore, a thorough survey. This survey determines three different aspects. First, it establishes the maximum possible split-up for each part of any job. Second, it optimizes the way each of these elementary works is done by eliminating any unnecessary movement. Finally, the exact time for the performance of each task is calculated (Taylor 1967, pp. 115ff.).

These times led to the second main principle of this theory, the calculated standard time for the completion of a specific task, or the standard performance in terms of quantities produced (Taylor 1967, pp. 38f.). This second principle had as consequence the development of 'piece-work-pay' as we know it today (Marr and Hofmann 1992, column 2147).

The third main principle of Scientific Management is a thorough personnel selection process in order to achieve an optimized fit between the position and the worker (Taylor 1967, p. 61f.).

A further aspect of Taylor's theory is that it also wishes to make use of the advantages of specialization on higher hierarchical levels (Taylor 1967, pp.

122ff.). This means, for example, having a superior for maintenance, another for materials management, etc. In contrast to the above-mentioned part of the Scientific Management, this part of the theory was rather unsuccessful (Kieser 1995a, p. 76).

The realization of Scientific Management has a number of significant consequences for organizational structures, as the differentiation of tasks reaches an extremely high level with this kind of organization. Therefore, organizational costs also climb significantly due to the increased need for integration and coordination (Kieser 1995a, p. 76).

Despite these negative effects on the organizational cost structure, Scientific Management was widely successful, since, as a consequence of the increased specialization, the positive effects outweighed the negative ones by far. This was due to an enormous increase in productivity, which was noticeable at least until the 1970s (Schreyögg 1999, p. 41; Kelly 1995, p. 506).

Negative effects of this kind of organization were observed mainly on the level of the individual workers (Kelly 1995, p. 506), as

- their work became increasingly senseless and monotonous in their perspective,
- they were subjected to omnipresent control.

Despite these negative side effects, Scientific Management was also rather successful among workers, as it very often provided them with a significantly increasing income (Kieser 1995a, p. 77).

To sum up, Taylor's theory was one of the first approaches to formalize organizational structures in a way that made it possible to reproduce the structures themselves as well as their successes. This aspect also gave this theory its name, because it claimed to be a scientific form of company management (Kieser 1992, column 1663f.).

The Administrative Approach proposed by Fayol

The second major classic organizational theory goes back to Henri Fayol. His theory, which was initially published in 1918, is to be seen more as a list of potentially advantageous ideas and principles, than an explanatory theory, like for example Weber's theory described below (Schreyögg 1999, p. 37).

These 'principals of administration', as he called them, are (Fayol 1984, p. 13) shown in Figure 3.1.

The term 'planning' describes the development of the long-term orientation of the company. It is basically intended to give the company its general goals for the future (Fayol 1984, pp. 15ff.).

'Organizing' is seen as an engineering task in which the layout and the implementation of the organizational structure are developed. This structure can be viewed as a technical arrangement of posts, initially without taking into account the people who are going to work within this structure. The main focus is the creation of the most efficient organizational machine (Fayol 1984, pp. 27ff.).

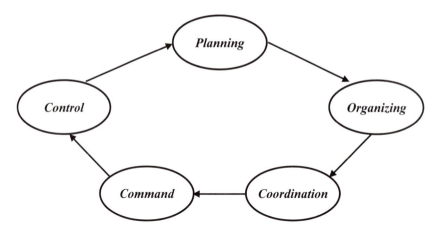

Figure 3.1 *Fayol's* **Principles of Administration**

Finally, integration is performed via 'coordination', 'command' and 'control' (Fayol 1984, pp. 45ff.). The people who fill the working posts in this engineered structure have to fit into it, not vice versa. The main means of achieving this is via command.

The basic guidelines of the Fayol theory can be seen in his 'General Principles of Managing the Body Corporate' (Table 3.1), in which his ideas of how to organize a company are outlined, and which he refers to as the managerial equivalent of the bible (Fayol 1984, p. 82).

The main focus of this work is obviously the way organizations should be structured. This part of Fayol's theory also received much attention in the academic world in its time and was subject to a number of further developments in various other countries during the years following (Schreyögg 1999, p. 38).

The problem of this theory is, however, that it is based solely on the above principles, which Fayol had derived from his experience as a manager. The almost total lack of empirical evidence for this theory, as well as the unclear meaning of the stated principles within the theory, led to a different orientation of organizational research in subsequent years, as can be seen in the following sections (March and Simon 1958, pp. 30ff.).

The Bureaucratic Organization according to Weber

Max Weber's (1864–1920) *Wirtschaft und Gesellschaft* can be seen as one of the most important theoretical works as regards the understanding of the way modern organizations function in state and society. In particular, his explanations concerning 'Bureaucratic Rule' were a major step towards the creation of modern organization theory (Kieser 1995b, p. 31).

The main characteristic of Weber's approach is that he does not set up certain principles, as for example Fayol did, but instead he proceeds to a comparison between the way organizations were structured in his time, and his proposed ideal structures

Table 3.1 *Fayol's* **Principles of Managing the Body Corporate**

---

1. Division of work: Division of work facilitates more and better work with the same effort.
2. Authority and responsibility: Authority represents the right to give orders and the power to receive obedience. Responsibility is the natural counterpart of authority; whenever authority is exercised, responsibility has to be present.
3. Discipline: Discipline is shown through obedience to the demands and conventions of the company.
4. Unity of command: Every employee should have only one direct superior.
5. Unity of direction: All the efforts, orders and actions within the company should be aiming towards a common goal.
6. Subordination of the individual's interests to the general interests: In business, individual interests should not prevail over those of the company.
7. Remuneration of personnel: The remuneration is the cost of services rendered by the employee; it should be fair, and satisfy both the employee and the employer.
8. Centralization: Centralization is a natural part of any organization; all the decisions finally have to end up in one place. The degree to which this centralization goes has to be determined individually for each company.
9. Scalar chain: The scalar chain leads from the top authority to the lowest ranks. It determines the route that all communication within a company has to take. Only in exceptional circumstances can direct interaction between two posts be realized, if the usual way of communication is too time consuming ('gangplank').
10. Order: All employees and everything within the company have to be in their place.
11. Equity: Equity results from the combination of respect and justice. The desire of equity and equality of treatment must always be taken into account in management's dealings with employees.
12. Stability of tenure of personnel: Instability of tenure is simultaneously the cause and the effect of mediocrity in operations and should, therefore, be minimized. Nevertheless it can be costly to retain employees who fall significantly short of their duty. Therefore each company has to find for itself the appropriate amount of personnel turnover.
13. Initiative: Encouraging employees to propose plans and take an active role in their implementation is a substantive task for managers.
14. Esprit de corps: In a company where esprit de corps prevails, each employee is motivated to do his best, to achieve the most positive outcome possible to all his actions, and he is loyal to his company.

Source: Fayol 1984

of an organization. These ideal structures are based solely on the above-mentioned Bureaucratic Rule (Kieser 1995b, pp. 38f.).

The starting point of Weber's work was the increasing importance of major organizations at that time, and their remarkable success (Kieser 1995b, p. 31).

In his approach, Weber develops a theoretical model in which he explains why, according to him, bureaucratically based rule is superior to any other kind of rule. He defines rule as 'the possibility to gain for specific (or for all) orders obedience within a specified group of people' (Weber 1976, p. 122). The basis of this rule can be found in the prevailing regulations of the organization. This definition distinguishes between rule and power, which he defines as 'the general possibility to force one's will upon somebody else' (Weber 1976, p. 542). In this sense, 'rule' is a specific regulation-based kind of power. Orders are only followed according to this logic if their base is considered to be legitimized. If this legitimization is missing, then Weber is not talking of rule, but of power, as the base of obedience.

Weber distinguishes three different kinds of legitimizing rule. These are (Weber 1976, p. 124):

- Legal Rule
- Traditional Rule
- Charismatic Rule

Legal (Bureaucratic) Rule is based on the belief in the legality of the defined structure of the organization, and the right of those who give orders to do so. The main idea is that obedience is not given to people but to regulations, which are equal for everybody within the organization (Weber 1976, p. 125).

The Bureaucratic Organization is characterized by the following traits (Weber 1976, pp. 125ff.). The discharge of office is based strictly on prevailing regulations. This means that, ideally, every action within the organization is regulation-based. Authority and responsibility are strictly separated and can be deduced from the positions. These positions are arranged in a clear hierarchy, which exactly attributes the importance and competence of each of these positions; this ideally excludes any form of arbitrariness. It also includes total neutrality in the discharge of office, which is ensured by the obligation to record in writing, every administrative action taken.

To achieve these goals it is necessary to employ specifically trained and educated people, because only then can it be ensured that the developed regulations are correctly used.

Weber considers this type of rule to be ideal: the one that every organization should aim to achieve, as it is, according to him, 'everywhere ceteris paribus, the most rational form [of organization] from a technical point of view', and that one only has the choice between 'bureaucracy and dilettantism' (Weber 1976, p. 128).

In comparison, 'Traditional Rule' is not considered to be based on rationality. The basis of this kind of rule is the belief in traditions and people and its authority is derived from these traditions (Weber 1976, p. 130). Therefore, the exact design of this rule depends largely on the underlying traditions and individual approach of each of the beneficiaries of these traditions. This kind of rule is obviously in clear contrast to the above described one, which is based solely on rational regulations.

'Charismatic Rule' is not based on rational considerations. As was outlined in Section 2.2.3, Charismatic Rule is based on the charismatic ruler. Charisma is defined by Weber (1976, p. 140) as 'an outstanding trait of a personality, because of which the person is attributed with supernatural, or superhuman powers, which are not accessible to others than the charismatic leader himself, and which render him to be a natural leader through these exemplary qualities' (Weber 1976, p. 140).

Here as well, obedience is obviously owed to the (charismatic) person, which is once again in clear contrast to Bureaucratic Rule and therefore, according to Weber, to be seen as less desirable.

This unconditional preference of Bureaucratic Rule has been the target of a number of critics. These critics are centred on the dysfunctionalities of a too strict following of the rules, the too narrow perspective of organizational relationships and the implied uniformity of ensuing tasks (Kieser 1995b, pp. 50ff.).

The dysfunctionalities of bureaucracy can be seen mainly in an auto-dynamic process in which bureaucracy focuses more and more on following the regulations, even if they are completely inadequate to the demands of the situation. This behaviour becomes especially apparent in situations of organizational change in which at least part of the regulations become obsolete and have to be altered consequently. This in turn leads to strongly opposing behaviour of the per definition regulation following bureaucracy (Schreyögg 1999, p. 35).

Finally, Weber sees social relationships in organizations as purely formal. This perspective excludes any kind of emotionally motivated actions among the employees; at the most these are seen as a disturbing and therefore undesirable phenomenon within the purely rational organization.

In view of the more recent insights gained by organizational research (see also the following sections), this position becomes rather untenable.

Despite the above-described shortcomings of Weber's theory, it ought still to be considered one of the most important works on organizational theory. In particular, the linkage of rule and legitimacy can be seen as a major advance in organizational theory and research. Besides that, it also represents the first theoretical examination of the above-described Charismatic Leadership, and therefore gave birth to one of the most important modern leadership theories, the Transformational Leadership.

3.1.2   Neo-Classical Organizational Theories

In the following, the two most important Neo-Classical organization theories are described. They are characterized by a significant change of focus compared to that of classic research (Robbins 1990, p. 38). In particular, the position of the employee within the organization underwent a significant change.

The Human Relations Approach

The Human Relations approach emerged as result of the so-called 'Hawthorne experiments' (Roethlisberger and Dickson 1947). These experiments were intended to examine the interaction between the working environment and the productivity of the workers. The aim was to establish a stable correlation between the factors that determined the working environment as independent variables on the one hand, and productivity as a dependent variable on the other.

The initial experiment was represented by variations in the lighting. The first results were fully as expected; the more light there was, the better productivity became. The interesting part started when the researchers tried to validate these findings and therefore decreased the lighting again. The results now achieved were totally unexpected: productivity increased even more. Even when the lighting reached a level close to that of moonlight, productivity still went on increasing.

More striking still was that even in the control group, which did not undergo any change, productivity constantly increased.

After attaining these confusing results, the researchers consulted a second research team from the University of Harvard, led by E. Mayo. They produced a comparable environment for the workers, but this time they did not vary the lighting but other variables. The same effect recurred: whatever was done, the productivity increased. Even when the initial working conditions were re-established, a significant productivity gain was still observed.

After thoroughly studying all available results, the researchers came to the conclusion that the variations of the work environment were not themselves responsible for the observed increases in productivity. In their opinion, the increased attention each worker was getting and the extensive possibility for social interactions within the working group were triggering the observed behaviour.

This was a significant change from a theoretical point of view, compared to, for example, the total neglect of any kind of social interaction within Weber's theory. The result of these findings was that, in a follow-up survey, a number of in-depth interviews were carried out. These interviews led to the conclusion that a significant number of employees' problems and complaints did not have their roots within the work process itself, but were the sign of problems not related to their work. Therefore, the social competence of the superiors emerged as a decisive quality, a fact that questioned another basic principle of the classical theories – the sole focus of order and obedience.

In 1931, a further set of experiments was carried out, this time with the explicit aim of gathering information concerning the importance of informal social relationships. In order to achieve this, three distinct working groups were set up. The results clearly showed the importance of informal social relationships. In particular, the emergence of distinct norms within the groups and the establishment of friendships beyond the boundaries of the different groups, even in violation of clear orders from the management, demonstrated the importance of these relationships for the satisfaction of the employees on the one hand, but also for their productivity on the other.

In summary, these works can be seen as a significant turn in organizational theory (Frese 1992, column 1723f.). A variety of hitherto unquestioned principles were challenged (Robbins 1990, p. 39). Furthermore, the focus of organizational research changed and increasingly emphasized the view of the employees. Finally, the established importance of informal social relationships can be seen as a basis of modern team-oriented approaches, of organizational theory.

As a further remark, it should be mentioned that the above-described disturbing influence of unexpected and consequently uncontrolled variables in an experiment was, for the first time, explicitly noticed within this research project, and hence gave the phenomenon its name of the 'Hawthorne effect'.

Theory of Organizational Equilibrium

The main focus of Chester I. Barnard's work, which was initially published in 1938 under the title *Functions of the Executive*, entailed a significant change of perspective compared with the Classical Organization theories (Barnard 1971). He saw the organization as a complex system of actions (Barnard 1971, pp. 65ff), which constantly had to ensure its ongoing existence. This could only be achieved through the maintenance of a number of equilibriums; formal and informal relationships, external and internal demands on the organization, incentives and contributions, etc.

Barnard was the first to define organizations as 'open systems', and thereby changed the classical perspective, which was solely oriented towards the internal organization (Schreyögg 1999, p. 48). Barnard considers every organization to be a cooperative system. His definition perceives any organization as a 'system of consciously coordinated activities or forces of two or more persons' (Barnard 1971, p. 73).

The central topics around which Barnard's theory revolves are the following. If organizations can only exist as far as their members are willing to cooperate and therefore to contribute, then the question is vitally important as to which incentives the organization has to provide to ensure this cooperation. From this perspective, the organizational goal achievement takes on the function of fulfilling the expectations of the members of the organization (Berger and Bernhard-Mehlich 1995, pp. 126ff.).

Compared with the classical approaches, this represents a major shift in the way the relationship between the individual and the organization is seen, and the consequences of this perspective go well beyond these considerations.

The balance between incentives and contributions is not restricted to the direct members of the organization, but extents to every individual whose contribution is vital for the ongoing existence of the organization. In the case of a company, this includes e.g. supplier, buyer, stockholder, etc. The consequence of this view is that the limit between an organization and its environment is vague and subject to constant change (March and Simon 1958, pp. 89f.). Therefore it is highly important, that the organization takes into account the expectation of every individual related to it. This view of the organization leads to one serious implication: if an organization were only based on constantly renewed coalitions, then this would imply a highly unstable nature of any kind of organization. That is why Barnard introduces a 'zone of indifference'. This zone can be understood as an area of acceptance of authority. Every participant of the organization accepts a certain amount of authority. As long as any order given by the respective authority is within this area of acceptance, it is not necessary to renegotiate existing coalitions (Berger and Bernhard-Mehlich 1995, pp. 128ff.; March and Simon 1958, p. 90). With this mechanism, it is possible to perform – to a certain degree – the necessary integration of organizational stability into Barnard's theory.

Another problem of Barnard's theory is the fact that the role of the formal structure of the organization is not made clear. His main interest is the communication within the informal structure of the organization. He considers the informal organization to be necessary for the functioning of the formal organization (Schreyögg 1999, p. 51).

Finally, his view that all the participants of the organization are equally powerful in the negotiations for the respective contracts seems to be, at least, problematic (Ortmann 1976 p. 38). Coalitions are often not the result of free negotiations, but merely a sketch of the existing power structures.

In summary, the 'Theory of Organizational Equilibrium' represents a significantly different view of the organization structure from that of classical approaches. In particular, the emphasis of the expectations of the employees can be seen as a highly important development within organizational research. Together with the results of the 'Hawthorne experiments', the integration of the individual and the organization was eventually seen as a distinct problem within organizational theory and research.

3.1.3 Comparative Evaluation of Classical and Neo-Classical Theories

Comparing the different presented approaches, one becomes aware of the shift of focus within that area of research in the first part of the 20th century. In the earliest theories the employee is seen mostly as some sort of biological machine that has to fit into the ideal organization structure.

This view of the employee underwent a significant change in the neoclassical approaches. The relationship between the individual and the organization became more and more important not only for organizational research, but also for management in general. These changes can be seen clearly in Figure 3.2, which illustrates the increased importance of behavioural sciences for organizational research.

In conclusion, it can be said that organizational theory and research underwent a significant change in the first half of the 20th century, and that these changes paved the way for the more recent theoretical approaches in which the classical understanding of 'organizing' as an engineering task was completely discarded.

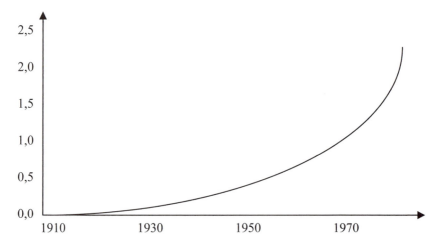

Figure 3.2   Use of Terms per page Originating in Behavioural Sciences in 28 Anglo-American Management Books

Source: Walter-Busch 1991

3.2   Modern and Post-Modern Organizational Theories

In the following, an introduction to the Modern and Post-modern theoretical approaches will be given.

'Modern' in this context means those theories developed after the Second World War that pursued the different directions in organizational theory and research as described above. 'Post-modern' approaches are those that have been developed in the very recent past; which point organizational research in a genuinely new direction compared with the previously described approaches (Weik and Lang 1999).

Observing a chronological order, we will begin with the Modern organizational theories.

3.2.1   Modern Organizational Theories

Modern Organizational Theory is composed of a vast variety of different theories. This implies that it is not possible to unite the different theories under one coherent theoretical concept; nor is it possible to introduce all the theories that have been developed in the past 50 years in a reasonable frame, as far as the present work is concerned.

The choice of theories taken in this section is therefore the result of a strict orientation to the demands of this book. This has led, among other things, to the discarding of various approaches that evolved around the term 'System Theory', since these approaches were never strictly speaking organizational theory, but served mainly as a supply of new ideas and perspectives (Schreyögg 1999, p. 90).

Hence, the reader will find below the three most relevant theories within this context, with the 'Neo-Human Relations Approach' being the bridge between the Neo-Classical and the modern approaches on the one hand, and representing the base for every team-oriented approach on the other. The second theory is specifically important in conjunction with the above-described charismatic leadership approach, whereas the third emphasizes the importance of external variables for the organizational structure. This aspect will prove to be especially useful in the context of the discussion of the Professional Cultures described below.

The Neo-Human-Relations Approach

As already stated, this theory is basically a further development of the Human-Relations Approach. But this further development enlarged that theory significantly as it included, as the main research focus, the organizational structure.

According to the proponents of this theory, the organizational structures were to be redesigned to match the motivational demands of employees (Vahs 2001, p. 31f.). According to this theory, traditional organizational structures, with their emphasis on obedience, suppress any kind of initiative and responsibility and lead to dependency and a lethargic following of regulations (Schreyögg 1999, p. 53).

A number of researchers led these critics, while at the same time developing possible solutions to the problems mentioned. The best known of them are McGregor, Argyris and Likert (see Section 3.3.1), who based their propositions on motivational considerations that went well beyond the mere social relationships of the classic Human-Relations movement. Their goal was to develop structural models that achieved a significantly better satisfaction of individual needs on the one hand and the economical considerations of the organization on the other (Scott and Mitchell 1972, pp. 27ff.). These structures were to be designed in such a way as to reach a maximum level of individual self-realization. In this theory, the way the human being is seen is based on the ideas developed by humanistic psychology, in which man is seen as having the need to develop personal growth (Völker 1980).

The idea behind this approach is to design the organization in such a way that the individual can, through the pursuit of his own personal goals, reach the organizational goals as well. According to this theory, work should no longer be a necessary evil but, on the contrary, a source of joy and self-fulfilment.

Furthermore, it should be noted that a special offshoot of this theory led to the research of organizational development and change (Thom 1992, column 1478). This was due to the fact that the implementation of the concepts of the Neo-Human-Relations school was faced with enormous problems, especially within bureaucratic organizations.

In summary, it can be said that the Neo-Human-Relations research represents a significant enlargement of the Human-Relations school. In particular, its focus on the development and maintenance of motivation is of significant importance; on the one hand, the motivation of the employees was recognized to be highly important, and on the other it was seen that this motivation could – and had – to be cultivated by the organization and its leaders.

The Cognitive-Symbolic Approach

The underlying considerations of this approach are mainly based on criticisms of rationality in the classical, objective sense. These critics claim that rationality is only one of a number of myths created and used by organizations to give themselves meaning, and that therefore a relativized and enlarged view of reality is necessary (Luhmann 1973, Peters and Waterman 1982, Quinn 1988).

These myths are intended to give the individual orientation and support through organizational significance. They are genuinely irrational, as they consider the organizational world to be entirely constituted through symbols. The complete set of these myths is combined in the term 'Organizational Culture' (see Chapter 4).

The theoretical base for this view is taken from a number of different theories; symbolic interactionism, symbolic realism, French symbolism, etc. (Czarniawska-Joerges 1997). The symbolic constitution of the organization is seen as a generic process (Morgan *et al.* 1983, p. 5) in order to emphasize that symbols represent not only the most apparent parts of the organization, such as the company logo, but that the whole organization is represented by symbols. Symbols are characterized by the fact that they possess a meaning that goes beyond their pure appearance (Weibler 2001, p. 381).

The transfer of this theory into practical use came to be defined as 'symbolic management'. It intends to create symbols and symbolic actions that can be exploited to increase organizational efficiency (Pfeffer 1981). This use of symbols has, on the other hand, been in the centre of a great deal of criticism, as the danger of an ethically unwanted manipulation of the employees is evident (Ulrich 1984).

In summary, the Cognitive-Symbolic theory represents a genuinely different theoretical approach to describe organizations and their structures; it led to the intensively pursued research of Organizational Cultures. Furthermore, through the above-mentioned symbolic management, it represents a potentially powerful tool to structure organizations in a highly efficient manner.

Contingency Theory

The main focus of this theory is the empirical determination of organizational structures and their differences on the one hand, and the explanation of these differences on the other. As a starting point, the theory of Weber was usually chosen, out of which measurement scales were developed. These scales served to determine and describe the different types of organization. Furthermore, for the first time in organizational research, the measurement device had to be objective, reliable and valid (Schreyögg 1999, p. 55).

The traits of the Bureaucratic Organization found during these research projects were interpreted as independently varying dimensions, with which it was possible to develop different structural profiles. These results led to further empirical research, through which the reasons for these differences were to be developed. One of the most important research projects in this context was the one pursued by the so-called 'Ashton-Group', which wanted to design a measurement tool that permitted the definition of the differences between the various types of organizations in a coherent manner (Pugh and Hickson 1976).

The starting point of their analysis was the six primary dimensions of organization structure, of which five were operationalized (Pugh and Hickson 1976, pp. 43ff.). These five dimensions are specialization, standardization, formalization, centralization, and configuration (Table 3.2).

The empirical part of the research project was done with a random sample of 46 organizations of different sizes and business sectors (Pugh and Hickson 1976, p. 79). The survey was realized through the construction and use of 64 component scales (Pugh and Hickson 1976, pp. 46f.). With the help of a factor-analysis, three factors were extracted from these 64 scales for further use (Pugh and Hickson 1976, pp.

Table 3.2   Dimensions and Scales of the Ashton Research Project

---

Specialization: The degree, to which work differentiation is pursued.

Standardization: The degree, to which organizational activities are pre-programmed in routine processes.

Formalization: The degree, to which regulations, orders, etc. are laid down in written form

Centralization: The degree, to which the authority to take decisions is concentrated at the top of the organization

Configuration: The design of the organizational structure, i.e. the number of hierarchical levels, percentage part of administrative posts, span of control, etc.

Source: Pugh and Hickson, 1976

103ff.). These factors are:

- structuring of activities
- concentration of workflow
- line control of workflow

They served to generate the seven organization structures of the Ashton-Group (Pugh and Hickson 1976, pp. 120ff.):

1. full bureaucracy,
2. nascent full bureaucracy,
3. workflow bureaucracy,
4. nascent workflow bureaucracy,
5. pre-workflow bureaucracy,
6. personal bureaucracy, and
7. implicitly structured organization

The base of this taxonomy (Table 3.3) is a reflection of the development of

Table 3.3 Taxonomy of Organizations

Full bureaucracy: Highly structured activities, centralized decision-taking, little line control of work flow.

Nascent full bureaucracy: Possesses the same characteristics as above, but to a lesser degree.

Workflow bureaucracy: Highly structured activities, but also highly decentralized, intensive use of impersonal control mechanisms.

Nascent workflow bureaucracy: Possesses the same characteristics as above, but to a lesser degree.

Pre-workflow bureaucracy: Same characteristics as the nascent workflow bureaucracy, but with considerably less structured activities.

Personal bureaucracy: Only a small amount of structured activities, centralized decision processes and highly line controlled.

Implicitly structured organisation: Same characteristics as personal bureaucracy, but decentralized decision-taking.

Source: Pugh and Hickson, 1976

organizations (Pugh and Hickson 1976, pp.124 ff.).

First, the implicitly structured organizations are relatively small in comparison with the fully developed bureaucracies. Therefore, the researchers argue, that with growing size, the structuring of the organization increases.

Second, the researchers stated that with increasing decentralization of authority, the intensity of personal ('line') control decreases, and the intensity of impersonal control mechanisms increases.

The logical consequence of these findings was to ask which the influencing factors were that had led to these results. This branch of research was later called 'Contingency Theory' (Schreyögg 1999, p. 59).

The three main influencing factors that were given by Contingency Theory were environment, technology and size (Freeman 1995, p. 105).

The main results are as follows.

With increasing size, specialization, formalization, and decentralization as well as the use of plans, increase (Kieser 1995c, pp. 162ff.).

In stable environments, bureaucratic structures prevail, while in unstable environments one can expect to find a more flexible organization based on fewer written regulations, less direct supervision, better trained personnel, etc. (Freeman 1995, p. 105; Kieser 1995c, p. 165).

The influence of technology is a lot less clear than that of the other two factors. Only for older production technologies was it possible to establish stable correlations between technology and organization structures (Kieser 1995c, p. 162).

A further development of the environmental branch of Contingency Theory considered not only complexity and dynamism to be the main influencing factors for organization structures, but also National Culture (Schreyögg 1999, p. 61). According to this approach (e.g. House *et* al. 1999) it is vitally important for an organization to create a Culture-Organization-Fit.

In connection with these results, it becomes clear why this theoretical approach was discussed in more depth. The present work will investigate the putative interconnection between prevailing Professional Cultures and efficient organization structures, which would also represent a kind of environmental influence.

Nevertheless, it has to be stated that the initial results of Contingency Theory were rather restricted, and that furthermore the results have not been overly consistent as far as environmental factors and technology are concerned (Schoonhoven 1981). Moreover, the approach was seen as too deterministic, since the role of the organization designer was reduced to a mere execution of external demands.

As a response to these critics, it will be mentioned that recently a major survey, the so-called 'GLOBE-Study', established a clear link between National Culture and required organization structure (e.g. House *et al.* 1999; Jesuino *et al.* 2002; Ashkanasy *et al.* 2002; Szabo *et al.* 2002). This indicates that environmental factors do in fact exercise an influence upon the organization structure, which in turn supports the findings of Contingency Theory.

In summary, it has to be stated that despite various critics, Contingency Theory contributed one major aspect to organizational research (and to this book). This aspect is the relevance of the environment in general, and culture in particular, to the organization and its structure.

3.2.2   Complexity Theory as an Example for a Post-Modern Theory

Complexity Theory represents a radically different approach to organization theory, in comparison to the above. This is because it relies on a distinctively new teleological base, which will be described below.

For the purpose of this section, the differing teleological frameworks define two elements (Stacey *et al.* 2000, p. 14). The first one concerns the kind of future that is to be reached ultimately and which can either be towards a known or an unknown state. The second one deals with the *purpose* of this movement.

Four different goals can be distinguished according to Stacey *et al.* (2000, p. 14f.). These are:

1. some optimal arrangement
2. a chosen goal
3. a mature form of itself
4. continuity and transformation of its identity

Five causal frameworks are then proposed; these are:

1. secular Natural Law Teleology
2. Formative Teleology
3. Rationalist Teleology
4. Adaptionist Teleology
5. Transformative Teleology

The main difference between these approaches is that the first three assume a movement towards a known future, whereas the last two assume a movement towards an unknown future.

The characteristics of the approaches that assume a known future can be described with reference to the work of Kant, who distinguishes between mechanisms and organisms (Stacey *et al.* 2000, pp. 25ff.). Mechanisms follow linear cause and effect links based on Natural Law Teleology, whereas organisms follow a pattern based on Formative Teleology.

The main idea of Natural Law Teleology is that the past, the present, and the future are all only repetitions of the same pattern, and that stability and change is registered through careful observation and by the subsequent formulation of 'if-then' structures. Time is irrelevant in this teleology, as is self-organization. Change is predetermined and therefore entirely predictable. The non-conformity between this view and organizations in reality is evident.

Formative Teleology implies two main aspects. The first is that the final state is already pre-given in an enfolded form and that any kind of novelty and change is therefore only able to cause the unfolding of this enfolded state. Consequently, there can be no true novelty in the change processes. The second aspect concerns the nature of change itself, i.e. the way the final (mature) state unfolds is dependent on the interactions between the concerned parts. Hence, variations are possible, but only within limits that are pre-assigned by the final, enfolded form.

The main problem of this approach is the pre-determination of the future, as this excludes the possibility of humans following autonomous choices. Kant therefore introduced Rationalist Teleology, which, according to his argument, permits autonomous human action so that stability and change are the consequence of these choices. True novelty is possible in this approach, but self-organization is not, which represents one of the main weaknesses of this teleology.

Adaptionist and Transformative Teleology consider the future to be unknown. They are based on the works of Darwin (Adaptionist Teleology) and Hegel, whose views can be seen as the direct opposite of those of Kant (Stacey *et al.* 2000, pp. 30ff.).

Adaptionist Teleology sees change as a process of chance change, sifted through natural selection, which leads to the survival of the most-adapted variations. This adaptive process can best be described through so-called 'fitness landscapes' or 'Evolutionary Stable States/Strategies' (ESS).

The notion of fitness landscapes, which goes back to Wright (1940), sees evolution as the movement across a landscape consisting of peaks and valleys. In this view, the peaks represent a fit and hence well-adapted collection of genes, whereas a valley represents the contrary. The higher the peak and the lower the valley, the more distinctive is the respective trait. In this process, nature is responsible for weeding out the downward moves, thereby keeping evolution (i.e. the chance movement in the landscape) moving towards new, unknown peaks.

According to the idea of ESS (Maynard Smith 1976), change is based on chance variation in the genes and subsequently on a competitive selection. This selection takes place through the search for an ESS. ESS is the biological application of the concept of Nash equilibria (Nash 1996); a Nash equilibrium being a state in which no participant of an interaction is able to increase his expected benefit by unilaterally changing his strategy. An ESS can therefore be seen as a state in which the individual agents' strategies are collectively stable. Hence, an ESS is present if no chance variation is able to produce a higher pay-off than the existing strategy in the interaction of the individual agents.

The main problem of this approach is the fact that it is – to a certain extent – of the Formative kind, as reference is given to some highest peak or optimum ESS that incorporates a certain pre-given best form reached through evolution. Although the Formative frame is always determined by the changing environment, this approach cannot be considered as representing a truly new teleology in comparison with the above (Table 3.4).

Considering the above given characteristics of Transformative Teleology, it can be stated that this approach represents a radically different view from that of the dominant management discourse that is mainly based on Rational and Formative Teleology, for the understanding of complex adaptive systems,[1] i.e. organizations (Stacey *et al.* 2000, pp. 106ff.; Lewin and Regine 2000, p. 6). According to Stacey *et al.* (2000, pp. 123ff.) this is due to the following six aspects.

It has to be stated that:

1. There are severe limitations as far as the predictability of the evolution of complex organizational processes is concerned. This means that creativity and uncertainty are inextricably linked, which represents a significantly differing role of managers in comparison to classic approaches, in which their role consists mainly of reducing uncertainty rather than using it creatively.
2. Self-organizing interaction is central as the transformative cause of emergent new developments of organizations. This also implies conflicts possibly being

---

1   'A complex adaptive system consists of a large number of agents, each of which behaves according to its own principles of local interaction. No individual agent, or group of agents, determines the patterns of behavior that the system as a whole displays, or how those patterns evolve, and neither does anything outside the system' (Stacey *et al.* 2000, p. 106).

Table 3.4   Comparison of Frameworks for Thinking about Causality

	Secular Natural Law Teleology	Rationalist Teleology	Formative Teleology	Adaptionist Teleology	Transformative Teleology
Movement towards a future that is	A repetition of the past	A goal chosen by reasoning autonomous humans	A mature form implied at the start of the movement. Implies a final state that can be known in advance	A stable state adapted to an environment that may change in unknowable ways	Under perpetual construction by the movement itself. No mature or final state, only perpetual iteration of identity and difference, continuity and transformation, the known and unknown, at the same time. The future is unknowable but yet recognizable: the known-unknown
Movement for the sake of/in order to	Reveal or discover hidden order, realize or sustain an optimal state	Realize chosen goals	Reveal, realize or sustain a mature or final form of identity, of self. This is actualization of form or self that is already there in some sense	Survive as an individual entity	Expressing continuity and transformation of individual and collective identity and difference at the same time. This is the creation of the novel, variations that have never existed before
The process of movement or construction, that is, the cause is	Universal, timeless laws or rules of an 'if-then' kind, that is, efficient cause	Rational process of human reason, within ethical universals, that is, human values. Cause is human motivation	Process of unfolding a whole already enfolded in the nature, principles or rules of interaction. A macro process of iteration, that is formative cause	A process of random variation in individual entities, sifted out for survival by natural selection. This is formative cause	Process of micro interactions in the living present forming and being formed by themselves. The iterative process sustains continuity with potential transformation at the same time. Variation arises in micro diversity of interaction, transformative cause
Meaning	Has no time dimension	Lies in the future goal	Lies in the past enfolded form and/or unfolded future	Lies in future selected adapted state	Arises in the present, as does choice and intention
Kind of self-organization implied is	None	None	Repetitive unfolding of macro pattern already enfolded in micro interaction	Competitive struggle	Diverse micro interaction of a paradoxical kind that sustains identity and potentially transform it
Nature and origin of variation/change	Corrective, getting it right, fitting, aligning	Designed change through rational exercise of human freedom to get it right in terms of universals	Shift from one given form to another due to sensitivity to context. Stages of development	Gradual change due to small chance variations at the individual level	Gradual or abrupt changes in identity or no change, depending on the spontaneity and diversity of micro interactions
Origin of freedom and nature of constraints	Freedom understood as conforming to natural laws	Human freedom finds concrete expression on the basis of reason and ethical universals	No intrinsic freedom, constrained by given forms	Freedom arising by chance, constrained by competition	Both freedom and constraint arise in spontaneity and diversity of micro interactions; conflicting constraints

Source: Stacey *et al.* 2000

the source of creative new developments. This also represents a difference from the managers' classic role in which they are supposed to reduce any kind of ambiguity and conflict as much as possible.

3. Individual choice is limited in complex systems according to the considerations presented here. Accepting the view that novelty emerges in relations between people, and that these are largely unpredictable, the idea that a small group can significantly alter or invent future developments becomes untenable. This

is also in stark contrast to the currently prevailing management discourse.

4. The source of stability is seen in Transformative Teleology to be emerging through the relationships of different agents rather than through somebody being in control. This also means that creative development cannot be controlled and that successful organizations have to combine stability and instability. The notion of the 'edge of chaos' is often used in this context. This once again does not conform to the classic view on management.

5. 'Difference' is seen as highly important, as complex systems only evolve when there is micro diversity or fluctuations; therefore, differences between people are also highly important. This does not fit the classic view of management in which harmony and consensus are considered to be the goal for any manager.

6. The movement of stability and change in an organization is a function of the human need to express individual and collective identity, rendering the expression of identity and difference central. In the prevailing management understanding, the central role lies in performance as the main motivating factor.

The main question, which will be considered in the following, is how the ideas of Transformative Teleology in connection with the notion of organizations as complex adaptive systems, can be put into reality.

The notion of an organization as a complex adaptive system leads to a non-mechanistic behaviour of organizations, which mainly implies unpredictable patterns, mostly developing in a non-linear way (Lewin and Regine 2000, pp. 40ff). This is because, as shown above, mutually interacting agents affect each other and every interaction might represent a possibly genuinely new, unforeseeable way. That is why a management guided by the principles of complexity science 'recognizes [...] that relationships are the bottom line of business', and is therefore highly focused on establishing a good and reliable base for relationships (Lewin and Regine 2000, p. 45).

According to Lewin and Regine (2000, pp. 263ff), the way this can be achieved is as follows. The first step for the individual leaders would be to accept that they have neither full autonomy nor control, and that they are neither supposed, nor able always to possess the required knowledge, to cope with every situation on their own. Therefore, in order to be successful, the leader has to develop into someone who works with and for the people, one who finds gratification in cultivating others; this is very much in line with the leader as a learning model in the above described SuperLeadership approach. Thus, the leader's role at the macro level is to recognize patterns, anticipate future developments and to be aware of external influences. On the micro level, the leaders have to see the connections and disconnections within the system and their task is to cultivate strong relationships and connections within but also beyond the system.

A successful leader in a complex adaptive system, one who practices what Lewin and Regine (2000, pp. 271ff.) call paradoxical leadership, has to be

(1) allowing; (2) accessible and (3) attuned.

1. 'Allowing' means, in this context, allowing things to emerge, i.e. not pushing too hard for a possibly premature solution to emerge, allowing paradox, ambiguity, contradiction, uncertainty and redundancies, and finally allowing experimentations, failure and mistakes. This in turn leads to the 'paradox of allowing: direction without directives; freedom with guidance; authority without control' (Lewin and Regine 2000, p. 276).

2. 'Accessible' means being accessible both physically and emotionally. In particular, the second point is highly important, as care is at the hub of building strong relationships, and genuine care demands that all parties concerned are emotionally open. The leader creates, for example, opportunities for people to learn, participate and contribute by allowing people to autonomously select the tasks in which they wish to participate (self-control, self-selection). Thus, according to Lewin and Regine (2000, p. 277), the paradox of accessibility consists of being visible when needed, and invisible when not; of being mutual, being one of the people, but not equal in power.

3. To be 'attuned', leaders have to empathize, listen and respond, be intuitive (not solely relying on facts), discriminative, and deliberate, and they have to have faith and trust in their people, which also means that information is shared without restrictions within the organization. The paradox of attunement can therefore be seen as 'knowing through hunches, intuition, senses and not knowing all the facts' (Lewin and Regine 2000, p. 278).

According to Lewin and Regine (2000, p. 281ff.), a second decisive base for the organization of complex adaptive systems is the creation of genuine teams. This can be achieved through an organizational design that is initially based on a participational structure. Out of this structure, a fluctuating authority in the sense of a heterarchy (e.g. Reihlen 1999) develops, which ultimately leads to collective steering; to teams guiding and controlling themselves. The advantage of a structure based on such teams is that they are more flexible, improvisational and resourceful than hierarchically structured systems, and therefore significantly more appropriate for the organization of complex adaptive systems (Lewin and Regine 2000, p. 299).

Through the achievement of the above-stated goals, an organization built on mutual care is created. This care is present among the people concerned, but also within each participant in the organization for the common cause, as each and every one of them, including suppliers, customers, etc., feels valued and therefore important for the success of the organization. This is particularly important, as because of the nature of complex adaptive systems, it is necessary for the adaptivity of this system that each person concerned is a real participant and not a mere member. This becomes especially clear with reference to the above-stated bases of Transformative Teleology.

Hence, assuming that organizations are in fact complex adaptive systems and that Transformative Teleology is the superior theoretical framework for them, it can be stated that a kind of organization that enhances teamwork, participation, and self-control, is the most adapted organizational design for the success of modern organizations.

As the above assumptions are both rather reasonable within the content of this section, it becomes clear why this theoretical approach was introduced at such length. Complexity Theory is, for the first time in organizational research, able to give a theoretical foundation for the human-oriented organizational 'theories' described in this chapter, and to offer propositions for their realization, as introduced below. Or, as Lewin and Regine (2000, p. 10) put it: 'But it is only now, and for the first time that there is a science [complexity science] behind this way of thinking that gives a realm of human-centered management'.

Furthermore, Complexity Theory is paving the way for an integrative view of Visionary and Team-Oriented Leadership, as it relies heavily on a leader giving the organization guidance and the 'reason why', as well as on a Team-Oriented, Participative approach. In addition, the notions of self-steering, self-control, differences within the organization, etc., and their described superiority support the thesis that it is necessary to adjust both organizational structures and leadership styles to the prevailing Professional Cultures and thus the present intra-organizational differences. In particular, this second aspect renders this approach extremely valuable for the further pursuit of the presented research project.

This is why a truly new and radical approach to organization theory can, according to Stacey *et al.* (2000, p. 55), only be achieved through the 'Transformative Teleology' described below, which avoids the risk of only re-presenting currently dominating explanations in a new terminology.

The main idea of Transformative Teleology, which goes back to Hegel's thinking, is that of a so-called whole, which is under perpetual construction and which therefore never exists in any kind of final state. It is formed by its parts, with which it has a mutual relationship, in so far as it is formed by the parts and also forms these very parts. The absent whole is therefore in the parts, but also emerges from the parts. The underlying idea of these thoughts is self-reference; a phenomenon creating itself. Thus, the identity incorporates the potential for continuity as well as that for change, this being due to two different aspects.

The first aspect is the known–unknown quality of interaction, which means that each interaction has the potential to create something genuinely new as well as just repeating the same thing. This is due to the iterative nature of communication, which can be seen as 'a movement from and toward an as yet unrecognized position that comes to be recognized (known) in the act of communication itself' (Stacey *et al.* 2000, p. 34).

The second aspect relates to time. In the above-described Kantian approaches, time was only related to the macro sweep of time, which consists of the (macro-) past, the (macro-) present, and the (macro-) future, with the present only representing a point in that sweep. In contrast, Hegel focuses on the present and renders it accessible to a living experience, which he splits up into a micro temporal structure.

This micro temporal structure can be subdivided into a micro-past, a micro-present and a micro-future. The micro temporal structure can be seen as a given set of interactions, so that a gesture takes its meaning from the response (micro-future), which only possesses meaning in relation to the gesture (micro-past), and the response potentially leads to a change in the gesture (micro-past). As a result, a circular temporal structure evolves in which the past changes the future and the future changes the past, which allows for the experience of meaning in the micro-present, as well as that of 'presentness'.

Through these thoughts, self-organization goes beyond the process of unfolding an enfolded, pre-determined, final state.

The source of change can be seen in this logic as lying in the detail of interactive movement in the living present which leads to a kind of self-organization that can be considered to be an iterative process of communication facilitating the emergence of true novelty. This is also the main strength of the concept of Transformative Teleology, as it permits the evolvement of the previously unknown.

3.2.3   The Different Modern and Post-Modern Organizational Theories in Comparison

Considering the different Modern and Post-modern organizational theories, it becomes apparent that the most important aspect is the further distancing of organizational theories from any form of scientific management. Although the theories presented emphasize to varying degrees the importance of the individual human being, it is clear that the understanding of the 'human being' as some kind of biological machine has vanished from all theoretical approaches.

As far as the differences among the theories presented in this section are concerned, a very interesting development can be observed. As incoherent as the findings of the varying Modern Organization Theories seem to be, when emphasis is placed on human motivation, symbols or external influencing factors, the findings become coherent once they are considered using the insights gained with Complexity Theory.

Complexity Theory is, in fact, able to integrate these different theories, as brief reference to the previous section proves. Although the creation of human motivation is indeed central to this theory, it does also incorporate the importance of symbols through the emphasis on 'creating meaning', on the one hand, whilst on the other, external influencing factors are also taken into account, since the organization, the complex adaptive system, is not seen to be a closed system, but – by necessity – incorporating every individual who comes in contact with the organization. Thus, the thoughts of Contingency Theory are also taken up in Complexity Theory.

Hence, it can be said in summary, that the differences between the modern organization theories, although viewed initially as significant, are in fact not what they seem to be. Considering the findings of Complexity Theory, they seem to be shedding more light on different parts of the same phenomenon than on the behaviour of complex adaptive systems as a whole. This in turn leads to the conclusion that a real comparison between the Modern Theories is rather pointless as this comes down to a comparison between things that simply cannot be compared.

This again shows the central importance of the findings of Complexity Theory for organization research and, in this respect, for the present book.

3.3   Examples of the Integration of the Individual and the Organization

In the following section, a variety of approaches of the integration of the individual and the organization will be described, which go beyond the classic way of performing this integration through order and obedience.

Here again, a chronological order will be pursued. The starting point will be those approaches that were a direct result of the insights gained in the course of the Neo-Human-Relations School. These theories are regrouped in the following section 'Classical Approaches'.

The three modern approaches described are of a rather different nature, as their bases are a little more diverse. They nevertheless represent a number of highly interesting insights for the further development of the presented research project.

3.3.1   Classical Approaches

As already stated, the integration models described here are a direct result of the Neo-Human-Relations researches. The main focus of these approaches is the above-elucidated inadequacies of order and obedience as the main tool for the integration of the individual and the organization.

The way this problem is tackled varies according to the approach. McGregor focuses on the individual need of growth, while Argyris sees the main importance as fulfilling one's desire to achieve personal maturity, whereas Likert's goal is to establish what he calls 'supportive relationships' throughout the organization. Hence, the way these authors want to achieve their aim varies, but the main question for all of them is how to create and sustain preferably intrinsic motivation.

Theory Y according to McGregor

One of the first researchers to put the insights gained by Maslow (1970, initially 1954) into a concept for organization structure was McGregor (1960, pp. 33ff.).

His starting point is the observation that the design of organizational structures is significantly influenced by the prevailing way employees are seen within a company by their employer. McGregor extracts two ideal types of theories that govern action within a company; Theory 'X' representing the traditional organization, Theory 'Y' representing its opposite (McGregor 1960, pp. 47f) – see Table 3.5).

McGregor postulates that people do not want to be treated according to Theory X. If nevertheless they are, it is probable that an auto-dynamic process will be initiated that will lead to the employees behaving in a defensive manner – according to Theory X. This behaviour is then interpreted by the organizational authorities as the rightness of them treating the employees according to Theory X. As a consequence, this treatment is pursued yet more intensively, which then leads to a stronger reaction of the employees and so on (McGregor 1960, pp. 38ff.); the above-mentioned auto-dynamic process is activated (Figure 3.3).

The solution to this problem is therefore, according to McGregor (1960) that the organizational authorities work on consciously dropping any mental link with a conception of man that resembles that of Theory X. In addition, McGregor

Table 3.5   Organization Action Theories According to *McGregor* (McGregor, 1960)

Theory X		Theory Y	
1.	Man has a innate dislike of work, and tries to avoid it whenever possible.	1.	Working mentally or physically is as natural, as play or rest.
2.	Because of this innate dislike of work, man (the employee) has to be led in a tight manner.	2.	To achieve goals that are self-set and that are considered to be reasonable, people are able to exercise self-direction and self-control.
3.	The dislike of work is that distinctive, that even monetary motivation is not sufficient to overcome it. One will accept the pay, but still demand more. Therefore money alone cannot sufficiently motivate the employee; only the threat of punishment in case of non-compliance to the rules is able to achieve the necessary employee motivation.	3.	The degree to which people feel themselves committed to pursue organization goals depends on the degree to which the achievement of these goals is helping to achieve personal goals at the same time.
4.	The average employee prefers to perform routine tasks, has relatively little ambition, and is mainly interested in security.	4.	The ability to actively participate in the solution of organization problems is widespread within the population, and not only restricted to minorities. The conditions of modern work are only making very restrictive use of the abilities of the average employee.
5.	Most people do not want to take responsibility.	5.	If the conditions are right, people are not only accepting to take over responsibility, but are even actively seeking it.

Source: McGregor, 1960

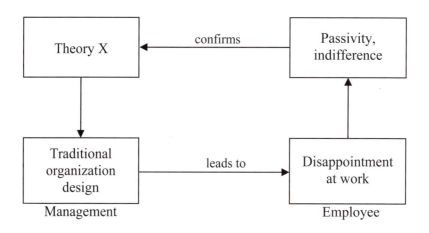

Figure 3.3 The Negative Auto-Dynamic Process
Source: Schreyögg

does not restrict his approach to stating what one should not do, but develops a counterproposal, which he calls Theory Y (McGregor 1960, pp. 45ff.).

Theory Y is also intended to create an auto-dynamic process, but this time a positive one. This can be achieved through the creation of an organizational design that allows the employees to reach their individual goals by pursuing those of the company. McGregor postulates that organizations become more effective if they are able to integrate organizational and individual goals (McGregor 1960, p. 50) see Figure 3.4.

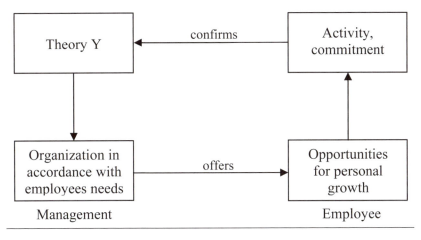

Figure 3.4 The Positive Auto-Dynamic Process
Source: Schreyögg 1999

McGregor does not specify how organizations should be designed but, as shown, puts an emphasis on any action that enhances self-control and the integration of the individual employee into organizational decision processes. This approach is in line with the need for personal growth, as stated in Maslow's theory.

Possible actions that aid the implementation of Theory Y are decentralization, delegation of responsibility, decision-taking in groups, etc. (McGregor 1960, pp.61ff.). The key factor for all these actions is that they create intrinsic motivation, as McGregor considers extrinsic motivation to be counterproductive for the achievement of an efficient organization pursuing the principles of Theory Y (McGregor 1960, pp. 56f.). This view is in accordance with a variety of findings in motivation research (Maslow 1970; Deci 1975; Thomae 1999), as was previously mentioned.

In summary, it can be said that McGregor's concept is a first attempt at the utilization of the insights gained by the Neo-Human-Relations movement. Although it does not yet give a complete model of how an organization should be structured, it does give an initial idea of what the Neo-Human-Relations movement considers to be important in organizational design.

The Maturity/Immaturity-Theory according to Argyris

A more specific proposal for the design of organizations is the 'Immaturity/Maturity-Theory' according to Argyris (1964). He bases his theory not on a need for personal growth, but on a striving for maturity, which is part of human development from childhood to adulthood (Scott and Mitchell 1972, p. 263).

This striving for maturity is seen by Argyris as psychological energy focused on the achievement of expectations, goals, and wishes (Argyris 1964, pp. 20ff). The striving for maturity is modelled by Argyris on the basis of seven dimensions (Figure 3.5):

Immature ————————————→ Mature	
a. Passivity	Increasing activity
b. Dependent on others	Relative independency
c. Only very limited behavioural patterns	Growing number of behavioural patterns
d. Erratic, shallow, superficial interests	Deeply rooted, consistent interest
e. Short time perspective	Long time perspective
f. Subordinate social position	Equal or superior social position
g. Lack of self-consciousness	Self-conscious, control of own personality

Figure 3.5 The Immaturity/Maturity-Continuum
Source: Argyris 1960

These dimensions can be seen as a specification of the human need for growth. The concept of maturity itself is based on Humanistic Psychology, in which man is seen as aspiring to have a fulfilled and meaningful life (Völker 1980).

As regards the importance of the maturity concept for organization design, it is important to understand that the striving for maturity springs not from intrinsic motivation, but is a function of external factors. For instance, the development of self-consciousness is obviously only possible in a social environment (Argyris 1960, p. 10). Therefore, the organization plays a major role in the process of maturing. 'Maturing' can be interpreted as a latent trait that is activated only in specific situations. Furthermore, Argyris views maturing as a process that cannot reach a maximum level. The parallels to Maslow's theory are obvious (Argyris 1960, pp. 9f).

In a further step, Argyris checks on how far the traditional organization is able to fulfil the need for employees' maturity (Argyris 1960).

In order to do that, he uses a model of the traditional organization, which is represented by the following four traits (Argyris 1960, pp. 12f.):

1. task specialization
2. chain of command
3. unity of direction
4. limited control span

Comparing these traits with the above described striving for maturity, it becomes clear that they are highly incongruent. Task specialization, for example, leaves little room for the use and development of individual competencies, whereas the chain of command is mainly intended to keep employees in a passive and subordinate state. The line control of workflow stops the employees from developing and pursuing individual goals, and the limited control span finally leads to the employees remaining dependent and relying on external control of their activities.

The traditional bureaucratic organization therefore inhibits the process of maturing as it leads to a passive and submissive state of mind, dependency, a very limited behavioural pattern, a short-term perspective, extrinsic motivation, and only minimum self-control of the daily work routines (Argyris 1960, p. 14).

The result of this incongruency between the individual needs and the requirements of the organization is frustration, apathy or even open aggression (Argyris 1960, p. 15). The symptoms are that the employees leave the organization if possible, or that they exercise passive resistance, concentrating all their energy on the fight for remuneration as the only means of achieving some kind of satisfaction (Argyris 1960, pp. 16f.).

The organization, on the other hand, tends to react to this with an increasing 'degree of directive leadership', an increasing degree of 'management controls', and an increasing number of 'pseudo human relations programs'. But this only leads to a worsening of the overall situation, as the employees usually react to this with an intensification of the above-described negative behavioural patterns, and so on (Argyris 1960, p. 18).

Argyris proposes the following solution to this problem, which is very much in line with the approaches of his fellows of the Neo-Human-Relations school: the organization design has to be such that individual and company goals can be integrated (Argyris 1964, pp. 272ff.). Specifically, Argyris proposes more individual responsibility, more variety of individual tasks, and more individual control for the individual working environment (Argyris 1964, pp. 228ff.).

As far as concrete measures are concerned, he differentiates between the organizational and the individual level.

On the organizational level, a decentralized, participation-oriented organization structure should be designed. According to Argyris, the degree to which these characteristics are developed is dependent on the situation (Argyris 1964, pp. 197ff.). He does not become more specific on this level, as his main focus is on the individual level.

Concerning the individual level, Argyris emphasizes in his theory the need for an enrichment of the individual work (Argyris 1964, pp. 228ff.). This is understood as a counterpoint to the way work is organized in Scientific Management. The so-called 'Two-Factor Theory' of Herzberg *et al.* (1959) represents the basis for this approach.

The key factor here is the 'individual room for manoeuvre', which is determined by the 'individual room for decision and control', and the 'individual room within the work activity' (Figure 3.6). The former can be interpreted as the degree of authority for planning, organization, and control, whereas the latter can be interpreted as the diversity of the work itself (Schreyögg 1999, p. 238).

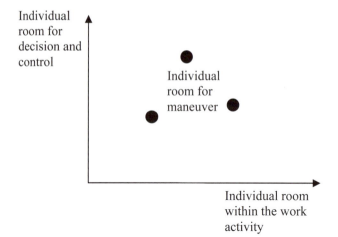

Figure 3.6 The Individual Room of Manoeuvre
Source: Schreyögg 1999

In summary, it can be said that the theory of Argyris is already more specific and precise than the one proposed by McGregor. Nevertheless, a certain lack of specific proposals for the organizational design has to be acknowledged. This specific topic will be dealt with in the following illustration of Likert's System 4.

Network Structures illustrated by Likert's System 4

The approach of Likert is based on three guiding principles (Likert 1967, pp. 47ff.):

1. the principle of supportive relationships
2. the principle of team-work, team-decision, and team-control
3. the principle of a multiple, overlapping group structure

These three principles are aimed at three different levels of the organization:

*   the first principle is aimed at the individual
*   the second at the group
*   the third at the organization as a whole

The main goal of the theory is to develop the organization into a highly cooperative, highly coordinated and highly motivated social system, which is able, under the full use of its technical resources, to integrate into the processes of the organization the needs and wishes of the employees (Likert 1967, p. 76). Therefore, once again, it is intended to make it possible for the employees to achieve, through the pursuit of organizational goals, their personal goals (Likert 1967, p. 47). Likert sees this type of organization in contrast to the traditional organization, which he calls 'System 1' (Likert 1967, p. 50).

One of the major tasks of the superiors within System 4 is to achieve the above-mentioned supportive relationships. Superiors always have to give the employees a feeling of esteem. This can be done by building trust, reducing any kind of distance to the group and giving encouragement to pursue new ideas and possible solutions (Likert 1967, pp. 48f.).

Another highly important factor in System 4 is the group (Likert 1967, pp. 49ff.). Likert proposes organizing as much work as possible as team-work. He argues that, through the group, one can achieve satisfaction of higher needs in the sense of Maslow's theory. In contrast to the classic organization, in which the 'man to man pattern of organization' reigns, System 4 is based on a 'group pattern of organization', which basically means that all members have the opportunity to interact with each other. The basic principle is that, whenever possible, all decisions taken should be based on a consensus; only when this is impossible should the superiors take the decision on their own.

What is more, the organization is to be designed as a network of interacting groups, this being achieved through the principle of the 'multiple overlapping group structure' (Figure 3.7). This principle is realized through the establishment of a vertical, a horizontal, and a lateral network (Likert 1967, p. 50).

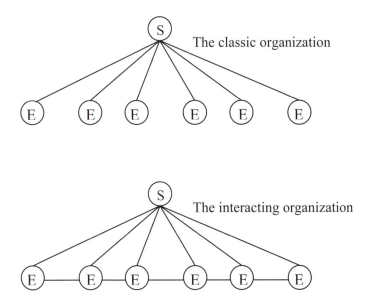

Figure 3.7   The Classic and the Interacting Organization in Comparison
Source: Likert 1967

The vertical network is built with the help of the so-called 'linking pins' (Figure 3.8). As the whole organization is structured in groups, there are groups on every hierarchical level. Therefore, the superior of one group is a member of another group, which consists of the superiors of this level, and so on (Likert 1967, p. 50).

This mechanism is intended to ensure that communication also takes place from bottom to top.

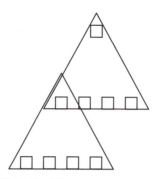

Figure 3.8 The Linking Pin Principle
Source: Likert 1967

The horizontal network is achieved through the establishment of 'cross function work groups' (Likert 1967, pp. 163ff.). These groups can be designed, for example, according to geographical areas or different products. The internal structure of these groups is comparable to those of the line groups. This leads to the individual employee having at least two direct superiors, which in turn guarantees that, in every decision taken, both line and cross function considerations are taken care of.

This design creates a structure somewhat similar to that of the so-called 'Matrix Organization', and therefore tends to develop the same advantages and disadvantages; for example, equal consideration of all parts concerned on the one hand, and strangulation of decisions on the other (see for further details Davis and Lawrence 1977).

The most important prerequisite for the success of this structure is that all the groups in an organization are highly cohesive and based on a significant amount of trust, as otherwise the intra-group friction would become extremely costly. This is due to the fact that every group is linked to a number of other groups, which causes one ineffective group to be a problem for the organization as a whole (Likert 1967, pp. 167ff.) – see Figure 3.9.

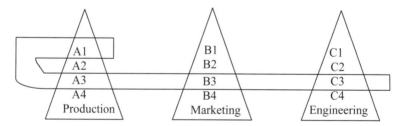

Figure 3.9 The Cross Function Group
Source: Likert 1967

Finally, the lateral network, is achieved through so-called 'cross linking groups' (Likert 1967, pp. 170ff.). These groups consist of members of various hierarchical levels and departments. Consequently, the power structure within the group is based mainly on knowledge rather than hierarchy. Nevertheless, the groups have a formal superior who is responsible for the group (Figure 3.10).

Here again, decisions are to be taken in a cooperative manner by the group. The establishment of such groups is projected if the existing communication and information routes are inadequate, and if the requirements of the problem ask for a rather unconventional competence profile.

In summary, System 4 proposes an organization design that permits vertical, horizontal and lateral coordination. The principle way decisions are taken within such an organization is through the group, and therefore in consensus. Hence, the integration of the individual and the organization is achieved by the group, which in turn leads to the fact that properly functioning groups are the key factor for the success of this design (Likert 1967, pp. 167ff.).

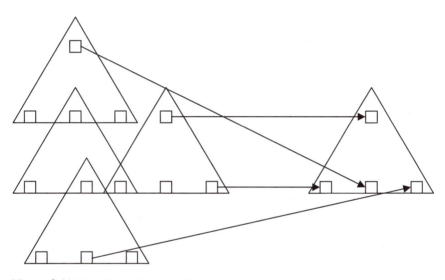

Figure 3.10 The Cross Linking Group
Source: Likert 1967

3.3.2   Modern Approaches

In the following section, an overview of newer organizational models will be given. They can be distinguished mainly by their focus. Significantly, Theory Z emphasizes team spirit as the decisive factor for organizational success, whereas Lateral Organization and Virtual Organization emphasize auto-coordination among the employees.

Theory Z according to Ouchi and Jaeger

Theory Z can be seen as a further development of the above-described motivation-based organization models.

Its starting point was the observation that most Japanese run companies in the US had been highly successful, whereas most US companies, trying to implement their structures in Japan failed (Ouchi 1981, p. 14f.). Therefore, the question arose as to what was the reason for this divergent success. In a further survey, it was discovered that the most successful Japanese companies in the US had adopted a hybrid style between the pure Japanese (Theory J) and the pure US (Theory A) model, which made the Japanese approach compatible with western societies (Ouchi and Jaeger 1978, pp. 306f.; Daft 1989, p. 558). This hybrid model was called Theory Z (Figure 3.11).

Theory A	Theory J
Short-term employment	Lifetime employment
Individual decision making	Consensual decision-making
Individual responsibility	Collective responsibility
Rapid evaluation and promotion	Slow evaluation and promotion
Explicit, formalized control	Implicit, informal control
Specialized career path	Non-specialized career path
Segmented concern	Holistic concern

Theory Z
Long term employment
Consensual decision-making
Individual responsibility
Slow evaluation and promotion
Implicit, informal control with explicit, formalized measures
Moderately specialized career path
Holistic concern, including family

Figure 3.11 Characteristic of Theory A, Theory J and Theory Z
Source: Ouchia and Jaeger 1978

Theory Z is therefore an approach that aims at achieving the attainment of individual motivation and responsibility coupled with team-oriented decision-making.

Because employment is based on a long-term perspective, appraisals are carried out a lot less frequently than in an A-type organization. Although the appraisals also contain formalized elements, they are mainly informal and personalized. Therefore, mutual trust and cooperation are the basis for work relationships. As far as individual qualifications are concerned, career paths are between those of Theory A and those of Theory J, as they are in principle specialized. This specialization, however, is intended to be relatively wide so as to prevent the individual employee from being as narrowly oriented as in type A organizations. Furthermore, the long-term orientation of the professional relationship, combined with the clear orientation towards common values, leads to strong bonds between the employees, their superiors and the company (Ouchi and Jaeger 1978, p. 311).

Theory Z therefore has most traits in common with the other approaches of the Neo-Human-Relations School. The main difference is, however, that the Z-

Organization is designed to create a very strong esprit de corps, which in turn creates a highly cohesive group. According to Ouchi and Jaeger (1978, p. 312) this is achieved via the fulfilment of basic human needs, such as affiliation, belongingness, and love (see again Maslow 1970). Hence, Theory Z proposes to integrate the whole organization into one highly cohesive group, which, according to this logic, evolves into a sort of clan, i.e. 'an organic association, which resembles a kin network but may not include blood relations' (Ouchi 1980, p.132).

In summary, it can be said that Theory Z represents an interesting further development of the classic approaches to organization design. In particular, the emphasis of the esprit de corps in conjunction with a strong Organizational Culture can represent a powerful tool for the efficient integration of the individual and the organization, and thus for creating a highly efficient organization (Daft 1989, p. 560). Ouchi himself favoured the use of his theory or, to be more precise, the use of a 'clan organization' in circumstances of high uncertainty or complexity, in which measures of external control of the employees are not practicable (Ouchi 1980, pp. 137ff.).

Integration through Lateral Organisation

The different approaches to achieving integration via 'Lateral Organization' are of a highly varying nature, but nevertheless all have as characteristic traits individual motivation and independently acting teams. The core of all of these approaches is the employee seen as entrepreneur (Peters 1993, pp. 226ff.). The aim is to reduce the need for hierarchical coordination and instead implement an organization based on lateral cooperation; lateral cooperation being defined by Wunderer[2] (2001, p. 468) as 'a goal and consensus oriented cooperation fulfilling tasks that go beyond the boundaries of single posts and which are fulfilled within a structured work-situation, as a rule by hierarchically and formally equal employees'.

The two main components of this approach are therefore:

* employees who are willing, and able to lead themselves,
* independently acting teams.

This should ideally lead to a high degree of self-control by the employees. Wunderer (2001, p. 489) considers self-control to be the most effective concept for achieving lateral cooperation.

A first step towards the achievement of a functioning Lateral Organization is measures to reduce the power difference between the employees and their superiors. Typical key-terms in this context are 'empowerment' and 'self-organization'.

Empowerment is to be understood as providing the employee with the tools, resources, and discretion to be capable of, and motivated to, furthering the interest of

---

2   'Laterale Koordination wird als ziel- und konsensorientierte Zusammenarbeit zur arbeitsteiligen Erfüllung von stellenübergreifenden Aufgaben in und mit einer strukturierten Arbeitssituation durch hierarchisch formal etwa gleichgestellte Organisationsmitglieder verstanden'.

the organization (Fenton-O'Creevy 1995, p. 155). The individual motivation of the employee is of major importance for the concept of empowerment. Its intention is to achieve an integration of the individual's motivation and the goals of the company: the parallels to the above-described motivation-based models are obvious.

Self-organization – as an independent coordination of different work-groups – is, on the other hand, to be seen as a consequence of successful self-control. The main prerequisite for achieving this successful self-control is adequate room for decision-making, action, and manoeuvrability, coupled with extensive qualification of the employees (Wunderer 2001, p. 617). That is also why empowerment and self-organization/self-control can hardly be dissociated.

Examples of this organization design are the above-described SuperLeadership of Manz and Sims (2001; see also section 2.2.2), the 'network structure of project groups' (Peters 1993), and the concept of 'Loosely Coupled Systems' (Orton and Weick 1990; Perrow 1984, pp. 89ff.).

From the perspective of Loosely Coupled Systems, the organization can be seen as a network of relatively autonomous entities (individuals, subunits, hierarchical levels, etc.) whose interactions are neither predetermined nor formalized. Interaction takes place through self-organization as to how to find the best possible answer to the present task. Because of the extreme flexibility of the organization's structure it is hoped that the flexibility of the whole organization and its ability to assimilate complexity can be increased significantly.

As individual demands on each employee also increase thanks to this increased flexibility, it can be assumed that individual motivation is also being influenced positively. This consideration is due to the fact that motivational variables such as self-control, task variety, etc. are directly positively influenced by this kind of organization.

In summary, it can be said that the concept of Lateral Organization is an interesting further development of the above-described motivation-based approaches. It uses them to develop a number of theories that are fairly well adapted to the demands of modern organizations. In particular, the emphasis on teamwork, independent interaction within the workforce, and Loosely Coupled Systems led to the development of highly recognized theoretical models such as the above-described SuperLeadership (see section 2.2.2 for details), or the theory of the Virtual Organization, described below.

The Virtual Organization

The 'Virtual Organization' is a rather new development in organizational theory. The beginnings of this approach can be traced back to the beginning of the 1980s. This theory can be seen as a further development of the above described Loosely Coupled Systems. A Virtual Organization is basically a network of independently acting entities, relying mainly on self-organization (Faucheux 1997, p. 51). These entities can be individuals, parts of organizations, or complete organizations (Shao *et al.* 1998, p. 305).

The characteristics of a Virtual Organization can be illustrated by the following model, which was developed by Saabeel *et al.* (2002, pp. 9ff.). It consists of the three elements:

1. Universe of Modules
2. Dynamic Web
3. Dynamic Organization

The 'Universe of Modules' can be seen as the set of all entities. This can be, for example, all automobile industry organizations including the supplier, the car producers, the customers and so on, in other words every entity that is in touch with that specific industry (Venkatraman and Henderson 1998). This universe is characterized by uncertainty, complexity and interdependence (Scott 1998, p. 229f.). To reduce these unwanted features of the Universe of Modules, the entities (the modules) can organize themselves into a Dynamic Web.

The 'Dynamic Web' is defined as all entities having a predisposition to work together (Goldman *et al.* 1995, pp. 220ff.). It is therefore not really a closed system, as new entities may join and others may leave. The base for the Dynamic Web can be already existing business contacts, realized partnerships, expectations for the realization of synergies, etc. Hence, these entities have some common ground, which leads to the expectation that cooperation could be beneficial to them in the future.

This common ground is characterized by Shao *et al.* (1998, pp. 309ff.) as:

- purpose
- connectivity
- boundary
- information technology

The 'purpose' is a result of a common view of the market and the expected beneficial consequences of sharing the different resources and competencies of the participants. The motivation to exploit those identified benefits is the 'connectivity'. The 'boundary' of the Dynamic Web is defined by the mutually agreed purpose. The key task of the Dynamic Web is the pre-selection of new members. It has to ensure that a new member actually strengthens the web, but also that it fits into the web. In principle, a new entity can be seen as having a high chance of qualifying for this web if it possesses new, partly overlapping competencies (Saabeel *et al.* 2002, p. 10f.).

Finally, it is important that the members are able to bridge even wide geographical gaps. That is why a coherent and highly powerful information technology in each entity is essential (Venkatraman and Henderson 1998, pp. 34f.; Shao *et al.* 1998, p. 310).

If then, at a certain point, the expectation of a beneficial cooperation becomes a real possibility – for example, thanks to a market opportunity, the Virtual Organization can be realized (Hardwick and Bolton 1997, p. 59) – the Dynamic Organization is born. The Virtual Organization (Figure 3.12) is consequently a cooperation between a part of the Dynamic Web and, furthermore, it is strictly goal oriented (Faucheux

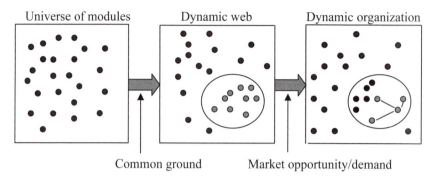

Figure 3.12 The Genesis of the Virtual Organisation
Source: Saabeel, *et al.* 2002

1997, p. 51; Mowshowitz 1997, pp. 33ff.). That means that after the beneficial outcome of the market opportunity/demand is achieved, or after it has ceased to exist, the cooperation ceases, and all entities concerned return into the Dynamic Web (Goldman *et al.* 1995, p. 172).

In summary, it can be said that the Virtual Organization is a highly interesting development in organization theory and research. This is especially true, considering the significant problems with the management of complexity as described in section 3.2.2.

The Virtual Organization can be seen as a possible solution to the problems stated in that section, and is therefore a highly promising theoretical approach for the future.

3.3.3   The Different Approaches in Comparison

The different integration models can be subdivided into two groups. The first group has as its main focus the 'human beings' and their 'motivation', whereas the second group focuses on 'auto-coordination'.

Regarding the first group, it should be mentioned that both the approach of McGregor and that of Argyris are lacking in sufficient focus on the organizational structures themselves, as they almost exclusively deal with the motivational base of the individual human being. This shortcoming can be seen as a direct effect of these models being developed with the help of the (Neo-) Human-Relations School, which admittedly explains it, but does not justify it. Likert apparently recognized this problem and developed a distinct organization model, through which he hoped to achieve the intended effects on the individual's motivation. It can be said that this trait of Likert's approach represents a significant further development of the approaches of McGregor and Argyris.

The second group of organization models, which consists of the concepts of Lateral Organization and Virtual Organization, is distinctively different from the first. Evidently, these equally want to achieve an increased motivation of the employees, but their focus is not solely on this mission, but on a genuinely different way of designing the organization. This revolves around the idea of team-based organization, which intends to make the best possible use of each employee, through higher flexibility, less line control, increased importance of competence in lieu of hierarchy, etc. That these measures also tend to increase the individual's motivation is, of course, a welcome by-product, but only part of the global goal of these models. From this aspect, they can be seen as a further development of the models in the first group, incorporating them into a broader global picture for the development of organizational structures.

Theory Z can, as already stated, be positioned between these groups, as on the one hand it focuses on teams, while on the other it cannot negate a certain proximity to the ideas of McGregor.

To sum up, it can be stated that the models for the integration of the individual and the organization evidently followed the development of the underlying organization theories, the most radical ideas being present in a Lateral Organization, and even more so in a Virtual Organization. In particular, the Virtual Organization with its small entities and its self-organizing modus operandi can be seen as an interesting approach for incorporating the insights gained within Complexity Theory, not only on a micro level (different individuals participating in one organization), but also on a macro level (different organizations interacting with each other).

Chapter 4

Professional Cultures

In this chapter, the theoretical construct 'Professional Culture' will be introduced. It will be shown why the existing concepts of 'culture' in dominant research, as being either National or Organizational Cultures, are not sufficient.

In order to do this, the term *Professional Culture* will first be defined: what are its characteristics and in what aspects is it distinct from concurring cultural concepts?

In addition, a short overview of the traditional perspectives of perceiving cultures will be given, in order to allow a comparison between the different cultural concepts.

Furthermore, it will be assumed that the approach of analytically exploring and thus explaining cultures in general is a viable way to understand this phenomenon. This also entails discarding voices that reject such a way of thinking altogether as being too 'reductionist' or too deeply rooted in standard western ways of thinking (e.g. Lowe 2002).

Thus, it will be demonstrated in this chapter that it is necessary to include Professional Cultures in cultural research in general, and in organizational and leadership research in particular, in order to obtain a more accurate understanding of the inter-subjective and intra-subjective processes within organizations.

4.1   Introduction of the Concept 'Professional Culture'

In order to elucidate the concept of Professional Culture and its importance for organizational and leadership theory and research, the term itself must first be defined. This will be achieved by examining the components of this concept. Following these introductory definitions, we will proceed to the description of the theoretical construct of Professional Culture as it will be used throughout this book.

Finally, a short evaluation of the results of this section will be given, to provide for a seamless transition to the following section.

4.1.1   The Components of a Professional Culture

The term Professional Culture comprises two distinct parts: 'Profession' and 'Culture'. These should be seen separately if they are to be fully understood.

The term culture has already been defined in Section 1.1 'as shared motives, values, believes, identities, and interpretations, or meanings of significant events that result from common experiences of members of collectives and are transmitted across age generations'. This definition is not tied to a specific understanding of culture as national or organizational and will therefore also be used in respect of Professional Cultures. However, the term 'profession' needs some further clarification.

Theories of professionalization and the derivative term profession can be traced back to four different basic views (Abbott 1991, p. 356f.):

1. the *relations to the state* view
2. the *functionalist* view
3. the *power* view
4. the *importance of knowledge* view

The first approach sees relations to the state as decisive for a profession and goes mainly back to continental European theorists (Abbott 1991, p. 357). The role of the state in this view is to regulate the profession and therefore limit outsider's access to it. Hence, the distinctive characteristics of the profession are established and protected by the state (e.g. Freidson 1986, pp. 63ff.; Georg 1993; Dingwall 1999). This limited access is, then, the base for the special importance the occupation may gain for the respective clients, depending on its actual importance for them.

The functionalist view sees a profession as the product of 'a special relationship between client and professional' (Abbott 1991, p. 356). This relationship is based on specific norms involving, for instance, expertise, competencies, social standards and ethics, which guarantee this relationship and the identification of each member with the profession (e.g. Raelin 1985, p. 9; Brien 1998, pp. 396f.). Expertise and competence are understood to be the product of extensive and prolonged specialized education in abstract knowledge. Social standards, on the other hand, lead to the professionals committing themselves to helping to police the conduct of fellow professionals, whereas 'ethics' implies an almost altruistic orientation of the professional in rendering the expected service.

Hence, the professional is seen here as practising an occupation that requires highly sophisticated education or training with the sole goal of producing the expected service.

The power view (e.g. Forsyth and Danisiewicz 1985) basically considers the same aspects, but from a different angle. Power, as it is understood in this theory, is based on the above-mentioned characteristics. It can either be seen as exercised by professional organizations, or as exercised by individual professionals. Either way, it sees the purpose of the exercise of this power as being the maximization of the social and economic benefit of the individual professional in the labour market. This maximization is intended to be achieved in the labour market through the use of the resulting monopolistic structure (Raelin 1985, p.10).

According to Forsyth and Daniesiewicz (1985), the degree of power and thus the degree of professionalization of an occupation can be deduced with regard to both the clients and the employing organization through the degree of autonomy an occupation has (Figure 4.1). A true profession is autonomous in both dimensions, whereas occupations that are only autonomous on one are called semi-professions and those that are autonomous on none are referred to as mimic professions.

It is important to note the significance of public recognition for the establishment of a profession. This is the reason why image building, by which means an occupation

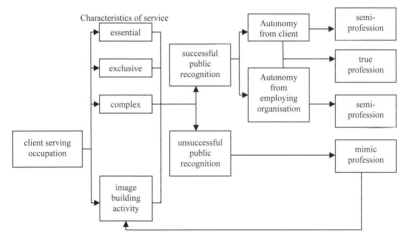

Figure 4.1 The Power View of Professionalisation
Source: Forsyth and Daniesiewicz 1985 (modified)

tries to persuade the public that it has the traits of a profession, is as crucial as the actual characteristics of the task in the above shown process.

The fourth view considers knowledge to be the base of professionalism (Freidson 1986, p.1ff.; Abbott 1991, p.357). This knowledge gives the profession a potential for differentiation and power over those not in possession of this specialized, or formal knowledge. Therefore, similarly to the functionalist view, knowledge serves to develop an exclusive and essential relationship between the client and the profession (Bloor and Dawson 1994, p. 282). The decisive difference from the functionalist view is the sole emphasis on knowledge as the common base and distinctive force of the profession.

For the purpose of this book, a profession will be understood as a mixture between the knowledge-based view and the functionalist view. The main aspect, however, is knowledge, taking into account the fact that from the functionalist view common norms will evolve within the profession, in one way or another. This will be especially important when the subject of the existence of a Professional Culture is discussed.

> A *profession* can therefore be seen as an occupational group that is able to provide an essential *client* service owing to its specialized *knowledge*.

The term *knowledge*, however, has to be seen in a broad way, as it is not intended to be limited to the theoretically highly qualified knowledge of an engineer or an IT-specialist, but should also be the know-how of a blue-collar worker or a clerk.

Therefore, the term *skill*, meaning job-related ability as a result of training or education would seem to be more appropriate (Freidson 1986, p. 24). Furthermore, according to van Maanen and Barley (1984, p. 311), knowledge is, despite the fact that it is 'scientific in origin and take[s] years to master, [...] subject to codification [whereas] skill is fluid and, to outsiders at least, mysterious'. Hence, as a basis for the special position of a profession, skill is apparently the more powerful concept, as skill resists codification.

The term *client* should also be seen in a rather general way. A client in the sense used here can just as well be located outside as inside the organization. This broad understanding is important, as certain professional groups do not have any direct contact to external clients, but nevertheless provide an essential service to clients within the organization (Figure 4.2). Such an essential service could be, for example, the phone service of a secretary or the production of a car component by a worker, equally as well as the development of a new machine by an engineer.

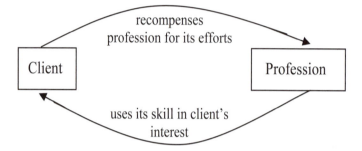

Figure 4.2 The Relationship between Profession and Client

The understanding of a profession presented here (Trice 1993; van Maanen and Barley 1984) is significantly less restrictive than that of dominating research in which more common occupations are either excluded by definition, or implicitly excluded by simply not taking them into consideration as relevant research entities (e.g. Raelin 1985; Bloor and Dawson 1994; Larson 1977; Davidson *et al.* 2001; Carayannis and Sagi 2001; Sheer and Chen 2003; Ulijn *et al.* 2001; Brockhoff 1989).

Under consideration of the goal of the present book, which is the development of appropriate leadership and organizational structures for the whole organization, this restrictive approach would be unacceptable, as it would necessarily lead to the exclusion of large areas of most organizations.

Therefore, the idea of differentiating between *profession* and *occupation*, which is quite common in dominating research, will *not* be followed here; instead, the terms will be regarded as being synonymous.

> Hence, a *profession* will be defined as an occupational group which is able to create a special *client service* due to its *occupational skills*; this in turn leads to a profound relationship between both, based on mutual needs.

4.1.2　The Theoretical Construct 'Professional Culture'

In this section, a complete presentation of Professional Culture, as an analytical tool and an indispensable part of research into culture will be given.

Initially, it is important to understand how a Professional Culture can evolve. The above definition of culture refers to members of collectives. These collectives can be nations, organizations, or, as argued here, professions (Trice 1993; Schein 1996; Hyland *et al.* 2001). Hence, the first distinctive trait of a collective forming a Professional Culture is that its members belong to a profession in the above-defined sense.

Furthermore, culture is based on shared motives, values, beliefs, identities, interpretation, or meanings of significant events that result from common experiences of members of collectives, i.e. in this case *professions*.

The crucial point lies in what aspects may generate common experiences for the members of a profession, which can lead to these shared motives, values, identities, or meanings of significant events. Here again, the problem arises that major research excludes a large variety of professions as already stated (van Maanen and Barley 1984). Nevertheless, it seems appropriate to include part of these findings, on condition that it is remembered that in crossing the boundaries of this research not all the mentioned characteristics have to fit each and every profession.

This is also true of the extensive work of Raelin (1985), who focused his understanding of members of a profession on university graduates and other highly educated occupations. Nevertheless, by allowing a certain flexibility to adapt the given characteristics of his view to all professionals according to our understanding, Raelin's (1985, pp. 85ff.) work gives important insights into the evolvement of a Professional Culture as regards the individual.

To describe this evolvement comprehensively, one has to refer as far back as the educational background of each professional, as he 'begins to identify with his profession and takes on some of the personal attributes associated with it' (Raelin 1985, p. 89). This identification is enhanced by peer groups, as well as – depending on the profession – titles, dress codes etc. Furthermore, a common language evolves, friendships are made, and again – depending on the profession – identification with great figures in the field develops. These aspects of professionalization tend to be reinforced during the professional's periods of education or training.

An example shows the importance of a common educational background in the behaviour of PhD engineers who 'place greater importance than those with bachelor's degrees on [...] belonging to a professional community, on contributing to knowledge in the field, and on challenges that are intrinsic to engineering work' (Raelin 1985, p. 95).

After the professionals have finished their education or training, the development of 'their' Professional Culture and, hence, their socialization and acculturation continues through the influences exercised by their job environment (Gottschalch 1999, pp. 703ff.; Mann 1969, pp. 5ff). Subsequent steps in this development include, according to Raelin (1985, pp. 96ff.):

- finding a niche
- digging in
- entrenchment.

'Finding a personal niche' represents the first step of professionals in their career. They try to find their spot within the organization, but most importantly within their professional environment. The chances at that time are that they are still changing employers because of a discrepancy between their expectations and their actual situation in the respective company. Hence, at this stage, the professionals' main focus will be their profession and their search for a job that fulfils their aspirations. Consequently, the commitment to their profession increases even more resulting in further strengthening of the value and belief system of the profession.

Here again, it should be noted that the degree to which this process takes place may vary according to the profession, but it is in no doubt that a main reference system for every young professional is his or her environment, which is significantly shaped by the profession.

The part of a professionals' development called by Raelin: 'digging in', takes place when the professionals are in their 30s to mid-40s. In this phase, their professional ability is at its peak. They will seek close contact with their fellow professionals and still have the profession as the main reference system for their personal development. At the end of this phase however, the professionals have to decide whether they want to become further specialized, develop their abilities towards a more general qualification, or whether they want to stay in their present professional situation.

It has to be kept in mind though, that not all occupations provide the scope for all of these possible developments. For example, consider factory workers who may only have the choice of specializing further in their job or simply continuing in their current position.

Nevertheless, it should be noted that the professional environment is still a major influence, even at this rather late stage of the professional's personal development. Therefore, their identity is still significantly shaped by their professional reference system, which is largely composed of professionals having the same occupation as them.

The last stage in the professionals' development is called by Raelin the 'entrenchment'. This phase can be seen either as the phase of decline of the professional's ability, and a consequence of them preparing themselves to leave their profession and retire, which is the more common case, or as them taking a more active role in mentoring and/or sponsoring young professionals. Either way, the process of *acculturation* has finished with the attainment of this stage. Furthermore, due to the entrenchment in their Professional Culture, the professionals may become more inclined to accept certain given facts of the organization.

Again, considering the above given definition of culture, it can now be seen that the professional development process has the typical traits of a process of acculturation, respectively socialization. Furthermore, this statement is independent from the profession involved. Professionals live through common experiences throughout their individual careers (van Maanen and Barley 1984). These experiences start with their training or education, and continue with them having a common environment, often a common (technical) language and dealing with the same professional problems. All this leads to them having their peers as their main professional focus, which often influences their private lives, leading to an even stronger enhancement of the importance of the profession in a professional's life (Figure 4.3).

Therefore, it can be stated that the professionals live through common experiences as members of a collective group, which potentially leads to the development of

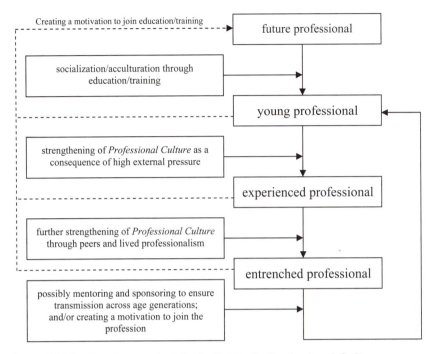

Figure 4.3 The Development of the Individual's Professional Culture

shared motives, values, beliefs, interpretations, or meanings of significant events. Furthermore, it can be stated that, because of the nature of these processes, they are transmitted across age generations (van Maanen and Barley, 1984).

Thus, Hypothesis 1 will be formulated at this point.

Hypothesis 1: Every profession leads to its members developing a genuine Professional Culture

After having analyzed the construct of Professional Culture on the individual level, we will now look more closely at the structure of these cultures at a group level.

Trice (1993) developed a model that can serve as a reference point for the internal structure of Professional Cultures. It is interesting to note that from a technical point of view it has a number of points in common with the well known model of Schein (1984, 1992) in dealing with Organizational Cultures, as described in detail in Section 4.2.2.

Trice (1993) sees 'ideologies' as the basis of Professional Cultures or 'occupational cultures', as he calls them. These ideologies start off as a 'self conscious belief and ritual system' (Trice 1993, p. 47). Through further utilization, the ideologies become 'taken for granted' and an 'inevitable part of life'. Finally, over time, they become guidelines for an individual's actions and moral convictions, and are semiconscious or completely unconscious and form, therefore, 'common sense'.

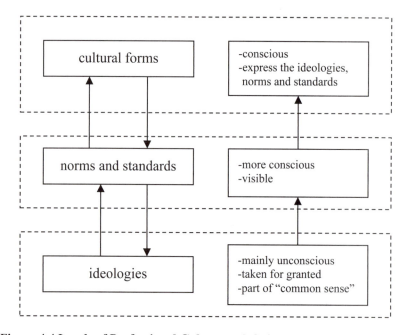

Figure 4.4 Levels of Professional Culture and their Interaction

One product of the ideologies is 'norms and standards' that form a value system for the group. In its turn, this value system forms the second level of Trice's model. Finally, Trice (1993) introduces 'cultural forms', which express the ideology and accordingly the basic assumptions and values of the culture (Figure 4.4). He cites as components of these cultural forms: 'myths and fictions', 'stories and songs', 'symbols', 'rites and ceremonies' and so on.

These cultural forms represent the third cultural level in Trice's model. In addition, they are the visible level of a Professional Culture.

Building upon this understanding of Professional Culture, Trice (1993) develops a two-dimensional classification scheme for Professional Cultures (Figure 4.5). These two dimensions are the group and the grid dimensions, which go back to the work of Douglas (e.g. Douglas 1982; Douglas Caulkins 1999).

The 'group dimension' defines how strong the cohesive forces are within a professional group (Douglas Caulkins 1999). Its main determinants are, according to Trice (1993, p. 26):

- esoteric knowledge,
- extreme or unusual demands,
- consciousness of kind,
- pervasiveness,
- ideologies that confer favourable self-images and social value to the task,
- the extent to which members of the occupation are members' primary reference group,

- the abundance of consistent cultural forms.

The 'grid dimension' defines the importance of (Trice 1993, p. 42):

- hierarchical authority,
- formal rules,
- impersonal relations,
- differential rewards,
- division of labour within the occupation.

The three main aspects of this dimension include ranking members' autonomy and the importance of the control they exercise over other workers, and, further, the imposed and formal rules that execute these arrangements.

low cohesiveness, assimilated in management ideology, strong structural features	strong cohesiveness prominent structural features
everyone has an equal role in every decision-process	mainly due to "one profession companies", profession develops its own way to administer the work process

Grid – Dimension (vertical axis)

Group – Dimension

Figure 4.5 The Two Dimensions of Professional Cultures

In the following, an outline will be given as to how these different cultural clusters deal with exterior influences, especially those of the managerial administration (Trice 1993, pp. 160ff.). The distinction presented here is also in accordance with Hofstede (2001, p. 414), who indicates that identification with the occupation and integration into the organization depend largely on the job.

Strong Grid/Strong Group cultures are accommodative, meaning that they try to reach a compromise between the definitions of their cultures and the demands of the organizations. The compromise itself will, however, always ensure that the culture will not be overly diluted by it; an example for such a culture would be corporate physicians, or corporate law.

Strong Grid/Weak Group cultures tend to be assimilated into the organization. This is usually either due to a relatively good compatibility of the ideology of the culture with the organization, or as a consequence of successful efforts of management to discern the idiosyncrasies of the respective jobs. This could be achieved, for example, by a redistribution of knowledge bases through implementation of computerized systems, or by a redistribution of tasks. An example for this kind of culture would be engineering, as its ideology is relatively compatible with the demands of management.

Weak Grid/Strong Group cultures tend to dominate organizational demands. Members of this culture try tenaciously to keep control not only over their work; but also over the way it is administered. Furthermore, they believe 'they must be vigilant about defending the boundaries of their occupation so as to prevent the uninitiated from performing their distinctive tasks' (Trice 1993, p. 171). In addition, the profession develops its own hierarchy, which is usually rather flat. This is due to the fact that all members underwent the same training, which generally ensures that all members have internalized the rules about how to perform their work; an example would be members of law or accounting firms.

Weak Grid/Weak Group cultures are usually relatively egalitarian. In such a culture everyone participates in the decisions as to which tasks are to be undertaken and in what way this should happen. In such a culture, the boundaries of the profession are weak, as they employ 'members on the basis of friendship, political attitudes and informally acquired knowledge rather than membership within the occupations' (Sonnenstuhl and Trice 1991, p. 308). Furthermore, in the absence of hierarchical means of channelling decision processes, members of the organization have significant control over each other, as decisions have to be reached through consensus. Due to the difficulties of maintaining such a democratic organization as a consequence of internal and external demands, very few of these organizations exist (Trice 1993, pp. 177ff.), and no general example can be given.

In summary, it can be said that the present section provides thorough insights into the concept of Professional Culture.

These insights are initially given with a set of definitions concerning this area of research. In addition, Professional Culture has been examined both from an individual point of view in the first part, and from an organizational/group point of view in the second.

Finally, a first classification of a number of Professional Cultures has been depicted, which already gives an initial idea of the possible differentiating factors to be found in the context of this cultural construct. Therefore, it can be stated that this section gives a sound foundation for the understanding of the theoretical concept of Professional Culture, which in turn serves as an important base for the present book.

4.1.3   The Construct 'Professional Culture' at a Glance

The concept of Professional Culture as it has been described in this section represents a significantly different view from current major research. This is a consequence of a significantly different understanding of the term *profession* on the one hand and, on the other, it is a consequence of the assumption expressed in Hypothesis 1 that professions can and will develop genuine cultures.

The second aspect has already found its way into research (e.g. Raelin 1985; Bloor and Dawson 1994; Schein 1996; Davidson *et al*. 2001; Hyland *et al*. 2001) but, unfortunately, frequently with a very restrictive differentiation between occupations and professions.

This approach is sustainable as long as the focus is concentrated on specific problems arising between specific occupations or between specific occupations and management. These specific problems usually also happen to be the most conspicuous ones, partly due to the strength of the underlying Professional Culture of the professions concerned (Schütz 2003). Nevertheless, such an understanding of Professional Culture is only able to explain a faction of the problems and frictions that arise in organizations, owing to the different Professional Cultures.

With the decision to include in this approach any kind of occupation that can be found in an organization this problem should be avoidable. It will facilitate the analysis of a large variety of inter-occupational and intra-occupational processes. The analysis of these processes is a necessary prerequisite for the development of appropriate leadership and organizational structures.

To sum up, it can be propounded that the rather unusual approach to professions and their cultures chosen here is arguably the most appropriate way of achieving the goal of the present work: the enhancement of both understanding and efficiency within organizations.

4.2   Professional versus Organizational and National Culture

In this section, an introduction to the dominant cultural constructs will be given. This is of considerable importance for fully understanding the already stated necessity for the development of a third cultural construct.

Initially, the approach of 'National Culture' will be presented, followed by that of 'Organizational Culture'. Both understandings of culture have been thoroughly researched in the past and are still being researched today. Furthermore, they are widely accepted as playing a major part in any organization. Consequently, an evaluation will be undertaken not only of the theories themselves, but also of their differences and similarities. This comparison is extremely important for an understanding of the shortcomings the restriction has on National and Organizational Culture, and in which aspects these shortcomings can be overcome by the introduction of a third theoretical construct, i.e. that of Professional Culture. Hence, this section serves to embed the idea of Professional Culture into current research and to point to the potential it has for the enhancement of organizational and leadership research.

4.2.1   National Culture

To start the overview of the two traditional ways of perceiving and analyzing culture, in this section National Culture will be presented with reference to the two most important projects in this field: those carried out initially by Hofstede (2001; 1980), and later within the context of the GLOBE-Study (House *et al.* 2004).

The above given definition of culture (section 1.1) will continue to be valid throughout this section. The term 'National' is not necessarily meant in a strictly political sense. The GLOBE-Study, for instance, has identified various cultural entities that did not match with political borders, but include a number of strong subcultures within one country (e.g. House *et al.* 1999, pp. 207ff; Ashkanasy *et al.* 2002; Szabo *et al.* 2002).

Initially, an introduction of the study carried out by Hofstede (2001) will be given, since a number of results here are also utilized within the GLOBE-Study.

Hofstede's study is based on data collected from 116,000 IBM employees. These employees had all kinds of hierarchical backgrounds and came from 40 different countries. The goal of this study was the development of a tool that could be used to compare different National Cultures in an identical and objective way across all cultural borders. The results showed that four interculturally valid dimensions could be isolated.

Hofstede called them

- Power Distance
- Uncertainty Avoidance
- Individualism
- Masculinity.

'Power Distance' indicates how far a society considers inequalities between its members in respect of power, prestige, status, etc. to be normal and worthwhile being stabilized. Low Power Distance leads among other things to a more consultative and caring leadership style, which employees reward with cooperative behaviour. Hierarchy is not seen as a means in itself, but in a rather functional way, and power is not usually overt (Hofstede 2001, pp. 79ff.).

'Uncertainty Avoidance' shows to what extent members of a society feel threatened by uncertainty and are trying to avoid it through rules, laws, etc. In societies with low Uncertainty Avoidance, change is easily accepted, seniority is rather unimportant, general rules are less valued, and so on (Hofstede 2001, pp. 145ff.).

'Individualism' can be considered the opposite to collectivism, and therefore it deals with the social structures within a society. In a collectivistic society, for instance, group decisions are preferred, an emotional bond to the employing organization exists, individual power is not highly valued, and so on (Hofstede 2001, pp.209ff.).

'Masculinity', finally, describes the degree to which a society is marked by stereotypically masculine traits. In a highly masculine society, e.g. more income is preferred over more leisure time, decisiveness and independency are highly valued, managers strive intentionally for commanding positions, etc. (Hofstede 2001, pp. 279ff.).

In a further work, Hofstede and Bond (1988) (see also Hofstede 2001, pp. 351ff.) added a fifth dimension, which was labelled 'Confucian Work Dynamic'. This dimension was a consequence of a survey that had been deliberately structured with respect to the Chinese value system, to correct a possible western bias in Hofstede's initial work. It could be shown that the dimensions Power Distance, Individualism, and Masculinity correlated to the dimensions 'moral discipline', 'integration,' and 'human orientation'. Uncertainty Avoidance, on the other hand, could not be found; instead, the above-mentioned fifth dimension was isolated. This dimension shows whether the society is mainly living on a long-term or a short-term orientation, or, in other words, if it is more oriented towards the future (long-term orientation) or the past and the present (short-term orientation).

To summarize, it can be said that the work of Hofstede and its subsequent refinement by Bond represents the first study that was able to give fundamental answers to the character of different National Cultures in an objective and interculturally comparable way. This led to Hofstede's work being the basis for a variety of different works in this area, including the GLOBE-Study, which is introduced in the following.

The GLOBE-Study is of significant interest as parts of its methodology and results are used for the empirical part of the research project presented here (House *et al*. 1999, 2004).

The works on the GLOBE-Study can be traced back to the year 1991, when the idea of a cross-cultural research project of greater magnitude was conceived. The beginning of the actual work on this study was in 1993 with the recruitment of 170 scientists from around the world, representing 62 cultures, and the development of an initial pool of questionnaire items. Up to today more than 17,000 members of 951 organizations and 62 cultures have been surveyed, both quantitatively and qualitatively. Furthermore, unobtrusive measures have been developed and used to locate each culture on the societal dimensions described below (House *et al*. 1999, pp. 199 ff.; 2004).

The societal dimensions isolated by the GLOBE-Study are:

- Uncertainty Avoidance
- Power Distance
- Collectivism I
- Collectivism II
- Gender Egalitarianism
- Assertiveness
- Human Orientation
- Performance Orientation
- Future Orientation

The first seven dimensions have their roots in the above-mentioned work of Hofstede (2001) whereas the eighth in that of Hofstede and Bond (1988)/Hofstede (2001). This is also the obvious reason why these works are described at relative length in this section.

'Uncertainty Avoidance' (Sully de Luque and Javidan 2004) and 'Power Distance' (Carl *et al*. 2004) are seen as analogous to the dimensions developed by Hofstede.

The dimension labelled Individualism by Hofstede needed to be split up into the two dimensions 'Collectivism I', and 'Collectivism II', corresponding to the results of Gelfand *et al*. (2004). Collectivism I 'reflects the degree to which organizational and societal institutional norms and practices encourage and reward collective distribution of resources and collective action', whereas Collectivism II reflects 'the degree to which individuals express pride, loyalty, and cohesiveness in their organizations or families' (House *et al.* 1999, p. 192).

Hofstede's dimension 'Masculinity' also needed to be split up, leading to the GLOBE dimensions 'Gender Egalitarianism' (Emrich *et al.* 2004), 'Assertiveness' (den Hartog 2004), 'Human Orientation' (Kabasakal and Bodur 2004) and also partly 'Performance Orientation' (Javidan 2004).

'Gender Egalitarianism' is 'the extent to which an organization or a society minimizes gender role differences' whereas 'Assertiveness' is 'the degree to which individuals in organizations or societies are assertive, confrontational, and aggressive in social relationships' (House *et al.* 1999, p. 192).

'Human Orientation' is 'the degree to which individuals in organizations or societies encourage and reward individuals for being fair, altruistic, friendly, [...]' (House *et al.* 1999, p. 192). This dimension can be traced back among others to the work of Hofstede (1980), Hofstede and Bond (1988) and that of McClelland (1985, pp. 333ff.), where it is labelled 'Kind Heartedness' and 'Affiliative-Oriented Behaviour' respectively.

'Performance Orientation' (Javidan 2004) goes back to the work of McClelland (1985, pp. 223ff.) concerning the individual's need for achievement, and is represented by the dimension 'Confucian Work Dynamism' in the work of Hofstede and Bond (1988). It 'refers to the extent to which an organization or society encourages and rewards group members for performance improvement and excellence' (House *et al.* 1999, p. 192).

'Future Orientation' (Ashkanasy *et al.* 2004) has its roots in Kluckhohn and Strotbeck's (1961) work, in which a distinction is drawn between the past, present and future orientation of a society. It indicates 'the degree to which individuals in organizations or societies engage in future orientated behaviors [...]' (House *et al.* 1999, p. 192).

In summary, it can be said that the GLOBE-Study represents the most important essay in cross-cultural research, resulting in extremely valuable findings in various areas. More details of the GLOBE-Study will be given later in this work. For the moment, the possible characterization of any National Culture by the nine GLOBE dimensions is the important point to retain in order to gather a sound knowledge of the construct National Culture.

Interestingly, the dimensions isolated are also valid on *both* the national ('societal') and the organizational level. Hence, an Organization Culture can be characterized and described using the Core Cultural Dimensions described in this section (Hanges and Dickson 2004; House and Javidan 2004). This trait of the GLOBE-Study is of significant importance for the present work, as will be shown in the following.

To sum up, the term National Culture therefore defines a culture that can be described by the above given dimensions and which relies primarily on a geographical definition. As already mentioned, this does not necessarily mean that each National Culture is defined by one country, as there may, for example, be more than one 'National' Culture in one country (e.g. Szabo *et al.* 2002, Ashkanasy *et al.* 2002).

Accordingly, political boundaries are only the decisive factor to a certain extent for establishing a National Culture (in our sense). This is also the reason why the GLOBE-Study uses the term 'Societal Culture' instead of National Culture. Nevertheless, the term National Culture will be retained throughout this work to give a clearer impression of the different cultural constructs treated, whilst keeping in mind the restrictions arising from the difference in the meaning of the term national in common language and in this specific context.

4.2.2   Organizational Culture

In this section, Organizational Culture, as a second traditional understanding of culture, will be described with reference to one of the most important models of Organizational Culture, which was developed by Schein (1992, 1984). Here, the basic definition of culture, given in Section 1.1, will also be used. This is well founded thanks to the findings of the GLOBE-Study (House *et al.* 2004), and also thanks to the definition of culture Schein (1992, p. 12) himself evolved, which is highly similar to the definition used in the present work. Despite these similarities, the construct Organization Culture has a number of specific characteristics that clearly separate it from National and Professional Culture.

In order to be able to illustrate these differences, a detailed description of Organizational Culture will first be given (Figure 4.6).

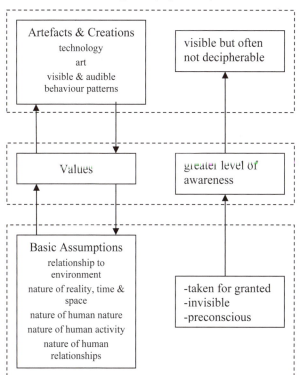

Figure 4.6 Levels of Organizational Culture and their Interaction According to *Schein*

Source: Schein 1984

Schein (1984) sees the internal structure of Organizational Culture as consisting of three different levels, which vary according to their level of individual awareness and visibility to both insiders and outsiders of the group, respectively the organization.

'Basic Assumptions' consist of a number of orientations and patterns of understanding in individuals. Referring to Kluckhohn and Strotbeck (1961), Schein (1992, pp. 94ff.) identifies six basic topics of human existence, which form the basis for cultural paradigms, which in turn formed the basis for the endeavours to build cultural typologies.

These six dimensions are

1. The Nature of Reality and Truth
2. The Nature of Time
3. The Nature of Space
4. The Nature of Human Nature
5. The Nature of Human Activity
6. The Nature of Human Relationships.

'The Nature of Reality and Truth' defines what is real and how it is possible to discover what is real. This concerns questions such as whether one relies more on facts or more on authorities, or whether one has a more academic or more pragmatic approach to solving a problem. Morality is also relevant here, as the question arises as to how it is decided whether something is morally right or wrong.

The dimension 'The Nature of Time' deals with topics like basic time orientation, which can be towards the past, the present or the future. Furthermore, it says something about how time is seen; as monochromic, which implies sequential working, or polychronic, which implies parallel working. Furthermore, it gives an understanding of what is considered to be punctual, etc.

'The Nature of Space' can be split up into three basic topics. These are 'distance and relative placement', 'space symbolics' and 'body language'. The correct placement of one in relation to others is highly important, as it has implications for status, social distance and membership.

Symbolics of space are important as organizations develop different norms for who should have how much space, where it should be located (e.g. office size and location), what kind of visual environment is chosen, including architecture, decorations, etc. Body language gives clues as to how individuals perceive a given situation, or how they relate to others in that situation.

'The Nature of Human Nature' is concerned with topics such as what it means to be human, what basic human instincts are, if humans are seen as principally good, evil, neutral etc. Furthermore, aspects of the organization of human life are dealt with, such as separation or non-separation of work and private life, or the individual's orientation towards a more individual or a more collective approach to life.

'The Nature of Human Activity' deals with aspects of the interaction of the individuals and their environment. This also defines the way a group should relate itself to the environment.

Schein (1992) distinguishes three basic orientations: that of

1. Doing
2. Being
3. Being-In-Becoming

The 'Doing' orientation sees no insurmountable obstacles; every problem is merely a question of effort rather than feasibility. The 'Being' orientation is the opposite in that it generally tries to adapt to the environment and finds its niche, whereas the 'Being-In-Becoming' orientation is located between the other two.

Another important aspect concerning human interaction with the environment is the relationship between work, family, and personal concerns, and the importance each of these has. In addition, the way the environment is seen is of relevance. It can be seen as, for example, controllable, demanding, threatening, invincible, etc.

Finally, 'The Nature of Human Relationships' incorporates expectations concerning individuals' behaviour in relation to their peers, in order to maximize the well being of the group. According to Schein (1992, p. 132), these expectations include (1) 'power, influence, and hierarchy' and (2) 'intimacy, love and peer relationships'. In this context, Schein (1992) mentions aspects such as individualism, groupism, participation, involvement, and characteristics of role relationships.

It is important to notice at this point that these basic assumptions are not to be seen as standing in an unrelated manner next to each other, but that they together form part of the *gestalt* represented by Organizational Cultures (Hofstede *et al.* 1990, p. 313). Their importance for the organization can best be understood in reference to the concept of Argyris and Schön (1978, pp. 10ff.; Argyris 1976) in which 'Espoused Theories' and 'Theories-in-Use' are differentiated. The difference between these two is that the former are merely officially prescribed action patterns, whereas the latter are those which actually guide individuals' behaviour. Therefore, it can be stated that Basic Assumptions are similar to what Argyris has identified as Theories-in-Use (Schein 1992, p. 22).

Furthermore, the definition Trice gave of ideologies has to be recalled within this context (see Section 4.1.2). He considers them to be semi- or completely unconscious and thus forming 'common sense'. This represents a significant resemblance to the definition of basic assumptions given here.

According to Schein (1991, pp. 19ff.), the next higher level of Organizational Culture is formed by the (Espoused) Values. These values and beliefs usually go back to founders, or leaders, and they serve to reduce uncertainty in critical areas. They are a precursor for the above-described basic assumptions, provided they are functioning satisfactorily on a continuous basis, leading to their ultimate transformation into basic assumptions.

The 'Values' remain conscious in that they serve to guide group members' behaviour in important situations by providing normative and moral standards (Wiener 1988). Furthermore, they play an important role in the socialization of new group members. The condition for them actually being lived, is, however, that they are based on prior learning, as otherwise they function merely as Espoused Theories in the sense of Argyris and Schön (1978, pp. 10ff.; Argyris 1976). This, in turn, results in these 'Values' only predicting what people say, but not what they actually think and do. An example of such behaviour would be a company officially pursuing a participative approach for the integration of the individual and the organization, whilst the actual approach is a rather authoritarian one, based on hierarchy.

Here again, it must be pointed out that this cultural level is also present in Trice's model of Professional Culture under the definition of norms and standards forming the 'Value System' of a Professional Culture (see again Section 4.1.2).

'Artefacts & Creations', finally, are all visible phenomena. They can be, for example, symbols, myths and stories, published values, rites and ceremonies (Trice and Beyer 1984). It should however be noted that here again this level cannot be seen independently from the other levels. Above all, it is not possible to decipher the true meaning of this level of culture without referring to the other levels, as any kind of interpretation of a single part of an Organizational Culture alone would be a reflection of one's own cultural system. Therefore, once more, it has to be emphasized that cultures are gestalts and only understandable as a whole. In addition, this third cultural level is already known from the model of Professional Culture as 'Cultural Forms' and has a very similar function in both models.

As far as the consequences of strong Organizational Cultures are concerned, it is noteworthy that they can be both functional and dysfunctional; the traits of a strong culture are for example that it is homogeneous, stable, widely shared, cohesive, fully articulated, etc. (Saffold 1988).

The most important positive and negative consequences of a strong culture will be given below (Saffold 1988; Wiener 1988; Trice and Beyer 1984; Deal and Kennedy 1982; Gussmann 1988, pp. 207ff.).

The positive consequences of strong Organizational Cultures can be:

- guidance for individual's actions
- fast decision-taking
- effective communication
- swift implementation
- little need for control
- stability
- high individual motivation and good team-spirit

Negative consequences on the other hand are, for example:

- barriers to organizational change
- barriers to the recognition of external demands on the organization
- development of a somewhat totalitarian way of dealing with individual's opinions

The important thing to remember is that the general statement that a strong Organizational Culture is necessarily good (e.g. Peters and Waterman 1982) cannot be upheld. The beneficial consequences of a strong Organizational Culture always have to be weighed up against their costs.

In summary, it can be stated that Schein's model is the most important approach to the understanding of the internal structure of Organizational Cultures (Schreyögg 1999, pp. 439ff.). Furthermore, this approach is also highly valuable for the research into Professional Cultures, due to its significant resemblance to the model developed by Trice, as outlined in Section 4.1.2. This high resemblance of the internal structure of the two cultural models leads to the following highly interesting option for research into Professional Culture.

In accordance with Trice (1993; section 4.1.2), because of these close similarities, the results and methodology developed in the context of Organizational Culture will be used for research into Professional Culture.

This in turn brings up the GLOBE-Study again, as the nine Core Cultural Dimensions developed in its context are, as stated, also viable for the identification of National Cultures and Organizational Cultures (House *et al.* 1999). This allows parts of the GLOBE-Study methodology and some of its results to be used for the research undertaken here into Professional Culture. This underlines once more the great importance that the GLOBE-Study has for cross-cultural research in general, and for the research into Professional Culture undertaken here in particular. Therefore, Hypothesis 2 is formulated as follows:

Hypothesis 2: After appropriate adaptation, the methodology and results of the GLOBE-Study can be used successfully for the research into Professional Cultures.

Hence, Schein's work provides a large variety of highly interesting insights, which will be an integral part of this book.

The link between Organization and Professional Culture is of such importance for the empirical part of this work, that this alone justifies the prominent position this model has been given in the present section.

4.2.3   A Joint Evaluation of the Three Cultural Constructs

In this section, the relationship between National, Organizational and Professional Culture will be treated in detail. This is highly important, as these three approaches have a number of similarities, but also a number of differences.

The most striking similarity is that, as has been shown, it is possible to use one single definition of Culture for all three approaches. This already indicates that the distinction made in research between the different constructs of culture is based, to a lesser degree, on a difference in principle, but mainly on a difference in perspective.

Furthermore, the internal structures of Professional and Organizational Cultures are highly similar, as has already been demonstrated in this chapter. They both reside on an unconscious and invisible, yet highly important base, form common values, norms, etc. and find their expression in rites, symbols, stories, etc. In addition, due to the fact that National Cultures and Organizational Cultures share the same operational definition, and in accordance with Hofstede (2001, pp. 391ff.) it can be stated that the internal structure of National Culture is very similar to that of Organizational Culture and thus to that of Professional Culture.

Therefore, it can be recorded at this point that the internal structure of all three cultural concepts is essentially the same. However, this does not mean that the importance of its components, i.e. the three levels of Schein's and Trice's model (Figure 4.4) is always the same. As, for example, Hofstede (2001, pp. 393ff.) pointed out, the importance of Values is significantly higher in National Cultures than in Organizational Cultures. Nevertheless, the components are present in all three approaches and they therefore represent three different kinds of one species rather than three different species altogether.

The question now arises as to where those differences lie, if there are so many fundamental similarities.

As already indicated above, the differences are on the level of the respective perspective. This difference in perspective is, however, highly important for analytical reasons, to enable cultural research to identify properly the influencing factors for the culture each individual actually possesses. From that aspect, the different theoretical approaches to culture are complementary to the overall understanding of this phenomenon (Hofstede 2001, p. 391).

This complementarity is due to the different entities that are researched in each of the cultural approaches, and which, according to the findings depicted, represent the most important influencing factors for the individual's culture. This is due to the fact that each cultural entity socializes the individuals in a distinct area and also at different times of their life (also Hofstede 2001, pp. 391ff.).

Socialization into National Culture, for instance, begins with the individuals' birth and, significantly, takes place outside of their workplace. Socialization into Professional Culture, in contrast, starts later in life depending on when the initial contact with the profession takes place, but still at a relatively young age. Furthermore, this socialization happens partly outside, partly inside the work organization.

Socialization into Organizational Culture, finally, may take place at any time of one's life between the first job and retirement, and happens mainly inside the work organization.

Culture, as shown in this chapter, represents an overarching construct composed of different influencing factors that can be subdivided analytically into three distinct 'sub constructs'. These 'sub constructs' are the National, the Organizational and the Professional perspective, and they have to be researched together to obtain a complete picture of the individual's Culture.

The idea of a complete Culture introduced here has to be understood from the individual level, as indicated in Figure 4.7, which in turn brings us back to the above point that the split into three different cultural constructs is mainly analytical.

This becomes especially apparent with reference to Hofstede (2001) and Hofstede *et al.* (1990) where it is stated that each of the three approaches has its main focus on a different cultural level. Although Hofstede uses a less detailed internal structure of culture with only two levels, in comparison to the here-preferred models of Schein, respectively Trice, that are composed of three, his classification is nevertheless useful.

The following statements are in reference to the model of Schein, although their content is equally valid in regard to the model of Trice.

The second and the third dimension of Schein's model can be produced by splitting Hofstede's (2001) level 'Values' into 'Values' and 'Basic Assumptions'. Furthermore, the second Hofstede level, 'Practices', is highly similar to what Schein defined to be 'Artefacts & Creations', as Hofstede sees Practices to be the 'manifestations of culture' in the form of 'Symbols', 'Heroes', and 'Rituals' (Hofstede 2001, pp. 9ff.) see Figure 4.8.

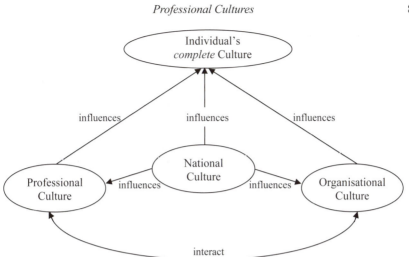

Figure 4.7   The Components of Culture and their Interrelationship

With this understanding, it becomes clear why the three different cultural constructs are complementary and should be seen as together forming the *whole culture* of the individual. This does not mean, however, that they are always in peaceful coexistence with each other. As has already been stated, there may be rather significant conflicts, for example between a Professional and an Organizational Culture, provided they are incompatible and strong enough. The same can obviously be true between all three constructs.

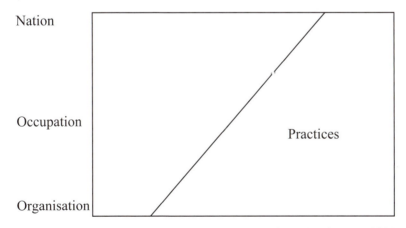

Figure 4.8 The Balance of Values vs. Practices (Hofstede, 2001, p.394, modified)

Source: Hofstede 2001 (modified)

The important thing to retain at this point is, nevertheless, that all three constructs together form the individual's culture. Depending on the individual's profession, organization and nation (society), this process is influenced to a varying degree (overall strength of the influence) and manner (cultural levels concerned) by the different cultural constructs, but a basic influence of all three constructs can always be perceived.

> Hypothesis 3. Professional Culture, Organizational Culture, and National Culture together form the complete Culture of the individual

To sum up this section, the similarities of the three cultural constructs are their common structural base and, following Hypothesis 3, their forming together the individual's culture, whereas their differences are to be found on the cultural level focused on by them, as well as the time and place of the individual's socialization.

4.3   Summarizing Evaluation of the Necessity to Include 'Professional' Cultures into Cultural Research

In this chapter, the importance of the Professional Culture construct for cultural research has been examined. In order to do that, initially the meaning of this construct was derived. Also, the significant shortcomings of existing research were shown.

As demonstrated, these are mainly due to a very restrictive way of defining what is to be considered a profession, which usually leads to the incorporation of only a very limited number of professions into any kind of existing research. This problem was also identified by Hofstede (2001 p. 414), who states that he knows 'of no broad cross-occupational study that allows us to identify dimensions of occupational cultures'.

Furthermore, it has been shown why it is necessary to see Professional Culture as an integral part of what we called the *complete individual's culture*, which is composed of Professional Culture and the well-known constructs of Organizational and National Culture.

This understanding of culture as being composed of a number of different influencing factors also clarifies why it is of such importance to include all relevant factors into cultural research if the intention is to obtain as extensive as possible understanding of a given culture. The inclusion of Professional Culture into the base that forms culture, at least enhances the chances of achieving this.

Hence, in summary, it can be stated that the inclusion of the construct Professional Culture, as it is defined in this chapter, into cultural research, will contribute to a deeper understanding of culture as a whole and therefore close a substantial knowledge gap in cultural research. This will, of course, in turn be highly beneficial to a wide variety of leadership and organisational tasks, as will be pointed out later in this book.

Therefore, in addition to being of significant academic interest, the introduction of Professional Culture is also highly valuable from a practical viewpoint.

PART 2
The Empirical Survey and its Results

Chapter 5

The Development of the Research Methodology

In this chapter, the methodology for the empirical phase will be described. Due to the complexity of the research issue, a multi-method approach was chosen. This multi-method approach is composed of a quantitative and a qualitative part.

In addition, a pilot study was performed, which served the validation of the questionnaire, the checking of the questionnaire's reliability and the generation of a number of demographical questions. The pilot study, including its results, is described in Section 5.1.1. The methodology of the main survey is described in Section 5.1.2. The quantitative part is represented by standardized questionnaires as already mentioned. The qualitative part, on the other hand, consists of open interviews, which will be explained later. In addition, the nature of the research sample is described in Section 5.2, followed by a final evaluation of the empirical methodology employed.

Thus, this chapter will give a complete overview of the methodology of the empiricals with all the implications for the survey itself and, in addition, an outlook on the expected insights to be gained in Chapters 6 and 7.

5.1 The Structure of the Empiricals

As already mentioned, the empirical study is subdivided into a pilot study and the main study. This separation is necessary both for analytical reasons and for aspects concerning the content of the survey.

The analytical reasons come down to the fact that it is not advisable to carry out a major empirical survey without a prior guarantee of the soundness of the chosen empirical tool so as to avoid problems ranging from general understanding of the questionnaire items by the respondents to the validity and reliability of the questionnaire itself (van Teijlingen and Hundley 2001).

As far as the content of the survey is concerned, a pilot study is advisable, as it has the potential to be an explorative precursor of the main study, thus enhancing the overall results of the survey (van Teijlingen and Hundley 2001). Therefore, the structure of the empirical study was arranged such that an extensive pilot study was initially carried out, followed by the main survey, in order to make the maximum use of the available research sample.

5.1.1   The Pilot Study

In the following, the contents and the results of the pilot study will be described.

The structure of the pilot study is based on two approaches (as is that of the main survey). On the one hand, a number of focus interviews was carried out, while on the other, the standardized questionnaire was tested on a significant number of individuals.

The results of the pilot study can be traced back to this approach. These results were the validation of the survey questionnaire, which required only a few minor changes and the generation of demographical questions for the main survey.

In addition, a high degree of reliability of the questionnaire could be demonstrated, further showing the high overall quality of the developed instrument. Thus, the pilot study can be seen as the basis for the main survey and its results, which are described later in this chapter and in Chapters 6, 7 and 8.

The Structure of the Pilot Study

The structure of the pilot study is, as already mentioned, twofold.

The initial part was composed of a number of focus interviews. These interviews were intended to create a first impression of the research entities and thereby collect preliminary data. A qualitative exploration of preliminary data is one of the fields in which a pilot study is highly useful (van Teijlingen and Hundley 2001). The goal of this data collection was to generate demographical questions and check for their relevancy. Therefore, the first goal of the pilot study was to narrow down and focus the research design in an explorative manner to enhance the quality of the survey with regard to its content. This goal was pursued with 12 focus interviews carried out with engineers, marketing representatives, buyers, sellers and with operatives from airlines.

The second part of the pilot study consisted of the evaluation of the quality of the developed questionnaire. As will be pointed out in Section 5.1.2, a previously validated tool was used for this part of the research project. Nevertheless, this tool had to undergo significant adaptive changes to render it adequate to the present survey. A thorough evaluation of the questionnaire had to be carried out to ensure the questionnaire itself was clearly understandable on the one hand, and valid and reliable on the other. Such an evaluation was necessary to ensure that the empirical research tool was able adequately to reflect the dimensions developed in the context of the GLOBE-Study. Such an evaluation necessitates the carrying out of an extensive pilot study (Black 1999, pp.188ff.).

This second part of the pilot study was carried out with a sample of 184 students from various disciplines. In detail, the sample consisted of 44 MBA students, 59 students in industrial engineering, 50 students in IT engineering and 31 students in human medicine. This choice was based on three considerations.

The first one was that it is advisable not to include participants of a potential pilot study in the following main survey so as to avoid problems in connection with contamination of the main sample with pre-exposed respondents (van Teijlingen and

Hundley 2001). Therefore, the participants of the pilot study were not to be included in the main survey. This decision led to the second consideration.

The number of possible respondents for a survey – especially in cooperation with the industry – is obviously rather limited. The problem here is that even for a pilot study to be able to produce meaningful results, it is necessary to incorporate quite a substantial number of participants if one wants to work quantitatively with the collected data. Hence, the decision was taken to choose a completely different population for the pilot study, which led to the third consideration.

The population that was to be chosen had to fulfil two criteria. The first was that it had to show the traits of a Professional Culture with a reasonable degree of probability if the questionnaire were to be properly tested. The very limited research results as regards Professional Cultures indicate that, among others, medical doctors and engineers possess a proper Professional Culture.

The second criterion was that the population had to be reasonably accessible for such a study.

These two criteria together led to the above-described composition of the sample for the pilot study. The MBA students were included because of the fact that these specific students are specialized in accountancy, which gives them a highly mathematical and technical and thus engineering-like approach to the knowledge field of business administration.

The questionnaire used was the questionnaire intended for the main study, except that some demographical questions, which did not make sense in a student environment, were replaced by questions relating to important aspects for the pilot study, such as how far advanced is the individual student in his or her studies.

To sum up, it can be said that the design of the pilot study and the way it was carried out permitted a thorough and appropriate test of the employed empirical tool. Furthermore, a number of highly interesting insights were gained in the course of the pilot study, as will be pointed out below.

The Results of the Pilot Study

The results of the pilot study are both of a technical nature as far as the fitness for use of the questionnaire is concerned, and of a content oriented nature as far as the generation of demographical questions is concerned.

Reliability was checked using Cronbach's Alpha (Cronbach 1990, pp.190ff.; Black 1999, pp.279ff.). Cronbach's Alpha represents a measurement to check for internal consistency of a given test, or – as in the present situation – a given dimension. It is a means of comparing the variances of the individual items of a dimension with the variance of the whole dimension.

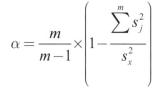

where m = number of items, s_j^2 = variance of the individual items, s_x^2 = variance of the dimension. Therefore, the closer Cronbach's Alpha gets to 1.00, the higher the reliability of the checked test/ dimension.

For the purpose of the current work, it was necessary to check individually the reliability of each Core Cultural Dimension. As each dimension is composed of a number of different items, the values given in Table 5.1 represent the above-mentioned comparison between the variance of the items of one dimension and that of the whole dimension.

It was noted that this coefficient from the beginning showed a remarkably high value. Only slight adjustments had to be made to the initially developed questionnaire – the most important being the addition of one further item for the Human Orientation Dimension.

The results of the last sample of the pilot study, using the final version of the questionnaire, showed the figures given in Table 5.1 for Cronbach's Alpha. According to these results, compared with those of the original GLOBE questionnaire, the reliability of the final questionnaire could be considered satisfactory (Black 1999; House *et al.*, 2004; Kopalle and Lehman 1997).

Table 5.1 Reliability of the Questionnaire According to the Pilot Study

Dimension	Cronbach's α
Uncertainty Avoidance	0.7733
Assertiveness	0.7344
Future Orientation	0.6600
Power Distance	0.7327
Collectivism I	0.7166
Collectivism II	0.7087
Performance Orientation	0.6885
Gender Egalitarianism	0.8530
Human Orientation	0.6512

Further analysis was aimed at the possibility of recreating the original GLOBE dimensions with the collected data.

In order to do this, a 'Bivariate Correlations' analysis was initially carried out with the most reliable items, as shown above. The results pointed strongly to the items of each dimension being correlated to each other. Furthermore, a factor analysis was carried out which strongly indicated that the different items do in fact create the nine Core Cultural Dimensions in the same way as in the GLOBE-Study. Therefore, a further 'Linear Regression' analysis was carried out with these items in order to check that they actually create the respective dimensions.

This course of action was chosen because the results of a factor analysis are never unambiguous, which is a consequence of the non-uniqueness of the factor loadings

(Mardia *et al.* 2003). This in turn implies a certain arbitrariness in the results of any factor analysis. Hence, a statistically more meaningful measurement technique was chosen: *Linear Regression Analysis*.

Linear Regression Analysis has the advantage of being able to attribute a statistical significance level to a linear correlation. As a linear correlation between the items of each Core Cultural Dimension was to be expected, this measurement technique provided the statistically strongest statement about the items of one dimension actually creating that dimension.

The values given in Table 5.2 were calculated in the following way.

Table 5.2 The Results of the Linear Regression Analysis

	Significance
Uncertainty Avoidance	0.000
Assertiveness	0.000
Future Orientation	0.028
Power Distance	0.035
Collectivism I	0.135
Collectivism II	0.000
Performance Orientation	0.000
Gender Egalitarianism	0.000
Human Orientation (1,3) N=31	0.050
Human Orientation (2,3) N=31	0.066
Human Orientation (1,2) N=31	0.344

For each Core Cultural Dimension, a Linear Regression Analysis was carried out with one of the items of that dimension being the independent variable, whereas the others of that dimension were the dependent ones. This procedure was repeated until each item of each dimension had been checked as an independent variable. Table 5.2 indicates the weakest value for all possible combinations of the items of one dimension as an independent and dependent variable.

It can be seen that, for most items of the respective dimensions, a strong correlation exists, clearly suggesting that they in fact recreate the various Core Cultural Dimensions of the GLOBE-Study. The items that did not match the 0.000 significance criterion will be discussed later in this section. Without going into any further details at this point, it can nevertheless be said that that these go back to the specific traits of the used sample.

The different results depicted in this section also show that, from a purely technical point of view, a number of items did not necessarily have to be included in the main questionnaire (e.g. Human Orientation 2).

From a content-based point of view however, retaining some of these questions was advisable as they focus on specific traits of the respective dimensions. As the total length of the questionnaire still remained within the reasonable frame of 30 questions, it was therefore advisable to use the slightly longer questionnaire in order to gather the maximum amount of data possible (Kopalle and Lehman 1997).

In considering those items that led to inconclusive results within the analysis undertaken above, a closer look has to be taken at the items themselves in connection with the used sample.

It has to be kept in mind that the sample is composed of students. Although students do share a number of traits with their counterparts from the professional world they will be joining after their studies, certain differences apparently exist. These differences surfaced in the responses to the items of the Collectivism I, the Human Orientation and, to a certain degree, in the Power Distance and the Future Orientation dimension.

The ambiguities within the Collectivism I dimension can be traced back to the fact that one of the items retained for the analysis of the pilot study asks for the degree of teamwork within the future profession. The responses to these questions are thus, for most students, based solely on apparently varying assumptions of a future situation.

Regarding the Human Orientation dimension, it has to be pointed out that, from a technical point of view, the second item should have been excluded from the main survey. It was however retained, as its focus is somewhat different from that of the other two items. It thus provides some highly interesting insights from a content-based point of view. This different focus is also at the source of the unsatisfactory results for the second item. The second question deals with the tolerance of mistakes whereas the others deal with human values such as warmth and generosity. Obviously, students do not see the link between Human Oriented behaviour and a tolerance for mistakes, a link seen *clearly* by the respondents of the main sample, as could be confirmed in various interviews and by the results of the standardized questionnaire.

The results of the eighth Dimension (Power Distance) point to a similar direction, as its content created some confusion, especially in the non-medical sample. This is because, at the present point (about 2–3 years of studying compared with about 5 for the medical doctors), it is not yet totally clear to the students whether they consider themselves as belonging to the future general management or to part of a special professional group. Therefore results of this dimension vary.

Furthermore, it has to be noted that the Power Distance dimension deals with an aspect of the students' life that they will not experience as such until they are actually in the job. The only power distance a student usually feels is towards the teaching body – a relation that can hardly be compared to that encountered in professional life after finishing university.

Finally, one item of the ninth dimension (Future Orientation) deals with meetings. As most students will not have a clear grasp of how meetings are generally organized in their future profession, it seems reasonable to attribute the non-conclusive results of this dimension to the lack of experience of the respondents therein.

It can therefore be said that the results of the pilot study were highly important and promising for the main study, both from a quantitative and a qualitative point of view, indicating a high validity and reliability of the employed research tool.

The reliability was checked – as indicated above – with Cronbach's Alpha, while the necessary validity was achieved with the help of the above-mentioned focus interviews and the described Linear Regression Analysis. In particular, the Linear

Regression Analysis was of key importance for the validation of the questionnaire. As could be shown, the Core Cultural Dimensions of the original GLOBE-Study could be recreated with the data gathered in the course of the pilot study. Therefore, the psychometric properties of that original questionnaire could be conserved with the newly developed questionnaire. As the main area of interest of the quantitative questionnaire was these very Core Cultural Dimensions and their valuation by the respondents, the highly satisfying results of the Linear Regression Analysis as depicted above clearly demonstrate the validity of the questionnaire.

This result is supported by that of the focus interviews, as respondents clearly confirmed the interconnection between the different items of each Core Cultural Dimension.

The demographical questions (see Appendix 2 for details) were developed on the basis of theoretical considerations and the above-mentioned 12 focus interviews. Theoretical considerations included, for example, the necessity to know which respondents belong to which organizations (Organizational Culture), their nationalities (National Culture), their gender (possible gender based bias), etc. The relevance of these questions was then cross-checked in the course of the mentioned focus interviews.

Hence, to sum up, it can be stated that, in connection with the results depicted in the following chapters, Hypothesis 2 can thus be considered to be confirmed (for details see Section 4.2.2) which supports the course of action undertaken for the development of the quantitative questionnaire.

Summarizing Evaluation of the Pilot Study

The pilot study, as described in this section, was a highly helpful tool in the development of the questionnaire used for the main survey.

The three main goals:

- the generation of demographical questions,
- the verification of the questionnaire's validity,
- the verification of the questionnaire's reliability,

were achieved.

In particular, reliability and validity as the two most important factors indicating the overall quality of a questionnaire were assured with the help of a variety of different techniques appropriate to the demands of this specific questionnaire (The American Educational Research Association *et al.* 1999, pp. 9ff.).

Therefore, it can be said that the pilot study was, together with the underlying theoretical work, able to provide the main study with a highly valuable tool to achieve the goals set out by the presented empirical study. In particular, the results of the pilot study strongly point to the possibility – already mentioned in the previous chapter – that it is possible to use a tool developed in the context of Organizational Culture research for research into Professional Cultures. Obviously, significant adaptations had to be carried out both on the level of the formulation of the items and on the level of the overall design of the questionnaire, but the basic psychometric properties of the questionnaire developed on the basis of the questionnaire of the GLOBE-Study remained unchanged in this new environment.

With regard to the following main study, this finding is probably the most important one, as the successful recreation of the GLOBE dimensions is a necessary prerequisite for the subsequent development of appropriate leadership and organizational structures. Therefore, it can be stated at this point that the pilot study fully achieved its goals within the development process of the questionnaire for the main study. It confirmed both the theoretical assumptions concerning the transferability of a tool originating in the context of Organizational Culture research and the quality of the newly developed questionnaire with reference to the tool used for the purpose of the GLOBE-Study.

Hence, in summary, the fitness for use of the questionnaire for the main study could be reached and subsequently demonstrated with the pilot study presented here.

5.1.2   The Main Study

The structural approach of the empiricals of the main study is, as already mentioned, twofold.

The standardized questionnaire that represents the first part is aimed at creating an objective overview of the number and traits of the Professional Cultures present in the companies researched. Their role is therefore to group the different Professional Cultures into clusters. Hence, the standardized questionnaire serves as a basis for the following open interviews.

The open interviews represent the second part of this first empirical phase. Their objective is to deepen the understanding of the cultural clusters identified with the help of the standardized questionnaires. The main objective is to get a better understanding of the Intra- and Inter-Professional processes that take place within the identified cultural clusters.

Hence, the structure of the empiricals is aimed at combining the advantages of both quantitative and qualitative research while avoiding the shortcomings of each of these. Consequently, this course of action leads to a significantly higher overall quality of the insights and results gained with the empirical work.

The Standardized Questionnaire

In this section, a detailed description of the standardized questionnaire used for the empirical part of the exploratory study will be given, starting with the underlying logic of the development of the questionnaire.

Two guiding principles governed the development of this questionnaire. The first was to reflect correctly the organizational dimensions isolated with the help of the GLOBE-Study. As already shown, a tool developed for use within an Organizational Culture environment can also be successfully implemented to answer the same questions within an environment of Professional Culture. Therefore, the adaptation and subsequent use of the methodology of the GLOBE-Study (Hanges and Dickson 2004, pp. 122ff.) was the most appropriate course of action for the research undertaken into Professional Culture.

However, it was not sufficient merely to adjust the original questionnaire to the new task, it was also necessary to shorten it. Originally, it comprised 39 items, which was not acceptable for the companies participating in the survey. Consequently, in the final version of the questionnaire the number of questions treating the Core Cultural Dimensions was reduced to 30 items.

The validity of this course of action was assured with the help of the above-described pilot study. Therefore, the qualities of the GLOBE Study (House *et al.* 2004) – namely the identification of the nine Core Cultural Dimensions – could be maintained despite the necessary adaptation to the current demands.

The second guiding principle was to render the collected data easily interpretable. Therefore, a number of demographical questions had to be developed, which were to allow for a meaningful interpretation of these data. Here again, the problem arose that the final questionnaire was not to be excessively long. Hence, nine of the most important demographical items were retained.

It can thus be stated that considerable work was carried out on the original GLOBE questionnaire to render it compatible with the demands of the current survey without, however, altering its core qualities. This work led to a questionnaire that combined a reasonable length with the maximum amount and quality of data collected.

The questionnaire itself is subdivided into two parts. This division is, on the one hand, due to the differing contents of the demographic- and the Culture-related questions. On the other it is due to the intended easier handling and improved visual impression of the questionnaire.

The demographical items that are, with a single exception, to be found in the second part, are composed of one open question asking for the individual's profession and eight multiple-choice questions. The decision to identify the individual's profession with the help of an open question was taken because of the intention to create professional groups as late as possible in the process of data analysis.

The first part, on the other hand, uses a seven point Likert (1932) scale. On this scale, the respondents were to indicate how they considered the cultural characteristics mentioned should be structured. In accordance with the GLOBE-Study (House *et al.* 2004) it was thus possible to measure cultural values as they are internalized by the respondents. These values were then used to extract the underlying Core Cultural Dimensions of Professional Culture of each respondent and thus isolate the different Professional Cultures.

Another consideration regarding the questionnaire was the intention to render its handling as easy as possible for the respondents. Therefore, an online solution was favoured that permitted the questionnaire to be filled in online, or printed out, filled in offline and returned by fax or mail. The latter, paper-based, solution was intended for those respondents who either did not wish to work on the questionnaires online or who did not have access to the internet at their workplaces.

Especially for the second group, the paper-based version was highly important as it was the only possible way to reach the substantial number of shop-floor workers present in the sample. The distribution and subsequent collection of the questionnaires for this group was always carried out by a person who was trusted by the members of the group, so as to respect guaranteed privacy (e.g. a member of work council). Furthermore, the questionnaire was available in the five languages most likely to be encountered within the research sample. The different versions of the questionnaire were easily accessible via the use of self-explanatory symbols (national flags) on the start page of the questionnaire.

The need for this approach has been raised on various occasions when carrying out research in different linguistic backgrounds. This is because respondents tend to have a systematic bias in their responses if they have to respond to a questionnaire that is not in their native language (The American Educational Research Association *et al.* 1999, pp. 91ff.).

The translations of the questionnaire were carried out with the help of two groups of people who are fluent in both the language of the original version of the questionnaire (English) and the language into which the questionnaire was to be translated.

The first group was responsible of the translation from English to the respective languages (French, German, Italian, Spanish). The second group independently carried out a back translation into English to ensure that, within the translation process, no bias in the meaning of the questions had occurred. To avoid such an unwanted bias in the meaning of questionnaire items due to their translation, an identical course of action was followed within the GLOBE-Study, strongly supporting the soundness of this approach (Hanges and Dickson 2004, p. 126; Brislin 1976).

To sum up, it can be said that the questionnaire used can be seen as the most appropriate approach for the measurement of the different Professional Cultures present within the surveyed companies. This assessment is due to its proven high reliability and validity in Organizational Culture research in combination with the demonstrated possibility to use Organizational Culture research tools for the purpose of Professional Culture research in accordance with the extensive pilot study undertaken.

Furthermore, the high flexibility in the way the questionnaire could be filled out in combination with the availability of the questionnaire in five different languages ensured not only a high return rate of the questionnaire, but also a high accuracy as to the agreement between the actual attitudes of the respondents and the collected responses.

The Open Interviews

The goal of the open interviews was to create a deeper understanding of the different aspects identified with the help of the standardized questionnaire. The main interest in this context was focused on the identification of possible problems between the different professions and to sharpen the characteristic traits of the different Professional Cultures identified. In addition, possible consequences as to the interaction between these cultures and organizational and leadership structures were treated in support of the development of appropriate leadership and organizational structures carried out in Chapters 6 and 7.

Due to these specific demands, a course of action was chosen that favoured an interview that was only slightly structured, leading to an informal atmosphere. This informality permitted not only a smooth evaluation of the interview, but allowed the interviewees to open up much more willingly than in a more formal setting. This, in turn, led to the intended better understanding of the underlying perceptions, wishes and attitudes of the interviewees.

The course of action undertaken was as follows.

Initially the content of each Core Cultural Dimension was explained to the interviewees. Subsequently, the interviewees were asked to locate their professional peer group on each dimension, and to give their reason for this placing. Finally, the interpretations based on the results of the quantitative part of the study were discussed with the interviewees to get as complete a picture as possible of the various Core Cultural Dimensions for the different Professional Cultures.

Audio recording of the interviews was unfortunately not possible. Although this is in contradiction to the recommendations given for qualitative research (Lamnek 1995b, pp. 97ff.) a different course of action was impossible. This was because, for the interviewees, a precondition for taking part in the interview process was that the interviews would not be taped. Therefore, notes were taken during the interview, followed by the compiling of an interview protocol immediately after the respective interviews.

A total of 84 interviews was carried out with employees from six companies representing each Professional Culture isolated within the quantitative survey. This number was sufficient to achieve the intended goal and gave a variety of highly interesting insights, as shown in Chapters 6 and 7.

To sum up, it can be said that the interview process employed was the most appropriate way to complete the results given by the standardized questionnaire. In particular, through its highly informal design, it ensured the interviewees were willing openly to disclose their views, feelings and wishes, which in turn permitted a truly deeper understanding of the underlying processes within the different professional groups.

Summarizing Evaluation

The present survey was carried out using a combination of empirical methods. These different approaches were highly complementary for the intended measurement of cultural characteristics of different professions.

The standardized questionnaire served to measure quickly and objectively the different Professional Cultures present within the sample. In particular, due to the size of the sample – 507 persons – this task could only be carried out with a standardized quantitative tool. A meaningful interpretation of the data gathered was, however, only possible with the help of a qualitative tool (Lamnek 1995b, pp.51ff.).

The combination of methods pursued in this survey, known as triangulation, was necessary due to the complexity and novelty of the researched entities. This assessment follows the assumption that, through a combination of qualitative and quantitative research methods, it is possible to avoid, or at least control, the weaknesses inherent in each of these techniques (Lamnek 1995a, pp. 250f.). Furthermore, it is expected that a significantly deeper understanding of the researched entity is possible (Lamnek 1995a, p. 257). Therefore, despite the significantly increased efforts required by the inclusion of interviews into the research process, this approach was nevertheless followed as it was the only one guaranteeing a satisfactory level of quality for the data gathered.

5.1.3   Closing Remarks

To finish this illustration of the development process and the subsequent use of the methodology of this research project, some central points have to be kept in mind.

To begin with, the specifically high demands of this research project led to the necessity of choosing a rather complex course of action both for the development process of the methodology and for its subsequent implementation. Initially, it was necessary to develop an empirical research tool that is able to measure the phenomenon investigated in this work. Because the special focus of this work required a specialized research tool, it was necessary to develop a new tool that could match these specific demands. Consequently, the development itself had to encompass significant theoretical work as well as extensive practical research to reach an adequate research tool for the presented survey.

Subsequently, it was imperative to test this newly developed research device in order to ensure it is valid and reliable. This step added significantly more complexity to the development process, but was nevertheless necessary to check for the quality of the newly developed tool.

These considerations led to the above-described pilot study. Furthermore, it was necessary to split the main study into qualitative and quantitative parts. This necessity was once more a direct consequence of the complexity and novelty of the research topic.

As was pointed out, only a mixture between a quantitative and a qualitative approach, known as triangulation, provides the necessary insights required to understand adequately the research topic under the given conditions. Therefore, it was necessary to choose the rather complicated method of first administering a standardized questionnaire followed by a subsequent phase of qualitative interviews, in order to be able to reach a sufficiently deep understanding of the research questions raised in this work.

As will be shown in Chapters 6 and 7, this complex approach did in fact produce highly satisfying results. In particular, a limitation to only quantitative or qualitative research would not have been able to provide comparable results, as each kind of research provided different and highly complementary insights into the research topic, creating a deep understanding of the phenomenon of Professional Culture.

Therefore, in summary, it can be stated that the complexity of the development process of the research methodology, as well as that of its subsequent use, are a direct reflection of the complexity of the research topic itself.

5.2   The Implementation of the Empiricals

In this section, the way in which the above-described research tools were used will be described.

In order to do this, first the course of action for choosing the companies sampled will be depicted. For this reason, the governing principles leading to the inclusion or rejection of a specific company will be illustrated. Subsequently, the way in which the sampled professional groups were selected will be described. The underlying logic for the specific composition of the sample of professional groups will also be given.

In summary then, the present chapter illustrates the profile of the research sample and the reason that led to this specific profile.

5.2.1   The Choice of the Participating Companies

The course of action for choosing the sampled companies followed a number of different aspects. The main one was to include the complete value creation chain of the aviation industry. This led to the necessity of sampling suppliers, producers and customers represented by the airlines. This aspect alone created considerable complexity as far as the organization of the sampling process was concerned.

Due to the total time of about one year being spent on the recruitment of the different companies, it was possible to gather five suppliers, nine producers and five airlines. Therefore, the main goal was achieved as far as the composition of the sample is concerned.

A second goal was to include not only major companies in the sample, but also a number of smaller ones, employing less than 1000 people. Out of the 19 companies/independent subsidiaries sampled, three have less than 1000 employees. Therefore, the second objective was also reached.

A third aspect concerned the composition of the pool of airlines being sampled. This pool was to consist of network carriers and low-cost carriers, because of the significant differences between the business models of network carriers on the one hand and low-cost carriers on the other. Charter airlines could be discarded as their business model increasingly leans towards the low-cost airline's business model.

Out of the five airlines sampled, two were network carriers and three were low-cost carriers. Therefore, the third objective could also be attained with the sampled companies.

The fourth objective concerned the national origins of the people sampled. To avoid a national bias in the sample it was necessary to gather companies originating from different national backgrounds. Therefore, considerable attention was paid to the goal, which was to have a nationally heterogeneous sample – an objective achieved through the representation of ten nationalities from Europe, North and Central America.

To sum up, it can be said that the sample used shows the necessary traits to successfully pursue the above-described survey. All the objectives identified as relevant for the selection of the research sample were reached. Furthermore, the sample not only satisfies the necessary qualitative demands, but is also highly satisfying in quantitative terms, as will be shown in the following section.

5.2.2   The Choice of the Sampled Individuals

Choosing the researched individuals followed a fairly straightforward logic, as described later. The reason for doing this was to avoid unwanted biases, namely those of Organizational and National Cultures. Basically there are two possible approaches to avoid these biases.

The first would be to sample only one single company from one country. Assuming that the characteristics of the relevant National Culture were known and assuming further that the characteristics of the relevant Organizational Culture were also known, it would most likely be possible to isolate a number of different Professional Cultures present within that company. Therefore, this seems to be a feasible approach.

The main problem with this research design is, however, its serious lack of generalizability, not to mention the practical difficulty in finding a sufficiently large company that would participate in such a research design. Assuming again that a number of different Professional Cultures were found pursuing this approach, a significant danger would exist that these 'cultures' were only an artefact due to some peculiarity of the surveyed company, leading to serious reservations as to the possibility of transferring the results gained to other companies.

Therefore, the opposite approach was chosen. The goal for the composition of the pool of people surveyed was to achieve a maximum degree of heterogeneity. This aspect has already been discussed in the context of the choice of the companies surveyed. The logic of this approach is to neutralize the different uncontrollable and, for a large part, unknown biases by using a sample that is as diverse as possible.

By pursuing this approach, the clusters isolated within the survey, being empirically based on different professional backgrounds, would be exposed to the least possible degree to unwanted systematic biasing influences.

In summary, it can be said that the composition of the sample of the researched professionals allows for a largely unbiased and therefore highly suitable research sample for the present purpose. At first glance, the logic followed may seem slightly unusual, but it is the only feasible way to gather data that allow the insights gained with the present survey to reach beyond the boundaries of a single company.

5.2.3   The Identification of the Different Clusters

The first question to be answered in the context of the identification of the different professional clusters concerned the basic way in which these were to be isolated, as two possible approaches exist to achieve this goal.

The first approach would have been to identify theoretically the professional groups that would most likely be formed by the professions present within the sample. Subsequently, it would have been possible to check for the differences that exist between these different groups and to create with these data the different Professional Culture clusters. This course of action would have had the significant advantage of being relatively easy to handle and would have produced results quite quickly.

The disadvantage would have been that this would not have matched exactly the demands of the survey. This is because, by limiting the number of professional groups in the questionnaire, a pre-selection is already being carried out before knowing any of the actual study's results. This course of action can hardly be regarded as compatible with the explorative nature of the survey.

Therefore, the first decision as to the identification of the different clusters had already to be taken at the level of the development of the questionnaire. At this stage we opted against a pre-classification of different professions and in favour of every respondent filling out an open question asking what is his or her profession. Although this way of carrying out the survey significantly increased the complexity of its analysis, it had a number of remarkable advantages.

First of all, the clusters were constructed independently from the underlying professions and were based solely on the responses to the Core Cultural items of the questionnaire. This has the significant advantage of grouping the different respondents together as a consequence of their relative position towards each other on the nine Core Cultural Dimensions only.

Furthermore, it was possible to gain a broader picture of the different professions present within the sample. Only after having analyzed the sample were these professions grouped into clusters. The main advantage of this course of action was the total openness of the research process to completely unexpected combinations of professions in the different clusters. This thus prevented the results of the study from being biased by misleading assumptions about the resemblance of different professions.

Technically, this was achieved with a 'Hierarchical cluster analysis' using 'Between-Groups Linkage' and by calculating the 'Squared Euclidian Distance' (Everitt 1993; Bühl and Zöfel 2002; Fahrmeier 1996; Bacher 2002). A Hierarchical cluster analysis was chosen because it represents the most appropriate method available in the area of cluster analysis for the present purpose.

Other possible approaches would have been a 'Two-Step' or a 'K-Means' cluster analysis. Both approaches were discarded on theoretical grounds.

For a K-Means cluster analysis it is necessary to pre-specify the number of final clusters. Obviously this information was not available before running the cluster analysis, so the K-Means cluster analysis was not being employed in the current environment.

Two-Step cluster analysis, on the other hand, is used if computer calculation power is critical at the expense of analytical accuracy. As, for the present study, accuracy was more important than computational restraints, a Two-Step cluster analysis was also discarded.

The choice of the Squared Euclidian Distance method is based on the following logic. The 'Euclidian Distance', for instance, is the shortest spatial distance between two points in a two- or three-dimensional space: $\text{distance}(x,y)=[\sum_i (x_i-y_i)^2]^{1/2}$.

This distance can also be calculated in n-dimensional space and is therefore also appropriate for the present case, which has nine dimensions. Using the squared Euclidian Distance has the advantage of taking larger distances into account more than smaller ones, which in turn provides clearer separations between the different clusters.

Other possible approaches would have been the City Block (Manhattan), the Chebychev or the Minkowski Distance.

The 'Chebychev Distance' takes the distance between the two furthest elements of two cases as the distance between these cases: distance(x,y)=Maximum $|x_i-y_i|$. This has the advantage of being relatively economical as far as computational demands are concerned. The problem is, however, that this technique implies a significant loss in accuracy as 'outliers' become disproportionally important for the actual clustering.

The 'Manhattan Distance' ('Block distance') is comparable to the Euclidian Distance with the exception that it does not calculate the direct distance between two points, but the distance as it is encountered in American city blocks: distance(x,y)=$\sum_i |x_i-y_i|$. The disadvantage this technique exhibits, among others, is that it does not emphasize larger distances at the expense of smaller ones, therefore leading to a less clear cluster solution compared with the Squared Euclidian Distance. As the main advantage of the Manhattan Distance is simply that it saves computation time, it could be discarded for the benefit of the Squared Euclidian Distance.

The 'Minkowski Distance', finally, is the general form of the above given distances (for Chebychev set $m=\infty$): distance(x,y)=$[\sum_i(x_i-y_i)^m]^{1/m}$. Therefore, the Minkowski Distance was used in the form of the Euclidian Distance.

By comparing the different possible approaches it becomes clear that the Squared Euclidian Distance represents the most exact and appropriate measurement technique for the current environment, as it calculates the actual distances in an n-dimensional space. Furthermore, it incorporates a slightly increased weighting of greater distances, which provides clearer results in the clustering process, without, however, overemphasizing them as, for example, would be the case with the Chebychev Distance. Finally, no standardization was necessary, as the scales of the standardized questionnaire are the same for every dimension.

The logic that led to the selection of the Between-Groups Linkage was the following.

The 'Between-Groups Linkage' method calculates the average distance between all possible pairs of items belonging to two clusters, to determine the distance between these two clusters. Therefore, it takes into consideration all inter-cluster pairs, thus providing a very high degree of accuracy. The peer technique of the Between-Groups Linkage is basically Within-Groups Linkage. In the current context, Within-Groups Linkage has the disadvantage of producing clusters that are too tight and the technique was therefore discarded.

Alternative techniques would have been Nearest and Furthest Neighbour, Centroid, Median Clustering and Ward's Method.

'Nearest' and 'Furthest Neighbour' have the disadvantage that either the closest (Nearest Neighbour) or the furthest elements (Furthest Neighbour) exclusively determine the distance between two clusters. This obviously implies a significant loss in accuracy for the final solution, as compared with the Between-Groups Linkage technique.

'Centroid' and 'Median Clustering' both determine the distance between two clusters as the (Euclidian) distance between the respective cluster means. Whereas Centroid Clustering takes into consideration cluster size when for example two clusters are merged, Median Clustering does not take into account size differences when joining clusters. The loss of accuracy when working with averages instead of raw data led to these techniques also being discarded.

Finally, 'Ward's Method' calculates the total sum of squared deviations for a given cluster and tries to minimize the increase of this value when adding elements. When two clusters have to be joined, those that produce the smallest increase in the total sum of squared deviations are joined. This approach was checked for appropriateness but, unfortunately, it produced less satisfying results than the finally retained Between-Groups Linkage method.

By comparing the different possible approaches it now becomes clear that the most appropriate technique for the current environment is the above-described Between-Groups Linkage method, as it is theoretically well adapted to the demands of the current study and produced the best overall results when actually employed.

The cluster analysis led to the identification of 12 Clusters. The number of clusters was determined based on two different features.

The first was the above-described statistical cluster analysis, which provides any number of clusters between 507 (the number of responses) and one single cluster, where all cases are united in this one cluster. As both of these results obviously do not make sense, a meaningful number of clusters had to be identified.

This goal was pursued with a content-based approach, which represents the second feature. This approach was favoured, as no clearly significant point regarding the distance coefficients could be observed within the cluster analysis. Furthermore, considering the nature of the current survey, it was advisable to focus on the actual content of a key question of the questionnaire, as pointed out below, than to base the clustering results on a mere technical figure.

Hence, the occupations of the respective respondents were used as reference points (see Appendix 2 for details). A level of aggregation (i.e. the number of clusters) was chosen on which the maximum number of similar occupations could be united in the minimum number of clusters. This course of action led to the above-mentioned 12 clusters; any further aggregation would have led to a significant loss of accuracy in the results, whereas any less aggregation would have counteracted the goal of this research to identify professional groups that form cultures instead of just defining the characteristics of certain occupations.

The different characteristics of these clusters will be described in the following chapter. It can, however, be taken that, at this point, the clear extraction of 12 clusters represents strong support for the thesis of the existence of the construct of Professional Cultures.

5.3   Final Assessment of the Development and Implementation of the Research Tool

The development and the management of the empirical survey followed the logic of providing the data necessary for the successful accomplishment of this study.

This goal encompassed two main objectives. The first was the development of a tool that possesses the necessary qualities to provide useful data of a sufficiently high quality for subsequent analysis. This goal was pursued and achieved with the efforts described concerning, on the one hand, the development of the questionnaire and, on the other, the design of the study. In particular, the design of the study, being divided into a quantitative and a qualitative part, played a major role in the achievement of this goal.

The second objective consisted of the kind and amount of data fulfilling certain requirements. The amount of data required is a direct consequence of the quantitative analysis undertaken, which requires a certain minimum amount of respondents. This goal could clearly be achieved, although the difficulties of reaching a sufficiently large sample in the industry should not be underestimated. Even more complicated was the kind of data necessary for the study. The data had to fulfil the various demands described in this chapter, ranging from the avoidance of any bias to the adequate representation of various countries, companies and possibly all professions present in this industry.

Notwithstanding these challenges, both objectives were achieved.

The questionnaire used in the survey fulfilled both the necessary criteria mentioned above and the necessary amount of data, with 507 respondents. Finally, the composition of the sample and therefore the kind of data collected also fulfilled all requirements, with the representation of the whole value creation chain of the aviation industry and that of a large variety of different Professions. Hence, it can be said in summary, that the presented exploratory study is able to generate insights into the area of Professional Culture research that are of a remarkable high quality and which open the door to a new and significantly deeper understanding of this highly important field of research.

Chapter 6

The Results of the Empirical Study I

In this and the following chapter, the results of the empirical survey will be described. These results are arranged around the clusters that could be isolated within this part of the research project. After the detailed description of the characteristics of the different Professional Cultures an appropriate leadership style and organization design will be developed for each Professional Culture identified.

A depiction of predominantly executing functions will be undertaken in this chapter, whereas in the following chapter the more guiding functions are described.

As mentioned, it was possible to isolate 12 clusters. These clusters were determined with the help of the previously described cluster analysis. Also, as pointed out in Section 5.2.2, a maximum degree of heterogeneity of the sample was aimed for so as to neutralize the influences that different systematic biases may exercise.

Three possible influencing factors were accounted for with the standardized questionnaire: national origin (determining National Culture), organizational origin (determining Organizational Culture) and gender. National and organizational heterogeneity were achieved for all Professional Cultures isolated. Gender-related heterogeneity is scrutinized within the analysis of the different Professional Cultures where appropriate.

Hence, the intended composition of the research sample was achieved, leading to the results of the current study being rather well protected against a systematic influence of the three factors mentioned above.

The clusters themselves unite 340 responses, which represents nearly 70% of all responses present in the sample. Unfortunately, due to the nature of the survey, no statement as to the return rate of the questionnaire can be given.

As already mentioned, the questionnaires were sent out in the form of an e-mail containing a link to the website of the survey. Technically, it was not possible to track the responses back to every individual respondent as this would have required a direct contact to each possible respondent with an individual key. This course of action was not acceptable for the participating companies, for two reasons.

One reason was the necessary choice with which the respective contact persons within the companies would have been confronted, to either publish internal e-mail distribution channels or to face an incredible amount of work to carry out the distribution of the questionnaires themselves. Neither of these choices was accepted.

Beyond that aspect, a second highly important reason led to the rejection of this course of action altogether. That aspect concerned the possible violation of privacy the distribution of individual access keys would have entailed for the surveyed employees. This clear possibility would have dramatically reduced the participation rate and, most likely, also the quality of the collected data.

Therefore, we opted against this course of action, thus leading to the unavailability of any firm figures concerning the return rate. Based on existing literature, however, it can be estimated that, with a distribution system such as that used for the current study, under consideration of the specific traits of the present situation, a return rate of about 15 to 30% can be expected, leading to an overall size of the sample of 1700 to 3400 persons (e.g. Meffert 2000; Scharf and Schubert 2001; Preißner and Engel 1997; Ott 1972).

As far as the technical quality of the collected data is concerned, it can be stated that it is highly satisfying. In accordance with the course of action of the pilot study, the reliability of the main study was verified with the calculation of Cronbach's Alpha for every Core Cultural Dimension. The exact results are given in Table 6.1.

Table 6.1 Reliability of the Main Survey

Core Cultural Dimension	Cronbach's Alpha
Uncertainty Avoidance	0.7213
Assertiveness	0.8272
Future Orientation	0.7879
Power Distance	0.6732
Collectivism I	0.6639
Performance Orientation	0.7702
Gender Egalitarianism	0.6886
Human Orientation	0.7542
Collectivism II	0.7321

The results are presented by joining the quantitative and the qualitative parts of the research project. This part of the analysis serves the identification of the different Professional Cultures represented by the various clusters isolated.

The actual interpretation of the differences between the various clusters was carried out with the help of the so-called *Test Banding* (Saltstone *et al.* 2001; Murphy 1994; Cascio *et al.* 1991).

Initially, this technique goes back, among others, to personnel selection and was used to determine a range of scores that cannot be distinguished from the top score present in the given sample.

In accordance with the course of action pursued in the GLOBE-Study, it is used in this work to determine a point at which the difference between two test scores is actually statistically meaningfully different (Hanges *et al.* 2004). The underlying assumption for this course of action is that an imperfect relationship exists between the measured scale score for a cultural cluster and the actual score if all members of that cluster had filled in the questionnaire. The main source for this imperfect relationship is random error. Therefore, the idea of Test Banding is to determine the values at which two cultures on a given cultural scale are to be considered statistically significantly different. These values are determined with the use of the confidence level the researcher wants to achieve and the standard error of measurement (SED).

According to Gulliksen (1987) the SED can be calculated with the following formula:

$$\text{SED} = S_x = \sqrt{2}\sqrt{(1 - r_{xx'})}$$

Here, S_x is the standard deviation of all the cultures on a given core cultural scale and $r_{xx'}$ represents the reliability that scale, expressed by the aforementioned Cronbach's Alpha. In order to determine the actual bandwidth, the SED has to be multiplied by a factor C depending on the confidence level sought. Here, a 95% confidence is opted for, leading to a factor of $C = 1.96$. Hence, the bandwidth is calculated in the present work with the formula:

$$1.96 \times S_x \sqrt{2}\sqrt{(1 - r_{xx'})}$$

This led to the identification of either two or three distinguishable bands for each Core Cultural Dimension, which we named following their scores 'High', 'Medium' and 'Low'.

The cut-off scores of these bands are given in Table 6.2. The top score given for each Core Cultural Dimension is the highest score observed in this survey for that culture; e.g. the score of 4.76 for the Power Distance dimension (PD) is the score of the Project Leaders' culture for that dimension and represents the highest score for that dimension out of all cultures present in the survey. The following cut-off scores are then calculated according to the individual bandwidths of the various Core Cultural Dimensions.

Table 6.2   The Band Width Values of the Different Core Cultural Dimensions

Dimension	Bandwidth values**		
UA	6.45 ≥ 1st group ≥ 4.77	4.77 > 2nd group ≥ 3.11	3.11 > 3rd group ≥ 1.43
ASS	5.87 ≥ 1st group ≥ 4.46	4.46 > 2nd group ≥ 3.05	3.05 > 3rd group ≥ 1.64
FO	6.23 ≥ 1st group ≥ 4.67	4.67 > 2nd group ≥ 3.10	3.10 > 3rd group ≥ 1.53
PD	4.67 ≥ 1st group ≥ 3.40	3.40 > 2nd group ≥ 2.14	2.14 > 3rd group ≥ 0.87
CI*	6.24 ≥ 1st group ≥ 5.16	5.16 > 2nd group ≥ 4.08	4.08 > 3rd group ≥ 3.00
PO	6.75 ≥ 1st group ≥ 5.50	5.50 > 2nd group ≥ 4.26	4.26 > 3rd group ≥ 3.01
GE	6.52 ≥ 1st group ≥ 5.45	5.45 > 2nd group ≥ 4.39	4.39 > 3rd group ≥ 3.33
HO	5.59 ≥ 1st group ≥ 4.42	4.42 > 2nd group ≥ 3.25	3.25 > 3rd group ≥ 2.08
CII	6.60 ≥ 1st group ≥ 5.57	5.57 > 2nd group ≥ 4.54	4.54 > 3rd group ≥ 3.51

UA: Uncertainty Avoidance; ASS: Assertiveness; FO: Future Orientation; PD: Power Distance; CI: Collectivism I; PO: Performance Orientation; GE: Gender Egalitarianism; HO: Human Orientation; CII: Collectivism II
* : 3rd group not occupied
** : 1st group represents 'HIGH', 2nd group 'MEDIUM' and 3rd group 'LOW' scores for the purpose of the following work

To visualize this, the graphical example in Figure 6.1 is given; a graphical overview of all Professional Cultures for all Core Cultural Dimensions will be given at the end of the next chapter. The title of the graphic indicates the name of the Core Cultural Dimension, which in this example is 'Uncertainty Avoidance'.

The legend next to the graphic indicates

- The name of the Professional Culture and its score for that Core Cultural Dimension visualized by the left bar;
- The 'bandwidths' of that Core Cultural Dimension, as calculated above, visualized by the right bar.

In the current example, the Blue Collar Workers group has, with a confidence of 95%, a higher 'Uncertainty Avoidance' than the Specially Qualified Production Experts. This is due to the fact that, in accordance with the above calculations, the Blue Collar Workers are located in the 'High' area of the 'Uncertainty Avoidance' dimension, whereas the Specially Qualified Production Experts only scored in the 'Medium' area.

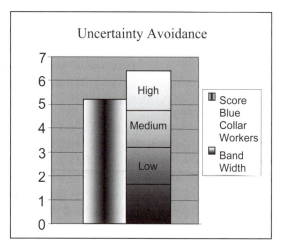

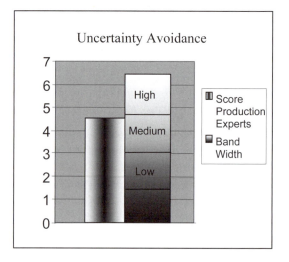

Figure 6.1 The Relative Positioning of the Different Professional Cultures

After having given a thorough description of the characteristics of the different cultural clusters, appropriate leadership and organizational styles will be developed for each cluster. These leadership and organizational styles constitute the basis for the remaining research project.

The leadership styles themselves go back to the findings of the GLOBE-Study, as six globally valid leadership dimensions could be identified in the course of this research project (House *et al.* 2004). These leadership dimensions, referred to as Culturally Endorsed Implicit Leadership Theories, are an extension of the Implicit Leadership Theory (ILT) of Lord and Maher (1991). ILT postulates that individuals have a set of beliefs that determine which kind of characteristics, behaviors and traits enhance or impede outstanding leadership. According to ILT, these beliefs determine to which degree individuals accept someone as a leader.

CLT extends this theory by arguing that these belief systems are shared among individuals of a common culture both on the societal and the organizational level (Dorfman *et al.* 2004, p. 669). In accordance with the aforementioned line of argument, that it is feasible to use findings originating within organizational research, these CLTs will be the basis for the development of appropriate leadership styles in the research project presented here. The six CLTs identified are labelled as follows (Dorfman *et al.* 2004, pp. 674f.):

- Charismatic/Value-Based Leadership
- Team-Oriented Leadership
- Participative Leadership
- Humane Oriented Leadership
- Autonomous Leadership
- Self-Protective Leadership

'Charismatic/Value-Based leadership' expresses the ability of a leader to lead people on the basis of firmly held core beliefs. An example for this kind of leadership is the 'Charismatic/Transformational leadership (e.g. Bass 1985; Burns 1978; see Section 2.2.3 for details).

'Team-Oriented leadership' is based on the creation of functioning teams and the creation of common team centred goals. An example for this kind of leadership is the SuperLeadership approach presented in Section 2.2.2 (Manz and Sims 2001).

Participative leadership is focused on the degree to which the leaders involve their employees in the decision-taking and implementation process (e.g. Lewin 1948; Tannenbaum and Schmidt 1958). Examples for this dimension can be found in Section 2.1.1, in which the degree of employee participation is the reference point for the leadership relationship.

'Human Oriented leadership' is centred on the question of how supportive and considerate leaders are of their employees and includes aspects such as generosity and compassion (e.g. Gagné and Fleishman 1959; Fleishman and Quaintance 1984; Blake and Mouton 1985; see Section 2.1.2 for details).

'Autonomous leadership' focuses on the degree of autonomy and individualism leaders show in the exercise of their function. Previously, this dimension had not been identified as relevant in leadership research.

'Self Protective leadership' is based on securing safety and security of the individual or the group member. In the context of the GLOBE-Study this dimension was also newly defined and incorporates the key traits of a leader, such as being self-centred, status conscious, a face saver or living in a procedural way.

The organizational styles will be developed on the basis of the findings of Chapter 3 and, obviously, the results of the empiricals described in this and the following chapters.

The appropriate leadership style for each group will be developed on the basis of Chapter 2, the leadership styles isolated within the GLOBE-Study and the empirical results as described in the following.

These results are focused on isolating the Core Cultural Dimensions developed in the course of the GLOBE-Study as described above. On the basis of these Core Cultural Dimensions, it is possible explicitly to develop appropriate leadership styles. To do that, the following key was used, which is an adaptation of the original GLOBE key to the needs of the present study.

Following the logic that empirical tools, developed for use in the context of Organizational Culture research, can be used in the current environment, only those in relation to Organizational Cultures were retained. For further details concerning the development of these keys refer to Dorfman *et al.* (2004).

Charismatic/Value-Based leadership follows if there is a 'High' rating of

- Performance Orientation
- Collectivism II
- Future Orientation
- Human Orientation

Team-Oriented leadership is a consequence of a 'High' rating of

- Uncertainty Avoidance
- Collectivism II
- Human Orientation
- Performance Orientation
- Future Orientation

Participative leadership is the appropriate leadership style in the presence of

a 'High' rating of

- Performance Orientation
- Gender Egalitarianism

and a 'Low' rating of

- Uncertainty Avoidance
- Assertiveness

Human-Oriented leadership should be preferred if there is a 'High' rating of

- Human Orientation
- Uncertainty Avoidance
- Performance Orientation
- Future Orientation

Autonomous leadership follows in case of a 'High' rating of

- Performance Orientation

and a 'Low' rating of

- Collectivism I

Self-Protective leadership should be employed if there is a 'High' rating of

- Power Distance
- Uncertainty Avoidance
and a 'Low' rating of

- Performance Orientation

Initially, these leadership and organizational styles serve to develop an approach as to how to lead effectively and organize each Professional Culture isolated in this work. Subsequently, an integrative approach will be developed that is focused on some of those Professional Cultures that are rather likely to work together. This is especially important to illustrate the enormous beneficial consequences the results of the present study have for cross-cultural work environments.

Furthermore, the developed leadership and organizational styles form the base for Chapter 8 in which the validity of these results will be scrutinized.

Therefore, it can be retained at this point that the present chapter, in connection with Chapters 7 and 8, is one of the core chapters of this work. It will unite all previous chapters around the results gained with the empiricals of this survey. Therefore, at various occasions, this chapter will be referenced to previous chapters in order to point to the underlying theoretical links.

Finally, it has to be noted that the present as well as the next chapter is not limited to uniting the empirical results gained in the course of this study with existing theories, but that it will also combine, alter and newly present existing theories of organizational and leadership research according to the specific traits of the different cultural clusters isolated.

Therefore, it can be said that the following chapters will be a highly interesting illustration of joining organizational and leadership theory with empirically gained insights in order to create a number of completely new approaches to this area of research.

6.1   The Blue Collar Workers

The first Cluster comprises Blue Collar Workers. According to the results of the survey these are employees such as mechanics with a lower qualification, storehouse workers, or individuals ensuring the company's internal transport of goods (e.g. fork-lift drivers, truck drivers on company ground etc.). In general, the Blue Collar Workers group comprises employees who are working in directly production related, auxiliary and/or supportive parts of the production process. Typically, these jobs require none, or only relatively little training and are therefore positioned in the lower levels of the hierarchy of a company. The Blue Collar Worker usually only has superiors but no subordinates and, depending on the specific job, can either work alone or in groups.

These characteristics of the work environment of Blue Collar Workers are reflected in the following results of the quantitative and the qualitative research carried out.

6.1.1   The Empirical Base

As mentioned, the results of the empirical survey are based on a quantitative and a qualitative part.

For this group the quantitative part has already delivered very clear results. Only people of the above-mentioned qualification could be found within this group. The group itself consists of 25 people originating from various countries and organizations. The only restriction as to the intended diversity of each sample has to be stated at the level of the gender composition, as primarily male respondents are present in this group.

The findings of the quantitative part were enhanced by those of the qualitative. Out of the seven interviewees, four were women in order to correct a potential bias occurring due to the composition of the quantitative sample. However, no such bias could be determined, which confirmed the results of the quantitative part.

Therefore, it can be retained that the empirical results for the Blue Collar Workers' group were highly coherent and satisfying.

The Quantitative Results

The results of the quantitative part are centred on the Dimensions of the GLOBE-Study as introduced in previous chapters. The 'Uncertainty Avoidance' Dimension is rated relatively high in this group with a score of 5.23. One reason for this can be seen in the relatively limited possibilities for the individual workers to influence their immediate work environment. They therefore prefer to live in a stable environment in which they are not constantly forced to adapt to changes they cannot influence. A further reason is to be seen in relation to the way the individual workers see their work and the importance this work has in their life. Usually, work is seen by members of this group as a means to earn the money necessary for a living and not as a means in itself. Therefore, stable environments are preferred that do not put too much pressure on the individual worker.

These aspects will be discussed later, as this relatively strong score on the Uncertainty Avoidance scale was one of the major topics in a number of interviews.

Related to the above-mentioned limitations as to the possibility to influence one's immediate work environment, the score on the 'Assertiveness' scale (2.07) has to be seen, which is positioned at the lower end.

Compared with the other Professional Cultures identified, the score of the Blue Collar Worker group is the lowest score of the whole sample. To characterize this as an expression of fatalism would be an exaggeration, but a certain indifference as to the work environment itself can certainly be deduced from this result. This assessment is due to the fact that it is non-assertive behaviour is usually the safest way to live a life in which one does not have the possibility of directly altering the demands to which one is subject, and so one can 'just do the job'.

Here again, a number of interesting insights were gained in the course of the interviews. 'Future Orientation' is positioned just at the border between the medium and the high band (4.76). This is a direct consequence of the job environment of this group.

Typically, 'Blue Collar jobs' do not require the people who do them to have a particularly long term horizon, as they usually get a certain piece of work that needs to be done in a certain time. On the other hand, they still need to have a clear concept of time as they have to make sure that they keep to their time schedules. These counteracting influences moderate each other to a certain extent, which leads to this dimension being at the rating shown.

The 'Power Distance' dimension is, compared with the other professional groups, rated in the very moderately positive area (3.6). A possible explanation, which will be pointed out below, can be seen in the area of tension between the individual's need for self-governance and independence, which every human being has to varying degrees, and the need for guidance and security exhibited here.

The 'Collectivism I' dimension is rated in the very low medium area (4.27). Furthermore, this rating represents the lowest score in comparison to any other cultural cluster (the Collectivism I dimension does not have any culture in the low area). This result can be seen as a consequence of the fact that the members of this group often do not really see the need for extensive team work. This will be further investigated in the following.

The 'Performance Orientation' dimension is likewise rated in the very low medium area (4.45), representing the second lowest value for this dimension out of all cultural clusters. This has to be seen in relation to the already-mentioned importance that work has in the life of the members of this group.

'Gender Egalitarianism' is valued in the lower medium area (4.72), and is the second lowest absolute value out of all groups. This rating may be seen as an artefact of the facts that it is predominantly men who are present in this group, and the relative indifference that Blue Collar Workers have towards matters that are not directly work related.

'Human Orientation' is scored in the higher neutral area (4.21). This can be seen as a consequence of the fact that, apparently, this Dimension has no significant meaning to the members of this group. The reasons for that will be pointed out below.

The 'Collectivism II' dimension finally is valued in the lower medium area (4.85). This represents the second lowest rating out of all Professional Cultures.

As this dimension is an indicator for pride in the group and the profession, these results have to be seen once more as a consequence of the place and importance that work has for the members of this group.

In the following section, these different insights will be deepened and clarified with the help of the results of the interviews.

The Qualitative Results

The results of the qualitative part described in this section are largely in line with those of the quantitative part.

According to the information gathered with the help of the interviews, the ratings on the Uncertainty Avoidance, the Power Distance, the Assertiveness and the Collectivism II scale have to be considered in correlation as they all relate to the following facts.

The regular Blue Collar Workers do not see the job as a source of pleasure in itself, but only as a way to earn the means necessary to fulfil their wishes outside the work environment. Therefore, their interest in the job is mainly to have a stable environment in which it is perfectly clear to them what they are supposed to do. The preference for a stable environment finds its expression in the high rating on the Uncertainty Avoidance scale and was clearly confirmed by the interviewees. The most important thing for the members of this group is to have a safe job, which stays stable over time. Any change in work routines or organizational structures is normally rejected. Very often, the initially stated reason for that is that existing structures are the best and that new structures are 'developed by people who don't know anything about the demands of the actual job'.

A little further down in the interview process it became clear that this is not the entire picture. Very strong resentment against any kind of change-related processes can be stated about this group. This resentment has to be seen in connection with the very strong emphasis on the value of leisure activities. The job itself is seen as a necessary evil only. Any activity that requires extra work and/or time of the individual worker is therefore rejected.

The rating on the Power Distance scale has to be seen in direct correlation with this aspect. At first sight, the slightly positive score of the Power Distance scale by a group that finds itself exclusively on the receiving end of the chain of command may surprise. With the results of the interviews, however, this becomes significantly more understandable. The individual workers do not necessarily consider a stronger hierarchy to be a means of oppressing them. If implemented and lived in a moderate way, it is seen as a relief instead. The leader gives guidance, help and structure to the workers' environment and therefore relieves them from the burden of having to worry about anything else except the occupational activity itself.

In this context, the low rating on the Assertiveness scale also becomes clearer, as it can be seen as an expression of the lack of ability and motivation to influence things that are not in direct connection with the individual's work. According to the interviews, the most appropriate course of action in this setting is to simply fulfil the job and behave in a friendly and cautious manner, particularly towards management.

This self-image of the individual workers, in which they see their job as nothing special or worth mentioning, is obviously reflected in the rating of the Collectivism II scale and could be confirmed by the interviews. Pride in the job only exists to a very limited degree in this group. This statement is hardly surprising for members of a group who explicitly do not attribute any deeper meaning to their jobs.

That view, however, cannot be seen as an expression of bitterness, but instead as a rational weighing of the possible satisfaction that can be extracted from the job on the one hand, and that which can be extracted from the individual's leisure time on the other.

A clear connection between the above results and the score on the Performance Orientation scale could be confirmed in the interviews. As already stated, the job has no further meaning beyond the income that can be earned with it, which is clearly extrinsic motivation (Maslow 1970; Deci 1975; Thomae 1999). In accordance with current motivational research, this leads to somewhat limited motivation to perform in an extraordinary manner on the job. Instead, the individual worker's goal is to maximize revenue while minimizing effort. This obviously does not mean that they do not perform their task properly, but it does mean that their motivation to do more than is expected is rather limited.

The medium to high rating on the Future Orientation scale can be explained by the nature of the job. On the one hand, most jobs in this group are of a quite simple structure, which implies that no particularly long-term horizon is needed in order to do the job properly. On the other hand, short term time schedules do exist in most of the jobs present in this cultural group. This is because, obviously, in most production processes one needs to keep to a clear sequence of activities. According to the results of the interviews, these two factors moderate each other, which leads to the rating on the Future Orientation scale.

The ratings on the Collectivism I and the Human Orientation scales are also a direct consequence of the nature of the jobs in this group. Usually, no real teamwork exists in this group. Even if people do not work completely alone, they work predominantly next to each other instead of actually working together. According to the interviews, this statement of fact is not seen overly negatively, as apparently most interviewees are rather satisfied with this kind of organization. Even when explicitly asked, an organization that is structured on the basis of real work teams was not considered to be necessarily more compelling than present organizational structures.

Human Orientation seems to be of less importance in this highly technical environment. According to the interviews, it is important for the workers to get along with each other well and to have a good and warm relationship with their direct leader. The interpersonal relationships do not really get beyond that point, though. This is possibly enhanced by the fact that the quantitative sample is composed predominantly of men, which does not overly favour the values that are expressed by the Human Orientation scale. Nevertheless, the neutral esteem for Human Orientation was confirmed by the female respondents of the interviews. In effect, these mutually influential factors moderate each other, which led to the neutral rating in the quantitative part.

Finally, the lower medium rating of the Gender Egalitarianism scale can be seen as a direct consequence of the composition of this group, the relative position work has in the Blue Collar Workers' life and the work environment. All of which favour the evolvement of a culture that is rather indifferent to criticism about gender egalitarianism and its values.

Summarizing Considerations

The empirical results for this cluster give a coherent and highly interesting illustration of the characteristics of Blue Collar Workers in the aviation industry.

The most interesting aspect for this cluster is without doubt the very clear separation between the professional activities of the individual workers and their private life. Apparently, life for this cluster is exclusively centred on leisure activities. Work itself has no intrinsically motivating quality for this cluster. At this point the question arises as to how far it is possible to change that situation. The answer to this will not be given here, as the main question is whether this situation *should* be changed.

It has to be kept in mind that the leadership style and the organizational structure that will be developed in the following are based on the opinion of the members of this group of 'how things *should* be'. Therefore, the data are a direct reflection of how Blue Collar Workers want their work environment to be structured.

According to the results of the quantitative and the qualitative part, members of this Cultural group are not overly interested in investing any more or any different energy into their work. The unambiguous emphasis on private life is a clear peculiarity of the members of the Blue Collar Workers' Culture.

The consequences of that for the appropriate leadership style and organizational structure are quite far-reaching, as will be shown in the following. However, it is important not to misinterpret the results presented up to now as an expression of a lack of understanding and motivation by the members of this cultural group.

The statements made in the interviews clearly show that the relative importance given to private and professional life is the direct consequence of a rational process in which work in general has a significantly different meaning in comparison to most other cultural groups. Furthermore, this interpretation is strongly supported by the results of the quantitative part.

In summary, it can be stated that the empirical results gave very interesting, although somewhat surprising, results, which represent an extremely valuable base for the following development of an appropriate leadership style and organizational structure.

6.1.2   *An Integrative Solution to the Found Characteristics*

An integrative solution has to take into account the very special characteristics of this Professional Culture. Especially for members of this group, the place the job has in their lives needs to be considered when developing leadership and organizational structures.

As will be shown in the following, it is necessary to create an environment in which the respective workers feel well without putting too much strain upon them, as far as demands that are not directly related to their job are concerned.

In summary, it can be said that this Professional Culture has a number of highly interesting and surprising traits that demand very special treatment of these employees in the professional world.

The Appropriate Leadership Style

According to the results of the empirical part and in connection with those of the GLOBE-Study (House *et al.* 2004), the following leadership style characteristics should be applied when working with members of the Blue Collar Workers' group.

The base of the leadership style should be centred on the 'Self-Protective Leadership Style' (House *et al.* 2004). This self-protection is, however, not to be seen as self-protection of the leader, but as self-protection of the group. As the main interest of the members of the Blue Collar Workers group is to do their job without having to worry about other things, it is important for the leaders to take that burden off their subordinates. While doing that, they have to make sure that their subordinates are protected as far as possible from any negative external influence. Obviously they will have to keep in mind the greater company interest, but it is vitally important that they give 'their people' the feeling that they are there for them, to protect and help them. For that reason it is furthermore necessary that the appropriate leadership style includes some elements of the 'Human-Oriented Leadership Style' (e.g. Gagné and Fleishman 1959; Fleishman and Quaintance 1984; Blake and Mouton 1985; House *et al.* 2004; see also Section 2.1.2). By adding some warmth and care to the leadership relationship the above-described group protection is rounded off at the group internal level.

In addition, the appropriate leadership style should incorporate elements of the 'Autonomous Leadership Style' (House *et al.* 2004). This is required as workers expect their leaders to do what is necessary in order to achieve the above-given leadership relationship. Furthermore, workers are conscious of the fact that this kind of leadership is not entirely usual for leaders on that leadership level.

In summary, an appropriate leadership style for the Blue Collar Workers' group should be as follows.

The leader should use a rather straightforward leadership style in which the individual workers always know what they are supposed to do. Furthermore, the leader has to make sure that the respective workers are shielded as much as possible from any further external influences that go beyond the boundaries of their immediate work environment. In that context, it is extremely important that the leader keeps up a good interpersonal relationship with the subordinates.

However, this good interpersonal relationship does not mean that the leaders are supposed to integrate their subordinates into each and every decision-taking process. It only means that they have to enhance the above-mentioned protection by giving their subordinates the feeling that they actually care about them and their well being.

This behaviour, however, is of such importance to the members of the Blue Collar Workers' group that they even expect their leaders to deviate from leadership behaviour that is usually seen and accepted in order to achieve the leadership style described here. In consequence, they grant them the freedom to behave rather individualistically if at least part of that individualism is focused on the realization of that warm, protective, but rather strict and detailed leadership style.

In summary, the leadership style favoured by the members of the Blue Collar Workers' group goes in the direction of the 'Patriarchal leadership' according to Wunderer (2001; see also Sections 2.2.1 and 2.1.1.2). For leaders of this cultural group it is, on the one hand, of the utmost importance to give sufficient guidance to their subordinates, which obviously excludes any overly participative leadership style. On the other hand, it is equally important to make sure that the individual workers always know that the leaders are actually giving the orders they are in order to help them, or if not to help an individual worker directly then at least the goal of the group. This should be achieved through the creation of a relationship in which the role of the leader is mutually perceived such that there is usually no discussion of whether a certain measure or decision is actually to be carried out.

Nevertheless, the leaders have to demonstrate clearly that they understand the worries and problems of their subordinates and that they will stand up for them if necessary. This means that they may have to oppose the implementation of certain measures if they see that they are clearly inappropriate for their subordinates.

Therefore, the term Patriarchal leadership is rather appropriate in this context, as the role of the leader is very much like that of a benevolent patriarch who makes sure that everybody does what he or she is supposed to do by ruling gently but firmly on the internal level, and by protecting everybody on the external level.

The Appropriate Organizational Structure

The appropriate organizational structure for this cultural cluster is somewhat in contradiction to the newer models described in Chapter 3.

Empirically, it has to be stated that the motivations of the members of the present group are not in line with a number of different assumptions of the above-described theoretical approaches. Instead, a more classical route has to be taken in order to match the expectations, wishes and needs of the members of the Blue Collar Workers' group.

The empirical results clearly point to a hierarchical solution in the sense of Fayol's Administrative Approach as the basis of an appropriate organizational structure (Fayol 1984; see also Section 3.1.1). But this hierarchical solution has to be adapted to the above-described needs of the present group. In order to achieve the necessary close relationship between the leaders and their subordinates it is necessary to opt for an organization in which the different work entities are not too big. The actual size depends, obviously, on varying factors, such as the nature of the task, the nature of the work space, etc. The decisive factor though is that a personal contact between the direct leaders and their subordinates is possible, in order to allow for the above-described leadership relationship.

According to the results gained in the empirical part, a Team-Oriented organization, which actually deserves this term in the sense given in previous chapters, is not necessarily advisable in this environment.

This conclusion may be somewhat unexpected as it is in contradiction to significant parts of organizational theory and research, but the results of the empirical part do not allow for any other conclusion. The appropriate organization structure according to the results of this study is the following.

The Blue Collar Workers are organized in relatively small groups. It is not necessary to create artificially a team-based work flow. Instead, it is important to have clearly responsible leaders as the hierarchical head of the group. These leaders need to be given the ability to actually lead their group. Therefore, it is necessary to give them the organizational freedom actually to take decisions for their group.

A holistic task structure should be striven for, in which the individual workers are able actually to see what they are building. This aspect is also in accordance with existing research that postulates that giving responsibility to the employees significantly increases motivation and therefore efficiency (e.g. Hackman and Oldham 1975, 1980).

Control mechanisms should be used in a very cautious manner only. Mostly, 'control' should be exercised through the close and trusting relationship the leaders are supposed to build up with their subordinates in order to achieve a state in which there is no need for formalized control in the work group (see for the relevance of trust, for example, Weibler 2001).

In summary, it can be stated that the Blue Collar Workers' group needs a rather classical organizational structure in which direct leadership is relatively important in comparison to indirect leadership. Furthermore, the task structure should be as close as possible to that of a tradesman, as this significantly enhances the individual motivation.

Summarizing Thoughts

The appropriate organizational structure for this cluster is based on a very personal way of leading people.

The role of the direct leader is of significant importance. This is due to the fact that the members of the Blue Collar Workers' group want and need a strong leader who is able to guide and help them. This renders it extremely important that the individual leader actually understands and uses the concept described above.

The organizational structure is of a more supportive nature in the present environment. It only gives the framework for the leaders in which they create the leadership relationship with their subordinates. This role of the organization is not without importance, but significantly less important than in a number of other cultural groups (see for example Section 6.2 'The Flight Attendants' or 6.4 'The Pilots').

Finally, the way members of this cultural group want their work to be structured has to be taken into consideration. It is not advisable to proceed to a too fragmented work process in which, for example, the individual worker exclusively tightens

50,000 screws a day. In general, it can be stated that the more holistic the work process is organized, the better it is from an organizational point of view.

In summary, it can be stated that the approach presented here is somewhat different from a number of other theoretical approaches. In particular, the low importance of Participative and Team-Oriented elements for the members of this cluster is remarkable. According to the empirical results of this survey, the consideration that these elements are appropriate in virtually any environment has to be rejected.

This result clearly shows again the importance of a culturally adjusted leadership and organizational structure for the success of any company, as no structure that is appropriate in all circumstances exists.

6.1.3   *Final Thoughts Regarding the Blue Collar Workers*

The results for the first cluster give a number of highly interesting and rather surprising insights into both the characteristics of the cluster itself and leadership and organizational theory altogether.

According to these results, it is indeed necessary to adjust both leadership and organizational design specifically to this Professional Culture. Furthermore, the characteristics of this group somewhat contradict the idea that some elements, such as teamwork or the non-existence of a hierarchy, are virtually always advantageous.

The quality of the empirical data gathered also suggests that these results are not the consequence of just some randomly influencing factors within the sample. The composition of the group is very coherent, as it consists only of employees with a rather low qualification who work in jobs relevant to this qualification in directly production-related parts of the companies surveyed.

Furthermore, as stated, these employees originate from a number of different companies and countries, which renders it highly unlikely that the results demonstrated are due to some national or company specifics. In addition, the above-demonstrated quality of the data itself as far as reliability and validity are concerned clearly shows the existence of different cultural clusters, which are a consequence of the respective Professional Cultures.

In summary, it can be stated that the empirical results of this first Professional Culture clearly indicate that not only do Professional Cultures exist, but also that it is vitally important for a company to take their characteristics into consideration. In particular, when dealing with Professional Cultures that strongly deviate from a number of standard assumptions in organization and leadership theory and research, not taking the peculiarities of these cultures into consideration leaves significant parts of the potential of a company unused.

6.2   The Flight Attendants

The second cluster is exclusively composed of Flight Attendants. Nevertheless, not all Flight Attendants are present in this group. A smaller, but significant, portion of the Flight Attendants have such differing views from the majority group represented here that they form a cluster with a number of other occupations (see Section 6.5 'The Service Providers').

This separation into two groups within the Flight Attendants' occupation is quite significant, especially considering the results for the two groups. Apparently, a highly differing view concerning the various aspects of the way this occupation should be exercised is present within this group.

The decision to call this group 'The Flight Attendants' was taken because a very clear majority of the Flight Attendants present in the sample are found in the cluster presented here (about 75%) and because this cluster is composed exclusively of Flight Attendants.

6.2.1   The Empirical Base

Both the quantitative and the qualitative parts of the survey generated a number of highly interesting results.

In this specific group, the quantitative part taken alone produced a very clear picture of the characteristics of the Flight Attendant's cluster. Its results are based on a sample of 50 respondents, originating from various countries and organizations. A majority of women can be seen in the sample, which is in accordance with the majority held by women for this specific occupation industry wide. Therefore, the overall composition of this sample is as intended.

The qualitative part of the survey, which was carried out with seven Flight Attendants, generated a number of interesting results as to why the Core Cultural Dimensions were rated the way they were by the members of this cultural group.

Finally, it can be retained at this point that the extremely homogeneous occupational structure of this group is only rivalled by that of the Pilots' cluster (see Section 6.4). This indicates that the flight crews' environment exercises a very unique influence upon the people working within it.

The Quantitative Results

The 'Uncertainty Avoidance Dimension' is rated positively (5.39). The reasons for this are similar to those of the Pilots (see also Section 6.4) and they have their roots in the fact that unforeseen and/or surprising events are considered to be a precursor for incidents or accidents.

Assertive behaviour is seen extremely negatively by the members of this group, with a value of 1.99; this represents the lowest value of all cultural clusters. The reasons for this result can be found in the specific composition of this professional group and the demands of its professional environment.

'Future Orientation' is valued even lower, at 1.66. Furthermore, this represents the lowest value out of all groups. The reasons for this rating are the importance and longevity the regular flight attendant attributes to his or her job and again the demands of the job itself, which favour short term thinking at the expense of long term planning. These aspects will be investigated in more detail in the following section.

The 'Power Distance Dimension' also receives the lowest rating of all groups (1.86). This result is mainly due to a mostly very flat to non-existing hierarchy in the cabin, combined with the fact that the regular flight attendant is always at the receiving end when it comes to the exercise of power. These aspects and some others will be described in significantly more detail later in this chapter.

'Collectivism I' is valued very positively (5.82). Teamwork is apparently seen to be a necessary part of the successful completion of the flight attendant's daily work routine. This result must be seen in connection with those of the Assertiveness and the Power Distance dimension. Therefore, more details will be given later.

'Performance Orientation' is scored the lowest out of all groups (3.75). To interpret this result simply as a lack of interest in the job would be quite unjustified, however. The reasons are more complicated and will be clearer after considering the results of the interviews.

'Gender Egalitarianism' receives a positive rating (6.19). Considering the composition of this cluster as far as age and gender are concerned, this result is hardly surprising.

The same reasoning is true for the result of the 'Human Orientation Dimension', which receives a significantly positive rating (5.5). Being nice and considerate with each other seems to be highly important to the members of this cluster.

'Collectivism II', finally, receives a clearly negative rating (4.02). Apparently, neither pride in, nor loyalty to, the profession are important to the members of this profession. But this result must be seen in connection with those of the other dimensions. Therefore, the insights gained with the help of the interviews will clarify the reasons for this rating given by the members of the Flight Attendant's Cluster.

The Qualitative Results

The results of the interviews for this cluster significantly broadened the understanding of the results of the quantitative part. Specifically interesting were those parts in which the similarities and differences with the Pilots' Culture were determined.

One of the major similarities is the view of 'Uncertainty' by the Flight Attendants. In this group, a strong antipathy exists towards anything unforeseen, unexpected or not anticipated. The reason for this view is the same as that of the Pilots' group; anything which has a co-notion of uncertainty is seen as a precursor of unsafe and potentially hazardous situations. Therefore, stable environments are always preferred.

The rating of the 'Assertiveness Dimension' has to be seen in connection with that of the 'Power Distance', the 'Collectivism I', the 'Gender Egalitarianism' and the 'Human Orientation Dimension'. According to the interviewees, generally a very friendly working atmosphere is preferred by the members of this group. This atmosphere should be achieved through equal treatment of every member of the cabin crew. If differences of opinions do occur they should either be accepted as an expression of that person's personality or, if necessary, be dealt with in a friendly and cautious manner.

In this environment there is no acceptance of assertive or aggressive behaviour. The same is true for any kind of behaviour that is intolerant towards persons' expression of their beliefs and convictions, whatever those may be.

This may seem at first sight somewhat contradictory with the previously mentioned clear rejection of any kind of assertive behaviour. In fact, though, a clear ranking within these aspects does exist. According to the interviews, basically any kind of opinion, behaviour and conviction is accepted as long as it does not conflict with the rejection of any form of intolerance. This leads to a unique working atmosphere in which everything is allowed as long as it does not disturb the governing peaceful way of dealing with each other.

This generally accepted framework for the Flight Attendants' work environment obviously has the inherent potential for significant problems when it comes to the exercise of power by others (for example the cockpit crew) and the acceptance of that by the Flight Attendants. However, this potential is usually kept under control by very specifically expressed and enforced work rules and procedures, which leads to a situation in which there is virtually no need for the exercise of power. This aspect is somewhat comparable to that found in the Pilots' culture, as described later.

The low rating on the 'Performance Orientation' scale can be partly explained on the basis of these results.

Owing to these very specific characteristics of the Flight Attendants' Professional Culture, benevolent, friendly and conflict free behaviour is favoured over the pursuit of outstanding performance. This obviously does not inhibit good performance on the job, but leads to it being merely a by-product of the 'right' mix of people working in one cabin crew.

Another very interesting aspect explored with the help of the interviews concerns the reason for the extremely low rating on the 'Future Orientation' scale. This result is due to two distinctive influencing factors, which tend to cumulate and strengthen each other in the Flight Attendants' group.

The first factor is the obvious lack of necessity for long-term planning in the Flight Attendants' work routine. Usually it is sufficient to have the next flight and its necessary service in mind, without having to think too much about any subsequent occurrences of the day. Interestingly, the second factor is an expression of the self-image regular Flight Attendants have about themselves and the job. A significant number of the interviewees do not see this job as an occupation for a lifetime. A typical statement in the interviews was 'I'll do this job maybe for another one or two years or so and then I'll have to see'. More stunningly still was that this kind of attitude was not only restricted to Flight Attendants who were new to the job, but could also be found among more experienced Flight Attendants. Apparently, members of this group have only a very limited time horizon as far as their professional development is concerned and are driven more by short-term motivations.

These two aspects strengthen each other over time and are obviously enhanced by the underlying group dynamics that consider this perspective to be the 'normal' perspective of a Flight Attendant's job and life.

Finally, the rating of the 'Collectivism II' dimension has to be seen in connection with this self-image. Considering this self-image it is virtually impossible to develop any kind of pride in, or loyalty to, the profession. Usually the most positive references about the job are those related to flight benefits, travelling and, sometimes, income (although this last aspect is highly dependent on the airline); i.e. those who have only an indirect link to the job itself and therefore create extrinsic motivation only (Maslow 1970; Deci 1975; Thomae 1999). Hence, a certain indifference towards the job and its consideration by outsiders can be stated for this Cluster.

In summary, it can be said that the interviews gave a number of very interesting insights into the motivations of the Flight Attendants to rate the different Core Cultural Dimensions the way they did. These results will be highly important in the following to develop an appropriate leadership and organizational structure.

Furthermore, the overall understanding of the results of the quantitative part was significantly enhanced, leading to a better interpretation for the purpose of their use in the following sections.

Summarizing Thoughts

The empirical results of this cluster gave a highly coherent picture, in which the interviews largely supported and further explained the results of the quantitative part. The main point of this culture is its extremely consensus-driven and harmony-oriented nature. As shown, this orientation is fully lived, even at the expense of performance on the actual job.

A further important factor is the image the Flight Attendants have of themselves and of their job.

As shown, members of this group do not attribute any long-term importance to their job. Instead, they see this job only as some sort of transitory phase in their life, which is limited to a couple of years only. Furthermore, this perspective does not have the tendency to change with the actual time the individual Flight Attendants have spent on their job. This strengthens the impression that the regular flight attendant does not have any long-term perspective as far as the job is concerned, which is partially due to the usually short-term orientation inherent in the content of the job itself. A direct consequence of this state of mind is the very low consideration the regular Flight Attendants have for their job as expressed in the interviews and the low rating on the Collectivism II scale.

Finally, uncertainty in any form is very strongly rejected by the members of this group. This finds its expression in the high rating on the Uncertainty Avoidance scale and is a direct consequence of the very strong insistence on safety that is inherent to any training for every single air crew member.

In summary, it can be said that the results of the empirical part show a very distinct culture for this group. This can be seen as a consequence of the very specific characteristics of the job itself and its environment. These characteristics have consequences that stretch into the whole life of a Flight Attendant, such as for example the high number of days away from home, or the significant problems in building stable social relationships on the job due to the crew members often changing.

These aspects also have to be taken into consideration when developing an appropriate organizational and leadership structure, as will be shown in the following.

6.2.2   An Integrative Solution to the Found Characteristics

Concerning the appropriate leadership and organizational structure for this cluster, a distinction has to be made that can also be found in the Pilots' cluster. This distinction concerns the leadership level of the solution, which has to take into account the difference between the operational leadership exercised by the head of the cabin crew and/or the Pilots on the one hand (in the following micro level), and that of higher cabin crew management on the other (in the following macro-level).

At the level of the appropriate organizational structure, a number of similarities with the Pilots' Cluster can be stated. Obviously, these similarities are a consequence of the closely related working environments of both groups, which share a number of common characteristics. This very special work environment is also responsible for the unique and quite homogeneous way respondents rated the different scales in the quantitative part and expressed themselves in the qualitative part.

The Appropriate Leadership Style

In accordance with the results of the GLOBE-Study (House *et al.* 2004) an appropriate leadership style should include the following characteristics.

It should be centred on a specific form of the 'Self-Protective Leadership Style' (House *et al.* 2004) including a number of elements of the 'Human-Oriented' (e.g. Gagné and Fleishman 1959; Fleishman and Quaintance 1984; Blake and Mouton 1985; House *et al.* 2004; see also Section 2.1.2) and the 'Participative Leadership Style' (e.g. Lewin 1948; Tannenbaum and Schmidt 1958; House *et al.* 2004; see also Section 2.1.1) and finally some elements of the 'Team-Oriented Leadership Style' (e.g. Manz and Sims 2001; House *et al.* 2004; see also Section 2.2.2).

Owing to the very low rating on the Power Distance scale though, the retained characteristics of the 'Self-Protective Leadership Style' differ somewhat from the prototype of Self-Protective leadership. The aggressive parts of this leadership style, which exclusively serve to 'self protect' the respective leader – such as status consciousness and conflict induction – have to be omitted. But those parts that reduce uncertainty and consequently enhance the procedural fulfilment of the job of the respective flight attendant need to be emphasized.

At the micro-level, the same is true for those parts of this leadership style that generate 'group protection' in lieu of 'self protection' of the respective leader. As the crew has only very limited possibilities of justifying any deviation from prescribed procedures on the one hand, but sees itself to be subject to very strong sanctions in case of any unjustified deviation on the other, any leadership action that leads to an enhanced protection of the group is viewed positively. This finds its expression, for example, in the very clear preference of the reduction in Uncertainty over an increase in Performance.

At the macro-level, the procedural parts of the Self-Protective leadership are more important as they give to the work environment of the Flight Attendants clear guidelines as to how to carry out the job.

The already-mentioned tendency of the individual flight attendant to strive for a conflict-free work environment that is based on good – although somewhat superficial

– interpersonal relationships, renders it necessary to include some elements of the 'Human-Oriented Leadership Style' into an appropriate leadership style. These elements exclusively concern the interpersonal level of this leadership style on a rather superficial level. This is due to the fact that normally there is no possibility of establishing a stable and deep working relationship as a consequence of the often changing team composition in the cabin and the very rare direct interaction between the individual Flight Attendants and their direct superior.

At the micro-level these aspects are obviously more important than at the macro-level, as interactions at that level are more intense than at the macro-level, owing to the close proximity in which crews have to work together.

'Participative leadership' needs be taken into account only at the micro-level, as – according to the interviews – this enhances a positive working atmosphere. If possible, crew members like and expect to be integrated into the decision taking process for decisions that directly concern them. Although true decisions are only rarely possible – owing to external restrictions and demands that cannot be solved at the micro-level – involving the respective flight attendant as far as possible into the decision-taking process seems to be highly important. This view is supported by the results for the 'Human-Orientation leadership style', because a positive and friendly atmosphere among crew members is of the utmost importance to this group.

This picture changes at the macro-level. As a consequence of the very limited occasions in which direct leadership is exercised and the rather high acceptance of given structures in this group (see also the Pilots' cultural cluster), a direct influence on the decisions of higher management is not significantly important.

Here again, the already mentioned focus of the regular flight attendant on a conflict and 'worry free' work environment in which good, but somewhat superficial interpersonal relationships exist, surfaces.

For the same reason, it is important for this group to feel part of a team. This aspect is, however, only relevant at the micro-level as, due to the number of Flight Attendants usually existing in bigger airlines, no real team spirit can develop at the macro level. This finds its expression, among others, in the very low rating on the Collectivism II scale and in the results of the interviews.

In summary, according to the results given, the leadership style on the micro-level should be as follows. A procedure-based and group-protective approach should be favoured. This is due to the already mentioned preference for a stable and 'worry free' work environment. Moreover, this approach should incorporate the individual Flight Attendants as far as possible into the decision-taking process for decisions that directly concern them. In addition, it is important to create a very warm and conflict-free environment. This can be achieved through a cautious and friendly leadership approach, which always has the individuals and their problems in its focus (Human Orientation). Finally, it is important to give every cabin crew member the feeling of being part of a team. Although this is not a top priority for the members of this cultural cluster, it still greatly enhances the positive impact when achieving the above-described leadership style.

At the macro-level, an appropriate leadership style would have the following characteristics. Owing to the very limited personal interactions between the Flight Attendants and their superior, indirect leadership is significantly more important than direct leadership (see below). In this respect, a clear parallel exists with the Pilots' cluster. For those occasions on which direct leadership is necessary, an approach based on rules and regulations should be pursued. With that logic, a leader should follow the 'Management by Exception' approach (e.g. Wunderer 2001; Bass and Avolio 1993; see also Section 2.2.3 where this leadership style is treated in the context and as a counterexample of Transformational Leadership). However, the realization of this approach has to take into account the specific characteristics of the regular Flight Attendant. Therefore, it is necessary to use, as much as possible, an 'Human-Oriented' approach to implement any kind of measure in the context of direct leadership. As already said, participation and team orientation are not overly important on this level.

To sum up, it can be said that the importance of direct leadership is remarkably higher at the micro- than at the macro-level. Therefore, at the micro-level, a successful use of the leadership style described here is vital for a motivated and, consequently, efficient cabin crew. However, at the macro-level, an efficient and appropriate way of indirect leadership, as exercised through organizational means, is significantly more important than direct leadership.

The Appropriate Organizational Structure

Owing to the highly repetitive nature of the Flight Attendants' job, combined with a quite strict regulatory framework from state authorities, rather tight guidance through rules and regulations seems to be the solution of choice. In that respect, the Flight Attendants' cultural cluster is similar to that of the Pilots, the difference here being, however, that not all aspects of the job are as well accessible to indirect leadership as with the Pilots' culture.

These parts are the ones that are directly related to the customer relationship, which requires flexible answers to the varying customer demands. For this part of the job, an organization in rather small work groups (as usually implemented with a standard crew, usually comprising between three and 18 crew members) is highly advantageous. This is because, within a given frame, each crew can find its own solution to these demands.

To try to get a crew to a point of self governance in the sense of Likert's System 4 (Likert 1967; see also Section 3.3.1) or Complexity Theory (Lewin and Regine, 2000; see also Section 3.2.2) would, however, not be appropriate. This is because the work of the Flight Attendants, very much like that of the Pilots, is embedded in a very tight regulatory framework by aviation authorities. This may initially seem to be a disadvantage, but can be transformed into an advantage if correctly used.

The regular flight attendant is used to receive a high number of unquestionable written orders in the form of aviation laws, relevant parts of airplane manuals, standardized emergency drills, and the like. Therefore, a certain predisposition to the acceptance of written standardized procedures can be stated in this professional group.

Furthermore, a huge portion of the Flight Attendants' work is highly repetitive. For example, the sequencing of the different service items is dependent only on the flight, but not on any unforeseeable events. Therefore, the above-mentioned predisposition to the acceptance of pre-established rules and procedures without a loss in individual motivation can be used to lead a Flight Attendant efficiently.

This also fits well with the already-stated need of the Flight Attendants for safe and predictable environments, which is obviously best coordinated through the use of rules and procedures. Therefore, an optimal organizational structure according to the results presented here would be the following. The base would be a rules and regulations oriented approach, which would incorporate a mixture of prescribed rules and laws on the one hand and company policies, procedures and goals on the other. The advantages of this course of action are, firstly, that it is not always clear to the individual where a certain law ends and a company procedure begins, and, secondly, the already-mentioned acceptance of rules and procedures.

These two aspects together lead to an extremely high acceptance of an approach using the logic of Weber's Bureaucratic Rule (1976; see also Section 3.1.1) in which the whole organization is based on rules and procedures. These job characteristics lead to the very high efficiency of this organizational design. A similar process takes place in the Pilots' cluster (see Section 6.4).

At the same time however, it is important to give enough manoeuvring room to the leadership at the micro-level to react appropriately to unexpected problems and demands. Although these events make up only a smaller portion of the regular work routine in this group, it is nevertheless necessary to have a structure that is able to deal efficiently with such problems. This structure should comprise crews that are self-governed by a cabin leader (often referred to as Purser; Chef de Cabine, etc.) who is directly involved in the Flight Attendants' work routine. However, this self-governance has to be restricted to occasions that are clearly inaccessible to prescribed rules, such as for example dealing with specific passenger demands.

In summary, it can be said that the best organizational structure according to the results presented here is one that is as close as possible to the Bureaucratic Organization according to Weber while keeping enough space for low level leadership to deal with unforeseen events efficiently. The right balance between these two aspects should lead to the most efficient organizational structure for the characteristics of the Flight Attendants and their work environment.

The Solution in Overview

The above-described solution is a unique approach to a professional group that has unique characteristics. These characteristics are comparable only to those of one other group; the Pilots. This is due to the fact that the work environment in civil aviation is significantly different from that of any other occupation.

The interesting point about the proposed leadership style and organizational structure is the extensive use of indirect leadership. As mentioned, this is a peculiarity that takes advantage of a set of given and unalterable traits of the Flight Attendants' occupation and their work environment.

With the application of the solution given here, it is possible to efficiently turn a potentially highly dysfunctional set of characteristics into a very helpful tool for the realization of company goals.

In particular, the right mix between indirect leadership with the help of the Bureaucratic Approach according to Weber, and direct leadership carried out on the crew level, is extremely important for efficiently leading the members of the Flight Attendants' group. A further important aspect when considering the results for this group is the distinction between the micro- and the macro-levels. This is again a peculiarity of air crews in general, as they have to deal constantly with both operational management (cabin crew leader/Pilot) and higher leadership (cabin crew management). These interactions take place in different time intervals and in different situations, but are both decisive in successfully leading Flight Attendants.

In summary, it can be said that, if correctly applied, the solution shown here is the best integration of the sometimes diverging interests of aviation authorities, the personal characteristics of the members of this group and the airlines' goals.

6.2.3   Final Thoughts Regarding the Flight Attendants

The results for Cluster 2 give a very compelling picture of the characteristics of this group and the way the members of this group expect their work environment and leadership to be structured.

When applying these results to a real-world scenario one major problem arises, however. This problem is a consequence of the fact that a significant minority of the Flight Attendants present in the sample are not part of the Flight Attendants' Professional Culture group. This minority can be found in the Service Providers' group (see Section 6.5) and shows quite different characteristics in comparison with those of the members of the Flight Attendants' group.

The problem here is that it is obviously impossible to know the composition of a flight crew with 'regular' Flight Attendants and with Flight Attendants that are part of the Service Providers' group. Therefore, by applying the solution found here, the danger always exists that one or more flight crew members are completely inadequately treated as far as their expectation towards organization and leadership are concerned. This obviously leads to a sub optimal efficiency of the flight crew.

The only possible solution to this problem is to increase the homogeneity of the workforce through personnel selection and training. At this point, though, the question arises as to which of the two 'kinds' of Flight Attendants is the superior kind, as that would necessary be the one to be favoured at this point.

This question will not be answered at this point, but the issue will be raised again in Section 6.5 to give a more complete picture of the possible solution of choice.

In summary though, it can be stated that despite the above-mentioned problem, an application of the leadership and organizational structures developed here has a very strong chance of being the best solution for an overwhelming majority of most flight crews. Therefore, it will be retained at this point as a possible approach for an optimum structure for Flight Attendants, pending the comparison with the Service Providers' Cultural group later in this chapter.

6.3 The Information Technology Experts

The cluster described in the following is composed of employees who are specialized in various kinds of information technology related tasks.

Two main groups are represented in this cluster.

The first group comprises people who are responsible for managing the computer systems within organizations. Typically, one may find IT technicians, administrators, or programmers here. The second group comprises people who are responsible for the actual development of new aviation computer systems. In this group, basically any kind of IT competence, hardware or software, can be found.

The strong similarity between these two groups also shows itself statistically, as they create one cluster, which was consequently called the 'Information Technology Experts'.

6.3.1   The Empirical Base

The quantitative part of the empirical survey gave clear results. Most of the employees present in this cluster have an unambiguous orientation towards an IT-related occupation. The sample comprises 20 employees, showing diverse organizational and national backgrounds. Nevertheless, a rather clear tendency towards a male domination of this culture has to be stated.

The qualitative part concentrated on deciphering the reasons for this specific orientation of people who work in an IT environment and was again composed of seven interviewees. One of the results of the interviews is that the above-stated male predominance in this Professional Culture is a consequence of the specific content of the different occupations in this sample, which is still significantly more appealing to men than women. Therefore, in accordance with the empirical results, it can be stated that the majority of male respondents does not negatively influence the insights gained in this section.

Initially, the results of the quantitative part will be presented, followed by those of the qualitative part.

The Quantitative Part

The valuation of the 'Uncertainty Avoidance Dimension' is very high in this group (5.72). Apparently, members of this cultural cluster prefer stable and predictable environments. This, at first sight probably somewhat surprising result, will be discussed later in the context of the illustration of the open interviews.

'Assertiveness' is seen to be neutral (3.98). No clear preference for either assertive or non-assertive behaviour can be stated in this group. The specific demands on the group, which are detailed later in this section, play a decisive role for this result.

'Future Orientation' scores high in this group (5.82). This result is a consequence of the fact that most IT tasks require a certain long-term orientation by the person carrying out that task in order to be successful.

'Power Distance' is rated in the positive area (3.9). Apparently this group strongly prefers to be in a structured environment, which leads to a positive view of

Power Distance. This score has to be seen in connection with that of the Uncertainty Avoidance dimension, which also scores strongly in this group.

'Collectivism I' scores in the medium range only (4.62). This is because tasks performed by members of this group have to be performed alone to a quite significant degree. Hence, collective values as expressed by the Collectivism I Dimension do not score particularly well.

'Performance Orientation' scores positively in this group (6.0). The relative position members of this group have in their respective organization and the peculiarities of their work are the decisive factors for this result. This aspect will be discussed further in the following section.

'Gender Egalitarianism' is rated in the positive area (5.72). As will be shown later, no specific importance is attributed to the content of this dimension, except for the fact that Gender Egalitarianism is considered to be something completely normal and not worth paying any further attention to.

'Human Orientation' is in the neutral area (4.23). In the technical environment in which this group finds itself, Human Orientation apparently does not play an overly important role.

'Collectivism II' is seen positively by the members of this group (6.0). Pride in the profession and a high degree of loyalty to the profession and to the other members of the profession prevail in the group.

The Qualitative Results

The following description of the qualitative part will give the reader a deeper and more detailed picture of the characteristics of the IT-Experts group.

The results of the 'Uncertainty Avoidance' and the 'Power Distance' scales have to be seen in connection with each other. Members of the present group prefer structured and stable environments. According to the interviewees, this is because the time horizon and importance of most IT-related tasks are quite considerable. The development of a new automated flight system, for example, takes years and necessitates significant investments. Such projects are usually significantly simpler to carry out in stable environments. Another example is the maintenance of computerized machines used in a production process. An unscheduled interruption of the production process due to a computer-related failure can be extremely costly for the company concerned. Here again, any unforeseen event is considered to be an obstacle for the successful fulfilment of the IT-Expert's task.

These factors lead to the above-described high rating of the Uncertainty Avoidance scale. At the same time however, they also lead to a high score on the Power Distance scale. This is because, in order to achieve the above-mentioned stable environments, it is necessary for the members of the present group to receive clear indications as to what is expected from them so that they can concentrate on the fulfilment of their task. This view finds its expression with the above-given positive score on the Power Distance scale.

The already-mentioned long-term orientation of most tasks shows itself in the positive view this group has about the values expressed with the Future Orientation Dimension. A long-term horizon is highly important for successfully carrying out the regular tasks of the members of this group. This does not exclude the ability to find ad-hoc solutions, but in connection with the results of the Uncertainty Avoidance and the Power Distance dimension it demonstrates a clear preference for anticipation and planning. This view is strongly supported by the results of the interviews.

The rating of the Performance Orientation scale should be seen in connection with that of the Collectivism II dimension.

According to the interviewees, a clear orientation towards excellence on the job can be stated. This is reflected in both the positive score of the Performance Orientation and the Collectivism II Dimension. The way members of this profession understand excellence gives them not only the motivation always to give their best on the job, but also a strong feeling of pride in that job. Furthermore, a very strong cohesion between the members of this group can be stated. This cohesion is not so much at the everyday working level, but mainly at the group level in a broader sense. Generally, a feeling of everyone being part of a very special profession is expressed. This consequently leads to the positive score of the Collectivism II scale.

The neutral rating of the Collectivism I scale is due to the nature of the work environment, which can be both teamwork oriented and focused on one person working alone. According to the interviews, this changing work setting leads to no clear preference as to the valuation of the Collectivism I scale.

Assertive behaviour does not receive a clear score, either. This is also a consequence of the specific demands that are exercised upon this profession. On the one hand, it is sometimes necessary to stand up, for example, for a solution or an idea that leads to a positive view of assertiveness. On the other, members of this Professional Culture in general prefer to find pragmatic solutions – an action that usually favours non-assertive behaviour in order to concentrate on the problem to be solved in that situation.

According to the interviewees, this becomes even more important when working with members of other professions (e.g. superiors or colleagues in adjacent fields) who do not necessarily always have the technical knowledge to fully grasp the IT-related problems in a given situation, but who do have some other knowledge or competencies necessary for the IT Experts to work out a successful IT solution.

Finally, owing to the highly technical nature of the work environment and the consequent priorities of the members of this cultural group, Gender Egalitarianism and Human Orientation trigger neither positive nor negative views in the interviews. According to their results, the content of these dimensions is not overly important, as technical competence and an efficient working style are much more decisive for this Professional Culture than the values expressed with these two dimensions.

Summarizing Thoughts

The empirical results give a number of very clear indications of the values and characteristics of the members of the IT-Experts group.

The quality of these results is remarkable, as the quantitative and the qualitative parts complement one another very well. The coherence of these two parts also renders the following development of an appropriate leadership and organizational structure significantly easier.

In addition, the empirical results again show the importance of combining quantitative and qualitative elements in order to gain meaningful results that go beyond a mere collection of figures; a statement already given a number of times in this work.

In summary, it can be stated that the empirical results of this cultural cluster are highly meaningful and will be very valuable for the following development of an appropriate leadership and organizational cluster for the IT-Experts cultural cluster.

6.3.2   An Integrative Solution to the Found Characteristics

In the following section, an appropriate approach for the successful integration of the members of the IT-Experts' cluster will be described.

Successful integration is particularly important for this specific Professional Culture, as the significant technical competence of the members of this cluster is a key competence for any company in the aviation industry. Furthermore, it is almost impossible for outsiders to monitor the work ethics of the members of this group efficiently.

Therefore, it is extremely important to create an atmosphere in which the individual IT-Experts do the best they can on their own initiative. This is helped by the already-mentioned tendency of the members of this group to strive for excellence.

In summary, it can be said that the goal is to create leadership and organizational structures that help the members of this cultural group to pursue their intrinsically motivated strive for excellence.

The Appropriate Leadership Style

According to the empirical results, and in accordance with those of the GLOBE-Study (House *et al.* 2004) an appropriate leadership style comprises significant elements of the 'Charismatic' (e.g. Bass 1985; Burns 1978; House *et al.* 2004; see also Section 2.2.3), the 'Team-Oriented' (e.g. Manz and Sims 2001; House *et al.* 2004; see also Section 2.2.2) and the 'Human-Oriented' leadership styles (e.g. Gagné and Fleishman 1959; Fleishman and Quaintance 1984; Blake and Mouton 1985; House *et al.* 2004; see also Section 2.1.2). These should be rounded off by some elements of the 'Autonomous' leadership style (House *et al.* 2004).

The special characteristics of this profession, which are focused on performing excellently in a demanding environment and, in consequence, being very proud of the profession and its achievements, point to a leadership style that is centred on the Charismatic/Value-Based leadership style. This is enhanced by the already-mentioned long-term orientation of most of the IT-Experts' tasks, which is accepted by the members of this culture (a high score on the Future Orientation scale).

A second central point of an appropriate leadership style is the Team-Oriented leadership style. Although the need often to work alone is acknowledged by the members of this culture, an orientation towards teamwork should be the aim as far as feasible. The results of the GLOBE-Study in connection with the empirical results, especially from the qualitative part, clearly indicate a preference for team orientation in the appropriate leadership style.

Thirdly, it is important for a leader of this group to incorporate significant elements of the Human-Oriented Leadership Style. This judgement is partially due to the quantitative results in connection with those of the GLOBE-Study, but also due to the qualitative part. Despite the fact that Human-Orientation itself was not considered to be overly important by the members of this culture, a clear indication of the importance to be recognized as a human being and of having good interpersonal relationships within the group could be seen in the interviews.

Apparently, the somewhat ambiguous rating on the Human-Orientation scale in the quantitative part can be attributed to the content of the questions that are centred on generosity, sensitivity and tolerance of mistakes. This wording most likely contributed to a picture in which the Human-Orientation dimension was seen somewhat ambiguously by people whose main focus is necessarily on technical matters. Nevertheless, the need for healthy interpersonal relationships both among the work group and with the direct superior was clearly expressed in the interview process and is rather clearly confirmed by most of the quantitative part.

Finally, the Autonomous leadership style also contributes partially to a superior leadership style in the current setting. This is due to the fact that the IT-Experts think of themselves as being different and that in order to match that difference it is sometimes also necessary for the direct leader to be different in comparison to the way other leaders are perceived by the members of the group presented here.

An appropriate leadership style according to the above given results would look like the following. The Charismatic/Value-Based leaders need to give a clear Vision and need to inspire their people, especially when it comes to long-term oriented and highly demanding tasks. They need to give a clear guidance to the people regarding where they want them to be in the mid- and long-term future and what they are supposed to do in order to achieve that.

Nevertheless, self-leadership in the sense of the SuperLeadership approach is a key issue as well. The Charismatic/Value-Based leader gives guidance and support as far as the 'big picture' is concerned, whereas the regular day-to-day business is independently handled by the people. Therefore, an emphasis on the Team-Oriented leadership style is also highly important.

Furthermore, the leaders' behaviour needs to be focused on the creation of healthy interpersonal relationships among the people as well as between themselves and their people. This can best be achieved with the help of warm and considered behaviour from the leaders' side in which all subordinates know that they are personally valued. In addition, the emphasis of teamwork and self-governance seems to be a valuable approach in connection with the creation of a credible Vision for all parties concerned.

Finally, the members of this Professional Culture expect their leaders to effectively live this behaviour even if that means that they will have to deviate from some commonly lived leadership style and autonomously create a new and different leadership style for themselves and their people.

In summary, it can be said that the specific traits of this culture can best be matched with a nearly equal use of the Charismatic/Value-Based and the Team-Oriented leadership style with the consistent use of the Human-Oriented leadership style if necessary. In certain settings, this leadership style needs to be supplemented by a few elements of the Autonomous leadership style in order to achieve a proper implementation.

The Appropriate Organizational Structure

The appropriate organizational design needs to take into consideration the special demands that the structure of the present cultural cluster creates. It is particularly important to give both the leader and the subordinates the room to manoeuvre that is necessary in order to create the above-described leadership relationship. Therefore, it is necessary for the retained organizational structure to permit a close and healthy relationship between the leaders and their subordinates on the one hand, and for the subordinates to pursue their tasks independently and self-responsibly on the other.

These demands can be best matched by an organization design that is based on that proposed in the context of the above-described Complexity Theory (Stacey *et al*. 2000; see also Section 3.2.2). The main point is the creation of teams in which the different competencies (e.g. hardware and software engineers) can be bundled. In these teams, members should be encouraged to pursue on their own initiative the search for an appropriate solution to the different problems arising during the completion of their tasks. The role of the leader in such an environment is mainly to guide and help.

To guide and help has to be seen as a double meaning in the present setting. The first meaning is on an individual level. The organization needs to give the leaders and their subordinates the freedom actually to work together. Working together means that the subordinate is not under a direct command and control scheme with the leader, but, on the contrary, under loose supervision in which the leader gives guidance and help when needed without putting any excessive control pressure on the subordinates. Therefore, formalized and standardized control mechanisms should be kept to a minimum, whereas the organization should encourage the individual IT-Experts to seek help on their own initiative when needed; either from a fellow IT-Expert or from their leader.

Furthermore, detailed planning of tasks should be replaced by the establishment of rough guidelines of when and in which form a task needs to be completed. The actual realization of the task should, however, be left entirely in the hands the individual employee or team.

On the group level, the organization has to give the leader the freedom actually to live the role described above. This means that it is necessary for the organization to permit the leaders to lead the subordinates, which means providing them with an appropriate power base. In detail, this means for example that overly restrictive planning, report and control systems have to be avoided, as this would impair the leaders' ability to take the necessary decisions on their own.

Furthermore, the chances are that the leader would exhibit the same kind of behaviour towards the team members that would obviously inhibit the necessary trust and harmony for the creation of a living organization in the sense of Complexity Theory.

Actual implementation of this organizational design could take, as a guideline, Likert's System 4 (Likert 1967; see also Section 3.3.1) or the above-described Lateral

Organization (e.g. Wunderer 2001; see also Section 3.3.2). The important point about both approaches is the realization of teams that work mainly independently. In these approaches, the leader is seen less as a commanding superior and more as a guide. Correctly applied, these structures also enable the above-mentioned key behavioural patterns of the leader to be allowing, accessible and attuned (see Section 3.2.2 for details). Furthermore, this kind of organization also permits the satisfaction of the above-detailed key needs of the subordinates – guidance, teamwork and healthy interpersonal relationships.

In summary, it can be stated that an organization that is designed around the principles laid down in the context of Complexity Theory is, according to the results obtained with the help of the empiricals, the most appropriate organizational design. The actual realization of this approach can be achieved through a team-based approach in the sense of Lateral Organization. Nevertheless, it is not appropriate to push the organization into a state of a heterarchy (e.g. Stacey *et al.* 2000; see also Section 3.2.2) as this would undermine the need of the IT-Experts' group to be guided clearly by a leader. Therefore, a very cautiously lived hierarchy should still be put in place, which would then be represented by the direct superior of the IT-Experts.

The Solution in Overview

The possible leadership and organization solution for the present cluster is quite different from that for the first two. It is significantly less based on a hierarchical solution and therefore a lot more in tune with current trends in leadership and organizational theory and research. This also leads to this solution being more complicated to implement, as it is significantly more demanding on the organizational and leadership level than, for example, a purely hierarchical solution that is rounded off by a Bureaucratic Organization.

Nevertheless, it is highly important for an organization to take into consideration these different aspects of the IT-Experts' culture, as only an appropriate leadership and organization structure is able to create an environment in which all IT-Experts actually do give their best.

As already mentioned, intrinsic motivation is of the utmost importance in the present setting, as direct control mechanisms are neither wanted by the members of the present cluster, nor are they efficient in this specific environment.

In summary, it can be said that according to the demonstrated results the integrative solution described here is the most appropriate way to design the organization and the leadership relationship for the present group. Therefore, any company having members of this culture within its workforce should strive for an implementation of the structures described here.

6.3.3   Final Thoughts Regarding the Information Technology Experts

The results for the third cluster are highly satisfying from both a technical point of view, and a content-related point of view. Technically, it can be stated that the employees present in the sample are nearly exclusively composed of members of IT-related occupations. This homogeneity as far as the profession is concerned is rounded off by the above-stated fact that members of the present sample do originate from various countries and companies. Therefore, the clustering that could be observed can be traced back to the professional background of the different employees present in the sample.

As far as the content is concerned, the results show the rather complex structure of this Professional Culture, which needs to be taken into consideration when leading and organizing these employees.

The successful implementation of the design developed here obviously is not without problems. In particular, the demands on the leaders of the IT-Experts are extraordinarily high as they need to be very open minded in order to embrace the developed leadership style. This is due to the fact that the style significantly deviates from the classic command and control structures still very often found in the industry. In particular, the fact that the leader should predominantly act as a role model and coach and not as a superior demands significant changes in the way leaders could possibly see themselves. Furthermore, as far as the design of the organization itself is concerned, it is not without problems to implement the presented design. This is due to the fact that, here as well, significant progress has to be carried out if a classical form of an organization is in place. In particular, the very loose command and control system potentially poses a serious problem for classical companies. This is a consequence of the fact that it is impossible just to integrate these trust-based structures into a classical and, by definition, not trust-based organization (for the relevance of trust see, for example, Weibler 1997b, 2001). Therefore, it is possibly necessary to alter whole divisions of concerned companies in order to match the needs of the IT-Experts cultural group.

In summary, it can be stated that the results of the present section are highly valuable for a more successful method of leading and organizing what is defined in this section as IT-Experts. Therefore, despite the fairly significant problems in integrating these findings into a classical organization, it seems to be advisable for any company to attempt to come as close as possible to the structures developed here.

6.4   The Pilots

Pilots make up a group of themselves. The unique structure in their responses leads to highly interesting insights into the mental make-up of the members of this Professional Culture.

The specific demands and the specific environment in which Pilots live and work are responsible for this. The present cultural cluster is, in a number of ways, significantly different from any other cluster present in this sample. In addition, the Pilots' cultural cluster is extremely homogeneous as there are no other occupational backgrounds found in this cluster. Hence, the separation between this cultural cluster and the other clusters is unambiguous and clearly shows the unique position the Pilots' culture has within the aviation environment.

The highly interesting peculiarities of the Pilots' culture and the consequences these have for the respective companies will be outlined in the following. In addition, a number of possible solutions for the successful integration of this culture into an organization will be given.

6.4.1   The Empirical Base

The description of the empirical survey is structured in the usual way throughout this chapter. Initially, the results of the quantitative part will be given, followed by those of the qualitative part.

The quantitative part alone gives a very clear indication as to the characteristics of the Pilot's cluster. The homogeneity of this group in comparison with the other groups of the sample is stunning. No other cluster is as unambiguously defined as the Pilot's cluster after evaluating the quantitative part of the survey only. The sample itself is based on 51 responses originating from various organizations and nations. As even today very few women are in this occupation, this sample is also nearly exclusively composed of men. As this is a reflection of the gender-related composition of the occupation as a whole though, this does not mean a restriction as to the validity of the findings of this section.

The qualitative part, which is as usual composed of seven respondents, deepened and strengthened the results of the quantitative part further and demonstrates why the Pilot's culture has developed the specific traits it has.

The Quantitative Results

The 'Uncertainty Avoidance' dimension is valued extremely positively in this cluster (6.45); no other group has the same high esteem of the values expressed by this dimension. Not surprisingly, an environment that is characterized by few unexpected events, and where future developments can easily be anticipated, is preferred by the members of the Pilots' culture.

The 'Assertiveness' dimension is valued very negatively (2.14). A number of reasons, which have their roots in different aspects of the Pilot's life, are responsible for this result. These aspects will be pointed out later in this chapter.

'Future Orientation' is valued in the very moderately positive area (4.88). The need to anticipate and the need to react swiftly to arising problems moderate each other in this dimension. These counteracting forces lead to the stated rating.

The 'Power Distance' dimension scores neutrally (2.63). This result is a little misleading though, as the Pilots' absolute score is the second lowest in the whole sample. Taking this fact into consideration, a certain aversion to the values expressed in the Power Distance dimension has to be stated at this point. An initial interpretation of this result, as being the expression of a preference for a low to non-existing hierarchical structure, has to be rejected. The reasons for this and some possible solutions will be given later in this chapter.

The 'Collectivism I' scale gets the *highest* rating out of all cultural clusters (6.24). The apparent need for effective teamwork in the cockpit leads to this clear and unambiguous result.

The 'Performance Orientation' dimension scores in the moderately positive area only (5.77). A number of reasons are responsible for that result. This dimension will be discussed further in the following section, as some highly interesting insights result from the more detailed investigation of this dimension.

'Gender Egalitarianism' is valued in the low area by the members of this culture (4.14), representing the lowest value present in the sample. Apparently, some rather old-fashioned views are still held in this predominantly male profession. This aspect will also be discussed in more depth in the following section.

'Human Orientation' scores the most negatively out of all cultures present (2.5). This rating is the consequence of two main aspects. The first is the extremely technical environment in which the members of this group live and work. The second aspect has already been mentioned in the context of the Power Distance dimension and has to be seen as a consequence of the hierarchical structures prevailing in this group. These aspects will be described in more detail in the following section.

'Collectivism II' is valued very positively in this Culture (6.16). It is hardly surprising, as members of the Pilots' Culture express significant pride and loyalty towards their profession.

The Qualitative Results

The interviews of the qualitative part generated a significant amount of highly interesting background information concerning the above-described quantitative results.

The already-mentioned preference for an environment that is marked by a minimum of Uncertainty could be confirmed. According to the interviewees, basically any kind of unforeseen event is usually seen negatively. Unforeseen events are considered to be responsible in large part for incidents and accidents. Therefore, Uncertainty is considered to pave the way for unsafe situations, which obviously is the last thing a Pilot wishes to have.

According to the interviewees, the low esteem Pilots have for Assertive behaviour has its roots in the fact that this kind of behaviour is rather unhelpful in most situations in which Pilots may find themselves. The clear dislike of Assertive behaviour is confirmed when it comes to the relationship between the Pilots and higher management. The Pilots usually do not have any significant influence on their work environment as it is largely pre-determined by others (Air Traffic Control, Revenue Management, Station Management, pre-established procedures etc.). Therefore, if they want to achieve something in this work environment it is a lot more useful to be nice and cautious, than to be assertive and aggressive. This extreme restriction as to the influence Pilots have on the final outcome of their work also leads to the only moderately positive rating the Performance Orientation scale receives in this group.

In addition, in the very few situations in which assertiveness could be helpful it is usually unnecessary to exhibit this behaviour. This is because, in situations in which the Pilot's opinion does matter, it mostly concerns the relationship between the Captain and Co-Pilot, and the Co-Pilot would usually rather give in to what the Captain wants and says, than force the Captain actually to exercise any kind of Assertive behaviour.

This second aspect leads to another very important topic, which is the way hierarchy is seen on the one hand and lived on the other. Officially, a 'flat hierarchy' policy is promoted for the cockpit crew. This official line is, however, ultimately not what happens. In the Pilots' culture, a very polite kind of a military leadership style is used. This is true for both the direct relationship between Captain and Co-Pilot and the relationship with higher ranking members of the flight operations management, which is also usually composed of Pilots. Therefore, despite the fact that, for the Pilots' culture, there is a high accordance between the way the members of the cluster would like to have their environment structured and the way they perceive it actually is structured (1.47; 1 showing a very strong correlation, 7 showing a very weak correlation; see also Section 8.4 for details), a restriction has to be made for the previously mentioned Assertiveness dimension in reference to the Power Distance dimension.

After due consideration of the results of the interviews, the relatively low rating on that scale can only be seen as an 'Espoused Theory' in the sense of Argyris and Schön (1978, pp. 10ff. Argyris 1976; see also Section 4.2.2), whereas the 'Theory-in-Use' is the military-like command structure in this environment.

The very low rating on the 'Human Orientation' scale perfectly fits this picture. According to the results of the interviews, the individual is seen much less as a person and much more as a sort of organic machine, performing various tasks.

Although these results may seem strange at first, they make sense to the Pilots themselves. They see themselves as being part of a machine and they want to adjust themselves as much as possible to the needs of this machine. For any Pilot, initially the machine is the airplane; later in their career though, the understanding of the 'machine' goes well beyond that point and reaches out to the whole operational environment or, in the case of the Pilots' management, even to higher management tasks.

For instance, to describe an efficient interpersonal work style, words that are usually reserved for technical specifications of machines, like standardization or function(ing) are used. Therefore, there is virtually *no* room for individuality. The positive view of team work as expressed in the high rating of the 'Collectivism I' scale has to be seen independently from these results to a certain degree. Despite the quite hierarchical structure of the Pilots' world, the need for effective team work at least in the cockpit, is acknowledged. Beyond the boundaries of the cockpit this becomes, to a certain extent, an Espoused Theory. Nevertheless, teamwork is considered to be necessary in the Pilot's profession.

The bridge between the highly hierarchical structure of this environment and the acknowledged need for teamwork can be seen in the already-mentioned rating of Assertive behaviour.

Usually *all* members of the air crew (see also the Flight Attendants' Cluster in Section 6.2) have internalized their role to such a degree, that the strong hierarchical elements are completely accepted by everyone concerned. This way of accepting hierarchy is thought to be unique to this Professional Culture (and to a certain extent to that of the Flight Attendants) and will be one of the key elements for an effective leadership and organizational style. Assertive behaviour, as already mentioned, is mostly useless in this environment.

The reasons for these results can be seen in a mixture of environmental demands, strong selection of personnel, training and the very strict way leadership itself is structured, which does not tolerate any kind of deviating behaviour.

Personnel selection is performed, to a significant extent, using psychological testing, which aims to select persons who fit into this command and obedience scheme. During initial and recurrent training, the following of pre-established procedures, rules and commands is emphasized again and again. Higher ranking operational management finally sanctions any behaviour that is not completely in accordance with that expected from the respective Pilot. Finally, environmental demands create the framework for putting people into this position, as the most important thing expected from a Pilot is the safe operation of the aircraft. Therefore, every measure taken is referred to as *safety relevant*, which inhibits any kind of further discussion. This is further strengthened by the fact that even if some sort of questioning could arise, this is answered by stating that the measure has been taken by some higher ranking authority that 'knows what it does, as it is the only one to have the necessary overview to take a decision'.

The results of the 'Gender Egalitarianism' and the 'Collectivism II' dimension have to be seen in connection with this.

The self-image of the Pilot is still governed to a certain extent by some sort of 'aviator romantic'. The fact that the job of a Pilot consists nearly exclusively of system control and not of actually flying is somewhat ignored. Instead, Pilots still think of themselves as performing the unique, and at times heroic, task of piloting the way it was done in the past. This self-image, in connection with a rather conservative basic state of mind, leads to Pilots having a rather low esteem of Gender Egalitarianism. At the same time, the Pilots see themselves and their profession as highly special, irreplaceable and extremely important. In connection with the high social prestige of the Pilot's profession, this obviously leads to the extremely high score on the Collectivism II scale.

The implications of these different aspects are quite far reaching. They will therefore be one of the main topics in Section 6.4.2, where an appropriate leadership and organizational structure for this cultural cluster will be pointed out.

Summarizing Thoughts

The empirical results show a highly interesting picture of the Pilots' Professional Culture. The Pilots' Professional Culture is characterized by the tension between a highly demanding and restrictive environment, a very strict hierarchical structure and a self-image that is still an artefact of the way this profession may have been in the past. This tension can be seen in the way the different Core Cultural Dimensions are valued and in the results of the interviews.

Apparently though, the regular Pilot can live with this tension rather well. The thorough selection and the tight guidance that is exercised throughout the whole professional life on both the group level (among the Pilots) and the management level ensures that the contradictions in the Pilots' culture never really surface. In particular, the nearly impossible symbiosis of a relatively high valuing of interpersonal collective values (Collectivism I) and a very strong hierarchy, is extremely interesting in this cluster. This symbiosis is, as already mentioned, a role model for the difference between an Espoused Theory and a Theory-in-Use in the sense of Argyris and Schön (1978, pp. 10ff.; Argyris 1976).

In summary, it can be said that the main point about the Pilots' culture is the way its contradictions can be kept under control, through the use of an appropriate leadership and organizational style. Apparently, in certain special settings, a hierarchical approach with specially adapted characteristics can be part of the solution of choice.

The next section will give a possible integrative approach to the leadership and organizational structure appropriate to the above-described Pilots' Professional Culture.

6.4.2   An Integrative Solution to the Found Characteristics

The following section is as usually divided into a leadership and an organizational part. This separation is especially helpful in this cluster as the difference between indirect leadership (the organization) and direct leadership from person to person is remarkable. This is thanks to the fact that the profession of a Pilot is especially suitable to the use of various kinds of prescribed procedures, continuously valid written orders etc. due to its repetitive nature. This part of the Pilots' profession is obviously governed with the help of the organization and not with the help of face to face, i.e. direct, leadership.

The very few occasions in which actual face-to-face leadership has to take place are special situations in which the pre-determined way of interpersonal interaction does not function as it should. As a consequence of the high degree of standardization and organization this rarely happens. Therefore, this culture can be used very well to demonstrate the difference between leadership and organization; a differentiation that is usually not as clean cut as here.

The Appropriate Leadership Style

In accordance with the results of the GLOBE-Study (House *et al.* 2004) and based on the results of the above-described survey, a possible approach to an appropriate leadership style would include significant elements of the Team-Oriented leadership style (e.g. Manz and Sims 2001; House *et al.* 2004; see also Section 2.2.2), some elements of the Charismatic/Value-Based (e.g. Bass 1985; House *et al.* 2004; see also Section 2.2.3), the Participative (e.g. Lewin 1948; House *et al.* 2004; see also Section 2.1.1) and the Human-Oriented leadership style (e.g. Gagné and Fleishman 1959; Fleishman and Quaintance 1984; House *et al.* 2004; see also Section 2.1.2) and finally in some very special settings certain traits of the Self-Protective leadership style (House *et al.* 2004). The mixture of these is going to be different at the micro-level (among the cockpit crew) and at the macro-level (higher management).

At the micro-level, Team-Orientation should be the base of the appropriate leadership style as all Core Cultural Dimensions except for Human Orientation point to this leadership style.

The Team-Oriented leadership style in this special setting must not be confused with that found in other professions. Usually, a Team-Oriented leadership style is used to integrate diverging interests and personal orientations in order to achieve the highest possible performance of the group. As already mentioned the given structure of the Pilot's work environment is characterized by a very strong hierarchy and very detailed rules and procedures that are highly internalized by this profession's members. Therefore, an integration of diverging interests and orientations is not necessary. Instead, the most important aspect of this leadership style is the creation of a work environment that permits an atmosphere in which every member of the cockpit crew feels able and willing to contribute to the safe and efficient outcome of the flight. This aspect is enhanced by the fact that the Participative and the Human-Oriented leadership styles can be seen to be effective in this work setting.

Therefore, the appropriate leadership style by the Captain towards the Co-Pilot would be the following. Based on existing rules and procedures an open and friendly work atmosphere should be created. Owing to the highly regulated nature of the work environment itself, no major problems should arise within the cockpit crew as usually any decision can be taken based on these rules and procedures, with the help of the accepted authority of the Captain. Therefore, usually it is sufficient for the Captain to be open and nice and to integrate the Co-Pilot into the decision-taking process in so far as the opinions of the Co-Pilot are considered and decision taking is based on the mutually accepted prescribed procedures.

In the very few situations in which there should exist any doubt about the way to proceed, Self-Protective leadership is considered to be helpful. Again, this is due to the fact that hierarchy, rules and procedures are the most important aspects when it comes to the Pilot's profession. Therefore, in these special settings, the decision that is likely to cause the least problems to the cockpit crew is the solution best accepted and consequently the solution of choice. Usually this will lead to a decision that deviates as little as possible from the solution proposed by 'the book'.

In summary, leadership at the micro-level is rather simple and straightforward. This is due to the fact that the person being led (the Co-Pilot) is usually alone with the 'leader' (it is only on some long- and ultra long-range flights the cockpit crew may comprise up to four Pilots). In this small and highly homogeneous environment, the need for actual leadership is very limited. Usually it is sufficient for the Captain to create a nice and positive atmosphere, as the work environment itself is mainly governed by prevailing rules and pre-established procedures. In this environment, a pre-dominantly Team-Oriented and Participative approach, in which joint decision-taking is undertaken, is the most appropriate leadership style. This should be supported by a gentle, friendly and hence Human-Oriented behaviour towards the Co-Pilot, as this enhances the acceptance of the overall decision-taking of the Captain. This is further helped by the fact that, as a consequence of the accepted hierarchical and procedural structure in the cockpit, a decision finally taken by the Captain is, in most circumstances, very likely also to be the solution of choice for the Co-Pilot.

Here, the above-mentioned contradiction again surfaces between the hierarchical structure in the cockpit and the high rating on the Collectivism I scale, which is overcome by the very high acceptance that this very structure has among every member of the cockpit crew.

At the macro-level, though, this picture changes significantly. The leaders simultaneously have to take into account the specifics of the underlying structure of the leadership culture of the regular line Pilot and those of leading a large corps of people. This leads to a somewhat different focus by the leadership structure. In particular, Team-Orientation and Participation change from lived behaviour to a more symbolic approach, as it is virtually impossible to lead such large divisions (depending on the company, up to 1000 Pilots and more) with these leadership styles. At that point, indirect leadership (see the next section) and Charismatic/Value-Based leadership become significantly more important, as it is vital to give the regular airline Pilots an idea about some greater purpose of their work.

Here again, the self-image of the Pilots plays a very important role, as it is highly useful for the creation of a 'Vision' that can show a higher purpose of the Pilot's Profession. This higher purpose lies mainly in the saving of human lives, which basically comes down to the safe operation of the aircraft at any time. Furthermore, this Vision can be extended to show the supposed importance the Pilot's work has for the efficiency of the company by operating the aircraft not only safely but also efficiently, etc.

In any case, it is important for the higher leaders of Pilots to create a Vision that is in line with the Pilot's work environment and which should incorporate parts of the above-described self-image of the Pilots. Using this self-image gives a number of hints on how to structure a Vision for the leadership of Pilots and therefore the creation of Charismatic/Value-Based leadership for this special professional group.

For the rest, a 'Management by Exception Approach' (see Section 2.2.3 for details) should be pursued in which the leader intervenes only in cases of unsatisfactory performances from an individual Pilot.

In summary, it can be said that, in accordance with the results of the empirical part of the research project, at the macro-level Charismatic Leadership together with indirect leadership is the most promising approach to leading Pilots. Depending on the size of the department, elements of Participative and Team-Oriented leadership may be included into this, although at that level their impact appears to be rather limited in comparison to the appropriate and efficient use of Charismatic/Value-Based leadership.

The Appropriate Organizational Structure

The appropriate organizational structure also has to take into account the very special traits of this Profession.

The three main aspects of this are:

- safety in the operation of the aircraft, including adherence to international aviation law;
- efficiency in the operation of the aircraft;
- interchangeability of the different Pilots among themselves.

In connection with the usually high span of control, particularly in larger airlines, all these aspects point to the unusually high importance of indirect leadership as exercised through the organization.

As mentioned in the previous section, direct leadership is exercised mainly at the micro-level. At the macro-level, it is necessary to create an organization that is able to generate a highly homogeneous work environment, which exactly follows prescribed rules without the need to constantly check for the obedience of these rules. This goal can best be achieved in this special setting through a set of very detailed and strictly enforced working rules. These rules have to be based on the very restrictive framework given by aviation law.

At first sight, this may seem to be an impediment. In fact, this framework can be used in a highly advantageous manner, as it is possible to create a mixture between state and company given 'law'. This mixture can be created in a way that, for the individual Pilot, it is largely impossible to discern where state law ends and company law begins. In connection with the already mentioned high acceptance of higher ranking authorities, this has the obvious advantage of giving the whole Professional framework of rules and regulations a significantly higher meaning than regular company rules alone can have.

In cases where state rules obviously do not cover a measure taken, it should normally be possible to find a reason for the safety relevance of that measure, or, as a last resort, the necessary efficiency of the flight operation. But this last resort is obviously not more binding than it would be in any other professional setting. This renders it the least advisable course of action considering the whole professional background of the Pilots. It has to be kept in mind that this background is focused on the application of certain pre-set standards according to aviation law and safety and not on the fulfilment of 'business administratively governed efficiency goals' (cumulative statement from various interviews).

Therefore, the appropriate organizational structure for the Pilots' environment should be as follows. Due to the above-mentioned specific characteristics, a deviation from most modern organizational solutions has to be favoured. In this special setting a classical approach is the solution of choice. In fact, this solution can be deduced virtually directly from the Bureaucratic Organization, according to Weber (1976; see also Section 3.1.1.3). This type of organization derives its justification from mutually accepted rules and regulations. As already stated, these rules and regulations are for a significant part pre-given by national authorities.

The pursuit of company goals should consequently be accomplished by integrating company rules and procedures into this framework of aviation law by preference, while giving a reference to the safety of the flight operation. Based on the Pilot's Professional Culture this will guarantee a very close adherence to these rules.

Thus, a very careful development of these rules and procedures has to be carried out. The realization of most company goals can and should be achieved by integrating them into the regulative framework for flight operation. As already mentioned, this should be achieved by referencing the different measures to either aviation law or safety of the flight operation; only as a last resort should business efficiency goals be mentioned, as they are the least effective in this environment.

In summary, it can be stated that this Professional Culture is probably the role model for a culture that can almost entirely be led by indirect leadership, i.e. organization. In that aspect, the results of this chapter are highly interesting in the overall context of the present work.

The Solution in Overview

As shown, the very special characteristics of the Pilots' Professional Culture demand very special solutions to the complexity of leadership and organization. First, a distinction has to be made between the micro- and the macro-levels of leadership: the organizational aspect is of interest only at the macro-level, as the organizational environment is not different for the Captain and the Co-Pilot(s).

At the micro-level, a highly Team-Oriented approach supported by Participative and Human-Oriented elements is the most appropriate leadership style: only direct leadership is of significance at this level.

At the macro-level however, direct leadership loses a significant portion of its importance, as it is reduced to a highly symbolic approach expressed by a Charismatic/Value-Based leadership style. In addition, at this level, direct leadership merely has a supporting function for the highly important indirect leadership through organization. Consequently, the importance of a thoroughly and carefully developed organizational structure cannot be overestimated at this level.

In summary, it can be stated that this Professional Culture exhibits a number of very special traits, which completely differentiates it from any other Professional Culture in the research sample.

6.4.3   Final Thoughts Regarding the Pilots

In this section, the most homogeneous and distinct Professional Culture of the whole sample in this survey was described. The high number of very distinctive traits in connection with their remarkable strength renders this cluster highly interesting in a number of aspects.

First, the extremely high importance of indirect leadership for the successful integration of this profession into the organization is extraordinary in comparison with any other Professional Culture. Any leadership and organizational approach has to take this very special trait into account.

Second, the high acceptance of hierarchy is another rather unusual trait for a Professional Culture. This second aspect, though, has to be seen in connection with the first and can be combined with it in a very advantageous manner. Thus, both aspects are of significant importance for the successful integration of the Pilots' Professional Culture into any company.

Third, the extremely homogeneous composition of this culture has to be kept in mind when developing leadership and organizational measures for this environment. Usually, it is necessary to allow for the fact that not all the members of a specific culture are accessible in the same way. This always gives direct leadership a more or less important role. In this special setting though, it can safely be assumed that all members of the present culture are virtually the same, permitting highly efficient ways of indirectly leading its members. Obviously, this has to be seen in connection with the first two aspects, pointing again to the extreme importance that indirect leadership has in this setting.

In summary, it can be said that this Professional Culture has practically no features in common with other Professional Cultures. This fact, in connection with the described high degree of self governance of this group (as mentioned the management of Pilots is usually done by Pilots) can sometimes lead to misperceptions as to the right way to handle its members, even triggering unnecessary disputes with the normally strong Pilots' unions. However, most of these disputes could easily be avoided through careful implementation of the above approach. This would obviously lead to a significantly better organization-internal understanding, which in turn would have highly positive effects on the Pilots' motivation. This stresses again the high importance that an appropriate mix of direct and indirect leadership has in general and for this Professional Culture in particular.

6.5   The Service Provider

The fifth cluster comprises people that are providing varying services to clients within and outside the company. Obviously, this view is not in accordance with that commonly held about service being exclusively a task dealing with outside clients.

Logically though, a discrimination between internal and external clients does not make sense as, for someone being in need of a service, it does not make a difference if that need is met by external or internal Service Providers. The same logic applies to the person providing the service as, in principle, there is no difference between providing service to an internal or an external party.

This understanding of service obviously leads to a significantly broader view as to which occupations should be included in the Service Providers' cultural cluster. In the present sample, such different occupations as internal business analysts, marketing analysts, supply chain specialists, customer support specialists, human resource specialists or Flight Attendants are present. Concerning the Flight Attendants in this group one has to keep in mind that they are significantly different from those representing the main portion of the Flight Attendants sample, who have their own group (see Section 6.2).

A problem with the Service Providers' group is that sometimes the limits between this group and the administration groups are not clear cut. This may become a problem to a certain degree, especially when practical applications of these research findings are planned. Nevertheless, this problem can be controlled if one keeps in mind the following points when deciding if a specific occupation or a team etc. should be assigned to this group or not.

The decisive factor as to the assignment to this group is the question of whether the specific occupation actually performs a real service activity and not primarily a mere administering one. If, for example, an analyst is working in a department in which primarily external data are collected, which then in turn are used to give the marketing division a sound decision base, this department and therefore this specific job is considered to be part of the Service Providers group. This is because the purpose of its activity is to provide information and therefore a service to someone else. If, on the other hand, analysts work in a controlling department and collect data as part of their department's controlling activity, then these persons and their department are not to be considered part of the Service Providers group as the focus of the task is its own activity. Therefore, the main question one has to ask when deciding if an entity is to be assigned to the Service Providers group is whether the task of that entity (an individual, a team, a department etc.) is focusing on the needs of another entity or not.

The traits that result from these demands and this focus of the Service Providers group are outlined in the following.

6.5.1   *The Empirical Base*

In this group, the role of the qualitative part was highly important. This is due to the enormous complexity of this group and the already-mentioned grey zone that necessarily exists between this group and neighbouring groups. Therefore, it was imperative for the correct interpretation of the results of this group to verify and deepen the understanding of the characteristics of this group resulting from the quantitative part. This was done with the help of the qualitative part.

The quantitative part itself is based on responses from 29 employees, originating from various national and organizational backgrounds. A majority of the respondents are female, which is once again a consequence of the composition of the employees present in this group.

The qualitative part is based, as usual, on seven respondents and significantly clarified the results of the quantitative part.

The Quantitative Results

Uncertainty Avoidance is seen very negatively in this group (2.3). This can be seen as a direct consequence of the specific demands on this group. A high degree of openness and flexibility is often expected of the members of this group by their clients. This constantly varying environment obviously does not really go along with people who express a strong inclination towards a stable and foreseeable life, as would be expressed with a high score on the Uncertainty Avoidance scale.

The Assertiveness scale is rated at the upper end of the medium area with a score of 4.39. This score clearly indicates the area of tension between showing a non-assertive behaviour towards the client and the need to sometimes show an Assertive behaviour towards others in order to meet the client's needs. More details concerning this dimension will be given in the following section.

The Future Orientation dimension is in the upper medium area (4.6). The reason for this ambiguous picture has to be seen in the area of tension that exists between the need to plan for the future in order to work efficiently and the need to stay as flexible as possible in order to meet the sometimes unstable needs and demands of the client. This aspect will be particularly interesting in the context of the open interviews.

The Power Distance dimension is valued very positively (4.38). This score can be traced back to the apparent need to have clearly set goals and to be able to set clear goals in the unstable environment in which members of this cultural cluster live and work. This subject is also going to be raised again in the course of the open interviews.

The Collectivism I dimension is clearly located in the positive area with a score of 6.21, representing the second highest value out of all Professional Cultures. The actual jobs carried out by most members of this group are centred on team work. Consequently, the very nature of the occupations present in this group leads to its members seeing collective values, as expressed in the Collectivism I dimension, being very positive.

In addition, Performance Orientation is valued very positively by the members of this group (6.32). Clearly, the successful accomplishment of the tasks arising out of the client's needs is a very important part of this specific Professional Culture. As will be shown, this interpretation is further enhanced by the results of the qualitative survey described below.

Gender Egalitarianism is also valued unambiguously in the positive area (6.02). This rating has to be seen in interconnection with the previous dimension and the actual task of this group, which leads to a self-image relying on a set of performance oriented, 'modern' values.

Human Orientation is clearly placed in the medium area by the members of this culture (3.95). Here again, two counteracting forces lead to this result. The first is rejection in everyday business of the values expressed by this dimension that revolve around the key issues 'warmth' and 'tenderness'. On the other hand, these very values are seen to be important when dealing with members of one's own culture, as will be shown further below.

The Collectivism II dimension, finally, is valued in the positive area (6.23). Members of this culture see themselves as taking a key role in professional life as they consider others to be frequently dependent on their work. Obviously, this leads to a very positive self-image of members of this culture and consequently gives them a feeling of pride and importance in comparison with other professions.

The Qualitative Results

The results of the Uncertainty Avoidance and the Future Orientation dimensions have to be seen in connection with each other.

According to the interviews, the low rating of the Uncertainty Avoidance Dimension is a consequence of the strong need for flexibility of this group. This need can be traced back to the fact that a lot of the demands members of this group face are due to external factors. Furthermore, members of this group actually like instability and they like to be forced to react swiftly to newly arising tasks. Therefore, they do not overly appreciate the values expressed with a high rating on the Uncertainty Avoidance scale.

For the same reasons, the Future Orientation scale receives a rating that is only in the upper medium area. Obviously, it is necessary to have a quite clear concept of future developments to be successful in this environment. This is due to the fact that, in order to satisfy the client's needs, it is very helpful to anticipate these demands. On the other hand, due to the above-given reasons in the context of the Uncertainty Avoidance scale, this positive view of the values expressed with the Future Orientation dimension is somewhat moderated. Hence, the rating of the Future Orientation dimension is a consequence of these counteracting influences.

The rating of the Power Distance dimension has to be seen against the setting of the above-described results. The high rating of this dimension is not to be understood as an expression of the wish of the members of this culture to be subject to tight guidance and control. According to the interviews, this high rating is a direct result of the expectation to receive clear guidelines and clearly set goals from the respective superiors. In order to interpret this particular dimension correctly, the open interviews were a great help.

According to the results of the open interviews, the results of the Assertiveness dimension are a product of three different influencing factors. The first factor is the Service Provider/client relationship, the second is the Service Provider/colleague relationship and the third the Service Provider/superior relationship. In their relationship with clients, the members of the Service Providers group clearly follow a non-assertive behaviour. This is in contrast to the behaviour they occasionally favour when dealing with colleagues from other professions. Here, somewhat Assertive behaviour is sometimes considered positive.

For the purpose of this study, however, the most interesting aspect is the relationship with the superior. When it comes to that relationship, members of the Service Providers' culture prefer behaviour that is, in principle, non-assertive. Nevertheless, they expect their superior to be able to exhibit assertive behaviour when necessary.

That can be seen in connection with the Power Distance dimension, where members of the present group clearly expressed the expectation that their leader is able to draw up clear guidelines and goals. As they are well aware of the fact that this may require action against a possible opposition, under the circumstances they expect the individual leader to show Assertive behaviour to actually take the necessary decisions. All these factors that partially neutralize each other lead to the above shown rating of the Assertiveness dimension.

The very positive rating of the Collectivism I dimension is a direct result of the nature of most tasks carried out by the members of the current group. According to the interviews it is virtually impossible to find a task that is not carried out in teams. This fact is also highly appreciated by the members of this group as, apparently, it fits rather well their expectations of how to work. These two factors – work necessities and personal preferences – lead to the extremely positive view of the values expressed with the Collectivism I scale.

According to the interviewees, the positive rating of the Performance Orientation scale is due to two factors. The first factor is the high intrinsic motivation that the tasks to be carried out have for the members of this group. The second is the highly competitive nature of the work environment itself.

The high intrinsic motivation is a result of the fact that, apparently, the members of the Service Providers culture usually do enjoy their work. There were practically no signs of frustration with the job, so there seems to be rather high congruence between the people carrying out a Service Provider job and certain elements of the job requirements themselves. Furthermore, respondents mentioned the highly competitive nature of the job environment. To cope with this competitiveness it is necessary for people working in this environment to be Performance Oriented, which in addition seems to be appreciated.

The high rating of the Collectivism II scale is a direct consequence of the above-mentioned factors. Members of the Service Providers' culture are proud of what they do and how they do it. According to the interviewees, this is due to two reasons. The first is that they perceive themselves to be extremely important for the good functioning of various parts of their respective companies. The second reason is that members of the current group consider themselves to be significantly more flexible and performing than a considerable number of other professional groups of their respective companies.

Finally, according to the interviewees, the ratings of the Gender Egalitarianism and the Human-Oriented dimension are closely interconnected as they are an artefact of the high Performance Orientation of the present Professional Culture. They clearly demonstrate that for members of the current Professional Culture it is not important who does the job as long as it is done well.

Summarizing Thoughts

The empirical results are once again of a highly satisfying nature. This is true for both the technical quality of the survey and the results gained based on the current data.

As desired, the composition of the sample is heterogeneous as far as national and organizational origins are concerned. The only possibly influencing factor besides the prevailing Professional Culture is gender. In this group, there is a majority of female employees. However, in the course of the interviews, it became clear that the responses to the questionnaires were not biased as mainly women completed them. Following the argumentation of the interviewees, the job profile of most jobs of this group is simply more attractive to women than to men, which leads to the underlying population of this culture being predominantly composed of women. Therefore, it can be stated at this point that, according to the empirical results, the characteristics of the present cluster go back to the specific traits of the prevailing Professional Culture.

In the present cluster once again, the quality of the data could be highly improved with the multi-method approach employed. The interviews proved to be highly useful for the better understanding of the results gained through the quantitative survey.

Finally, the results themselves are of a highly interesting nature. The sheer existence of a Service Providers culture was quite surprising. Furthermore, the traits of this culture are rather extraordinary and have to be taken into account when designing a work environment for its members. This is strengthened by the fact that members of this culture are often placed in key positions for the successful operation of the companies concerned.

In summary, it can be said that once more the main survey delivered very interesting and highly important insights. These insights will now be used to develop an appropriate work environment for the members of this culture, which will be beneficial for both the members of the Service Providers' culture and the companies involved.

6.5.2 An Integrative Solution to the Found Characteristics

In the following, an integrative leadership and organization design solution will be developed. As always in this study, the appropriate leadership style will be developed, followed by the appropriate organizational style. It should be kept in mind that this particular group is one of those groups where positive motivation towards the job is of the utmost importance. This is due to the fact that it is impossible to command, for example, a smile towards a customer. Therefore, a leadership style and organizational structure that harmonizes well with the needs and expectations of the present group is extremely important to use fully the potential of the members of the Service Providers' culture.

The Appropriate Leadership Style

According to the empirical results, and in connection with those of the GLOBE-Study (House *et al.* 2004), the appropriate leadership style should be based on the Participative leadership style (e.g. Lewin 1948; Tannenbaum and Schmidt 1958; House *et al.* 2004; see also Section 2.1.1) and should furthermore contain some elements of the Team-Oriented (e.g. Manz and Sims 2001; House *et al.* 2004; see also Section 2.2.2) and the Charismatic/Value-Based leadership style (e.g. Burns 1978; Bass 1985; House *et al.* 2004; see also Section 2.2.3).

Three out of the four Core Cultural Dimensions of the Participative leadership style point to this style, whereas one is in the neutral area. This picture is enhanced by the results of the qualitative part, as members of the current Professional Culture clearly expressed the expectation to participate in the development of decisions regarding their professional environment. It was mentioned at various occasions that decisions by superiors that do not adequately reflect the knowledge of the 'people in the field' have significant acceptance difficulties. This view seems to be in contradiction to the above-mentioned relative appreciation of the Assertiveness dimension. But, as a matter of fact, the relatively positive view of the Assertiveness dimension is only conditional and depends on the consideration of the Service Providers' professional opinion.

Two out of the four Core Cultural Dimensions of the Charismatic/Value-Based leadership point to this leadership style, whereas two are in the neutral area. As already mentioned, it is of some importance to the members of the Service Providers' culture to have loose guidance in their day-to-day work. This guidance can be achieved partially through the creation of a Vision for this group. Nevertheless, the importance of this leadership style is not as high as for a number of other groups in the sample. This is due to the fact that the current group is more focused on carrying out the tasks at hand successfully than on the possible consequences their work may have in the middle and long term future.

Finally Team-Oriented leadership is important as well. Two out of the five Core Cultural Dimensions point directly to this leadership style, whereas two are in the neutral area and one in the negative one. The importance of team work for this group has already been mentioned on various occasions in this chapter. The one Core Cultural Dimension, which is in contradiction with the Team-Oriented leadership style (Uncertainty Avoidance) is a little misleading in this context, as teams are not seen as a means to reduce uncertainty; a goal which is, in any case, not overly valued by the members of this group.

An appropriate leadership style for the Service Providers culture would therefore look like the following.

The leaders have to establish a highly participative leadership relationship with their team. In detail, this means that the leader has to make sure that the team members are always included in any major decisions regarding the team. This also includes decisions concerning individual team members only. Obviously, such a highly participative course of action will not always be possible. Nevertheless, a leadership relationship should be strived for that is as Participative as possible.

This Participative leadership relationship should be supported by the above-mentioned Team-Oriented leadership. The establishment of a functioning team orientation in the sense of SuperLeadership, according to Manz and Sims (1995, 2001) is extremely important in the present setting. This is due to the fact that the members of the Service Providers culture see themselves as 'natural born team workers'. A leadership style that does not take this into consideration would not be able to liberate all the potential present within this group.

Finally, a valid Vision should be established. As the members of the current culture are not too interested in far-fetched Visions, this Vision should be as close as possible to their actual work environment. This could, for example, mean that the Vision incorporates elements such as comparisons with competitors. In a further step, the Vision could then clearly show how it would be possible to be superior to these competitors in a reasonable amount of time thanks to the efforts of the group. In summary, however, the importance of the Charismatic/Value-Based elements should not be overestimated.

To sum up, the appropriate leadership style for the present Professional Culture is highly consensus driven and steered by collective values. Any successful leadership in this environment has to take these two main components into consideration. A leader who is not able to be a team player will not be in a position to lead the members of the Service Providers' culture efficiently, possibly even inflicting dysfunctionalities that will gravely undermine the potential the team has in reality. The Charismatic/Value-Based part is, in that aspect, just an additional point that can transform a good leader into a somewhat better leader.

The Appropriate Organizational Structure

Considering the above complex and team-driven characteristics of the present Professional Culture, the starting point for the development of an appropriate organizational design will, once more, be Complexity Theory (Stacey *et al.* 2000; see also Section 3.2.2).

As already shown, Complexity Theory is the most appropriate theoretical approach when it comes to designing an organization for Professional Cultures that have a preference for being organized within independently acting entities. In the present case, this is even more important as a significant number of traits of the present Professional Culture are in clear agreement with the basic ideas of Complexity Theory. For example, a highly important point of Complexity Theory is the acceptance of Uncertainty in the professional environment. As shown, the members of the Service Providers' culture see Uncertainty as something inherent in their work environment, which they highly appreciate.

Another point is diversity. The characteristics of the work environment necessitate often working with people of very different backgrounds. This again is highly appreciated by the members of the current culture. Diversity is seen by them as a tool for enhancing the quality of their work, a point that is very much in line with the basic ideas of Complexity Theory.

Finally, the above-mentioned preferred organization into independently acting entities is one of the core ideas of Complexity Theory. Therefore, it can be stated that it is not only the underlying basic preferences of the members of the Service Providers culture that point towards Complexity Theory. Also, one of the key elements for the successful implementation of this theoretical approach is highly appreciated by the members of this culture.

The implementation of this approach should be carried out following Lewin and Regine (2000; see also Section 3.2.2) through the implementation of true work teams that can act independently of restricting influences due to external command and control mechanisms. The teams have to be organized around the competencies needed to carry out the specific task at hand. This may, for example, mean that a department responsible for the supply of a technical company is composed of people who have more of a technical background together with people who have more of a business background. Another example may be a HR development department that may be composed of psychologists for the development of new theoretical approaches to HR development and of experienced trainers for the actual teaching of these new approaches, etc.

Another important point is the installation of means to facilitate Lateral Organization – e.g. the network structure of project groups (Peters 1993); the concept of 'Loosely Coupled Systems' (Orton and Weick 1990; Perrow 1984, pp. 89ff.; see also Section 3.3.2).

In the current setting, the importance of this is the facilitation of the mobilization of required resources. If one team does not possess the capabilities it needs to complete a task successfully, it should have direct access to other teams to tap into their competencies. Doing so without having to go through some superior is extremely important for the members of the Service Providers culture.

Depending on the situation, a very interesting further organizational option should be considered: the Virtual Organization (e.g. Saabeel *et al.* 2002; see also Section 3.3.2). As this is a special form of Lateral Organization for geographically dispersed entities it cannot always be implemented, but in certain settings it has the potential to be highly beneficial.

Command and control systems should be kept to a minimum. In principle, it is sufficient to give a rough guideline to the team and control it only via the achievement of these goals. The role of the superior in this setting is Participative, Team-Oriented and in a guiding role only; or to put it into the words of Lewin and Regine (2000) the leader should be allowing, accessible and attuned.

In summary, it can be said that the appropriate organizational structure for the Service Providers should be highly decentralized, Team-Oriented and as free as possible from hierarchical influences.

The Solution in Overview

The possible solution proposed for the Service Providers culture points to a very non-hierarchical structuring of the work environment for its members.

This may incur radical changes for some companies, but the empirical results are unambiguous. A classical leadership and organization scheme for the present professional group is highly inappropriate, potentially leading to the performance of any Service Providers team being seriously inhibited. Therefore, the implementation of the described leadership style and organizational structures should be sought. Although a parallel implementation of both is to be preferred, they are not completely contingent upon each other. If, as a first step, only the implementation of the described leadership style is possible, this should be undertaken. Nevertheless, the appropriate organizational design should follow as soon as possible.

An isolated implementation of the organizational structure is, however, not advisable, as a combination of the described organization structure with a 'classic' leader, would most probably lead to significant fractures within the internal structure of the concerned team.

Therefore, joint implementation of the appropriate leadership style and organization design should be aimed for. After due consideration of the results given in this section, the benefits should by far outweigh the costs for the proposed change.

6.5.3   Final Thoughts Regarding the Service Provider

As already mentioned, the existence of a Service Providers' culture is extremely interesting. Especially for highly service-oriented companies such as airlines, knowledge about the existence of such a professional group is very important.

Particularly for airlines, this group has a special significance. This becomes clear when comparing the traits of the current culture with those of the Flight Attendants' culture (see Section 6.2) as, for example, the clear Performance Orientation of the members of the Service Providers' culture is in stark contrast to that of the Flight Attendants' culture. Hence, looking at the results of this section, a recommendation for airlines would be to strive for the promotion of this culture at the expense of that of the regular Flight Attendants culture, with the help of both personnel selection and training. Despite the fact that the demands on leadership are significantly higher in the present Professional Culture, the companies concerned would most probably gain greatly from a predominantly service and performance driven corps of Flight

Attendants, even if that means that the Professional Culture itself is more demanding as regards the accepted leadership structures.

For other companies, however, it is important to know about the specific traits of the members of this culture. This is true both for Service Providers for external clients and Service Providers for internal clients. The reason for this is clear: Service Providers for external clients are responsible for selling the company product, whereas Service Providers for internal clients are responsible for the smooth operation of a company.

The quality of the data collected was once again remarkable, giving the recommendations of this section a sound empirical and theoretical base. Hence, despite the already-mentioned difficulties when attempting to implement the proposed structures, one should also consider the possible negative consequences inflicted on a company by not implementing them. As stated above, a smile cannot be ordered, and therefore the performance of the members of the Service Providers culture is largely dependent on themselves and their motivation.

It can therefore be stated at this point that anything that could impair that motivation should be avoided and anything that can enhance it should be aimed for – a recommendation that may not always be easy to realize, but which will most likely pay off in the long run.

6.6   The Middle Administration

The sixth cluster is composed of the members of the Middle Administration. These employees are what is usually referred to as 'the administration'. Typical jobs that can be found in this cultural cluster are supporting activities of all kinds in various departments such as marketing, controlling or sales.

These employees always perform office jobs that require a low-to-medium qualification as opposed to the members of the Higher Administration group (see Section 7.4). Time spent in training is therefore rather limited, while total time spent on the job is highly varying.

Although there are a number of commonalities between the two administrative Clusters, there are also quite a few differences, and these are highly interesting and will be explored in the following.

Initially, an isolated description of the Middle Administration cluster will be given, beginning with the empirical survey.

6.6.1   The Empirical Base

In this group, the written part of the empirical survey gave interesting insights on its own. The study uses 20 respondents originating from various countries and organizations. The gender-related composition is also well mixed. Therefore, it can be stated that the required heterogeneity is achieved for this cultural cluster.

The distribution of occupations and the ratings on the different dimensions gave a clear picture as to the nature of this cluster. Nevertheless, looking at the already-mentioned differences in comparison with the Higher Administration group, a number of highly interesting questions remained to be solved with the help of the interviews. These were, as usual, carried out with seven respondents from the above-mentioned companies. As always, initially the results of the written questionnaire will be given, followed by those of the verbal interviews.

The Quantitative Results

Uncertainty Avoidance is rated in the neutral area (4.0). The reasons for this rating will be given in the following section.

Assertiveness is placed in the upper medium area (4.17). According to the results of the present survey this score is the consequence of a variety of influences which all revolve around the perceived importance of the occupations exercised by the members of this group in combination with their relative position in the organizational hierarchy. These aspects will be examined further in the following.

Future Orientation is scored in the upper medium area (4.43). Members of this group seem to exhibit a mixture between a rather short time horizon dictated by the regular day-to-day schedule of this group and a rather long time horizon as far as other factors – for example personal development within the bureaucratic environment of this Professional Culture – are concerned.

Power Distance is rated in the lower positive area (3.7). As with the score for Assertiveness, this has to be seen in connection with the relative position of this cluster in the organization, which while it exposes members of this group to the exercise of power, it also gives them the possibility to exercise power over others.

Collectivism I scores in the lower medium area (4.43). Keeping in mind that for this dimension there is no Professional Culture placed in the low area and that this rating is the second lowest of all Professional Cultures present in the sample, it seems like team-related issues are of less importance to the members of this cluster.

Performance Orientation is found in the medium area (5.12). Here again, the specific work patterns of this cluster play a major role for this result. More details concerning this dimension will be given in the following.

Gender Egalitarianism is placed in the higher medium area (5.22). This score does not seem to be the result of specific influences from the professional environment, but rather of a certain indifference towards the contents of this cultural dimension. This assumption is also supported by the results of the verbal interviews given in the following.

Human Orientation is in the slightly positive area (4.55). The values of this dimension though, seem to be of less importance to the members of this cultural cluster, as will be pointed out further below.

Collectivism II is finally rated in the upper part of the medium area (5.34). Members of this Professional Culture seem to have a certain positive notion about their profession, although it is not too strongly expressed. Further indications for that can be found below, where the views members of this culture have of their respective occupations will be discussed in more detail.

The Qualitative Results

According to the interviews, the ratings of the Assertiveness, the Power Distance and the Uncertainty Avoidance scale have to be seen in connection with each other.

The Assertiveness dimension is rated in the neutral area. This is due to the fact that members of this culture do appreciate Assertive behaviour to a certain degree in certain settings. Sometimes they feel the need to be Assertive towards other professional groups, especially when it comes to the enforcement of certain prescribed rules and procedures. Interestingly, sometimes they also do consider Assertive behaviour advantageous when it is exhibited by their direct superior. These situations usually involve the necessity for the superior to take some decisive action. Owing to the very bureaucratic environment of this Professional Culture, these situations seldom arise, but when they do it is expected that the superiors use their position to take the decision.

For the same reasons, the Power Distance dimension is rated in the positive area. Members of the current culture sometimes appreciate the exercise of power towards other professional groups and sometimes they expect their direct superiors to use the power they have to take a decision. This positive view of Power Distance though is conditional. According to the interviewees it is seen positively only when the superiors use their power to do something in favour of the Middle Administration group. Especially in situations where other professional groups are involved, this becomes highly important.

The Uncertainty Avoidance dimension is rated in the neutral area only. This should not be interpreted as an insignificance of the values expressed by this dimension though. Following the interviews, Uncertainty Avoidance seems to be a given fact to the members of this group and is therefore not of any major concern to them. Indeed, living in a structured environment governed by enforceable rules and procedures is highly important for the members of the Middle Administration culture.

In connection with this, the rating of the Future Orientation scale has to be seen. According to the interviews, members of this culture do not have to be overly concerned about their future. The only thing that is somewhat important for them is their future development within their profession. The tasks themselves carried out by the members of the Middle Administration culture usually do not require an overly long time horizon. Therefore, Future Orientation is rated in the medium area only.

Collective values, as expressed by the Collectivism I scale, do not play a major role for the members of this cluster. This is mainly due to the fact that a significant portion of the tasks carried out by the members of this group do not require teamwork. Therefore, members of the current culture neither feel the need for nor have the habit to work in teams. Jointly, these factors lead to the very low relative rating of the Collectivism I scale, which is the second lowest out of all Professional Clusters present in this study.

The Gender Egalitarianism dimension does not have any particular meaning for the current cluster. According to the interviewees this is due to the fact that Gender Egalitarianism as an idea is achieved in practice. This can also be seen with reference to the sample. Within the sample, a very even gender distribution can be stated, strengthening this interpretation. Therefore, the members of the Middle

Administration culture scored the Gender Egalitarianism scale in the medium area only.

The importance of the Human Orientation scale is also rather limited. According to the interviewees this is due to the fact that the rules- and procedures-driven environment does not overly require good interpersonal relationships beyond a certain level of superficial politeness. Therefore, the values expressed with the Human Orientation dimension are seen to be without too much meaning, leading to a certain indifference as to the content of this dimension.

The medium score of the Performance Orientation scale is a direct consequence of the bureaucratic environment and its socializing effects on the members of the Middle Administration culture. They neither feel the urge to do more than necessary, nor the desire to do significantly less. A satisfactory fulfilment of the tasks expected from them is apparently sufficient to satisfy the members of this culture. This does not mean that they do not like their jobs or that they want major parts of the jobs to be changed. It simply means that for the members of this culture performing in an extraordinary manner in their job is not a top priority. Therefore, the values expressed with the Performance Orientation dimension are not overly relevant for the members of this culture, neither in a positive nor in a negative way.

The rating of the Collectivism II scale has to be seen in connection with this. Members of the Middle Administration culture do like their jobs and they are also somewhat proud of what they do. One thing that can be stated though after the interviews is that they are realistic about the relevance of their jobs. Members of the Middle Administration know that they are not unimportant, but they also know that their individual importance is limited to a relatively small area only. This is further enhanced by the fact that their influence on most things is rather small as often a prescribed course of action exists. Again this does not mean that the members of the Middle Administration culture dislike this situation. Apparently, they appreciate the fact that they do not have to worry too much about what they do and why they do it. The only medium rating of the Collectivism II scale and the statements collected with the help of the open interviews are solely a consequence of the very realistic self-image the members of this professional group have.

In summary, it can be said that the Middle Administration culture is a rather bureaucratic professional group. Furthermore, members of this culture have a very realistic self-image, which is rather positive for leading and organizing this group. Finally, it is once again interesting to see how professions attract certain people and subsequently shape them even more according to that Profession. For example, it is highly unlikely that a member of the Innovation and Development culture could be happy in the setting of the Middle Administration culture and vice versa.

Summarizing Thoughts

In summary, it can be said that the results are once again highly instructive. Furthermore, as shown above they are also satisfying from a technical point of view.

The results themselves are highly interesting as they give a number of very important insights into the core of the administration of virtually any company.

Owing to the high number of Core Cultural Dimensions rated in the neutral area, the interviews were of a special importance to interpret correctly the opinions and expectations of the members of this culture. The undertaken multi-method approach proved once more to be the only adequate approach to tackle this highly complex area of research successfully.

The importance of the findings themselves should not be underestimated. Despite the fact that the members of the Middle Administration cluster are positioned relatively low in the hierarchy, it should not be forgotten that it is almost impossible to run any company successfully without a smoothly running administrative base. Taking into consideration the expectations of the members of the Middle Administration culture and translating these expectations into an appropriate leadership style and organization structure is therefore highly important.

In summary, it can be said that the underlying logic of Professional Cultures being structured along functions and not professional terms, for example as 'engineers', shows itself again very clearly in the present Cluster.

6.6.2   An Integrative Solution to the Found Characteristics

In the following, a closer look at an appropriate leadership style and organizational structure will be undertaken.

As usual, this will be done by initially developing the leadership style, which will be followed by the corresponding organizational structure. In this case, special attention will have to be given to the results of the open interviews as the high number of medium ratings in the quantitative survey means that here it is even more important than usual to consider both quantitative and qualitative analysis.

Nevertheless, joining quantitative and qualitative research will allow for the development of a comprehensive solution for the successful integration of the Middle Administration culture into its professional environment.

The Appropriate Leadership Style

As far as an appropriate leadership style is concerned, the current Professional Culture is relatively special. This can clearly be seen with reference to the results of the empirical survey.

Members of this group show no clear preference for any of the six Culturally endorsed Leadership Styles isolated within the GLOBE-Study. According to the interviews though, this does not mean that one has to search for a seventh leadership style, but that the appropriate approach is somewhat special in comparison to most other Professional Cultures isolated within the current study.

As a matter of fact, the results of the empirical survey point to a rather low consideration of direct leadership in general. Members of the Middle Administration culture do not overly appreciate any kind of regular personal intervention from their direct superior altogether.

As can be seen with reference to the Power Distance dimension, only in exceptional circumstances, and then only to a very limited degree, is direct leadership appreciated by the members of the current culture.

One aspect that was mentioned at various occasions in the course of the open interviews was the relevance of clearly expressed guidelines, rules and procedures that are stable over time. Obviously, as long as this condition is achieved, there is no need for any direct intervention by the superior. In fact, most of the time, a direct superior will be useless altogether.

As will be shown in the following section, the importance of indirect leadership through an appropriate organizational design is such that, in accordance with the empiricals, any direct superior should intervene in exceptional circumstances only. These exceptional circumstances in turn would only arise in the very rare occasions where employees fail to adhere to the requirements of their respective tasks. Therefore, the present group is a role model for the existing necessity to sometimes employ a special kind of transactional leadership: 'Management by Exception' (e.g. Bass and Avolio, 1993, p. 52; see also Section 2.2.3 where transactional leadership in general and Management by Exception in special is treated as the counterexample of Transformational Leadership).

Management by Exception postulates the need for any direct intervention by a leader only in case of unsatisfactory results achieved by the subordinates. According to this leadership approach, it is advisable for the leader to be virtually absent from the scene as long as all subordinates carry out their respective tasks as expected.

Therefore, the role of the leader is extremely limited in the current setting and is more that of an administrator than that of an actual leader.

In the case of a necessary intervention, it is advisable for the leaders to have a relatively clear and straightforward approach with which they clearly indicate the problem and a possible solution. This can be derived from the above-mentioned relative appreciation of the exercise of power. As expressed in the course of the interviews, members of the current culture do expect their leaders to indicate clearly what they expect in the rare occasions where a direct intervention is appropriate. Therefore, no particularly sophisticated leadership style is necessary in the current setting. It is sufficient for a leader to supervise the subordinates.

However, the leader has to make sure not to give them the feeling of being constantly controlled. In the case of a deviation from given goals or procedures, the leader has to take corrective action and should do so in a clear and unambiguous way. Except for these special occasions, the leader should keep a clear distance from the day-to-day business of the subordinates. Hence, in summary, it can be said that the demands on a leader of the Middle Administration culture are among the most limited ones of all the Professional Cultures described in this book.

The Appropriate Organizational Structure

In the current setting, the appropriate organization design will be straightforward and is based on one of the classic approaches. In fact, the most suitable organizational design is the Bureaucratic Organization according to Weber (1976; see also Section 3.1.1). This is due to the above-described appreciation of a rules- and regulations-based professional environment. Members of the Middle Administration culture explicitly expect to live a bureaucratic life in a bureaucratic organization.

At first sight, this result may seem to be somewhat surprising as it is in clear contradiction with more modern approaches of organizational design. Considering the results of previous sections of the current book, it becomes clear that, for some Professional Cultures identified, a classic approach is more suitable than the significantly more demanding (for all parties concerned) Modern or Post-Modern Approaches.

This obviously does not mean that these Professional Cultures are more simplistically structured than others. It only means that, as mentioned at various occasions throughout the present work, different Cultures require different treatments.

For the Middle Administration Culture this different treatment is a clearly bureaucratically designed organization, as expressed with the Bureaucratic Organization developed by Weber (1976).

It is important though that an organizational design based on this theory also takes into account the potential problems and shortcomings already mentioned by Weber (1976). In particular, the tendencies of a bureaucracy blindly to follow inadequate rules and to be increasingly occupied with itself have to be avoided. Therefore, it is important that surfacing dysfunctionalities within the organization, which can be traced back to an inadequate organizational design, are taken care of and are not ignored. Most likely, this aspect is the most important role for the leaders of a Middle Administration group. They need to detect, in a timely fashion, such dysfunctionalities and have to take corrective action within the organizational design to alter the factors leading to these dysfunctionalities.

In summary, it can be noted that if one is aware of the potential problems that are inherent in a Bureaucratic Organization, this kind of organization design is – according to the results of the current study – the most appropriate one for the Middle Administration culture. This view is also clearly supported by the results of the development of the appropriate leadership style, where the role of leadership is very much in line with that proposed by Weber (1976). Hence, the Middle Administration culture is another example of a Professional Culture to which a more classical approach in organization design is more adequate than the more complex approaches developed in the recent past.

The Solution in Overview

The above-developed solution is one more example of the necessity to consider more classic approaches in leadership and organization theory when designing a professional environment. This also supports once more the basic underlying idea of the present work, which states that there is no such thing as one leadership style or organizational design that fits all circumstances.

In summary, it can be stated at this point that the results given in this section are once again somewhat surprising as they are in opposition to a number of ideas brought forth in recent years. Nevertheless, these results are in accordance with those of a number of other Professional Cultures that also do prefer more classic approaches when it comes to leadership style and organizational design.

6.6.3   Final Thoughts Regarding the Middle Administration

The above-given results show a very interesting picture of the characteristics of the administrative base of an organization. As already mentioned, it is highly important to integrate this group into the organization appropriately, as its efficient functioning is crucial for the success of any company. Furthermore, the results clearly show that it is not always necessary to strive for the most complicated approach when designing leadership and organizational structures.

In the current setting, this is especially relevant as the structures required by the Middle Administration culture are relatively simple. Therefore, besides the fact that more sophisticated approaches may have counterproductive effects, using them would be nothing more than a serious waste of precious resources.

As the current culture is, for example, quite undemanding when it comes to direct leadership, and instead is heavily reliant on indirect leadership, it is possible to have a rather big control span. This in turn leads to the possibility to eliminate a number of positions for higher paid superiors.

On the other hand, the importance of an adequately designed indirect leadership is crucial in the current setting. This is due to the already-mentioned inherent weaknesses of the Bureaucratic Organization. Furthermore, it may not always be simple to formulate certain demands in a comprehensible and unambiguous way in written form so that employees clearly know what is expected from them.

In summary, it can be stated that the current group is rather easy to integrate into an organization on the condition that the organizational structure is designed with the necessary care and precision adequately to match the requirements of the respective tasks.

Chapter 7

The Results of the Empirical Survey II

In the following, the analysis of the empirical results will be continued. This splitting into two of the illustration of the empirical results is mainly to enable easier access to the various sections of this illustration. After having dealt with the predominantly executing functions, the more guiding functions will be described in this chapter. One more aspect of the current chapter is a cross-evaluation of the possibilities of integrating various Professional Cultures in one work team. This evaluation is important in order to get an idea of the possibilities of leading and organizing successful cross-functional teams. Mainly it will serve to demonstrate whether and how it is possible to integrate different Professional Cultures in one work team.

In summary, therefore, the current chapter continuous the work undertaken in Chapter 6 while introducing another highly interesting and important aspect of the complex of Professional Cultures.

7.1   The Specially Qualified Production Experts

The seventh cluster comprises people who have a very high qualification level and who are working directly in a technical production process.

Employees who fulfil this definition are, for example, various kinds of engineers, such as aerospace/space and mechanical engineers, but also highly qualified and specialized technicians. In order to decide whether or not specific persons belong to this group, one therefore has to answer two questions.

The first one is whether the qualification level of these persons is that high and rare that their contribution is vital for the success of the production process. This distinguishes a member of this group, for example, from a member of the Blue Collar Worker group.

The second question is whether that person's job is directly production related in a technical discipline. That aspect, for example, differentiates members of this cluster from that of the Innovation and Development cluster.

These two factors are also the reason why there is no cluster that could unite all, or at least a significant majority of engineers present in our sample, because within the engineering group one can state a clear distinction between the 'creative and inventive' engineers and the 'applied knowledge' engineers. Both have their own particularities that have to be taken into account if one wants to work with them the best way possible.

7.1.1   The Empirical Base

For this Professional Culture, the standardized survey produced results that only indicated a certain direction for the characterization of the group. These results needed to be clarified in the course of the verbal interviews, as most of the ratings of this group are in the neutral area. The quantitative part itself is based on 37 respondents originating from various countries and organizational backgrounds. Hence, the intended heterogeneity could be achieved. The rather male-oriented nature of the present professional environment is reflected by the composition of the current sample, which is largely male dominated. Therefore, this male domination does not impair the quality of the findings of this section as it is merely a reflection of the actual composition of this Professional Culture.

Owing to the large number of neutral ratings within the quantitative part, the interviews (based as usual on seven interviewees) are once again highly important for the complete understanding of the traits of this cultural group and hence for the development of an appropriate leadership and organizational style.

The Quantitative Results

Members of this group score the 'Uncertainty Avoidance' scale in the higher neutral area (4.54). The reason for that can be seen in the necessity to be able to react swiftly within the production process to cope with unforeseen events. This is moderated by the wish to avoid such situations since, to a certain extent, they always mean a disruption in the production process itself. Among others, these two counteracting forces lead to the above-given rating.

'Assertiveness' is placed in the higher medium area (4.12). This can be traced back to the need for the members of this group to maintain a smooth production process, which requires them to be moderately assertive every once in a while.

'Future Orientation' is placed in the lower high area (4.92). This rating has to be seen in connection with that for the Uncertainty Avoidance scale. Here also, the area of tension between the need to be flexible in order to meet exterior demands and the need to plan ahead to ensure a smooth production process is responsible for this score.

'Power Distance' is rated in the positive area (3.97). This score is a direct consequence of members of this group usually being in some position of power. Apparently, the use of power is seen to be rather positive. The score has to be interpreted in connection with that for the Uncertainty Avoidance scale. That interconnection will be discussed further in the following.

Collectivism I scores positively (5.46). Members of this cultural cluster do apparently recognize the need for efficient teamwork. Considering the work environment for the Production Experts and its demands, these results are not overly surprising.

'Performance Orientation' scores positively (6.14). High performance on the job seems to be of significant importance to this group. This result is especially interesting in connection with the Assertiveness and Power Distance dimension and will therefore be a central subject further down.

'Gender Egalitarianism' scores positively (6.04). In the present setting, this result mainly indicates that job-related performance is considered to be more important than gender-based considerations.

'Human Orientation' is rated neutrally (4.03). Considering the highly technical nature of the different jobs carried out by the members of the present group, this result is not overly surprising. Nonetheless, in connection with the results of the other dimensions, this score strengthens the impression that this culture is very result and efficiency driven, without paying too much attention to individual concerns. Once again, the open interviews were of crucial importance for the understanding of the rating.

Finally, 'Collectivism II' scores positively (6.04). Looking at the key function that members of this cluster have for the success of their respective companies, this result is hardly surprising.

The Qualitative Results

The results of the qualitative part further deepen and clarify the findings of the quantitative part. As already mentioned, in particular, the frequently found medium scores in the quantitative part needed some further clarifications as to the reasons for these ratings.

According to the interviews, the rating of the Uncertainty Avoidance scale has to be seen in close connection with that of the Future Orientation scale. Both are an expression of the need for flexibility in any production process, while still being very critical when it comes to unforeseen events that are considered to be at the source of this need for flexibility. These counteracting influences moderate each other in both dimensions.

The medium rating of Uncertainty Avoidance is a clear expression of the above situation. On the one hand, a certain level of uncertainty is accepted and seen to be a necessity in the production process. On the other, this very uncertainty is considered to be the reason for a significant number of problems in the production process. Therefore, ambivalence is felt when it comes to uncertainty. For the members of this group, uncertainty is not a bad thing in itself, but rather something that has to be kept in balanced control. Too much uncertainty is considered to be problematic, due to the negative consequences it has on the production process. At the same time, too little room for flexibility is seen to be counterproductive, as it inhibits a swift and appropriate reaction to demands originating in the production process. These two influencing factors virtually neutralize each other, leading to the given rating on the Uncertainty Avoidance scale, which gives a slight preference to a somewhat more stable professional environment.

According to the interviewees, a similar line of argument leads to the rating of the Future Orientation scale. On the one hand, it is necessary to have a certain long-term perspective in order to carry out a production process successfully. On the other, it is impossible to control completely a production process through the sole means of long-term planning. Thus, a certain level of flexibility is needed, which moderates the rating on the Future Orientation scale.

The high rating of the Performance Orientation scale is due to the relative position this Professional Culture has in its environment. The regular Production Experts consider themselves to be largely responsible for the success of the production process. As this is a core-function of practically all companies sampled (including the airlines) it gives them the feeling of being highly important, which leads to a high motivation to perform well on the job. This in turn is the reason for the stated high rating of the Performance Orientation scale.

The rating of the Assertiveness scale has to be seen in connection with that of the Performance Orientation scale. The very high motivation to perform well on the job sometimes leads to a lack of tolerance for other professional groups who do not necessarily share the same view as to how to carry out a certain task. Especially when dealing with lower ranking employees, the members of the present group sometimes feel the need to behave assertively. Another example where assertive behaviour is occasionally necessary is when dealing with people of a comparable relative position within the organization. According to the opinion of the interviewees, it is 'often problematic to reach an appropriate agreement with these co-employees due to their lack of technical knowledge which is paired with an excessive drive to influence the production process'. At the same time, it is acknowledged that excessively assertive behaviour is counterproductive when dealing with both lower ranking employees and people of the same relative position. These influences virtually neutralize each other with a very limited tendency in favour of assertiveness. With their superiors, they accept assertiveness as long as it is paired with reasonable judgments and is not excessively frequent and strong.

The positive view of Power Distance is also a direct consequence of the relative position of the members of the Production Experts in the organization. Very often they are in situations in which they have to express clearly what has to be done. At the same time the employees who receive these orders often do accept and do expect their superior actually to give them clear guidance (e.g. see Section 6.1). However, this specific way of leading people is not accepted when it comes to being led by the direct superior. The present group expects to be led in a way that is marked by low Power Distance and high consideration for the opinions and views of its members. This phenomenon is not a peculiarity of the present group, but can be found with a number of higher ranking Professional Cultures. The exercise of power is considered to be helpful and right only when the respective group is not on the receiving end of this exercise. So the interpretation of the positive rating on the Power Distance scale as an acceptance of a leadership and organizational concept based on Power Distance would be seriously misleading and cause significant dysfunctionalties in the respective departments.

A positive view of teamwork, which already shows itself in the positive rating of the Collectivism I dimension, was confirmed in the course of the interviews. Although the need for real team work is sometimes seen to be limited, it is largely acknowledged that in certain settings a team-based approach is necessary. Therefore, it depends largely on the respective situation, whether or not there should be a team-based approach. Nevertheless, if the work setting is such that it permits such an approach, this course of action should be favoured.

The high rating of the Gender Egalitarianism scale is, on the one hand, a consequence of the fact that the present group is extremely result and efficiency driven. On the other, it is a consequence of the fact that the clear conviction exists that superior results can only be achieved if there are no gender-based prejudices.

The same reasoning is at the core of the neutral rating of the Human Orientation scale. The technical background and the large emphasis on efficiency lead to a certain indifference towards the values expressed with the Human Orientation scale. This does not necessarily mean that they are seen to be negative, but according to the interviewees it does mean that these values are not part of the main concerns of the members of the group.

Finally, the score on the Collectivism II scale is a clear expression of the pride that members of this Professional Culture feel in being part of the group. This pride is a consequence of the perceived importance each group member has for the success of their respective companies and therefore the importance felt within the company. As already mentioned, they sometimes also feel certain pressure from other professional groups, which adds a notion of loyalty towards the profession and its members.

In summary, it can be said that the results of the qualitative part significantly deepened the insights gained with the quantitative part. Furthermore, for the correct understanding of the results of the Power Distance scale the results of the qualitative part were actually crucial, as without them a complete misinterpretation of this Core Cultural Dimension would have been possible.

Summarizing Thoughts

The empirical results gained in the course of the research project give a very detailed picture of the characteristics of the Specially Qualified Production Experts.

As shown, technically, the present sample is highly satisfying. This is due to the fact that, on the one hand, it comprises a rather large number of people, and on the other the sample itself is highly diverse as far as nationality and organizational origins are concerned. The quality of the results themselves is also clearly satisfying. In fact, they will be more than sufficient to develop a fitting leadership style and organizational design to integrate this Professional Culture efficiently into any organization.

In addition, one particular quality of the present section is the demonstration of the clear necessity to join quantitative and qualitative research methodologies in order to gain a correct and complete picture of a Professional Culture. Neither research approach alone would have been sufficient for the full understanding of the present culture; even worse, this could have led to wrong conclusions. Therefore, in summary, it can be stated that the empiricals delivered highly satisfying results both from a technical and a content focused point of view. Thus, they are highly adequate to achieve a clear identification of the characteristics of the present Professional Culture on the one hand, and to ensure the development of an appropriate organizational structure and leadership style on the other.

7.1.2   An Integrative Solution to the Found Characteristics

The development of an integrative solution to the characteristics found will be undertaken as usual. Initially, an appropriate leadership style for the direct leader of the present group will be described. Subsequently, an organizational structure that fits the characteristics of the present group will be developed.

Jointly, these two approaches form the solution to integrate the members of the present cluster successfully into an organization according to the results of previous chapters, the empiricals and the GLOBE-Study (House *et al.* 2004).

The Appropriate Leadership Style

An appropriate leadership style, according to the results found here, will comprise elements of the Team-Oriented (e.g. Manz and Sims 2001; House *et al.* 2004; see also Section 2.2.2), and the Participative leadership style (e.g. Lewin 1948; Tannenbaum and Schmidt 1958; House *et al.* 2004; see also Section 2.1.1), while being centred on the Charismatic/Value-Based leadership style (e.g. Bass 1985; Burns 1978; House *et al.* 2004; see also Section 2.2.3).

The relatively high degree of flexibility that is needed in order to carry out the tasks of the present group successfully, in correlation with the high motivation to perform well on the job, calls for its members to be given a significant amount of freedom. Nevertheless, it is necessary to keep up this high level of motivation. The best way to do that in the present setting is to create a very clear idea of where the direct superiors want the department and its people to be in the middle and long term; thus they need to create a clear Vision that inspires their people. At the same time, the leaders should stay out of the way of the subordinates when it comes to their day-to-day business. Therefore, Charismatic/Value-Based leadership has to be at the core of the appropriate leadership style.

In addition, Team-Orientation is also quite important. This Team-Orientation is necessary because of the expressed need of the members of this group to be free from too much influence from their respective superiors on the one hand and, on the other, due to the explicitly expressed preference for a team-based approach wherever possible. Therefore, elements from the above-described SuperLeadership (Manz and Sims 2001; see Section 2.2.2) should be employed whenever possible, which includes the actual implementation of the three aforementioned core roles of the respective leader (coach, referee, entertainer).

Finally, Participative leadership has also to be considered. This is because the extremely high qualification level connected with the high Performance Orientation leads to members of the present group to expect their superior to take their respective opinions into consideration.

As already mentioned, the relatively high score on the Power Distance scale is oriented solely towards other employees led by the members of this Professional Culture and is not an expression of a preference for themselves being led that way.

Therefore, an appropriate leadership style for the present group would have to look like the following. The leader creates an appropriate vision, which inspires the employees on a long term basis. Unfortunately, this vision cannot be specified more clearly at this point as it depends on various factors such as competitors, traits of the company, technical challenges, etc. The important thing is, however, that it actually inspires the members of this group in the sense outlined in Section 2.2.3.

The leaders keep out of the day-to-day business as much as possible and serve primarily as a counsellor to their subordinates. They guide and help them when needed, but do not impose their view if not absolutely necessary. The leaders should always try to lead their people with a team-based approach if the task permits. In connection with the above mentioned inspiration, it is highly important that the leaders are actually able to convince their subordinates of the rightness of their vision. This can be achieved more easily if the leader embodies the above-mentioned three core roles of SuperLeadership.

Furthermore, thorough participation in the decision-taking process is crucial for the motivation of the members of this group, as this directly touches their self-image as being among the most qualified to judge technical matters in the production process. By taking the subordinates' opinions, concerns and ideas seriously, the leader further enhances the acceptance of the vision formulated.

If the leader is able to join the different elements of these three leadership styles, an appropriate match between the used leadership style and the needs of the subordinates should occur. It is crucial, though, that the leader is able to supply the correct mixture of these three leadership styles. In particular, the joining of Charismatic/Value-Based on the one side and Team-Oriented and Participative leadership on the other may prove difficult. This is due, on the one hand, to the fact that actually 'learning' Charismatic/Value-Based leadership is rather hard. On the other, successful leaders in the present setting will have to step back somewhat and permit their subordinates to go their own way and give them the feeling of actually participating in the various decision taking processes instead of simply imposing themselves by virtue of their charisma.

In summary, it can be said that the demands on the leaders are very high in the present setting. Not only have they to be charismatic, which is already a challenge in itself, but in addition it is necessary to avoid fully exploiting that charisma to their own advantage. This will often put enormous strains on the character of the respective leaders. Thus, a very important aspect is the careful selection of an appropriate leader for the Specially Qualified Production Experts' group.

The Appropriate Organizational Structure

Concerning the appropriate organizational structure, the particularities of the present cultural cluster point clearly to an adaptation of Complexity Theory to the needs of this cluster (Stacey *et al.* 2000; see also Section 3.2.2). According to the logic of the Complexity Theory, it is necessary to build a living complex system (Lewin and Regine 2000; for details refer also to Section 3.2.2). As far as leadership is concerned, this can be achieved through the leadership style developed above.

The organization needs to be structured with a team-based approach. Here, this team-based approach does not, however, necessarily have to be understood in the strict sense it is usually used in the present work. For the Production Experts' culture it is more appropriate to use a broader understanding of teams.

In the present setting, a team can be understood as a group of people working for a common goal, without necessarily working together in a physical sense. As an example, consider a leader in charge of 20 production engineers, each of whom is responsible for a different part of the production process or working in a different location. For organizational purposes, they may still be considered to form a team if they work for that same common goal.

At that point, as already mentioned, it is necessary for the leaders not to exercise too much influence upon the day-to-day business itself. Organizationally, their role becomes twofold and genuinely more complicated. To the outside, they have to be the representative of the team, collecting information, being 'the face of the team', articulating the interests of the team towards outsiders, etc. To the inside, the main role is to ensure good relationships between the team members, give guidance and help, ensure that external demands are well understood by the team members, and so on. In short, their role is to create out of the different team members one entity that works closely together towards the common goal.

Besides the above given leadership style, this implies the creation of an organization in which the individual team members have all the autonomy they need, in order to decide for themselves if a certain task can be accomplished alone, or if any help is needed. Therefore, boundaries between the responsibilities of the different team members will fluctuate, rendering fixed organizational structures obsolete. These are replaced by capacities and competencies of the individual team members and the groups/teams/departments they lead. As a consequence, this becomes an organization that is oriented to a solution of 'Integration through Lateral Organization' (e.g. Peters 1993; Wunderer 2001; see also Section 3.3.2) in which the individual team members organize themselves in order to pool the competencies needed for a specific task. The leader is only involved in case no such pooling is possible, be it due to a lack of such competencies or due to a lack of the will to pool these competencies, etc.

Organizationally, this also means that it is necessary for the leaders of the Specially Qualified Production Experts to have the necessary competencies actually to give this freedom to their subordinates. As most of the time this leader will be part of Strategic Management (see Section 7.6), this should usually be assured. However, should a situation arise in which the leader is closer to Operational Management (see Section 7.5), which may happen if, for example, a group of highly qualified technicians is led by another technician who, in turn, is not part of the higher echelons of management, it is crucial to provide this leader with the above-described imperative freedom.

In summary, the necessary organization for the present cultural cluster will have a flatter hierarchal difference between the superior and the members of this culture, and more competencies located at the level of the members of this culture than a classical organization. As a rough guideline, it can be stated that any competence that can be reasonably located with the members of the Specially Qualified Production Experts' culture should be located with them.

The Solution in Overview

The possible integrative solution for the present cluster is quite complicated, especially when it has to be realized within a classical organization. For one thing, it is necessary to select people who are actually capable of filling out the highly demanding leadership role that this culture requires, and for another it is necessary to give that leader thorough training in dealing with the peculiarities of the present cultural cluster. For the organization, the demands are of the same magnitude. The rejection of hierarchy, control, etc. as the main organizational features in favour of empowerment and an increase of responsibilities at the level of the Production Experts can be extremely demanding, depending on the type of organization in use.

Despite these problems, it has to be stated that a non-adaptation of the organizational and leadership structures developed here can have highly negative consequences. This is because the preference for the above described structures could be identified clearly in the course of the research project. In connection with the objective importance that the members of this group have for the success of virtually any company, this can lead to disastrous consequences if ignored.

Therefore, despite possible problems when implementing these structures, the beneficial consequences will far outweigh these potential inconveniences.

7.1.3   Final Thoughts Regarding the Specially Qualified Production Experts

The results of cluster seven show a very complex and highly interesting Professional Culture. Furthermore these results are highly satisfying from a technical point of view.

The complexity of this group shows itself in connection with the results of the 'Innovation and Development' group (see Section 7.2). These results were quite surprising, as they clearly indicate that there is no such thing as one homogeneous group of engineers, but two distinctively different groups for the production part and the development part. In addition, neither of these two groups is exclusively composed of engineers, further undermining the idea of a common 'engineering culture'.

Especially for companies that have large development and large production divisions, these results are highly important. Even more so as the two groups have a number of quite significant differences, rendering common treatment of both not only less efficient, but also potentially harmful for the whole company.

In that sense, the results gained in this chapter go well beyond this one single Professional Culture and point to an aspect that has already been mentioned at various occasions in this book. This aspect is the necessity to take properly into account the different characteristics of the various Professional Cultures present in a company. Furthermore, it is of the utmost importance not to base these judgements on some rule of thumb, but on a thorough and well-founded database and an appropriate evaluation of these data.

Another interesting aspect of this section is the further demonstration of the enormous benefit that can be achieved through the combination of quantitative and qualitative research methodologies.

A purely qualitative research approach would not have generated the necessary details to truly characterize this culture, while a purely quantitative approach would possibly have led to erroneous results. Here again, the above-mentioned necessity to combine these two research methods in this highly complicated environment has been demonstrated.

In summary, it can be said that in this section a number of aspects show up that have an importance that goes well beyond this single chapter. Therefore, this section is highly interesting for a number of points regarding the understanding of the whole meaning of the present work.

7.2   Innovation and Development

According to the results of the empirical survey, people working in Innovation and Development related areas create an independent group which is not restricted to that of development engineers. This is due to the fact that Innovation and Development are not necessarily exclusively due to somebody exercising a technical profession.

This can already be seen when considering the composition of this group, which incorporates not only engineers, but also members of a variety of professional groups such as consultants, HR managers, or members of management and, obviously, engineers. The results given in this section have far-reaching consequences for any organization that depends largely on innovation for its success, because creativity and innovation cannot be decreed in the same way as can, for example, an increase in working hours per day. Therefore, the appropriate treatment of this key group is hugely important for optimizing its results.

Considering the fact that in the aviation industry virtually any company is highly dependent on innovation in order to survive, this insight is even more important in the present context than in most other industries.

7.2.1   The Empirical Base

The results of the empirical survey are presented as usual, beginning with the results of the quantitative part of the survey.

The quantitative part of the survey played a key role in determining the main characteristics of the Innovation and Development culture. It is based on responses from 26 respondents originating from various countries and organizations. The gender-related composition shows a male majority. This majority is, once again, a reflection of the composition of the occupations themselves present in this cultural group.

The qualitative part, which as usual is composed of seven respondents, played once more an important role in understanding the underlying processes leading to the results of the quantitative part.

Therefore, this dual approach proved once more to be the most appropriate way to gain the maximum amount of information and therefore the best insights possible into the research object.

The Quantitative Results

The Uncertainty Avoidance dimension is placed at the lower end of the medium area (3.53). This result is hardly surprising for a professional group that has to search for new ways of doing things, as this necessarily creates an environment of high uncertainty.

Nevertheless, total uncertainty is not the goal of this cultural cluster as its members still need stability to a certain extent in order to pursue their respective tasks successfully. The items of the Assertiveness dimension score positively in this group (4.79). This result has to be seen in relation with the role of the members of this group in their respective organizations. These employees are at the source of most new developments and innovations in every organization. As will be elucidated below, it is often impossible to push through any innovation without a certain amount of persistence and assertiveness leading to the given result.

The Future Orientation dimension receives in this group one of the highest ratings out of all groups (6.22). This result is rather obvious as the values formulated by this dimension are at the core of the self understanding of this group. Further details concerning this will be given below.

The Power Distance dimension gets a positive rating within this group (4.17). Again, the reasons for this will be elucidated below. The one thing to be retained at this point though is that this rating is to be seen in connection with the needs to have clearly set goals and the ability to push through developments if necessary against opposition.

The Collectivism I dimension is clearly rated in the positive area and gets the second highest score of the whole sample (6.08). This result is a clear reflection of the need for effective team work in this group, which is a direct consequence of the highly demanding work environment.

The Performance Orientation dimension is also valued strongly positively (6.41). This rating should not be a surprise, as in the highly demanding environment in which this group is placed only individuals who strive for excellence can succeed.

Gender Egalitarianism is rated positively (6.24). This rating can be seen as an expression of the fact that the most important aspect when judging a person in this environment is that person's performance. As will be pointed out further below, this dimension should therefore be seen in connection with the Performance Orientation dimension.

Human Orientation is valued strongly positively (5.29). With reference to the details given in the following section, this rating reflects the understanding of the members of this group that an efficient and creative way of working together also necessitates good and healthy inter-personal relationships. This highly interesting aspect will be investigated further in the following section.

The Collectivism II dimension is rated at the limit between the medium and the high area (5.46). Considering the key role this professional group plays in any company, such a result should not be overly surprising, although it does not completely reflect the view that members of this group have about themselves. As will be pointed out below, the self-image of the members of the Innovation and Development group is very positive, partially leading to the given result.

The Qualitative Results

According to the interviews, a balanced mixture between stability and instability is an important prerequisite for the successful accomplishment of the tasks of the group.

An area of tension thus exists between these two factors. On the one hand, some instability is necessary for any kind of creative process, on the other, too much instability is potentially counterproductive for any long-term development process. The interviewees stressed more than once the importance of freedom and, specifically, the freedom from unnecessarily restrictive rules and procedures. That does not mean, however, that every kind of rule and procedure is considered to be negative. The important point for the members of this group is the above-mentioned balance between stability and instability, which finds its expression in the low to medium rating of the Uncertainty Avoidance scale.

Another interesting point concerns the relatively high rating on the Power Distance scale. This, at first sight somewhat surprising, rating is a direct consequence of a very specific understanding by the members of the Innovation and Development group of the way in which power should be used. They expect their direct superior to give them clear and unambiguous guidelines without, however, influencing their day to day work. This can be seen in direct connection with the results of the Uncertainty Avoidance scale, where some stability and guidance is appreciated. According to the interviewees this relative stability can be achieved by setting up goals and clearly communicating them, while at the same time relying on the individual Innovator/Developer to actually reach them independently.

The result of the Assertiveness scale has to be seen in this connection. Its positive rating is a consequence of two aspects. The first is the way members of this group think they should behave, especially when dealing with other professional groups. Here, the impression prevails that sometimes it is necessary to be somewhat Assertive in order to 'push through' certain new developments successfully. The second aspect concerns the behaviour they expect from their superior. Here, it is thought that it is advantageous for a superior to be able to be Assertive when necessary. 'When necessary' means for the members of the present group that they sometimes expect their superior to take a decision and thus to give the above-mentioned guidelines. That is also true when this means pushing something through against opposition.

This aspect is especially important when it comes to long term decisions, as Future Orientation is highly important for the members of this group. As most Innovation and Development tasks in the aviation industry have a rather long-term orientation, the overall time horizon of the concerned professionals needs to be long-term oriented as well. This latent long-term orientation is highly significant for the members of the present group as it can be seen in connection with the already clearly expressed need for guidelines. Therefore, the rating on the Future Orientation scale was the highest out all Professional Cultures.

Team-Orientation is also very important for the members of this group. Such a result is hardly surprising as most innovative tasks would be largely impossible without properly functioning teams. This result finds its expression in both the quantitative part of the survey with the high rating of the Collectivism I Dimension and the qualitative part, where the importance of teamwork was mentioned more than once.

This impression was further enhanced by the results of the Human Orientation scale. The quantitative part of the survey showed a clear preference for the values expressed with this dimension. Furthermore, the interviews clearly indicated the importance that good interpersonal relationships have for the members of this group. A direct reference was made to the above described importance of efficient teams. Members of the Innovation and Development culture are convinced that caring about the other team members and having a true relationship with them is a necessity for the successful implementation and actual experience of teamwork.

Performance Orientation is high for the members of the current group. According to the interviewees, the task itself is usually extremely *intrinsically* motivating, leading to a very high motivation to perform in an outstanding manner. This is usually strengthened if these performances can be achieved within one of the above described functioning and harmonious teams.

The result of the Gender Egalitarianism scale has to be seen in direct connection with that of the Performance Orientation scale. The positive rating of this scale can be interpreted once again as a clear expression of the preference for performance in comparison to any gender-based questions, further strengthening the above stated importance of performance.

Finally, a positive view of the Collectivism II Dimension could be confirmed, which is not completely clear when only the score of the Collectivism II scale is taken into consideration (as shown, it is on the limit between medium and high). This positive rating is, on the one hand, a direct consequence of the stated high intrinsic value the profession itself has for the members of the Innovation and Development group. On the other, it is a consequence of the perceived importance the work carried out by the members of this group has for the companies concerned. The perception is that most tasks carried out are vital for the future of the company, giving this work even more intrinsic value than it already has thanks to its unique character.

In summary, it can be said that the interviews gave a number of very interesting insights that went well beyond those gained in the course of the quantitative part of the survey. Once again, it was only possible with the help of the interviews to join the findings of the quantitative part into one coherent and detailed picture of this specific Professional Culture.

Summarizing Thoughts

Jointly, the empirical results gave a very interesting and detailed picture of the characteristics of this Professional Culture. For the appropriate interpretation of the quantitative results it was necessary once again to proceed to a thorough qualitative survey. Only by taking full advantage of the results of both research methodologies is it possible to correctly develop an appropriate leadership style and organizational structure as undertaken below.

A very interesting second aspect concerns the composition of this group. This is due to the fact that the present group comprises the second part of the group of engineers present in the survey. In comparison with the production engineers (Section

7.1) the characteristics of this group are remarkably different. This is a consequence of the fact that the engineers present in this group are development engineers, and thus have a quite different work environment than that of the production engineers.

Furthermore, this group is not only composed of engineers, but also of people working in HR development, as consultants, in coaching, etc. Therefore, as already stated, the differentiation between two Professional Cultures is not necessarily possible with reference to what is usually called an occupation or a profession, but rather with reference to functional aspects. The importance of these results cannot be overestimated in the context of the present study as it clearly shows that a Professional Culture may develop in a quite different manner from what usually may be expected.

In summary, it can be stated that the present Professional Culture exhibited a number of highly interesting and important traits in the course of the empirical study. As mentioned, these results are based on responses from employees originating from various countries and working for a number of different organizations. Hence, here again the found characteristics are not an artefact of some national or organizational cultural influences, but apparently of the mentioned underlying mental processes being a consequence of the prevailing Professional Culture.

7.2.2   *An Integrative Solution to the Found Characteristics*

In the following, an adequate leadership style and organizational design will be developed. Based on the rather detailed picture gained in the course of the empirical study, the appropriate leadership style will initially be developed. Subsequently, an organizational design will be proposed that will be in line with the results gained in this section.

The results presented in the following are of high importance as they concern one of the key Professional Cultures of this very demanding and dynamic industry, as each company is dependent on the successful and constant development of new solutions.

Owing to the fact that it is hardly possible to order creativity, it is of the utmost importance to appropriately treat the members of the Innovation and Development group.

The Appropriate Leadership Style

According to the above results, an appropriate leadership style is based on the Charismatic/Value-Based leadership style (e.g. Burns 1978; Bass 1985; House *et al.* 2004; see also Section 2.2.3). Large parts of the Participative (e.g. Lewin 1948; Tannenbaum and Schmidt 1958; House *et al.* 2004; see also Section 2.1.1), the Human-Oriented (e.g. Gagné and Fleishman, 1959; Fleishman and Quaintance, 1984; Blake and Mouton, 1985; House *et al.*, 2004; see also Section 2.1.2) and the Team-Oriented leadership style (e.g. Manz and Sims 2001; House *et al.*, 2004; see also Section 2.2.2) need to be included into the final solution in order to create a leadership style that appropriately reflects the above preferences of the members of this group.

All relevant Core Cultural Dimensions clearly point to the Charismatic/Value-Based leadership style as the leadership style of choice. The only exception here is the inconclusive quantitative result for the Collectivism II Dimension. As already mentioned the interpretation of the Collectivism II Dimension became much clearer with the open interviews. The resulting positive interpretation of this dimension leads to the very high importance attributed to the Charismatic/Value-Based leadership style.

Four out of the five Core Cultural Dimensions that are relevant for the Team-Oriented leadership style indicate the necessity to incorporate elements of this leadership style into the final solution. Only the result of the Uncertainty Avoidance scale is in contradiction to this leadership style. Considering the fact that four dimensions are in accordance, and the nature of the tasks carried out by the members of this group, the importance of Team-Oriented leadership cannot be denied.

Concerning the Participative leadership style, all relevant Core Cultural Dimensions, with the exception of the Assertiveness scale, indicate the importance this leadership style has for appropriately leading the members of this Professional Culture. Furthermore, reflecting the professional competencies present in this culture, it is evident that its members expect their superiors to be participative in their leadership style.

Finally, Human-Oriented leadership has also to be taken into account. As already mentioned, good and healthy interpersonal relationships are extremely important to the members of the Innovation and Development culture, as they consider these to be necessary in order to create well-functioning teams. In connection with the results of both the quantitative and the qualitative empirical part, and the already stated importance of teamwork in general for the members of this Professional Culture, it becomes clear why Human-Oriented leadership necessarily forms part of the appropriate leadership style.

An appropriate leadership style would therefore look like the following.

The leaders would have to develop a compelling Vision that inspires their subordinates. It is important that the Vision is realistic and that the leaders have the credibility that the subordinates actually believe in them and the Vision. The Vision itself should be closely related to the Innovation and Development task so that the link between the successful completion of the task and the fulfilment of the Vision is clearly visible to the employees concerned.

Furthermore, it is extremely important that in their day to day business the leaders take a strictly Team-Oriented leadership approach. A very promising approach in this setting is the above-described SuperLeadership (Manz and Sims 2001; see also Section 2.2.2). The leader should always strive to transfer as much decision competency as possible into the team in order to demonstrate clearly that it is the team's responsibility to find the appropriate solutions to the problems at hand.

In that context it is also vitally important when the leader has to take a decision, that the decision-taking process itself is as participative as possible. This is a consequence of the usually extraordinarily elaborated specialized knowledge members of this Professional Culture have. A decision that does not truly reflect this existing knowledge has a very high chance of not being accepted. Owing to the already-mentioned impossibility to order creativity, unaccepted decisions taken by the leader have potentially disastrous consequences for the results of the whole department concerned.

In addition the leaders have to make sure that they create the above-mentioned positive interpersonal relationships. To achieve this, it is necessary for the leader to value all members of the team as human beings beyond the limits of their professional function. The intention has to be to create a true bond between the team members and the leader so as to facilitate the leader's role outlined in Section 2.2.2. Furthermore, strong positive interpersonal relationships between the leader and the team members, greatly facilitate the internalization of the above-mentioned Vision. Hence, the significance of Human-Oriented leadership must not be underestimated in the current setting.

In summary, it can be stated at this point that the leadership pattern to be exhibited by the leader of an Innovation and Development team, is quite demanding. Failure to do so, however, may result in a greatly diminished efficiency of the concerned team. Due to the importance of this professional group for their individual companies, this is an outcome that should be strictly avoided.

The Appropriate Organizational Structure

Due to the above-given characteristics of this Professional Culture, Complexity Theory will serve again as guideline for the appropriate organizational structure of this culture (Stacey *et al.* 2000; Lewin and Regine 2000; see also Section 3.2.2). The actual characteristics of this organizational structure should be very close to the theoretical approach given in Section 3.2.2.

In detail, this means that the whole organizational structure has to be centred on largely independent work teams. Superiors should exist, but depending on the size of the respective team not necessarily one for every single team. They should exhibit the three main traits of a leader in a complex system mentioned in Section 3.2.2, which are allowing, accessible and attuned.

The hierarchy, if one still wants to call it that in the present setting, should be very flat. On the regular day-to-day basis, the members of the Innovation and Development Culture should not feel that a true hierarchy really does exist. Instead, they should get their day to day guidance from their intrinsic motivation, the above mentioned Vision and their fellow team members.

Therefore, self-governance is a key issue for this organizational design. It is of the utmost importance that the different teams get the tools into their hands, which actually allow them to lead their teams themselves.

When it comes to the creation of the different teams it is to be made sure that all necessary competencies are present within the group. If, after a while, it becomes clear to the team that a competence is missing, the initiative for adding that missing competency may, and obviously should, come from the team itself.

Control mechanisms should be kept to a minimum. As a principle, the teams should only be measured by the degree to which they actually reach their goals not on how they reach them. Here also, the basic idea of self-governance shows up again, as true self-governance obviously implies self-control.

Any measure that facilitates the exchange of knowledge among the different teams should be undertaken. In the present setting this should provide the different teams with the possibility to have unrestricted access to the knowledge of other teams if needed. This topic is to be seen again in the context of self-governance.

In summary, it can be said that the present Professional Culture does require a lot of freedom in order to perform efficiently and at the level of its potential. As shown, this freedom can best be achieved with the consequent use of the approach described in Section 3.2.2. One of the things though which should not be attempted is the implementation of a true heterarchy, as this clearly collides with a number of points given above. Therefore, the solution is not a blind implementation of some organization design that goes back to Complexity Theory, but the adequate use of this design to the here-described needs of the present Professional Culture.

The Solution in Overview

The proposed solution is, on the one hand, highly demanding and, on the other, rather straightforward.

The leadership part puts enormous demands on the respective leaders as they have to display a large number of highly challenging behaviours in order to achieve the above-described leadership style. The organizational design part, on the other hand, is relatively straightforward and, in theory, easy to implement. The main problems would probably arise due to superiors not getting along with this kind of organizational structure or possibly even outright fighting it.

Therefore, the most challenging part is to have leaders who can actually successfully live the above developed leadership style. The problem here is similar to that in the previous section although somewhat even more distinct.

Hence, the importance of a thorough selection of future leaders for this Professional Culture and continues training with these leaders seems to be a necessity. In particular, the leader selection process is extremely important as not all the behaviours described above are actually learnable; e.g. persons who are not able to adjust their behaviour to build the mentioned positive relationships with their subordinates lack a key competence, which they need to effectively lead a team in the present setting.

In summary, it can be said that the solution proposed in this section may not be the easiest to implement, either due to a lack of qualified leadership personnel or due to political opposition within the company against such radical change in organizational design. Nevertheless, the importance an outstanding performance of the members of this Professional Culture has for the companies concerned should, after due consideration, of the costs and benefits clearly demonstrate that the benefits outweigh the costs.

7.2.3   Final Thoughts Regarding Innovation and Development

The results of this eighth Cluster show a Professional Culture that has a very special standing in most companies.

The members of this culture are not necessarily hierarchically highly placed in their respective companies, but due to their importance for the future of these companies they often do have a very special position.

This special position finds its expression in the clearly articulated demands for independency and freedom that the members of the Innovation and Development culture expect to have in their companies. There is no doubt that an overly restrictive leadership and organizational design has potentially highly negative consequences for the performance of the members of this culture.

Therefore, the results gained in this section are highly important. Often, companies may be tempted to structure Innovation and Development departments in a more classical way. According to the results given here, such a structure would be highly inappropriate and most likely harmful for the success of the concerned companies.

It is for that reason that it becomes once again clear why it is of such importance to take the specific requirements into consideration that different Professional Cultures and therefore professions have. As demonstrated at various occasions in this book, failure to do so leaves large parts of a company's resources unused. This should be avoided with all Professional Cultures present in a company, but in particular with those cultures that have such a key importance for the success of many companies.

7.3   The Project Leaders

The ninth cluster reunites people whose focus is on managing and integrating projects. Depending on the projects themselves, these employees had varying backgrounds before they started managing projects. Nevertheless, the very activity of being responsible for projects has been exercised by these employees for a number of years. Apparently this time span and the specific demands of project management are sufficient to create a genuine Project Leaders culture.

The existence of a Project Leader culture is highly important for a number of reasons. First, it clearly indicates that for the integration of employees with different professional backgrounds very specific qualifications and approaches are required. This represents another strong indication for the existence of different Professional Cultures, as stated and empirically shown in the present work.

Furthermore, the existence of a Project Leaders culture and its characteristics will be useful in Section 7.7, when an integrative solution to a number of rather common cross-cultural encounters will be developed. Obviously, these encounters are very often to be found in project-type environments.

Finally, the tasks that are organized in projects are frequently of a key importance for organizations. Their success is therefore often critical for the concerned organizations. Hence, the meaning of the results of this section cannot be overestimated due to their relevancy for both the present work and the success of organizations in general.

7.3.1   The Empirical Base

In this Professional Culture, the written questionnaire gave highly satisfying results based on 18 respondents from various national and organizational backgrounds. Therefore, the intended heterogeneity of the sample was achieved.

A tendency towards a cultural cluster that is virtually exclusively composed of Project Leaders was already clear after the evaluation of the written data. These results were further enhanced with the help of the interviews in which the underlying reasons for these results also became increasingly understandable. This part was, as usual, based on the statements from seven interviewees.

As usual, the results of the written questionnaire will be given first, followed by those of the interviews and some further insights.

The Quantitative Results

The rating for the Uncertainty Avoidance scale is neutral (3.57). The reason for this can mainly be traced back to the specific demands the members of this culture have to deal with. Further highly interesting details concerning this aspect will be given in the following.

Assertive behaviour is seen to be relatively positive (4.5) with a score just on the limit between a medium and a high ranking. The sometimes highly diverging interests among the members of a given project lead, among other outcomes, to the need to integrate through consensus building, but also to the need sometimes to take decisive action if this consensus is not achievable.

Future Orientation is valued positively in this group (5.35). This score is influenced by two demands. These two demands are a result of the need for the Project Leaders to have a precise long-term perspective in order to achieve the goal of the project on the one hand. On the other, this long-term perspective is slightly moderated by the necessary flexibility most projects require from their leaders. This area of tension will be discussed in more detail later in this section.

The Power Distance dimension is valued very positively by the Project Leaders (4.67), representing the highest score out of all dimensions. This result has to be seen in connection with that for the Assertiveness dimension. Sometimes decisions have to be taken despite diverging views among the members of the project. These decisions necessitate, at that point, the use of power to a certain extent, which leads to the above given score.

The values expressed with the Collectivism I dimension are seen positively by the members of this group (5.5). This is obviously a consequence of the need for teamwork in complex environments, which shows itself in a positive score for the Collectivism I dimension.

The Performance Orientation dimension is valued positively by the members of this group (6.39). As will be pointed out below, the nature of projects results to the need for performance-driven personalities to lead them.

Gender Egalitarianism is valued slightly positively (5.81). Here again, the nature of Project Leadership is responsible for this rating, as the values expressed by that dimension are not seen to be overly relevant. This is due to the fact that people are judged according to their achievement without taking into consideration their gender.

Human Orientation, as expressed with the respective dimension, is valued very positively by the members of the Project Leaders group (5.59). This score, which is the highest in the whole sample, can be traced back to the need for the individual Project Leader to strive for decision taking by reaching a consensus. Although this approach may not always work, chances are significantly enhanced if the decision takers express some affection for their co-workers, including their needs and desires.

The Collectivism II dimension is scored positive (6.06). As will be shown in the following section, this rating is due to the perceived importance of the tasks carried out, which in turn leads to a feeling of pride and loyalty towards the respective project and thus to the occupation of project leadership.

The Qualitative Results

According to the interviewees, the neutral score on the Uncertainty Avoidance scale is a consequence of two counteracting influences. The first is the need for stability in order to create a functioning project team. This influence is moderated by the necessity to have a certain flexibility so as to cope with the varying challenges this professional environment has. These two influences neutralize each other and lead to the above-given neutral score on the Uncertainty Avoidance scale.

This picture gets even clearer when put into the context of the Future Orientation and the Power Distance scales.

An orientation that is based on a long-term strategy is very much appreciated by the members of the Project Leaders culture. This result is rather obvious as most projects in the aviation industry show a very long time span from their initiation until their completion. This supersedes the above-mentioned need for flexibility in the rating of this dimension as a clear concept of time is of the utmost importance for the successful completion of any major project.

The very positive rating on the Power Distance scale further strengthens the impression that, to a certain extent, a clear and stable environment is preferred by the members of this group. Furthermore, according to the results of the interviews, this rating also shows a clear appreciation of understandable and responsible hierarchical structures. It is seen to be a necessity that superiors are able to formulate clearly what they want to achieve, so that the people working for those superiors have a clear idea of what is expected from them. The same reasoning is applied when it comes to the treatment of the project members by their respective Project Leaders. Therefore, if properly used, power is considered to be positive and thus the Power Distance scale was rated in the way shown.

In connection with this aspect, the rating on the Assertiveness scale has to be seen. The integration of a number of sometimes diverging interests leads to the necessity to show, on occasion, a somewhat assertive behaviour. According to the interviewees, this is not the 'regular' course of action. Nevertheless, if a consensus cannot be reached, a more decisive behaviour has to be used to come to a solution. The same kind of behavioural pattern is expected from the direct superiors. It is expected from them that, initially, a consensus-driven approach is followed. Nevertheless, if this approach does not work, it is expected that the superior is able to take a reasonable decision if necessary also against opposition. Therefore, Assertiveness is seen to be positive to a certain degree, but only if it is exercised with the necessary caution, in order not to slip into an autocratic behaviour.

This, in turn, has to be seen in connection with the results for the Collectivism I scale. According to the results of the interviews, it is extremely important to build functioning teams in these professional environments, as this is the only way truly to mobilize all available resources, which is a prerequisite for the success of any project team. Therefore, an approach that initially favours a consensus-driven way to solve problems is always the approach of choice. Only if that does not work may the above-mentioned assertive behaviour be employed in order to find and take a reasonable decision if the team is not able to do so. Therefore, teamwork and, in consequence, the Collectivism I scale receive a highly favourable rating from the members of the Project Leaders' culture.

This is in line with the results of the Performance Orientation scale. The very positive rating of this scale is a clear expression that the members of this group always strive to perform in an outstanding manner in their jobs. This performance-driven behaviour, as already mentioned, leads to the activation of all available resources, which in turn favours the above-mentioned team orientation. According to the interviewees, this Performance Orientation is a key element of the Professional Culture of the Project Leaders.

Linked with these insights, the results concerning the Gender Egalitarianism scale have to be seen. According to the interviews, the only slightly positive rating is an expression of the fact that there is no special importance attributed to gender-based questions. In comparison to those groups in which exists a clearly positive rating on the Gender Egalitarianism scale, this is an even stronger verdict, as it clearly shows that there is no importance at all attributed to the values expressed by this dimension. Or to put this into the words of one interviewee 'it is not important who does the job, a man, a woman, or whatever, it is important that the job gets properly done in our team-based atmosphere'.

The results of the Human Orientation scale have to be connected to those of the Collectivism I scale. The very high appreciation of the values expressed with this Dimension shows that if one wants to create well functioning teams, the necessity to create good and healthy interpersonal relationships is understood by the members of the present culture. Therefore, this extremely positive rating for the Human Orientation scale is once more an expression of the perceived importance teamwork has for the members of this group. In addition, they also do expect their direct superior to behave in the same manner, as they consider this behaviour to be a prerequisite for an effective leadership style and, therefore, for the success of the company as a whole.

The positive rating of the Collectivism II scale is a clear exhibition of pride in the profession. This is a direct consequence of the perceived importance Project Leaders have in their respective companies, but also a direct consequence of the content of the job itself. Being responsible for a project gives the Project Leaders the possibility to see clearly what they achieve, to influence significantly the very outcome of the project and to work relatively independently. Therefore, the results of this dimension have to be seen in connection with those of the Performance Orientation Dimension, as both results unambiguously point to a very high intrinsic motivation of the members of the Project Leaders' Professional Culture.

In summary, it can be said that the open interviews gave a number of highly interesting and important insights into the processes that take place within this Professional Culture.

Summarizing Thoughts

The empirical results clearly show a number of distinctive traits of the Project Leaders' Professional Culture. The most interesting ones are the highly performance driven nature of this culture on the one hand, and the extremely interesting mixture between human values, team spirit, etc. and assertive power based behaviours on the other.

These, at first sight somewhat contradictory aspects, will be extremely important when it comes to the development of the appropriate leadership style and organizational structure. This is even more true as the results gained on the basis of this Professional Culture, will be very useful in the context of the development of the appropriate leadership and organizational styles for cross-cultural encounters undertaken in Chapter 7.7.

Hence, at this point it can be stated that a genuine Project Leader culture does exist and that this culture does show a number of very distinctive and highly interesting traits. Furthermore, the importance of these results clearly goes beyond this section as these results will be very helpful for the correct handling of cross-cultural encounters.

In summary, it can be said that the present section is, in a variety of aspects, extremely important for the correct understanding of the processes that take place in most companies in the aviation industry.

7.3.2   An Integrative Solution to the Found Characteristics

In the following, an appropriate leadership style and organizational structure will be developed.

As already mentioned, some results of this section will be picked up again in the context of Section 7.7. Special attention should therefore be given to the findings outlined below.

As usual, the leadership style will be developed first, followed by that of the appropriate organizational structure.

The Appropriate Leadership Style

The appropriate leadership style is unambiguously based on Charismatic/Value-Based leadership (e.g. Bass 1985; Burns 1978; House *et al.* 2004; see also Section 2.2.3), which needs to be supported by Team-Oriented (e.g. Manz and Sims 2001; House *et al.* 2004; see also Section 2.2.2) and Human-Oriented leadership (e.g.

Gagné and Fleishman 1959; Fleishman and Quaintance 1984; Blake and Mouton 1985; House *et al.* 2004; see also Section 2.1.2). If necessary some elements of Autonomous leadership (House *et al.* 2004) should be added.

All relevant Core Cultural Dimensions for Charismatic/Value-Based leadership show either high or very high ratings in the quantitative part. This view was confirmed in the course of the open interviews. On the one hand it was confirmed with the views expressed concerning the Core Cultural Dimensions themselves. On the other, the necessity to show clearly the goal of the company and, in that context, the goal of the respective project, was considered to be extremely important. In addition, aspects such as decisiveness, integrity and the formulation of a persuasive Vision for the future were mentioned again and again. These aspects together lead to the necessity to base any leadership style for this group on the Charismatic/Value-Based leadership style.

Team-Oriented leadership is a second very important factor for appropriately leading this professional group. In the present circumstances though, this should not be understood as the necessity to create artificially a team out of all Project Leaders present in a company (an undertaking that would necessarily be fruitless anyhow). It is to be seen as Project Leaders expecting their direct superiors to give them the freedom and support to build effectively and lead a true team for the benefit of all parties concerned. Therefore, this rating has to be understood as a demand to transfer as much decision competency as possible into the hands of the Project Leaders, in order for them to redistribute these competencies among the project/team members.

Human-Oriented Leadership is the third main component of an appropriate leadership style for the present Professional Culture. Members of this culture do praise this kind of leadership in both the standardized questionnaire and the open interviews. They highly appreciate the beneficial consequences that an integration of this leadership style into the appropriate leadership style for the current Professional Culture potentially has if correctly carried out. Therefore, they expect their direct superior to behave in a similar, although more subtle, way towards themselves. This includes, for example, the creation of good and healthy interpersonal relationships among the leading personnel in the company, instead of a rules- and regulations-based approach.

Finally, they do expect their superior to actually live this kind of leadership style, even if it means that a deviation from classic patterns of leadership has to be undertaken. This finds its expression in the moderate support for some elements of the Autonomous leadership style.

Hence, an appropriate leadership style for the Project Leaders' Professional Culture looks like the following.

The leaders formulate a compelling Vision via which they inspire the Project Leader; this could, for example, be a Vision concerning the extreme importance the project has for the future success of the company. The superiors are reliable and honest in their dealings with the Project Leaders so that the Project Leaders always know that they can trust their superiors.

The superior places as much responsibility as possible into the hands of the Project Leaders. Often, this will be a necessity through the demands of the project itself, but if there is any room to manoeuvre for the superiors they should use that room to give the maximum decision competency to the respective Project Leader. Furthermore, they should make sure that the respective Project Leaders actually feel encouraged to use that extra competency.

The relationship between the leader and the Project Leader should be governed as much as possible by a healthy and warm way of dealing with each other. The leader should focus this relationship on the individual Project Leader, so that its characteristics approach those of a friendship without losing the balance between this friendship and the necessary difference between superior and subordinate. It is important though that this difference is not perceived as being a problem in the establishment of the mentioned friendship, like the relationship between the superior and the Project Leader.

If necessary, the leader should exhibit a leadership behaviour that may be somewhat uncommon if it supports the actual implementation of the above-described kind of leadership style. This is due to the fact that Autonomous leadership is perceived to be an advantage if it is beneficial for the interests of the members of the Project Leaders' Professional Culture.

In summary, it can be said that the appropriate leadership style needs to be based on a compelling Vision that guides the individual Project Leaders in their day-to-day business. The superiors have to give the Project Leaders as much decision competency as possible and they have to make sure that the respective Project Leader feels appreciated not only as a professional but also as a human being.

The Appropriate Organizational Structure

The appropriate organizational structure in the current setting is relatively straightforward.

The most efficient way to structure an organization for the needs of a 'project', is described below. How the internal structure of the different projects looks is a different story and depends mainly on the professional composition of the project itself (for some examples see Section 7.7). In this section, a project is considered to be a sort of black box, whose internal structure is not the subject of this section. Only the treatment by outside actors of the respective Project Leaders is of interest at this point.

Considering the above-described appropriate leadership style, an organization design that is based on self-governance with an emphasis on auto-determination of the different project groups is the best.

Therefore, Complexity Theory (Stacey *et al.* 2000; Lewin and Regine 2000; see also Section 3.2.2) is once again the approach of choice. It is of the utmost importance to create an organizational structure that renders the project team and its leader as independent as possible. If the project is important and large enough it should be treated like an independently acting entity within the company, very much like a subsidiary.

The organization that actually employs the project team should only set the framework and distribute the task(s) to the project team. The manner in which the project team members tackle those tasks should be entirely up to the team itself.

The project team should not be subject to any kind of external control, except for occasional checks to see whether goals actually are achieved. An impression of being under direct and constant control of the parent company has to be avoided. Therefore, one should aim for a very Loose Coupling between the project team and the parent company, which always respects the need for independency (for more details concerning Loosely Coupled Systems see e.g. Orton and Weick 1990; Perrow 1984; see also Section 3.3.2). Any unnecessarily close interference with the project team and especially its leader has potentially highly negative consequences.

The appropriate organizational structure for a project team can best be brought down to one single guideline: when in doubt give more freedom.

The Solution in Overview

The possible solution worked out here is probably not as much of a surprise as some of the preceding ones. This is because the organizational part of this solution is very close to what is usually referred to as Project Organization. How far these results are actually in line with what is to be found in reality will be left to Section 8.6.

Nevertheless, these findings are relatively comforting as they show once more that it makes sense to create for different demands and different professional groups different organizational structures. Obviously no one would intend to use some organizational structure that is commonly used in a non-project type setting for the organization design of a project-type environment. Therefore, the hypothesis that different Professional Cultures require different organization and leadership structures is once again supported.

The leadership part though may be a different story, as it is highly dependent on the individual characteristics of the respective leader. Nevertheless, it does not seem to be overly unlikely that the described leadership style may be found in reality.

The main problems arise most likely out of the necessary close and trusting personal relationship between the superior and the Project Leader(s). This is due to the fact that, possibly, not all leaders are able to build such a bond with their subordinates. Nevertheless, it is of the utmost importance that the superior of one or more Project Leader(s) is able to live the above described leadership style, as this is the leadership style of choice for this Professional Culture.

In summary, it can be stated that the structures developed in this section are relatively straightforward and simple as far as the organization part is concerned and potentially very demanding as far as the leadership part is concerned. Nevertheless, an implementation does seem to be possible with an appropriate selection and possibly some training of the leaders, to render them more in line with the requirements of this specific cultural group.

7.3.3   Final Thoughts Regarding the Project Leaders

The results gained for cluster nine are once again of a highly interesting and qualitatively very satisfying nature. As already mentioned, the importance of the results gained in this section go well beyond the Professional Culture treated here. A number of the insights gained will be of great interest within the context of Section 7.7.

Another important aspect is the clear preference for a very interesting mixture between direct and indirect leadership.

The demand for a maximum degree of freedom as far as indirect leadership is concerned is joined with an expectation of a very cordial, warm and caring kind of direct leadership. This statement is enhanced by the expectation of the Project Leaders that this cordial relationship is built by a strong and visionary personality who is able to give clear and unambiguous meaning to the work of the Project Leaders. At the same time, it is expected that this leader does not overly interfere with the Project Leaders' interests.

This mixture is rather uncommon as it demands a strong but, at the same time, cautious and caring leader. However, this precise mixture possibly represents the biggest obstacle to the realization of the solution developed in this section. This is particularly true in comparison to the organization design, which is relatively simple to build.

Technically, the results are again highly satisfying. The professional group extracted is highly homogeneous, with most members having actually carried out the task of a Project Leader for years. Therefore, the results gained here are seemingly apt as regards Project Leaders as a whole.

In summary, it can be said that this section serves to identify a highly interesting and, in some aspects, quite demanding Professional Culture that nevertheless possesses enormous importance for the success of most companies in the aviation industry.

7.4   The Higher Administration

The tenth cluster, called 'The Higher Administration', comprises all those individuals who are working in purely or predominantly administrative functions, but who are not part of top management. In that sense, members of this group are still in executing functions. This does not exclude the possibility that these positions also imply management and decision-taking functions, but the main focus of this group's work is administrative on a higher qualification level. Typical jobs in this group would be those in leading positions in a finance department, an executive secretary, or also higher positions in a controlling department.

In reference to the Service Providers, the same problem surfaces here regarding the boundaries of the Higher Administration group. The Higher Administration group shares a number of similar traits with the Service Providers group, so that the decision as to which group a certain entity should be assigned is not always evident.

The solution to this problem is obviously similar to the one above, but inverted. As soon as a task carried out by an entity does not provide a service for another entity, but is part of its very core function and requires extensive training and in-depth knowledge of the subject, this entity should be assigned to the Higher Administration group.

7.4.1   The Empirical Base

In this group again, the qualitative part of the survey was of significant importance in order to render the results of the quantitative part correctly understandable.

The quantitative part itself is based on 23 respondents from various organizations and countries, exhibiting a balanced mixture between male and female respondents. As always, the qualitative part is based on seven interviews.

With the present cultural group the importance of the qualitative part mainly originated from the above-mentioned difficulty in drawing a clear limit for this group based on quantitative analysis only. This made it necessary to verify the findings of the quantitative part thoroughly and to check their validity.

So, in this group, the findings outlined out in the quantitative and the qualitative parts are also heavily interdependent. Hence once again, it can be seen why a combination of both methods is of such extreme importance in highly complex environments.

The Quantitative Results

The Uncertainty Avoidance dimension was rated neutrally (4.32). Here again, an area of tension between the need to react swiftly to arising situations and the rejection of an unstable and/or unforeseeable environment that creates these very situations has to be stated.

Assertive behaviour is placed on the boundary between the medium and the high area (4.48). This can be seen in direct interconnection with the jobs present in this group. They are often located in positions where a purely consensus driven approach does not lead to the desired outcome (e.g. controlling), whereas an excessively assertive approach has equally disadvantageous consequences. This aspect will be studied closer in the following section.

As the members of this culture usually need to keep in mind the long term consequences of nearly every topic they have to deal with, the Future Orientation dimension is valued strongly positively (6.03). This score is one of the highest in the sample, expressing the high importance that members of this culture attribute to long-term orientation.

The Power Distance dimension is valued positively by the members of this group (4.35). This rating can be traced back to the fact that the members of this Professional Culture are usually in a position of power and apparently appreciate the exercise of that power. The reasons for this will be evaluated later. It can be kept in mind, however, that the characteristics of the Higher Administration's work environment play a major role for this specific rating.

The Collectivism I dimension is in the upper neutral area (5.08). Apparently, members of this group do appreciate teamwork, although the need for it does not always seem to be obvious to them. The reasons for this somewhat contradictory score will be clarified later; the important thing to keep in mind at this point is the ambiguity with which this dimension is rated.

Performance Orientation is rated neutrally (5.03). This rating apparently has to be seen in connection with a tendency that all bureaucracies, private or state run, seem to incorporate. This tendency is that, sometimes, outstanding performance is not the first priority, but more of a by-product of the efficient application of existing rules.

Gender Egalitarianism, on the other hand, is valued strongly in the positive area (6.52), showing the highest rating out of all professional groups. Possibly this is a consequence of the relatively high number of women in this group, but probably also of the above-mentioned strict application of rules by this group. These aspects will also be discussed in more detail later.

The Human Orientation dimension is scored neutrally (4.06). A possible explanation, which has to be seen in connection with the already-mentioned application of rules and procedures, will be pointed out below. At the moment, it is sufficient to keep in mind that the values of the Human Orientation dimension have no significantly important meaning for the members of the Higher Administration group.

Finally, the values expressed with the Collectivism II dimension seem to be rather important for this group. The rating of 6.2 is one of the highest in the sample. This is a clear indicator for pride in, and loyalty to, the group.

The Qualitative Results

According to the interviews, the results of the Power Distance and the Assertiveness scale have to be seen in correlation.

The high rating of the Power Distance scale is the consequence of the relative position that members of the Higher Administration culture have in their respective organizations. Usually it is up to them when it comes to the exercise of power. Obviously this leads to a positive view of power in general. Nevertheless, this positive view is not restricted to members of the current cultural group exercising power, but interestingly it is also accepted when power is exercised upon them. This does not include the arbitrary use of power, but it is acknowledged and expected that sometimes it is necessary for the direct superiors to give clear guidelines. This in turn implies the appropriate use of their power base.

The rating of the Assertiveness dimension is in close connection with this reasoning. The use of power may obviously incorporate assertive behaviour. This is not to be seen as the acceptance of some blind assertive behaviour, however. According to the interviewees, it is important that the superiors are able not only to formulate clearly their expectations, but also to push certain decisions through. Therefore, weak and hesitating leadership behaviour is not accepted by the members of the Higher Administration culture.

Somewhat interconnected with these considerations is the rating of the Collectivism I scale. According to the results of the interviews, teamwork is not considered to be a priority in this group. Sometimes it may be necessary, but very often the tasks carried out do not favour a team approach. In addition, considering the above-given reasoning in respect of the Power Distance and the Assertiveness scales, an affinity towards hierarchical solutions has to be stated. Therefore, the values expressed with the Collectivism I scale are seen to be only marginally positive.

The scores of the remaining Core Cultural Dimensions are, apart from the Collectivism II scale, closely interconnected.

Members of the Higher Administration culture see themselves to be in an area of tension between the need to be flexible in the short term and the urge to have stability in the long term. These influences neutralize each other and thus the values expressed with the Uncertainty Avoidance scale are considered to be neutral.

The very high rating of the Future Orientation scale has to be seen in that context, as it is a clear expression of the mentioned urge for long-term stability. Members of the current culture prefer to be able to rely in the long term on clearly set rules and regulations. If these rules and regulations are to have long-term validity, it is obviously necessary to have long-term orientation. Therefore, the values expressed with the Future Orientation scale are seen to be very positive.

However, this orientation on rules and regulations has a second consequence. It leads to the surprisingly low score of the Performance Orientation scale, which is medium only. As members of the current culture prefer to live in an environment based on rules and regulations, they do not necessarily see the need to perform extraordinarily, in the sense expressed with the Performance Orientation scale. This is due to the content of the Performance Orientation items themselves and the self-image that members of the Higher Administration have. The items of the Performance Orientation scale stress aspects such as continuously searching for ways to be innovative and continuously improving performance. According to the interviewees, the sole emphasis of these aspects is counterproductive for the specific environment in which they live. They consider the exact following of rules and procedures as well as stability and predictability to be at least of the same importance. Therefore, the above-mentioned importance of rules and procedures shows itself once more, leading to the neutral rating of the Performance Orientation scale.

This is also true for the very high score on the Gender Egalitarianism scale. In part, this score is due to the fact that in the present sample a very balanced gender distribution can be stated. Mostly though, this score is again a consequence of the emphasis of rules and procedures as, in most companies, Gender Egalitarianism is part of company policy, which is obviously strictly followed by the members of this group.

The score of the Human Orientation scale can also be traced back partly to this central trait of the Higher Administration culture. In a rules- and regulations-based environment, there is not much room for the values expressed with the Human Orientation scale. Furthermore, according to the interviewees and considering the above-mentioned view of the Collectivism I scale, there is no real need for the members of the current group to moderate this view. Still, they do not see the Human Orientation values to be negative; they simply do not attribute any importance to them. Therefore, a neutral rating is the logical consequence.

Finally, the positive view of the Collectivism II scale is a direct consequence of the relative position that members of this group have in their respective organizations and their resulting self-image. Usually, members of the Higher Administration culture are placed relatively highly within their organizations. Furthermore, they consider themselves to be one of the key groups for the success of their respective company. Therefore, to a considerable degree, they feel proud of their own work and that of their peers. This is further enhanced by the fact that members of the current group sometimes feel they are subject to some sort of underlying hostility by members of other professional groups. In connection with the pride they exhibit in their work, this leads to a strong feeling of loyalty towards their professional group, which is the second aspect of the Collectivism II scale.

In summary, it can be said that the results of the interviews clearly show one highly specific trait of the Higher Administration Culture: the perceived importance that rules and regulations have for the work environment of this culture.

Summarizing Thoughts

The empirical results show a highly interesting picture for a very important group of employees. In particular, the highly rules- and regulations-based nature of the current group is quite stunning considering the relative position its members have in their respective companies. This trait will be of a significant importance for the development of an appropriate organizational and leadership design.

In summary, it should be noted here that the specific characteristics of the Higher Administration culture exhibit a remarkable number of similar traits to the Middle Administration, but also a number of highly interesting differences, as will be shown in the following.

7.4.2   An Integrative Solution to the Found Characteristics

In the following, the appropriate leadership style and organizational structure for the Higher Administration culture will be developed. In particular, compared with the above-shown very special traits of this culture, this undertaking is highly significant. This is even more important as the relative position members of this culture usually have in their organizations is such that their successful integration into the organization is crucial.

As always, the development of an appropriate leadership style will be undertaken first, followed by that of an appropriate organizational style

The Appropriate Leadership Style

As far as the development of an appropriate leadership style is concerned the Higher Administration interestingly shows similar traits to those of the Middle Administration, as no clear preference for any of the six CLT Dimensions exists. This similarity is rather surprising, as both cultures do have rather significantly different professional environments. Apparently though, administrative processes seem to develop auto-dynamic processes, which are independent from hierarchical positions and actual tasks.

This result obviously has far-reaching consequences and strengthens once again the insight gained in the current work, which is that Professional Cultures do structure themselves around different functions. Therefore, the appropriate leadership behaviour should be very non-intrusive into the regular day-to-day work of the members of the Higher Administration culture. Only a very limited tendency towards Charismatic/Value-Based leadership can be stated.

Jointly, these two aspects would lead to the superior developing some greater idea, which would give some specific underlying meaning to the actual task the members of the current culture carry out. Nevertheless, this greater idea should not be understood like a genuine Vision, as the Higher Administration culture does not have any affinity towards such idealistic approaches. It is sufficient if this greater idea puts the individual tasks into the greater context, which is very much based on the present situation.

For the rest, the direct superior, which is often going to be found within the executive board, should follow a 'Management by Exception' approach (e.g. Bass and Avolio 1993, p. 52; see also Section 2.2.3 where transactional leadership in general and Management by Exception in special cases is treated as the counterexample of Transformational leadership, and Section 6.6 where the Middle Administration culture is treated).

As members of the current culture do take their jobs very seriously, situations in which the leader would have to intervene in the sense of the Management by Exception Approach arise extremely rarely. Therefore, the role of the superior is even more limited than that of the leader of members of the Middle Administration culture. Hence, a possible leadership solution should look like the following.

The leader of the Higher Administration develops a greater picture, which clearly shows the importance of the respective tasks carried out by its members. Depending on the actual task, however, this may not always be necessary, it is definitely not harmful and has potentially beneficial consequences.

The leader sets up clear goals and guidelines and exhibits in that aspect clear and unambiguous leadership. As long as the goals are achieved and the different guidelines followed, the leader does not interfere with the day-to -ay business of the subordinates.

Control mechanisms have to be kept to a minimum as they interfere with the self-image the Higher Administration has. Furthermore, tight control mechanisms will prove to be useless as, in principle, the current culture inherently follows existing rules and regulations.

In summary, it can be said that direct leadership can be considered to be almost unnecessary in the current setting. Except for the extremely rare occasions in which an unjustified deviation from existing rules and procedures has to be stated, the leaders will not have any direct role in their subordinates' work environment. Therefore, it is highly questionable if a leadership position that is exclusively dedicated to the lead members of the Higher Administration is necessary altogether. Often it will be sufficient to have these leadership functions as a sideline only in addition to some other function within the organization.

The Appropriate Organizational Structure

The appropriate organizational structure for the Higher Administration culture is a reflection of that developed for the Middle Administration. It should be based on the Bureaucratic Organization developed by Weber (1976; see also Section 3.1.1).

Therefore, full use should be made of a detailed and appropriate set of rules and regulations to design the organization in the current setting. For the same reason, it is of the utmost importance to avoid any incongruent or inconsistent parts within this organizational design.

Nevertheless, it has to be ensured that the organization does not become too rigid and tight. It has to be kept in mind that most people present in this culture have a rather high educational background as well as a rather high self-esteem. Therefore, the organization has to give them the freedom to decide themselves how they want to achieve the given goals and the feeling that they can act to a significant degree autonomously within their work environment. For that reason the already-mentioned necessity to avoid, as much as possible, control mechanisms is of such an importance.

Finally, it is necessary to check regularly the organizational design in general and the underlying rules and regulations in particular, for adequacy and relevancy to avoid any dysfunctionalities within the organization resulting from a non-adapted organizational design.

In summary, it can be stated that, for the present culture, it is sufficient to almost exclusively exercise leadership with the help of indirect leadership. Therefore, it is crucial not to underestimate the importance that the development of a task-appropriate set of rules and regulations has for the successful integration of this culture into a company. Doing so will lead to a very autonomously and efficiently operating Higher Administration, which in turn is of the utmost importance for the success of the whole company.

The Solution in Overview

The solution proposed relies heavily on indirect leadership.

Considering the characteristics of the present culture, this seems to be the most appropriate approach for the integration of the current culture. The heavy reliance of this approach can be an advantage though. If used appropriately it renders the integration of the members of the current culture into their respective organizations relatively simply. This is because, by using the organization as the primary means for integration, it is to be expected that members of the current culture act relatively autonomously within that organization while striving for the achievement of the given goals.

Therefore, in summary, it can be stated that if the necessary provisions are taken, the present culture is one of the easier ones to be integrated into the organization.

7.4.3 Final Thoughts Regarding the Higher Administration

The most interesting aspect about the results of the tenth cluster is the high similarity it exhibits with the Middle Administration culture.

Apparently, administrative processes of all hierarchical levels share a common set of characteristics, which clearly finds its expression in the very similar leadership and organizational structures required for these two clusters. This does not mean that both clusters are the same, but it does mean that they show a number of similar traits, which leads to them being receptive to very similar leadership styles and organizational structures.

The importance of these results potentially stretches far beyond the boundaries of the current study and even the industry in general. This is due to the fact that jobs that show the characteristic traits of an administration can be found in practically all parts of the state and economy.

Therefore, the insights gained in this section and those in Section 6.6 serve the better understanding of administrations and their integration into the value creation process in general.

In summary, it can be said that the results of the tenth cluster may be surprising at first sight. This is especially true as members of the Higher Administration usually can be found within the higher echelons of their respective companies. Nevertheless, administrative processes seem to be exercising such a high degree of influence upon the employees carrying them out that certain basic patterns can be found throughout any administrative environment.

7.5   The Operational Management

The cultural cluster that is presented in the following is composed of employees who perform tasks that can be subsumed under the term Operational Management. Typically, these individuals perform management tasks on a low-to-medium level in an organization, leading a rather small number of other people.

Examples for such occupations are a team leader in an operational centre of an airline, lead buyer in a smaller company, but also foremen or team leaders in technical departments.

As can be seen from these examples, employees in this group are qualified to a medium level. The difference to other groups in the present sample is that members of this group are directly implied in the production processes on the one hand, and they have to perform an actual management task in the day-to-day operation of their respective organization on the other.

In summary, the task of the members of this group is to assure that decisions that have been taken at some higher position within the organization are actually implemented and to guarantee a smooth operation on the 'field level'.

7.5.1   The Empirical Base

As always, the results of the empirical survey are based on a quantitative and a qualitative part.

The quantitative part is composed of 21 respondents originating from various countries and organizations. As a reflection of the actual composition in reality of the occupations present in this sample, a majority of male respondents has to be stated. The intended heterogeneity is therefore achieved.

For this group, the qualitative part, which is based on seven interviews, was of significant importance in determining the actual characteristics of the cluster.

The quantitative part obviously gave an indication as to the basic orientation of the cultural dimensions.

In this specific case, however, it was imperative to determine the underlying processes that led to these results in order to determine correctly the characteristics of this cultural cluster.

The Quantitative Results

The Uncertainty Avoidance dimension is rated neutrally in this group (4.06). This result can be seen as a consequence of the fact that members of this group often have to react to exterior influences on the one hand, but also seem to need at least some stability. This apparently favours rather mixed esteem for the values expressed in the Uncertainty Avoidance dimension. The Assertiveness dimension scores the highest of all groups in the present group (5.87). The extremely high demands exercised on the members of this group in connection with the sometimes only limited means to achieve the set goals are at the source of this result. This highly interesting aspect will be detailed further in the following.

Future Orientation is considered to be moderately positive (4.84). On the one hand, this result has to be seen in connection with the already-mentioned fact that this group has to be flexible enough to react – always efficiently – to exterior demands. On the other, a certain long-term orientation has to exist in order for other people to be led effectively. This topic will also be raised again in the context of the interviews.

Power Distance is considered to be positive (4.27). This score has to be seen in connection with the already-mentioned problem for the members of this group to actually achieve what they have to achieve with the limited possibilities they have. One of the means to do that is obviously the use and the appreciation of the power base they have.

Collectivism I is rated positively (5.56). The need for functioning teamwork is obviously appreciated by the Operational Management. That result is a clear consequence of the placement which members of this cultural group have in their respective organizations, as they head small teams, assuring constant personal contact to their subordinates. This aspect will be treated further in the following.

Performance Orientation scores very high in this group (6.57), representing the second highest value out of all Professional Cultures. Apparently, members of this group want to perform in an outstanding manner. The very interesting reasons for that though will be described in the context of the results of the following section.

Gender Egalitarianism is seen positively (5.71). In connection with the high score on the Performance Orientation scale, it becomes clear that members of this culture predominantly value performance and do not appreciate gender-based judgements.

Human Orientation is rated neutrally (3.78). This has to be seen in connection with the results of the Assertiveness dimension as well as that of the Power Distance, Gender Egalitarianism and Performance Orientation dimension. All these interconnections point to the strong emphasis of performance by the members of this culture if necessary, even at the expense of human values such as warmth and tenderness.

Collectivism II is located on the edge between the medium and the high area (5.56). Members of the Operational Management cluster seem to be moderately proud only of what they themselves achieve and loyalty to the other members of their professional group seems to be somewhat limited. This result is a direct consequence of the special position members of this group have in their respective organizations and will be discussed further below.

The Qualitative Results

The results for the Uncertainty Avoidance scale and for the Future Orientation scale have to be seen in correlation.

According to the interviews, members of the current culture see themselves to be in an area of tension between the need to stay flexible in order to carry out successfully their day-to-day business and an urge for long-term stability, which takes away as much uncertainty as possible. These two factors neutralize each other, leading to the medium score on the Uncertainty Avoidance scale.

The slightly positive score for the Future Orientation scale is a direct consequence of these conflicting influences. The need for flexibility is well acknowledged by the members of this group, but is somewhat superseded by the already mentioned urge for long-term stability. So the values expressed with the Future Orientation scale are seen rather positively, leading to the above-mentioned score.

The scores of the remaining Core Cultural Dimensions are all interconnected and centred on the very high Performance Orientation of the Operational Management culture.

Both the results of the quantitative and the results of the qualitative part clearly indicate that members of the current culture are very performance driven. According to the interviewees, performing in an outstanding manner is highly important in their environment and part of their understanding of their work. The score of the Assertiveness scale must be seen in connection with this Performance Orientation. Due to the relative position that members of the Operational Management have within their respective organizations, they have to fulfil two highly conflicting roles. The first is their role as leader. The second is that of a subordinate to the next higher management level. According to the interviewees, the room for manoeuvre to achieve their goals is extremely small, sometimes leading to a situation in which members of the Operational Management culture feel responsible for outcomes they did not have any possibility to influence. Therefore, the tendency is to use existing possibilities to their fullest extent to influence any possible outcome. Hence, assertive behaviour is seen very positively in this group. Furthermore, this acceptance of assertive behaviour also leads to members of the current group expecting their direct leader to show assertive behaviour when necessary towards themselves. This in turn has as a consequence that Assertiveness is also relatively highly valued when it comes to members of the Operational Management being subject to assertive behaviour of their leaders.

The relatively positive view of Power Distance goes back to the same reasons. According to the interviews, members of the current culture need to use their (rather limited) power as much as possible in order to achieve what is expected from them.

At the same time, they consider it to be necessary for their direct superiors to express clearly what they expect. In case of arising conflicts, the use of power is accepted if it is necessary in order to develop and implement these clear guidelines.

Nevertheless, the need for efficiently functioning teams is also acknowledged. It may not be necessary always and for every task, but when it is, its use is appreciated. That is true on both the level of Operational Management subordinates and on the level of the members of Operational Management itself. Therefore, the values expressed with the Collectivism I scale are seen relatively positively.

The high rating on the Gender Egalitarianism and the medium rating on the Human Orientation scale both have their roots in the above-described prevailing Performance Orientation. Jointly, these two dimensions clearly indicate that it is of the utmost importance to the members of this group that the respective tasks are carried out well, irrespective of who executes them. Furthermore, in the technical environment in which this culture is positioned, human values as expressed with the Human Orientation scale are not overly important. As stated, the main focus is that 'the job gets done, regardless of who gets it done'. These two dimensions further strengthen the high Performance Orientation of the Operational Management culture.

Finally, the rating of the Collectivism II scale indicates the pride felt in the current group in the respective tasks carried out and the loyalty towards the group as a whole. Statements clearly demonstrating pride were mentioned at various occasions throughout the interviews. The reason for that is the feeling that, given the very limited possibilities, the achievements of the members of the Operational Management culture are rather remarkable.

Summarizing Thoughts

As shown above, the results are technically of a rather satisfying nature. The double methodology employed proved its superiority yet again in comparison to a purely quantitative or a purely qualitative approach, as both the width and depth of the results are extremely satisfying.

Concerning the content of the results, it can be stated at this point that the most interesting aspect of the current culture is its *extreme* Performance Orientation. This Performance Orientation shows itself in nearly all Core Cultural Dimensions and additionally in the interviews. Consequently, this specific and very positive trait has to be taken into consideration when designing an appropriate leadership style and organizational structure as undertaken in the following.

7.5.2   An Integrative Solution to the Found Characteristics

In the following, an integrative leadership and organizational solution will be developed. The way of proceeding will be as usual: initially the appropriate leadership style, followed by the appropriate organization structure.

The most important aspect for this Professional Culture as far as leadership and organization are concerned is the support and promotion of the Performance Orientation of its members. Therefore, provision has to be made in order to free them from any unnecessary restraints that may hamper the unfolding of this Performance Orientation.

The Appropriate Leadership Style

According to the empirical results and those given by the GLOBE-Study (House *et al.* 2004) an appropriate leadership style for the current Professional Culture would have to be based on the Charismatic/Value-Based (e.g. Burns 1978; Bass 1985; House *et al.* 2004; see also Section 2.2.3) and the Team-Oriented leadership style (e.g. Manz and Sims 2001; House *et al.* 2004; see also Section 2.2.2). Furthermore it would contain certain elements of the Participative (e.g. Lewin 1948; Tannenbaum and Schmidt 1958; House *et al.* 2004; see also Section 2.1.1) and the Human-Oriented leadership style (e.g. Gagné and Fleishman 1959; Fleishman and Quaintance 1984; Blake and Mouton 1985; House *et al.* 2004; see also Section 2.1.2).

All Core Cultural Dimensions with the exception of Human Orientation, which is in the neutral area, point to the Charismatic/Value-Based leadership style. Furthermore, the need for guidance and 'reason why' expressed in the course of the interviews is a very strong indication for the appropriateness of that leadership style. Therefore, Charismatic/Value-Based leadership will be retained as the appropriate solution.

Three out of five Core Cultural Dimensions point to the Team-Oriented leadership style, whereas two are in the neutral area. This relatively positive view of team orientation was confirmed in the open interviews. Members of the current culture consider functioning teamwork to be essential for their professional success. This positive view is not unconditional, however, as teamwork is not promoted in all circumstances but only when 'it makes sense'.

The quantitative part gave some indication as to the appropriateness of Participative leadership with two Core Cultural Dimensions being in favour of it, whereas one is neutral and one in contradiction. With the help of the interviews, this tendency could be focused more precisely. Members of the current culture do not expect or even wish to be included in every little decision taken. Nevertheless, they expect their direct superiors to listen to them and appreciate their opinion when they consider their professional knowledge and experience to be helpful.

Despite the fact that the Human Orientation scale itself is valued only neutrally, Human-Oriented leadership should be part of the appropriate solution, but only to a limited degree. Hence, only some particular elements should be retained, as only two out of the four Core Cultural Dimensions are in favour of this leadership style, with two being in the neutral area. Furthermore, Human Orientation surfaced within the interviews in only one precise aspect, indicating the existing but limited use of this leadership style in the current setting.

An appropriate leadership solution for the Operational Management culture would thus look like the following. The leaders develop a Vision that inspires the members of this culture. This Vision should also clearly show the importance of each individual's contribution for the achievement of the Vision. The leaders have to show integrity and they have to be decisive. In particular, integrity and decisiveness are very important in that context, as they reflect the personal characteristics of the leader, which are highly appreciated by the members of the Operational Management culture. If possible, the leader should support this Visionary approach by a predominantly Team-Oriented leadership style, as proposed by Manz and Sims (2001). 'If possible' means in the current context that the task structure itself needs to be favourable to team organization. According to the empirical results, it is not advisable to push through a Team-Oriented approach at all costs, but appropriately realized, such an approach can be very beneficial.

Participative elements need to be included for two reasons. The first is that the professional expertise of the members of the Operational Management culture is highly valuable for a significant portion of the various decision-taking processes. Furthermore, as already mentioned, members of the current culture do expect to be heard when they have a contribution to make. Jointly, these two factors clearly indicate that it is advantageous to include the Operational Management into decisions regarding their direct professional environment.

Human-Oriented leadership, finally, should be included only in a very precise way. Members of the current culture do not necessarily need an overly warm and understanding leader. What they need are leaders who clearly show that they are on their side and are willing and able to protect them if necessary. Most probably, this attitude is an artefact of the 'Blue Collar Worker' origins shared by a substantial number of members of the current culture. Nevertheless, this aspect needs to be taken into consideration in order to lead the Operational Management culture adequately. This is a consequence of the fact that even for those individuals who do not have a 'Blue Collar Worker' background, a slightly Human-Oriented leadership is potentially beneficial.

In summary, an adequate leadership style is based on a Charismatic/Value-Based approach enriched by strong Team-Oriented influences. Participative and Human-Oriented leadership need to be integrated into this approach in the highly focused way illustrated, in order to adjust the global leadership style to the needs of the Operational Management culture.

The Appropriate Organizational Structure

The appropriate organizational structure needs to incorporate two different aspects.

The first is the need for guidance by a responsible and decisive superior, whereas the second deals with the decision competence given to the members of the Operational Management culture.

These two aspects jointly lead to an organizational design that is a mixture of certain elements of the Administrative Approach according to Fayol (1984; see also Section 3.1.1) and Complexity Theory (Stacey *et al.* 2000; Lewin and Regine 2000; see also Section 3.2.2).

The base of the organizational approach is Complexity Theory. It is important that one of the main concerns for the members of this Professional Culture gets addressed and taken care of. That main concern is the perception that responsibility and competency sometimes are seriously misbalanced. Therefore, it is necessary to give members of the current group a decision-taking competence that is in agreement with their responsibilities. Furthermore, it is advisable to tap into the professional expertise these employees typically have by giving them a rather far-reaching operational decision power. In that way, a significant part of the mentioned imbalance between responsibility and decision taking competency should be taken care of. Therefore, on the operational level, the organization should be relatively close to that proposed in the context of Complexity Theory. Consequently, the entities led by the respective Operational Manager should be relatively independent from other entities on that same operational level.

Strategically though, the organization needs to bewould be a lot closer to that proposed by Fayol (1984; see also Section 3.1.1), as a relatively clearly structured administration is preferred by the members of the Operational Management.

These two aspects are in line with the results demonstrated above. Members of the Operational Management culture expect their leaders to keep their distance from day-to-day business, which they consider to be their own area of competency. On the other hand they explicitly expect their leader to give clear guidance and to be responsible for strategic decisions. That clearly shows a preference for a more hierarchical solution.

Therefore, the organizational design should be as follows.

Operationally, full responsibility and decision-taking power should be with the Operational Managers. They need to have the ability to actually take decisions. Having provided the Operational Managers with the tools to achieve the given goals, it is then possible to give full responsibility for operational decisions to them.

Strategically though, the organization needs to be arranged such that the direct superior is present and responsible for decisions taken on that level. It is absolutely crucial that the Operational Manager does not have the feeling of being left alone by the direct superior.

Those decisions, which are neither clearly operational nor clearly strategic, should be taken in a joint approach by the Operational Managers and their superiors. Therefore, the organization needs to be relatively flexible to cope with various demands. Depending on the nature of the decision, it may be completely in line with the organization design according to Complexity Theory, but it may also be very close to the organization design according to the Administrative Approach. Between these two extremes, it may be possible to find situations in which the organization design has to provide the means for a joint and Participative decision-taking between the superior and Operational Manager. Hence, the organization design is extremely important in the current setting. In particular, the differentiation between strategic and operational design and the resulting decision competency is of the utmost importance for an efficient organization. Failure to do this will be at the source of constant problems and conflicts about competencies and responsibilities.

Opting for the concentration of the decision-taking power either in the hands of the Operational Management or the next higher hierarchical echelon cannot be the solution to the above problem. This is due to the fact that the members of the Operational Management culture will either feel left alone if they have to bear the responsibility and competency for practically all decisions taken or they will feel like their professional expertise is not appropriately valued if they are excluded from the decision-taking process.

Therefore, according to the results of the empirical survey, only the above given solution appears to be feasible. Although the clear definition of the terms 'strategic' and 'operational' will be rather complicated, it is still the most promising approach to the efficient integration of the members of the Operational Management culture into the organization. Furthermore, this organization design will have to be closely tracked in order to make sure it evolves over time with altering demands.

If these potential problems are being taken care of though, in the form of a clear and appropriate distribution of competencies and the constant tracking of that appropriate distribution, the proposed organizational structure is the most appropriate organization for the members of the Operational Management culture according to the results of the current study.

The Solution in Overview

The proposed solution is rather demanding at both the leadership level and the organization design level. At the leadership level, the most demanding part is for a leader to be able to exhibit a number of completely different leadership styles according to the prevailing situation. As shown, a large variety of leadership styles is required from very 'Team-Oriented', via 'Participative' to significantly 'Hierarchy-Based'.

The leader faces two challenges with this demand.

The first is the correct interpretation of the situation to decide which kind of leadership style may be required. The second challenge is to be able to live all these different leadership styles appropriately. Therefore, as far as leadership is concerned the present Professional Culture is one of the most demanding cultures present in this study.

Concerning the organizational level, the challenge is to create an organization that is flexible enough to cater for both the need for a rather hierarchy based organization, and the need for a team- and autonomy-based organization.

The challenge here is to create an organizational framework that gives the leaders the possibility actively to choose the situation-adequate organizational background in accordance with the situation-adequate leadership style at their discretion. This aspect shows once more the extreme importance competent leadership has for the Operational Management culture. Nevertheless, the appropriate organization design is highly important, as a non-supportive or, even worse, counterproductive organization design renders it – even for the most competent leader – impossible to fulfil the demands of the current culture.

In summary, it can be stated that owing to the highly diverse requirement as far as leadership style and organization design are concerned, the Operational Management culture is among the most demanding ones present in the current sample.

7.5.3   Final Thoughts Regarding the Operational Management

The results for cluster 11 show a culture that exhibits a significant number of different characteristics at the same time. The rather concurring nature of these different characteristics renders the current culture extremely interesting to study, but also extremely difficult to organize and lead. These different characteristics are a reflection of the relative position members of the Operational Management culture have in their professional environment.

They are located at an intermediate level between a predominantly executing and a predominantly ordering function, with a slight tendency towards the first in their respective organizations. Therefore, to cater for the varying demands that come along with this intermediate position, members of the Operational Management culture consequently require varying organizational and leadership approaches. However, the efforts required to match the needs of this culture, should be undertaken by all companies concerned. This is due to the fact that the performance of the Operational Management potentially makes the difference between a smoothly and efficiently running organization and one that is largely struggling with itself. Therefore, any effort necessary to enhance the performance of the current culture should be undertaken.

In summary, it can be stated at this point that the Operational Management culture demonstrates once again that a universal leadership and organization approach for all members of an organization leads to a less than optimum performance of the organization. As this is a clear waste of valuable resources, any organization should strive to avoid this situation and take the varying demands of the varying Professional Cultures into consideration.

7.6   The Strategic Management

Cluster 12 unites those employees who are responsible for Strategic Management. A different term for this cluster could have been 'Executive or Top Management'. The term *Strategic Management* though is more descriptive in showing what members of this group actually do, and was therefore favoured.

Strategic Management as it is understood here means that members of this culture have the possibility actually to decide in which direction the organization is to go. Their influence therefore is so significant that their performance has direct consequences for the future of the concerned organization.

Typical occupations found in this cluster are therefore, directors of subsidiaries, leaders of whole divisions, or CEOs. Due to their place in the respective organizations, the results described for this cluster get a somewhat different meaning in comparison to the other groups in this sample. This is because, to a certain extent, this group can actually make its work environment the way it wants to have it. This important aspect will be investigated further in later sections.

7.6.1   The Empirical Base

The results of this part are again based on both methodological approaches of the survey. Only with the simultaneous use of quantitative and qualitative elements was it possible to gain actual meaningful results.

The quantitative part is based on responses from 20 individuals originating from various countries and organizational backgrounds. Once more the actual composition in reality of the underlying population for this sample finds its reflection in the gender-related composition of the present sample as it exhibits a male majority. The needed heterogeneity of the sample in order to avoid any unwanted biasing influence therefore, can be considered to be achieved.

The qualitative part, as always, is based on seven respondents from the above-mentioned companies.

Initially, we will have a closer look at the quantitative results and then at the qualitative before a complete picture of this final cluster is going to be given.

The Quantitative Results

Uncertainty Avoidance is valued neutrally (3.63). This result is a consequence of two opposing influences. The first is the obvious need for members of this cluster to be open for new solutions in order to keep the organization competitive, which necessarily leads to the rather low esteem of the values expressed by the Uncertainty Avoidance dimension. This factor though, is moderated by the high responsibility members of this cluster have, which prevents them from scoring low on the Uncertainty Avoidance scale.

Assertiveness is considered to be moderately positive (4.73). This score is to be seen in connection with the need for members of this group to sometimes take decisions against opposition and to push these decisions through.

The Future Orientation dimension gets the highest rating out of all cultural clusters from the Strategic Management culture (6.23). The obvious need constantly to take long-term decisions in order to assure the future of the organization leads to this rating.

The values expressed with the Power Distance dimension are considered to be positive (4.02). This result has to be seen in connection with the already stated need to sometimes be assertive and take decisive action against possible opposition. This obviously leads to a positive view of the values expressed by the Power Distance dimension.

A similar logic is the reason for the score of the Collectivism I scale, which is rated only moderately positive (5.3). Two influencing factors can be stated here. The first one is the already stated necessity to take decisions and sometimes to take them alone, which leads to a rather negative view of the Collectivism I dimension. Nevertheless, this view is compensated by the understanding that to be truly successful in the current environment a functioning team is a prerequisite. These different aspects will be further investigated later in this chapter.

The Performance Orientation dimension gets the highest rating out of all cultural clusters (6.75). Obviously, the need for the members of this group to perform in an outstanding manner in their respective organizations leads to this result.

Gender Egalitarianism is viewed positively (6.05). This rating can be traced back to the understanding that true success requires the optimum use of all available resources in an organization. It is clear that such a view is not compatible with any kind of judgment due to a person's gender. On the other hand, this fact is seen to be so obvious by this group that the rating itself does not truly reflect the actual feeling of the members of the Strategic Management. This aspect will be further detailed in the following as a number of interesting connections can be drawn to other dimensions, in particular the Performance Orientation dimension.

Human Orientation is valued neutrally (4.07). Apparently, the large emphasis on performance does not leave too much room for an orientation that would lead to a higher score in this dimension. A number of further details concerning this explanation will be given later in this chapter.

The Collectivism II dimension finally, gets the highest rating out of all clusters (6.6). Members of this group are apparently very proud on what they do and they feel an extreme loyalty towards their professional cluster. Considering the relative position members of this group have in any organization this result is hardly surprising.

The Qualitative Results

According to the interviews, the score of the Uncertainty Avoidance and that of the Future Orientation scale have to be seen in connection. Members of the current culture see themselves to be subject to two counteracting influences. On the one hand, they need and want to be open to new solutions. That leads to a rather negative view of the values expressed with the Uncertainty Avoidance scale, as new solutions usually come with uncertainty and instability.

This view though is moderated by the high responsibilities members of the Strategic Management have, as – according to the interviewees – that aspect leads to a somewhat positive view of the values expressed by the Uncertainty Avoidance scale.

These two counteracting factors virtually neutralize each other, leading to a neutral rating of the Uncertainty Avoidance scale.

The rating of the Future Orientation scale is connected to the above. According to the interviews, members of the Strategic Management culture clearly appreciate thorough long-term planning. This is a consequence of the already mentioned high responsibility they have. Therefore, the values expressed with the Future Orientation scale are seen to be very positive, leading to the, as shown, outstandingly high rating of that scale.

The results for the Assertiveness, the Power Distance and for the Collectivism I scale are also interconnected.

It is an accepted fact for the members of the Strategic Management culture that sometimes it is necessary to take decisions against opposition. According to the interviewees, this view is not only shared when it comes to pushing decisions through to lower ranking members of the organization, it is also accepted in situations in which decisions have to be taken by other members of the organization, e.g. a joint-board decision or the CEO in person. Therefore, the Assertiveness dimension received a relatively positive rating in this culture. The score of the Power Distance dimension needs to be seen in connection with that reasoning.

Pushing decisions through against opposition sometimes requires the use of force. Use of force in a professional environment comes down to the use of power. As already shown, members of the Strategic Management culture consider that kind of behaviour to be an integral part of their job. Furthermore, members of the current culture expect their superior (CEO, etc.) to give some guidance and 'reason why' to them. Therefore, the values expressed with the Power Distance dimension are seen to be positive. Finally, the results of the Collectivism I scale have to be considered in connection with the above-described two dimensions. In principle, teamwork is seen to be very positive by the members of the Strategic Management culture. However, due to the fact that sometimes it is necessary to take swift and decisive action, a sole reliance on teamwork is viewed to be counterproductive. Therefore, the values expressed with the Collectivism I scale are seen to be moderately positive only.

The score of the Performance Orientation, the Gender Egalitarianism and the Human Orientation dimensions build another group that has to be considered jointly.

Performance Orientation scores the highest out of all Professional Cultures. This is clearly confirmed by the statements of the interviews in which the need to perform outstandingly is mentioned at various occasions. This already very strong statement though is supported by the results of the Gender Egalitarianism and the Human Orientation scale. According to the interviewees Gender Based prejudices are so obsolete that there is no acceptance for such an attitude. Furthermore, the need to fully use all available resources in order to achieve the best possible outcome to a given problem clearly prohibits any gender-based discrimination. This clearly goes along with the above-given extreme Performance Orientation.

Human Orientation is not a priority for the members of the Strategic Management culture. The reasoning for that given in the interviews is once again the prevailing Performance Orientation. Values such as warmth and tenderness apparently have no room in such an environment. They are neither seen to be positive, nor negative, but simply without any special meaning. Therefore, the Human Orientation dimension is rated only neutrally.

Following the interviewees, the extremely high score of the Collectivism II scale is a reflection of the view members of the Strategic Management culture have about themselves. As they see it, it is them who constitute the key group for the success of their companies. Furthermore, they are very proud on what they and their fellow group members do. This in turn obviously leads not only to feelings of pride, but also to group loyalty, which is another contributing factor to that score of the Collectivism II scale.

Summarizing Thoughts

Technically, the empirical results are of a highly satisfying nature for the present cluster. The results themselves show a quite interesting set of characteristics for the present culture. In particular, the high Performance Orientation and the relatively important role Assertiveness and Power play are very important aspects for the members of the current culture.

These two aspects need special attention in order to integrate successfully the members of the present culture into their respective organizations. Considering the relative positions these individuals have, this is a goal of the utmost importance for every company.

In summary, it may be retained, however, that the results for the current cluster are probably less surprising than those for some other Professional Cultures depicted in the current study.

7.6.2   An Integrative Solution to the Found Characteristics

In the following, an appropriate leadership and organization solution will be proposed.

Obviously, one may argue about the purpose of such an undertaking, as the members of the Strategic Management culture are placed in positions in which it appears as if there were no more need for leading them. Nevertheless, even at the executive board level, appropriate leadership and organizational structures are needed to integrate successfully this very important group into the organization. Furthermore, even at that level it is not always possible for the members of the Strategic Management culture to create their own leadership and organizational approach, as for example this may be imposed by some higher ranking authority. A typical example for that is the board of a subsidiary. Therefore, even at such high levels of organizational echelons, it makes sense to have a clear idea about an appropriate leadership and organization approach for the successful integration of the members of the present culture into their respective companies.

The Appropriate Leadership Style

Considering the quantitative and the qualitative results simultaneously, with reference to House *et al.* (2004), an appropriate leadership style for the current culture is based on the Charismatic/Value-Based leadership style (e.g. Bass 1985, Burns 1978; House *et al.* 2004; see also Section 2.2.3), which is supported by elements of the Team-Oriented (e.g. Manz and Sims 2001; House *et al.* 2004; see also Section 2.2.2) and the Participative leadership style (e.g. Lewin 1948; Tannenbaum and Schmidt 1958; House *et al.* 2004; see also Section 2.1.1).

Three out of four Core Cultural Dimensions relevant for the Charismatic/Value-Based leadership style point to it being part of the retained solution. This is strengthened by the fact that these three dimensions show the highest score out of all Professional Cultures in absolute terms. Furthermore, the need for guidance and 'reason why', even at the current relative position within the organization, was expressed more than once in the course of the open interviews. Therefore, Charismatic/Value-Based leadership is the core of the proposed solution.

Three out of the five Core Cultural Dimensions relevant for the Team-Oriented leadership style point towards this leadership style being favourable for the current culture, whereas two are in the neutral area. This is again strengthened by the fact that these three dimensions score the highest out of all Professional Cultures in absolute terms. Therefore, Team-Orientation plays a supportive but nevertheless very important role within the proposed solution.

Two out of the four relevant Core Cultural Dimensions are in favour of Participative leadership, whereas one is in the neutral area and one in the negative area. Nevertheless, Participative leadership needs to have a supportive role in the current context, as members of Strategic Management clearly expect to be heard when decisions are taken. Therefore, Participative leadership will be part of the proposed solution.

Although Human-Oriented and Self-Protective Leadership would have to be included in the final solution on the basis of the quantitative part of the survey, these two leadership styles were discarded. This decision was taken after due consideration of the results of the qualitative part, which gave a number of strong indications as to these leadership styles not being part of an appropriate solution.

Hence, an appropriate leadership style for the Strategic Management culture would look like the following. The leader develops a Vision that is clearly inspiring and which gives higher meaning to the tasks carried out by the members of the current culture. It is important that each and every individual feels to be of significant importance for the achievement of this Vision. The leaders have to be decisive when implementing the Vision and have to show integrity in their day-to-day actions.

When it comes to the implementation though, this decisiveness must not be overdone, as the actual implementation has to include Team-Oriented and Participative elements. Members of the current culture explicitly expect to be integrated into decisions. Therefore, the actual implementation process should be done in an atmosphere of teamwork as proposed, for example, by Manz and Sims (2001; see also Section 2.2.2). Here, it is important that the leaders pick up the roles proposed in that approach, which are those of a coach, a referee and an entertainer. Therefore, they have to explain, decide and sell their Vision to the members of the current culture.

Furthermore, if, for example, concerns are expressed about the way of the actual implementation, or well-founded objections exist, it is imperative to hear and take into consideration the opinion of the members of the Strategic Management culture. These are the above-mentioned participative elements that have to be included into the appropriate solution proposed here.

Hence, in summary, the leaders have to develop a captivating Vision which they implement for both the development of the initial Vision and its actual implementation by means of a clearly Team-Oriented approach and with the help of Participative elements.

The Appropriate Organizational Structure

The appropriate organizational structure has to be supportive of the above-proposed solution.

In the current context, this means that despite the strong emphasis on Visionary leadership, it is advisable to implement a strongly Team-Oriented organizational structure. It is important that the Strategic Management feels and acts like a team. That can best be achieved with an approach in the logic of Complexity Theory (Stacey *et al.* 2000; Lewin and Regine 2000; see also Section 3.2.2). The most significant factor is that, despite the importance of the charismatic leader, the organization must not be based on a hierarchical solution. The task of the leader in this setting is, as mentioned by Lewin and Regine (2000), to be allowing, accessible and attuned. Therefore, it is advisable to create an organization that clearly supports those roles.

Hence, hierarchical elements should cater for highly exceptional cases only. In general, an extremely flat to non-existing hierarchy should prevail. The superiority of this approach becomes clear when considering the empirical results shown above. By implementing a strictly Team-Oriented approach following Complexity Theory, it is possible to satisfy simultaneously the Strategic Management's need for team orientation and participation. But if, in addition, the leaders are able to communicate their vision successfully, all requirements the members of the current culture share can be matched. Therefore, the organizational solution for the Strategic Management culture is rather simple and straightforward.

The appropriate solution is a predominantly Team-Oriented approach with virtually no hierarchical elements. The leaders' role in this organization design is primarily that of a team member. Hence, the organizational design needs to be such that it clearly favours a Team-Oriented behaviour, in particular of the respective leaders. This means that every team member has a very strong position within the team. Nevertheless, the organization has to give the leaders the possibility actually to take decisions on their own if necessary, due to some situational demands such as lack of intra-group agreement etc. Consequently, the leadership position within this kind of organization should only be moderately equipped with a means of power, so that the leader is not tempted to pursue arbitrarily a solution based on the use of power.

In summary, it can be said that the appropriate organizational solution is very close to that proposed in the context of Complexity Theory. The main aspect to be kept in mind is the strong need of the current culture for Team-Orientation and Participation in the various decision-taking processes of the respective organizations.

The Solution in Overview

The solution proposed in this section is focused significantly on Team-Oriented elements.

Despite the fact that the appropriate leadership style is based on Charismatic/Value-Based leadership, Team-Oriented elements play a key role in the successful integration of the members of the Strategic Management culture into their respective organizations.

Concerning the organizational solution, it is remarkable how close this solution is to the approach presented in the context of Complexity Theory. The main aspect for this culture is the necessity to give each member a voice within the actual decision-finding and decision-taking process. If, at the same time, it is possible to formulate a compelling Vision, a true activation of the potential of the Strategic Management will be possible.

Despite the relatively high demands that the mixture between Charismatic/Value-Based leadership on the one hand and Team-Oriented and Participative leadership on the other puts on the leader, the implementation of the above-mentioned approach should be attempted. This is due to the key importance members of the current culture have for their respective companies. Therefore, any measure that potentially increases the efficiency of the current group should be undertaken.

In summary, it can be said that the demands on the leader, especially on a personal level, are relatively high, whereas the proposed solution on the organizational level is relatively straightforward. Therefore, considerable attention has to be paid to the qualification and personal abilities of the leaders in Strategic Management.

7.6.3   Final Thoughts Regarding the Strategic Management

The results of this final Professional Culture are highly interesting and extremely important, although somewhat less surprising than some of the results of preceding cultures might have been.

One of the most interesting parts of this section is the fact that, even at such a high level within the organization, people still expect leadership and a congruent organization within their work environment. Although the leadership style favoured is relatively cautionary, it is nevertheless expected from a leader to be present and to exhibit clear leadership if necessary. Even at the current level, a heterarchy is apparently not overly appreciated.

Hence, it can be stated at this point that on all hierarchical levels and for all Professional Cultures present in the current survey, leadership and organization are of significant importance. Furthermore, the kind of leadership and organization varies within the different cultures, as well as the balance between leadership and organization.

In summary, the results of the Strategic Management culture are highly interesting and reflect the relative position that members of this culture have in their respective companies.

7.7   An Integrative Approach for a Number of Common Cross-Cultural Encounters

In this section, a selection of possible solutions for situations in which a number of cultures have to work together in order to carry out a specific task will be presented. The following list does not claim to be exhaustive as not all possible multi-cultural encounters can be treated at this point. It is to be understood primarily as a guideline to how the different results of the current work can be combined in order to lead and organize a number of cultures successfully at the same time. Furthermore, it obviously gives a direct solution to a number of rather likely Cross-Cultural encounters in professional life.

7.7.1   The Specially Qualified Production Experts and the Information Technology Experts

These two Professional Cultures (Section 7.1 and Section 6.3 respectively) have a number of similar views as to the way they expect their leadership relationship to be structured. For both groups, a Charismatic/Value-Based (e.g. Bass 1985; Burns 1978; House *et al.* 2004; see also Section 2.2.3) and a Team-Oriented Leadership approach (e.g. Manz and Sims 2001; House *et al.* 2004; see also Section 2.2.2) are highly important. This means that if these two Professional Cultures have to work together they would be very responsive to a Team-Oriented leadership style, which would be strongly supported by a convincing Vision emphasizing the importance of succeeding in the task that is carried out by this bi-cultural group.

Taking into account the importance of Participative (e.g. Lewin 1948; Tannenbaum and Schmidt 1958; House *et al.* 2004; see also Section 2.1.1) and Human-Oriented leadership (e.g. Gagné and Fleishman 1959; Fleishman and Quaintance 1984; Blake and Mouton 1985; House *et al.* 2004; see also Section 2.1.2) have for the Specially Qualified Production Experts and the Information Technology Experts respectively, it is advisable also to integrate these two leadership styles into the final solution.

Theoretically this can be achieved in a rather simple manner, as the Production Experts culture does not have a negative view of Human-Oriented leadership, and the IT-Experts culture does not have a negative view of Participative leadership. Therefore, it would be possible for a leader to join both approaches into a considerate, listening, warm and helpful leadership style.

In practice however, this combination may be a little more difficult to achieve. This is due to the fact that it is rather demanding for a leader to exhibit traits of Charismatic/Value-Based, Team-Oriented, Participative and Human-Oriented leadership at the same time. Nevertheless, in order successfully to lead a work team with the current composition it is advisable for the leader to strive to be as close as possible to the following leadership style. The leaders develop a clear and compelling Vision. They have to live that Vision and have to lead by example. Furthermore, they need to use Team-Oriented leadership in the sense of Manz and Sims (2001) for the actual implementation of the Vision. Finally, it is highly important that the leaders are available as a person if and when they are needed. The need for the leader as a person arises when there is a requirement for Participation and/or Human-Orientation as described at various occasions throughout this work.

If a leader actually manages to combine and employ appropriately all these different leadership styles, a superior leadership style would be achieved for the current combination of Professional Cultures. Despite the difficulties mentioned in actually living this combination, it is nevertheless highly beneficial for an organization to have such a leader available if there is a need for the Specially Qualified Production Experts and the Information Technology Experts to work together.

Concerning the appropriate organization design, an appropriate solution is rather simple to develop, as both cultures rely on Complexity Theory (Stacey *et al.* 2000; see also Section 3.2.2) as the base for their appropriate organization design. Therefore, it is advisable to structure the organization very much in line with that proposed by Lewin and Regine (2000; see also Section 3.2.2), as this kind of organization clearly supports the above-developed appropriate leadership style.

It is of crucial importance to create an organization that actually permits self-governance of the work team and which gives the members of this work team the freedom truly to work together on the success of their respective tasks without outside interference. At the same time though, it is not advisable to aim for a heterarchy as this is in clear opposition to the need for guidance expressed by both Professional Cultures. They still do expect their leader to be present and intervening if necessary, for example if there is an external challenge with which the team cannot deal directly, or a persistent lack of agreement within the team as to how to solve a specific problem.

In summary, it can be stated that the demands on the leaders are very high in the current situation. They have to exhibit outstanding leadership qualities in order to lead successfully these two Professional Cultures jointly. The required organization design is a little more straightforward, but its implementation may still represent a challenge in classical organizations. Nevertheless, it is advisable to make this extra effort as, on the occasions on which these two cultures work together, their success is usually of significant importance to the company concerned.

7.7.2   The Specially Qualified Production Experts and Innovation and Development

An appropriate leadership solution for a work team composed of Specially Qualified Production Experts (Section 7.1) and members of the Innovation and Development Culture (Section 7.2) can be relatively straightforward. This is because the differences between both cultures predominantly concern details, whereas the major aspects as far as leadership is concerned can be joined relatively simply.

As, for both Professional Cultures, Charismatic/Value-Based leadership (e.g. Bass 1985; Burns 1978; House *et al*. 2004; see also section 2.2.3) represents the basis for an appropriate leadership approach, it is necessary to use this leadership style as the basis for the solution retained for the present work team.

Participative Leadership (e.g. Lewin 1948; Tannenbaum and Schmidt 1958; House *et al*. 2004; see also Section 2.1.1) was another key leadership trait mentioned by both groups. This is due to the extremely high professional knowledge present in both cultures. Due to this qualification level, members of both Professional Cultures obviously expect to be integrated in the decision-taking process. Hence, Participative leadership will be part of the retained leadership solution.

Team-Oriented leadership (e.g. Manz and Sims 2001; House *et al*. 2004; see also Section 2.2.2) is a little more problematical. Despite the fact that both groups consider this leadership approach to be important, they do have a slightly differing understanding of teamwork. For the Innovation and Development culture it is very much understood in the sense outlined by Manz and Sims (2001), in which teamwork shows itself not only in an idea, but very concretely by the way members of this culture work together. The Specially Qualified Production Experts, on the other hand, see Team-Orientation as more of an underlying idea that may also link geographically dispersed entities to behave like one team.

For practical matters though, this different understanding is not necessarily problematic. This is due to the fact that, even for the Production Experts, an affinity towards Team-Oriented leadership can be stated, which simply needs to be slightly supported and focused on the respective teams by the respective leader.

The preference for Human-Oriented leadership (e.g. Gagné and Fleishman 1959; Fleishman and Quaintance 1984; Blake and Mouton 1985; House *et al*. 2004; see also Section 2.1.2) expressed by the members of the Innovation and Development culture does not represent a major obstacle in the development of a joint leadership solution, as members of the Production Experts culture have neither positive nor negative feelings about the content of this leadership style. Therefore, integration of Human-Oriented leadership into the retained leadership solution can easily be undertaken.

In summary, an appropriate leadership solution would look like the following. The leader develops a compelling Vision for the team. The implementation is undertaken with the help of a strictly Team-Oriented approach. For both the development of the Vision and regular day-to-day business, including the implementation of that Vision, a Participative approach should be chosen by the leader. Finally, this approach needs to be rounded off by Human-Oriented elements, such as warmth and care for the employees, to satisfy the expectations of the Innovation and Development members of the team.

As far as an appropriate organization design is concerned, the solution is even more straightforward, as both Professional Cultures rely heavily on the theoretical framework proposed by Complexity Theory (Stacey *et al.* 2000; see also Section 3.2.2). Therefore, it is advisable to structure the organization along the lines proposed by Lewin and Regine (2000; see also Section 3.2.2). It is important to design the organization in a way that supports the Team-Orientation of the people present in the current combination. At the same time though, it is important that the organization provides a position to the team leaders that gives them the possibility to actually live the leadership style described above.

This means, in particular, that there is still the need for a leader to be present and to be able actually to take decisions if necessary. In that context, the implementation of a heterarchy, even if it were possible, would constitute a serious flaw in the organization design for the current setting. Therefore, an appropriate organization design would look like the following in the current setting.

Members of both cultures should be put into teams, in which they have to work together in order to be successful in the completion of their task. The teams themselves should be able to work as independently as possible from the rest of the organization. That also means that control mechanisms should be kept to a minimum and they should be goal-achievement oriented instead of process oriented. Nevertheless, it is necessary to place at the top of each team a leader who needs to have the power base to actually take decisions if necessary. This power base has to be structured in a way that also permits the leaders to take decisions regarding the whole team without always having to clear their decisions with some other superior before proceeding.

To sum up, it can be said that the current combination is very close in its requirements for an appropriate organization design to that outlined in Section 3.2.2, except for the fact that it is not advisable to even attempt to implement heterarchy. This is due to its clear contradiction to the expectations of the two Professional Cultures present in the current setting.

Finally, it can be stated that the leadership and organization design proposed in this section is once again relatively demanding on the leadership level. This is due to the fact that the successful leader in the current environment needs to be able to combine a number of sometimes conflicting leadership styles. In particular, the highly complicated mixture of Charismatic/Value-Based on the one hand and Participative and Team-Oriented leadership on the other is very demanding on the character of the leader. As far as the organizational design is concerned, this is somewhat easier to implement, but nevertheless can pose a major challenge for more traditional organizations.

7.7.3   *The Specially Qualified Production Experts and the Service Providers*

For the current setting, the leadership solution is relatively simple to establish as, for both Professional Cultures (see Sections 7.1 and 6.5 respectively for details), it is based on the same components only with a differing emphasis on the different components. Whereas Charismatic/Value-Based leadership (e.g. Bass 1985; Burns 1978; House *et al.* 2004; see also Section 2.2.3) is a key component for members of the Specially Qualified Production Experts, it only represents an extra for the Service Providers. Nevertheless, both cultures having a positive view of this leadership style renders it part of the retained leadership solution.

Team-Oriented leadership (e.g. Manz and Sims 2001; House *et al.* 2004; see also Section 2.2.2) is highly important for both cultures. As mentioned previously, members of the Production Experts culture understand Team-Orientation in a somewhat unconventional way. As already stated though, this understanding does not hamper them in integrating into a true team if the task asks for it. Therefore, Team-Orientation in the sense of Manz and Sims (2001) will be retained for the leadership solution of the present setting.

Participative Leadership (e.g. Lewin 1948; Tannenbaum and Schmidt 1958; House *et al.* 2004; see also Section 2.1.1) finally, represents the most important aspect in the leadership relationship for the Service Providers culture. As it is also part of the appropriate leadership style for the Production Experts as outlined in Section 7.1, it will be retained for the current setting as well. Therefore, an appropriate leadership solution for the current setting would look like the following.

The leader develops a Vision around the task of the group. This is particularly important as, on the one hand, members of the Production Experts expect Charismatic/Value-Based leadership to be part of 'their' leadership. On the other, this Vision has to be relatively close to the actual task at hand in order to reach the Service Providers.

Participative elements have to be included in both the development and implementation of the Vision and the regular day-to-day business in order to cater for the demands of both Professional Cultures, but in particular that of the Service Providers'. Finally, Team-Orientation is very important in the day-to-day business to successfully melt these two distinct cultures into one functioning entity.

In summary, joining these two Professional Cultures is relatively easy from a leadership point of view, as both share the same key expectations only with a different emphasis when it comes to an appropriate leadership style.

As far as organization design is concerned, Complexity Theory (Stacey *et al.* 2000; Lewin and Regine 2000; see also Section 3.2.2) is once again the solution of choice. This is due to the fact that both Professional Cultures have a preference for an organization designed according to this theoretical approach. Both cultures need independence and freedom to meet their expectations as far as organization design is concerned. In addition, the Service Providers often already have experience with working in professional settings that are rather close to those proposed by Complexity Theory (Lewin and Regine 2000; see also Sections 3.2.2 and 6.5).

As already mentioned at various occasions throughout this work, the Production Experts do not see working in teams as a necessary prerequisite for successfully carrying out their tasks. Nevertheless, the stated preference for a Team-Oriented approach renders this Professional Culture very receptive to them being organized in teams as proposed by Complexity Theory. Therefore, the appropriate organization design is once again a rather straightforward adaptation of Complexity Theory. The important point is that the Service Providers and the Production Experts need to be put into an independently acting entity in which they have the freedom and feel the necessity to actually work together without interference from outside actors.

The importance of achieving this kind of team lies in the fact that when these two Professional Cultures work together, usually all the professional knowledge of every single team member is needed. If, for example, a supply team is set up, it is crucial that both business and technical knowledge are available at 100% to reach a successful outcome. Hence, it can be retained that Complexity Theory is the most promising approach to successfully organize a team consisting of Production Experts and Service Providers. The only aspect of Complexity Theory that should not be introduced is the creation of a true heterarchy, as this clearly conflicts with the preferred organization design of the Production Experts' culture and does not have any positive co-notation for the Service Providers' culture. Nevertheless, a rather flat hierarchy as proposed by Complexity Theory should be pursued as this caters for the expectations of both cultures concerned.

In summary, it can be said that the retained joint leadership and organization solutions are very close to those proposed for each Professional Culture individually. Obviously each culture has a different focus of the various details. Nevertheless, both having the same key elements for a successful leadership and organization approach in common is rather helpful for their integration into a joint team.

Finally, Complexity Theory proved once again its superiority when it comes to the organizational integration of different Professional Cultures into one functioning team.

7.7.4   *The Specially Qualified Production Experts and the Operational Management*

The appropriate joint leadership solution for the Production Experts (see Section 7.1) and the Operational Management (see Section 7.5) is very close to the isolated solutions for these two Professional Cultures. This is because both often share a production-related technical background. Therefore, differences in the isolated solutions are notable, but do not represent an insurmountable obstacle for the development of a joint solution.

Both Professional Cultures base their respective preferred leadership style on Charismatic/Value-Based leadership (e.g. Bass 1985; Burns 1978, House *et al.* 2004; see also Section 2.2.3). Both express the need for guidance and reason why, expressed in a compelling Vision. Furthermore, both Professional Cultures have a strong preference for Team-Oriented leadership (e.g. Manz and Sims 2001; House *et al.* 2004; see also Section 2.2.2) when the task demands it. Hence, the acceptance of a Team-Based approach for the integration of these two cultures is assured.

Participative leadership (e.g. Lewin 1948; Tannenbaum and Schmidt 1958; House *et al.* 2004; see also Section 2.1.1) is viewed very positively by members of both Professional Cultures. This is mainly due to their professional expertise and, to a lesser degree, their perceived importance for the whole organization. Therefore, Participative leadership needs to be part of the retained solution.

Finally, Human-Oriented leadership (e.g. Gagné and Fleishman 1959; Fleishman and Quaintance 1984; Blake and Mouton 1985; House *et al.* 2004; see also Section 2.1.2) is considered to be of some significance to the members of the Operational Management. In accordance with the results of Section 7.5 this Professional Culture mainly expects the Human-Orientation of its leaders to show itself in the form of a group protection against external threats and a supportive behaviour of group members if needed. To the members of the Production Experts, Human-Orientation is of no specific significance, neither positive nor negative. Hence, Human-Oriented leadership will be part of the retained solution. Therefore, an appropriate leadership solution for a team consisting of Specially Qualified Production Experts and Operational Management looks like the following.

The leaders develop a compelling Vision, which clearly shows why the successful completion of the tasks the team has to carry out is of such vital importance to the organization as a whole. They implement the Vision with the help of a Team-Oriented approach in the sense of Manz and Sims (2001). For both the development of the Vision and its day-to-day implementation and realization, it is highly important that the leaders clearly take into consideration the ideas and suggestions of the team members. Finally, they have to make sure that their people feel protected and supported.

Owing to the very similar preferences, as far as leadership is concerned, it can be retained at this point that a leader who successfully runs one of these two Professional Cultures will most likely be able successfully to run both cultures jointly.

As far as organization design is concerned, matters are somewhat more complicated. This is due to the fact that the Operational Management culture needs a joint design, consisting of the Administrative Approach (Fayol 1984; see also Section 3.1.1) and Complexity Theory (Stacey *et al.* 2000; Lewin and Regine 2000; see also Section 3.2.2). The main problem in this setting is the need expressed by the members of Operational Management for strategic leadership. This need gives a clear preference for an organization that is very much in line with that proposed by Fayol (1984) for strategic matters, an in-between solution with Complexity Theory for matters that are not clearly operational and a Complexity Theory based approach for operational matters (for details see Section 7.5).

A possible solution to this problem is the implementation of an organization that is based on Complexity Theory, but deviates somewhat from that proposed by Lewin and Regine (2000). This deviation mainly concerns the role of the leaders. They have to be significantly more present and, in that aspect, more powerful than they would have to be in a purely Complexity Theory based organization. Therefore, for the sake of the members of the Operational Management Culture, to a certain degree it is necessary to dilute the solution proposed by Complexity Theory without touching its core.

On the other hand, if the solution proposed in Section 7.5 for the Operational Management was to be directly implemented, serious dysfunctionalities would have to be expected as well. This is due to the strong emphasis the Production Experts put on the implementation of an organization, which is congruent with Complexity Theory.

Therefore, the role of the leaders is of the utmost importance in the current setting. They have to make sure that they fulfil the expectations of both groups at the same time, which means that they will have to fill appropriately the manoeuvring room the organization design gives them. This design would have to look like the following.

Its base is Complexity Theory. Nevertheless, hierarchical elements have to be present in the organizational layout in order to give the members of the Operational Management the required guidance and support. At the same time it is necessary to implement structures that satisfy the expectations of the Production Experts. Therefore, the appropriate balance between the Administrative Approach and Complexity Theory is of the utmost importance.

In the current setting, this appropriate balance would be principally to structure the organization according to Complexity Theory. Nonetheless, the position of a powerful leader position has to be implemented into this design, so as to permit the leaders to take decisions if necessary. In the present setting, 'if necessary' means that they will mostly restrict the use of this power to strategic decisions for which no team internal solution can be found. These decisions will have to adequately reflect positions of both Professional Cultures. In such situations, they may be reasonably sure that acceptance among the Operational Management will be the highest. With this high acceptance of one culture they may also expect members of the Production Experts to at least partially accept their decision.

In virtually all other situations it is advisable that the leaders keep as much as possible out of the way of their team members. The situations in which they will be needed will most likely involve members of the Operational Management culture. If such assistance is necessary, it should be given while keeping in mind the freedom members of the Production Experts' culture expect. Hence, in summary, the following should be noted.

The position of the leaders is of the utmost importance in the current setting. They will have to make sure that they always find the right balance between favouring Complexity Theory and favouring the Administrative Approach while pursuing the leadership style developed above. Finding this balance will probably turn out to be quite demanding, but together with the appropriate leadership style this is the key to the successful integration of these two Professional Cultures.

7.7.5 *Information Technology Experts and Innovation and Development*

The Information Technology Experts' culture (for details see Section 6.3) and the Innovation and Development culture (for details see Section 7.2) share a number of traits, but also exhibit a number of differences as far as their preferred leadership style is concerned.

For instance, both share a high esteem for Charismatic/Value-Based (e.g. Bass 1985; Burns 1978; House *et al*. 2004; see also Section 2.2.3), Team-Oriented (e.g. Manz and Sims 2001; House *et al*. 2004; see also Section 2.2.2) and Human-Oriented leadership (e.g. Gagné and Fleishman 1959; Fleishman and Quaintance 1984; Blake and Mouton 1985; House *et al*. 2004; see also Section 2.1.2). The IT-Experts on the other hand value Autonomous leadership (House *et al*. 2004) relatively highly whereas Innovation and Development exhibits a relatively positive view of Participative leadership (e.g. Lewin 1948; Tannenbaum and Schmidt 1958; House *et al*. 2004; see also Section 2.1.1).

In the current setting and in accordance with the empirical results it seems to be advisable to favour the leadership styles that are viewed positively by both Professional Cultures simultaneously and to add some elements of the Participative leadership style. If at all, the Autonomous leadership style should be used, but very cautiously only.

An appropriate leadership style would therefore look like the following.

The leaders develop a compelling Vision that demonstrates the importance the success of the team has for the whole company. They live the Vision and lead their people by example. The Vision itself should be implemented by using a Team-Oriented approach. Giving team members the choice to participate in both the development of the Vision and its subsequent implementation and realization is a plus, but no team member should feel forced to do so. This is due to the fact that the IT-Experts do not express a particularly positive view of Participative Leadership, which renders it advisable not to force them to participate. On the other hand, members of the Innovation and Development culture unambiguously expressed their preference for Participative leadership, which clearly shows that having the possibility to participate without being forced to do so is the best course of action in the current setting.

In addition, the leaders have to make sure that they develop a leadership relationship that permits a warm, friendly and caring relationship. Achieving that Human-Oriented leadership is extremely important, and is strongly favoured by both Professional Cultures. In summary, it can be retained at this point that the appropriate leadership style for the current combination is once again rather demanding.

As has been stated at various occasions throughout this work, the combination between Charismatic/Value-Based leadership on the one hand and Team-Oriented, Participative, and Human-Oriented leadership on the other is very difficult to achieve. Nevertheless, this combination is the most appropriate way to lead a combination of the Information Technology Experts' culture and the Innovation and Development culture successfully.

Concerning the appropriate organization design, a solution that is significantly easier to implement will be proposed. As, for both Professional Cultures, Complexity Theory (Stacey *et al*. 2000; Lewin and Regine 2000; see also Section 3.2.2) is the approach of choice, an actual implementation of this approach should be undertaken. The team has to operate as independently as possible from the rest of the organization and the perceived hierarchy should be very flat.

Nevertheless, given the fact that both cultures are, in a number of aspects relatively different, it is advisable to create a hierarchical leadership position, which possesses the power base to actually take decisions if needed. 'If needed' means in this setting, for example, that an internal consensus by the members of the team is not possible or that the team needs somebody to represent it to the outside, etc.

The respective leader though has to make sure not to misuse this power base and not to turn the organization into a classical hierarchical organization. The basic underlying orientation of the appropriate organization design always has to be towards that proposed within the context of Complexity Theory. Here again, the competency of the leaders is of the utmost importance as it is up to them to choose the appropriate course of action and to make sure that the characteristics of the organization are not altered from the ones given above.

As far as the organization design is concerned, it is important that it gives the leaders the possibility to actually implement the organizational design outlined in Complexity Theory, while at the same time giving them the power to temporarily switch back to a more hierarchical solution. Therefore, once again, the leaders have an extraordinary importance for the success of the team. The organization can only help them to achieve the results aimed for and is, in that respect, setting a rather loose framework for the leaders only. The leaders themselves have to make sure that the organization and their leadership are in line with the above outlined expectations of the members of both Professional Cultures.

7.7.6   *Innovation and Development and the Service Providers*

An appropriate leadership solution for a team consisting of members of the Innovation and Development Culture (see Section 7.2) and the Service Providers' Culture (see Section 6.5) would have to incorporate elements of the Participative (e.g. Lewin 1948; Tannenbaum and Schmidt 1958; House *et al.* 2004; see also Section 2.1.1), the Charismatic/Value-Based (e.g. Bass 1985; Burns 1978; House *et al.* 2004; see also Section 2.2.3) and the Team-Oriented leadership styles (e.g. Manz and Sims 2001; House *et al.* 2004; see also Section 2.2.2). This is because both Professional Cultures expect these leadership styles to be part of 'their' leadership style. The problem in the current setting though is that the different leadership styles are valued differently by the two cultures. The base of the appropriate leadership solution is Charismatic/Value-Based leadership for the Innovation and Development culture, whereas the base for the appropriate solution for the Service Providers' Culture is Participative leadership.

Therefore, for the retained solution, it is not possible to concentrate on one leadership style, but it is necessary to join the Charismatic/Value-Based and Participative leadership in order to match the expectations of these two cultures. Furthermore, Team-Orientation has to be part of that retained solution as it is valued positively by both cultures.

Finally, Human-Oriented Leadership (e.g. Gagné and Fleishman 1959; Fleishman and Quaintance 1984; Blake and Mouton 1985; House *et al.* 2004; see also Section 2.1.2) is to be part of the final solution as it is seen positively by the members of the Innovation and Development culture and neutrally by those of the Service Providers' culture. Hence, an appropriate leadership solution for the current setting looks like the following.

The leaders develop a compelling Vision jointly with their team members. For the acceptance of this Vision, in particular by the Service Providers, it is highly important that the final Vision is the end product of a Participative development process. The leaders only have to make sure that the Vision itself is relatively closely connected to the task at hand, as otherwise it may not be sufficiently credible to the members of the Service Providers' culture. On the other hand it still has to be Visionary enough to be compelling to the members of the Innovation and Development culture. Therefore, finding the right balance for the Vision is one of the first major tasks of the leader in the current setting.

The actual implementation of the Vision as well as the following day-to-day business have to be carried out in a Team-Oriented setting in the sense of Manz and Sims (2001) and obviously in addition the continued use of Participative leadership. Finally, this should be supported by Human-Oriented elements so as to satisfy the expectations of the Innovation and Development culture.

Joining all these leadership styles into one is obviously quite demanding. Nevertheless, the key to successfully leading members of both cultures jointly lies in the correct application of the above-developed leadership style. The appropriate organization design is once again based on Complexity Theory (Stacey *et al.* 2000; Lewin and Regine 2000; see also Section 3.2.2). This is due to the fact that both Professional Cultures favour this organization design. Therefore, the appropriate organization design needs to give the team a maximum degree of freedom to carry out its tasks. The leadership position does not have to be overly strong as far as its power base is concerned. As the function of the leaders is mostly to help the team find and implement a superior solution to a given problem, they cannot rely on power to push a decision through, but have to aim for acceptance and subsequent implementation of a found solution.

The organizational design should only provide in exceptional cases a possibility for the leader to actually push a decision through. At the same time though, this does mean a rejection of a heterarchy as, in particular, the need of the members of the Innovation and Development culture would not be overly matched with such an organization design. In particular, the expressed expectation for Visionary leadership clearly shows the need for a present and charismatic leader.

Finally, it is important that the overarching organization design allows the leaders actually to implement the above-described features. The leaders and their teams need to be able to operate independently from the rest of the organization. Control mechanisms, for example, should be avoided as much as possible and centred on goal achievement and alike.

In summary, it can be said that the solution proposed here for a combined team of members of the Innovation and Development culture and the Service Providers' culture requires a fairly elaborated leadership style, whereas the appropriate organization design is rather straightforward.

The same phenomenon seen at various occasions in this section reoccurs. The demands on the leader in a Cross-Cultural setting are enormous, whereas the demands on the organization design are not significantly more challenging than in various single culture environments. Therefore, once again, it is of the utmost importance to choose the right leaders for the current setting and to provide them with the organizational tools necessary to lead their teams successfully.

7.7.7 The Information Technology Experts and the Service Providers

As far as an appropriate leadership solution for the Information Technology Experts (see Section 6.3) and the Service Providers (see Section 6.5) is concerned, it should be based on the Charismatic/Value-Based (e.g. Bass 1985; Burns 1978; House *et al*. 2004; see also Section 2.2.3) and the Participative leadership style (e.g. Lewin 1948; Tannenbaum and Schmidt 1958; House *et al*. 2004; see also Section 2.1.1). Furthermore, the Team-Oriented leadership style (e.g. Manz and Sims 2001; House *et al*. 2004; see also Section 2.2.2) represents a significant part of the retained solution. Finally, some elements of Human-Oriented leadership should be (e.g. Gagné and Fleishman 1959; Fleishman and Quaintance 1984; Blake and Mouton 1985; House *et al*. 2004; see also Section 2.1.2), and of Autonomous leadership may be (House *et al*. 2004), included.

The challenge for the appropriate leadership style in the current setting is very similar to the one in the previous section. This challenge is due to the need of the Charismatic/Value-Based and Participative leadership to jointly build the core of the common leadership style. Therefore, a similar approach for the development of the appropriate leadership style will be pursued.

The development of a compelling Vision is undertaken jointly between the leaders and their team members. For the acceptance of this Vision by the Service Providers it is highly important that the final Vision is the end product of a Participative development process. None of the team members should be forced to participate though, as Participative leadership is not part of the leadership style set of the IT-Experts culture.

The leader has to make sure that the Vision itself is not overly removed from the task at hand, as otherwise it may not be sufficiently compelling for the members of the Service Providers' culture. Nevertheless, it still has to be sufficiently visionary in order to truly be a source of motivation for the Information Technology Experts' culture. Therefore, finding the right balance between Participative and sufficiently, but not overly, Visionary elements in the leadership style is one of the major tasks of the leader in the current setting.

The implementation of the developed Vision as well as the following day-to-day business have to be carried out in a Team-Oriented environment. Team-Orientation was mentioned by members of both Professional Cultures to be an integral part of outstanding leadership.

Human-Orientation should be part of the retained leadership solution as members of the IT-Experts' culture mentioned this leadership style to be an important aspect of 'their' leadership style. The inclusion of Human-Oriented leadership at the initiative of only one of the two Professional Cultures present in this combination is possible because members of the Service Providers' culture did not show an antipathy towards this kind of leadership.

Finally, Autonomous Leadership may be included in the retained solution, if the leader has to be significantly different from other leaders in the organization in order to live the following appropriate leadership solution for the current setting.

The leader develops, in a Participative manner, a Vision that is compelling to members of both Professional Cultures. Both the implementation of the Vision and the subsequent day-to-day business are strictly Team-Oriented. Finally, it is important that the leader is able to exhibit Human-Oriented behaviour such as warmth and empathy towards the team members. This is due to the fact that, to the members of the IT-Experts culture, a healthy relationship to their superior is important. Furthermore, it may be expected that the resulting positive relationship to those team members who are receptive to Human-Oriented leadership will also have beneficial consequences for the members of the Service Providers' culture.

As far as an appropriate organization design is concerned, it needs to be based on Complexity Theory (Stacey *et al*. 2000; Lewin and Regine 2000; see also Section 3.2.2) as, for both Professional Cultures, this represents the preferred organization design. This organization design is also compatible with the above-developed leadership style as it gives the leader and the team members the freedom to build the described leadership relationship.

The actual implementation should be carried out according to Lewin and Regine (2000) with the implementation of true work teams. In that aspect, the organization design should be very much in accordance with that described in Section 7.7.6.

In summary, it can be said that the current combination requires a relatively complicated leadership style. Nevertheless, here again it is necessary actually to live this leadership style if one wants to use all the resources the team has to offer.

As far as organization design is concerned, once again the only possible solution to a joint approach lies in Complexity Theory. The fact that Complexity Theory proved again and again to be the solution of choice in the current section will be examined further below. The implications of this finding are rather far reaching though, and will be of significant importance for virtually all Cross-Cultural work teams. Therefore, it is advisable that even classic organizations make the extra effort to implement Complexity Theory based structures where appropriate.

7.7.8   *The Service Providers and the Middle Administration*

Finally, an example of a combination between two Professional Cultures that do not permit a joint solution is given.

The characteristics of the Service Providers (Section 6.5) and those of the Middle Administration (Section 6.6) are so different that it would prove virtually impossible to create leadership and organization structures that fit both Professional Cultures at the same time.

As far as leadership is concerned, an approach focused on the individual could possibly be a way to circumnavigate the differences in the cultural traits of these two cultures. The leaders would have to adapt their leadership style to the one developed for the Service Providers or Middle Administration respectively, depending on the actual situation. Therefore, depending on an individual being part of the Service

Providers or the Middle Administration culture, the leaders adopt the appropriate leadership style.

Despite the inherent high complexity that such a split in leadership behaviour incurs for the respective leader, this approach would be the only way to engender a valid leadership approach in the current setting. Therefore, despite its complexity, this approach represents at least a possibility of leading both Professional Cultures jointly.

More serious problems arise from the incongruity of the organization structures expected by both Professional Cultures. The Service Providers expect to be organized in an environment governed by Complexity Theory (Stacey *et al.* 2000; Lewin and Regine 2000; see also Section 3.2.2), whereas the Middle Administration expects to be organized in an environment inspired by the work of Weber (1976; see also Section 3.1.1). The significant differences between these approaches render it impossible to fuse these approaches effectively into one joint approach. It would therefore seem inadvisable to actually put both Professional Cultures into a single organizational environment.

Thus, a possible solution to a setting in which the two Professional Cultures have to act jointly could, for example, be to keep them separated organizationally, but to give them one joint leader who can oversee that the efforts of both cultural groups lead in the same direction.

In summary, it can be said that it will not always be possible to find leadership structures and organization designs that simultaneously fit two or more Professional Cultures in a cross-cultural setting. Therefore, it is highly important always to check thoroughly the characteristics of each Professional Culture concerned before joining a number of Professional Cultures in one team. Failure to do so will result in at least one of the Professional Cultures not being treated according to its characteristics, with the possible negative consequences mentioned at various times throughout this book.

7.7.9   Summarizing Evaluation of Cross Cultural Leadership and Organization Design

Three main aspects should be retained from the above insight into the appropriate way to lead and organize cross-cultural teams. The first aspect is the apparent frequent superiority of an organization design based on Complexity Theory (Stacey *et al.* 2000; Lewin and Regine 2000; see also Section 3.2.2) when it comes to organizing cross-cultural teams. This is due to the demonstrated flexibility such an organization design has in order to adapt itself to the needs of the teams concerned. Obviously, this does not mean that the approach proposed by Lewin and Regine (2000) can be implemented directly. But it does mean that a well considered adaptation of Complexity Theory is at the core of a substantial number of functioning cross-cultural teams.

A further highly important consequence of Complexity Theory's flexibility is that this flexibility permits the leaders of the concerned work team to adjust their leadership style to the requirements of the situation. As shown, leadership is highly demanding and hugely varying across the different cross-cultural settings. Therefore, it is of the utmost importance that the organization design does not restrict the leaders in their leadership approach. As was also shown, even within one team it may be necessary to slightly alter the leadership style in order to match the Professional Cultures present in the team.

Hence, leadership selection and training are of the utmost importance in order to lead cross-cultural teams successfully. In such settings, the competence of the respective leaders is the key to success or failure as they have appropriately to occupy the role given to them by the respective organization design and the requirements of their professional environment. Finally, it has to be retained that it may not always be possible to join two or more Professional Cultures to make one single team. These situations arise when the characteristics of the Cultures to be joined are as contradictory as those described in Section 7.7.8. In such situations forcing different cultures into one team has potentially disastrous consequences and should therefore not be attempted.

This last finding once again clearly demonstrates the importance of research into Professional Cultures, both from an academic and a practical point of view. Neglecting the differences in cultural perceptions based on the respective professions leads to the same potential dysfunctionalities as neglecting differences in Organizational or National Cultures.

7.8   Final Assessment of the Found Results for the Different Clusters

Probably the most important point about the findings outlined in this chapter is the fact that Professional Cultures are not structured along what is usually referred to as professions or occupations, but along functional lines. This became especially clear with the engineers, who are split evenly into two groups, but also isolated from most other Professional Cultures in the current work. Nevertheless, professional functions do shape genuine cultures according to the results of this book. Therefore, Hypothesis 1 (for details please refer to Section 4.1.2) is clearly supported by the results of the current study. How far it is actually correct has to be left to future research; however, its basic statement is significantly strengthened by the results of the current study.

These findings alone are extremely important, as they demonstrate that the function that is carried out by a person clearly shapes that person's cultural system. Therefore, it can be stated at this point that the construct of Professional Cultures as introduced in previous chapters does exist and that it needs to be taken into account in addition to National and Organizational Cultures if one wants to get a more holistic picture of a person's cultural setting. Therefore, Hypothesis 3 (for details please refer to Section 4.2.3) can be considered to be confirmed by the empirical results gained in the course of the current study.

A further important finding concerns the complex of cross-functional or, as referred to in the current work, cross-cultural work teams. It could be demonstrated that it is highly important to analyze thoroughly the characteristics of each Professional Culture present in the team in order to make sure that these cultures can work together and, if they can, what kind of leadership and organization they need.

Furthermore, it could be clearly demonstrated that it is of the utmost importance to have outstanding leadership in cross-cultural settings. This aspect is specifically important for setting up virtually any kind of project, as most likely a project-type environment will tap into the competence of more than one Professional Culture. As demonstrated, it is vital for the success of such teams that the leader is able to exhibit a number of different leadership attributes and fuse them into a flexible and situation-adequate leadership style.

In that context it is important to note that the organizational design for such environments will in all probability be centred on Complexity Theory, as apparently this is the only organizational design that is able to give the necessary degree of freedom to the teams concerned.

Finally, it is important to note that it will not always be possible to combine two or more Professional Cultures efficiently into one team. These situations arise if the characteristics of the Cultures concerned are too different to find a solution that can cater for all of them at the same time. Forcing a joint team in such a situation will most likely have disastrous consequences for all parties concerned. Therefore, another interesting result is the insight that sometimes work teams are beneficial and sometimes they are not. This is true for both single cultural settings and cross-cultural settings. Hence, before implementing a team structure it is necessary to check for the appropriateness of this setting.

Jointly, all these points clearly demonstrate the importance that research into the construct of Professional Cultures and its subsequent appropriate use has both for academic and practical purposes. Neglecting the differences between the cultural traits each profession has potentially leaves large parts of the resources of each organization untapped; a situation that is obviously to be avoided.

To close this chapter, an overview of the results of this and the preceding chapter will be given in a graphical form. Figures 7.1–7.9 show the relative position of each Professional Culture on each of the Core Cultural Dimensions. A numerical overview of the results is given in Appendix 3.

Leadership and Organization in the Aviation Industry

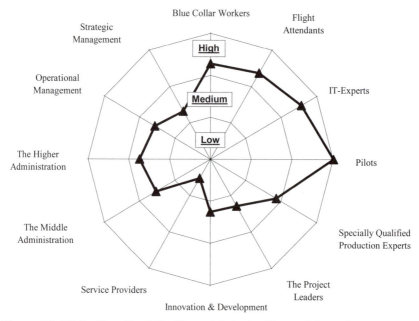

Figure 7.1 All the Results of the Uncertainty Avoidance Dimension

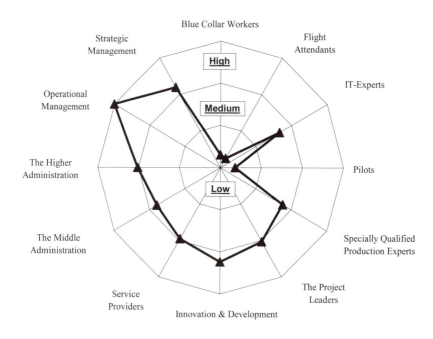

Figure 7.2 All the Results of the Assertiveness Dimension

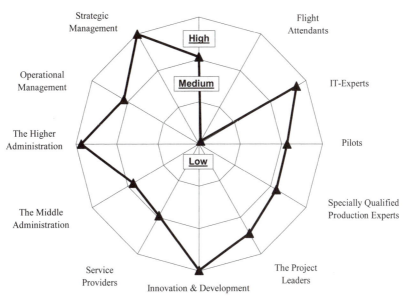

Figure 7.3 All the Results of the Future Orientation Dimension

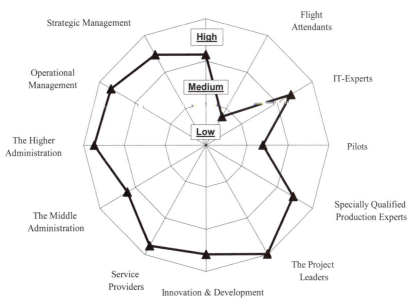

Figure 7.4 All the Results of the Power Distance Dimension

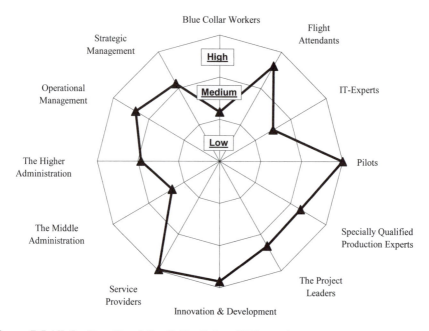

Figure 7.5 All the Results of the Collectivism I Dimension

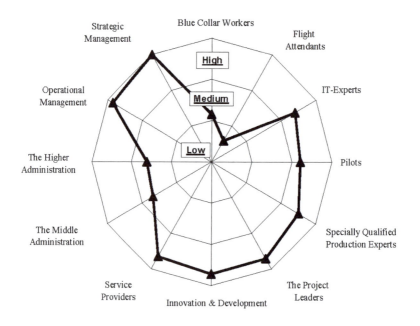

Figure 7.6 All the Results of the Performance Orientation Dimension

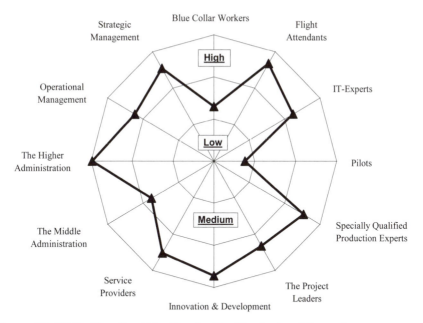

Figure 7.7 All the Results of the Gender Egalitarianism Dimension

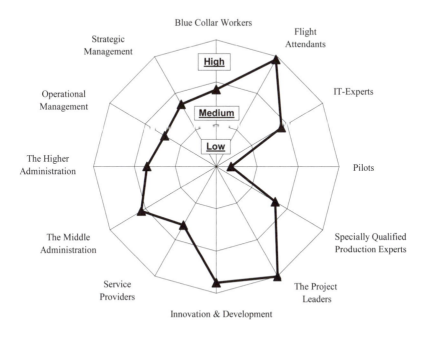

Figure 7.8 All the Results of the Human Orientation Dimension

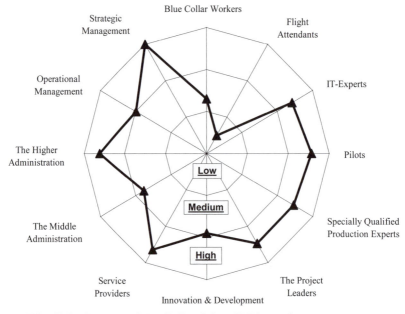

Figure 7.9 All the Results of the Collectivism II Dimension

Chapter 8

A Cross-Evaluation of the Results Depicted

In the following, a cross-evaluation of the possible superiority of the developed leadership and organizational structures will be undertaken. This will be carried out with the help of two questions to be found in the standardized questionnaire.

The first question asks for the agreement between the current situation as it is and the overall opinion expressed in the questionnaire of how things should be. The second question asks for the perceived efficiency of the professional peer group. Therefore, the values for efficiency given below are exclusively based on the assessment of the individual respondents and not on some objectively valid measurement scale. Thus, in the current context, efficiency is not to be understood as a clearly defined scientific construct, but merely a reflection of the respondent's opinion regarding the efficiency of the Professional peer-group (see also the exact wording of Question Six in Appendix 2).

Linking these two questions, however, gives an indication as to the superiority of the developed leadership and organizational structures, as will be pointed out below.

In the context of the following explanations, it has to be kept in mind that the leadership and organizational structures proposed for the different Professional Cultures are directly related to the answers as to how things should be. Therefore, these 'should be' answers represent the link between the developed structures and the different current situations in which the various Professional Cultures find themselves. This current situation is then matched with the efficiency as perceived by the members of the different Professional Cultures.

Four different possible situations have to be distinguished, each representing a different indication as to the appropriateness of the structures designed.

The first situation is a high agreement between the current situation and the 'should be' situation as perceived by the respondents. In connection with a perceived high efficiency of the professional peer group (Professional Culture) this result can be interpreted as an indication of the superiority of the developed leadership and organizational structures. This is because a high perceived efficiency of the current situation, which is in agreement with the situation as it should be, clearly points to a high appropriateness of the leadership and organization structures based on these 'should be' questions.

The second situation is a low agreement between the current situation and the 'should be' situation in connection with a low perceived efficiency. Following the above, this indicates a high appropriateness of the developed leadership and organization structures.

This assessment is due to the fact that, if the agreement between the current situation and the 'should be' situation is low, the current leadership and organization structures are also most likely different from the herein proposed solution. In connection with the low perceived efficiency, this can be interpreted as an indication of the superiority of the developed and an inferiority of the current structures, although this is weaker than in the first situation.

In this situation, the indication is weaker because it shows only that the current situation is perceived to be sub-optimal while at the same time differing from the one proposed in Chapters 6 and 7. Nevertheless, in connection with the strong empirical base of the solution developed in those chapters, this result can be seen as an indication for the soundness of the leadership and organization approach developed there.

The third situation is a low agreement between the 'should be' situation and the current situation in connection with a high perceived efficiency. This situation is not as easily interpretable as the former two because of the fact that this result does not give any further indication as to the appropriateness of the leadership and organization structures developed in Chapters 6 and 7. In addition, such a result would indicate that there is at least one more set of appropriate leadership and organization designs besides the one proposed in Chapters 6 and 7.

Obviously, such a result does not exclude the possibility that the leadership and organization designs developed in Chapters 6 and 7 are appropriate, but it would show that they are not the sole leadership and organizational solution appropriate for the Professional Culture concerned. Therefore, in these situations, no clear statement as to the superiority of the developed structures can be given.

The fourth and final situation is a high agreement between the 'should be' and the current situation in connection with a low perceived efficiency. Following the above, this would indicate that the developed leadership and organization structures do not represent an advantageous approach.

This result ensues from the fact that these structures are developed based on the 'should be' answers, which are in accordance with the current situation as it is, which in turn is perceived to be inferior. Clearly, it is also possible that a Professional Culture rates a question neither positively nor negatively. In these situations a cautious interpretation under due consideration of all available empirical data will be undertaken. To be sure, this situation is the least desirable one as it implies the weakest statements about the topic of interest.

Nevertheless – as will be demonstrated – even in these situations it is possible to extract some meaningful information about the respective Professional Cultures and their perception of their Professional environment and its efficiency.

Figure 8.1 gives an overview of the four possible combinations of positive and negative ratings on the agreement scale (agreement between 'should be' and 'is') and the efficiency scale (perceived efficiency of the direct professional environment) and their implications for the leadership and organizational structures developed in Chapters 6 and 7.

Technically the decision regarding efficiency and agreement being low or high was carried out with the help of a statistical analysis that is based on the so called t-test (e.g. Schlittgen 2000; Kühnel and Krebs 2001; Hartung 2002). This test provides information on the relationship between parameters. In the present case, it was used to check if the value given by each Professional Culture to the 'agreement' and the 'efficiency' scale differed significantly from the overall mean exhibited by each of these two scales within the whole sample.

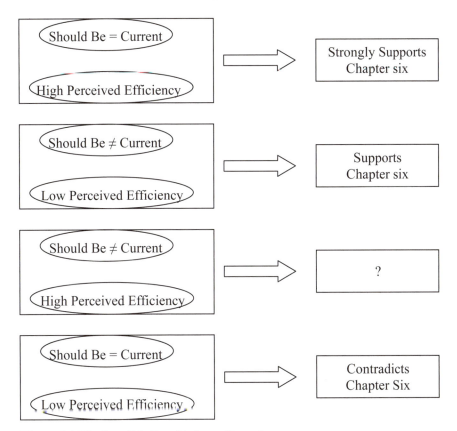

Figure 8.1 The Possible Results in an Overview

The t-test is the most appropriate test in the current environment, as it clearly answers the question of whether a given value differs statistically significantly from the sample mean (Bühl and Zöfel 2002). Furthermore, it is quite robust towards deviations from a normal distribution. Despite the fact that, due to the large sample size (340), normal distribution can be assumed, this trait of the t-test is another aspect favourable for its choice.

Therefore, a t-test was run for the values given by each Professional Culture for both questions. The test itself used the average rating each Professional Culture showed for each question. If a significant deviation from the mean of the whole sample could be stated, the Professional Culture was grouped into either high agreement or low agreement and high efficiency or low efficiency. Finally, in the absence of any further comments, the significance level is always at 0.000 in this section, if a significant deviation is stated.

In summary, it can be said that the approach taken for a cross evaluation in this chapter is not intended to give a final answer to the question of efficiency of the different leadership styles and organization designs developed in Chapters 6 and 7. The goal of this chapter is to check whether there are any more indicators favourable to the solutions in Chapters 6 and 7, or if there are some that may weaken these solutions and in so doing make them questionable.

A clear and unambiguous answer as to an empirically proven superiority of the approaches developed in Chapters 6 and 7 has to be left to future research. In this context, the current chapter will point out the possibilities and necessities for future research.

In the following, there will be analysis of what the actual situation for each Professional Culture isolated in Chapters 6 and 7 is in the light of the above-described possible interaction between the 'should be' and the current situation, on the one hand, and the perceived efficiency of the professional peer group, respectively Professional Culture, on the other.

8.1   The Blue Collar Workers

The Blue Collar Workers rated the question for the agreement between the current situation as it is and the one they think should be with an average of 2.4 (the highest would have been 1, the lowest 7). This does not represent a significant deviation from the overall mean of 2.4765.

Therefore, the Blue Collar Workers are neither part of the high agreement nor the low agreement group. Considering the results of the open interviews as described in Chapter 6, this score can be interpreted as the opinion that there is partial agreement and partial disagreement between the situation as it is and as it should be in this Professional Culture.

The rating of the question regarding the efficiency of the Professional peer group is at 2.72, significantly lower than the average, which is 2.35 (1 is the highest and 7 the lowest possible rating). Therefore, Blue Collar Workers are part of those Professional Cultures that consider their work efficiency to be relatively low.

Following the above-described line of argument, these results indicate a strengthening of the results of Chapter 6 and the developed leadership and organization structures. This is because the partial disagreement between the current situation and the one that should be is an indicator for the leadership and organizational designs not being in accordance with those developed in Chapter 6. This result, in connection with the low perceived work efficiency of the Blue Collar Workers' Professional Culture, leads to a strengthening of the result of Chapter 6.

In summary, it can be said that the joint evaluation of the perceived efficiency and the agreement between the current and the 'should be' situation points to a confirmation of the results of Chapter 6. This confirmation is not overly strong, as the low efficiency is paired with a neutral rating of the agreement scale. Nevertheless, considering all empirical results, this partially negative view of the current situation in connection with the negative perceived efficiency has to be seen as a favourable indicator for the superiority of the leadership and organization styles developed in Chapter 6.

8.2   The Flight Attendants

The Flight Attendants see a high agreement between the situation as it is and as it should be. They rate this question at 1.6, which is significantly higher than the overall average of 2.4765.

This result strongly suggests that the leadership and organization structures in use are relatively close to those developed in Chapter 6. This interpretation is strengthened by the fact that the score of 1.6 on this scale is the second highest of the whole sample after that of the Pilots. The perceived efficiency of the Flight Attendants' Professional Culture is, at 1.56, just as positive as the average of the whole sample, which is 2.35. This score is once again the second highest after that of the Pilots.

Jointly, these two results strongly support the findings of Chapter 6. This is because the very high agreement between the situation as it is and as it should be is a strong indication for the leadership and organization design in use being relatively close to that developed. This closeness in connection with the very positively perceived efficiency indicates a superiority of the structures developed in Chapter 6. In summary, it can be retained that the Flight Attendants perceive their Professional Culture to be relatively efficient. Furthermore, a very high agreement between the way the Flight Attendants would like their professional environment to be structured and the way they perceive it is structured can be stated.

In summary, it can be retained that the results of this section strongly support those of Chapter 6 indicating that the leadership and organization design developed in fact do represent a superior approach to the needs and characteristics of the Flight Attendants' Professional Culture.

8.3   The Information Technology Experts

According to the empirical results, the agreement between the situation as it should be in the opinion of the Information Technology Experts and the way it is, is relatively low, with a score of 2.85. This represents a significant deviation from the overall mean of 2.4765.

Therefore, members of the Information Technology Experts' Professional Culture see a significant deviation from the way they think things should be and the way they actually are. In addition, a non-significant deviation from the overall mean can be stated concerning the perceived efficiency of the present Professional Culture. The value of 2.5 is located within the lower end of the non-significant area around the overall mean, which is 2.35.

Jointly, these two factors can be considered to be favourable towards the findings described in Chapter 6.

Following the usual line of argument, a low agreement between the situation as it is and as it should be points implicitly to a difference between the leadership and organization structures developed in the previous chapter. Moreover, considering the, at most, neutrally perceived efficiency of the current Professional Culture, serious doubts surface as to the appropriateness of the leadership and organizational structures in use. Therefore, according to the results of the present chapter, a leadership and organization approach that is centred on the one developed in Chapter 6 seems to be advisable.

In summary, it can be retained that the Information Technology Experts' Professional Culture is a relatively weak example for the second possible situation (current ≠ 'should be', and low perceived efficiency) described in the introduction to this chapter. Nevertheless, the results presented here point to the leadership and organizational solution developed in Chapter 6 as being superior and the most appropriate for the needs of the Information Technology Experts' Professional Culture.

8.4   The Pilots

The Pilots see a very high agreement between the way they think their Professional environment should be and the way they think it is structured. The value of 1.4706 is not only a significant deviation from the overall mean, but also the highest value of all Professional Cultures present in the current sample.

The efficiency perceived by the Pilots of their own Professional Culture is also very high. Here again, the value of 1.5098 not only represents a significant deviation from the overall mean, but is also the highest score out of all Professional Cultures in this study. These two factors taken together strongly support the findings laid out in Chapter 6.

The extremely high agreement between the situation as it is and the one that should be, according to the Pilots, is a strong indicator for the current leadership and organization structures being in agreement with those proposed in Chapter 6.

The also-stated extremely high perceived efficiency indicates that the approach used to lead and organize this Professional Culture leads to highly satisfying results. Hence, the empiricals of the current section indicate that the leadership and organization structures developed in Chapter 6 do indeed represent a superior approach for the current Professional Culture.

In summary, it can be retained that once again the Pilots' Professional Culture produces very clear and unambiguous results. Clearly, Pilots embrace their current situation as being extremely close to the one they wish to have. Furthermore, they consider this situation to be highly efficient. Therefore, the results of the current section strongly support those gained in Chapter 6, which in turn supports the leadership and organizational solution for the needs of the Pilots' Professional Culture proposed in that chapter.

8.5 The Service Providers

The Service Providers' Professional Culture is an example of a Culture that scores both questions in the significantly lower area of the respective scales.

The agreement scale is valued with 4.6552. This value not only shows a significant disagreement between the situation as it is perceived by the Service Providers and the way they consider it to be appropriate to their culture, but it also represents the lowest value in absolute terms of all Professional Cultures sampled. The perceived efficiency scale is also clearly positioned in the negative area. Its score of 3.0345 is not only significantly lower than the overall mean but, furthermore, it is the second lowest value in absolute terms.

Jointly, these results support the findings laid out in Chapter 6, as will be pointed out in the following.

As a consequence of the fact that the statements of the current Professional Culture show considerable differences between the 'should be' situation and the current situation, the support for the results of Chapter 6 is not as clear cut as in the previous section. As pointed out earlier, this is due to the fact that, in connection with the low perceived efficiency, this result only shows that the current structures are apparently sub-optimal.

Nevertheless, considering the empirical evidence depicted in Chapter 6, the strong rejection of the currently prevailing situation and the above given line of argument regarding leadership and organizational structures, the results of the current section strongly indicate that the structures developed in Chapter 6 are advantageous and therefore advisable.

Hence in summary, it can be retained that the current situation is seen extremely negatively and considered to be inefficient by the members of the Innovation and Development Professional Culture. Therefore, the results of the current section clearly strengthen the results gained in Chapter 6 although in a more indirect way than, for example, those of the previous section.

8.6 The Middle Administration

The agreement scale is scored in the neutral area by the members of the Middle Administration. The score of 2.45 is very close to the overall average of 2.4765. Therefore, apparently both similarities and differences exist in comparison to the 'should be' situation.

The perceived efficiency scale is rated in the negative area. The value of 2.55 is significantly lower than the average of 2.35. The significance level itself is a little lower than usual, but at 0.012 well within the significant area. Jointly, these results support the findings of Chapter 6, but only to a very limited degree.

The line of argument is comparable to that in the previous section. Apparently there are differences between the situation as it is and as it 'should be'. As the 'should be' situation is the base for the development of the various leadership and organizational structures, it is assumed that the leadership and organizational structures in use differ from those developed in Chapter 6. This is paired with a relatively low perceived efficiency.

Following the logic of this chapter, the simultaneous occurrence of differences between the proposed leadership and organizational structures on the one hand and low perceived efficiency on the other is an indicator of the superiority of the structures developed in Chapter 6. It has to be remembered, however, that the differences between the 'should be' and the current situation are relatively small. Therefore, the strength of the argument is somewhat limited.

Nevertheless, in connection with, and under due consideration of, the empirical results of Chapter 6, the recommendations will be upheld as to the appropriate leadership and organizational structures for this Professional Culture.

In summary, it can be said that the results of the current Professional Culture are an example of a relatively ambiguous picture of the evaluation of the results of Chapter 6 undertaken here. Despite this ambiguity, the results still, to a certain extent, support the statement that the leadership style and the organization design developed in the previous chapter are an appropriate approach to leading and organizing the members of the Middle Administration culture.

8.7   The Specially Qualified Production Experts

Unfortunately, the ratings given by the Specially Qualified Production Experts are rather unsatisfying in the current context. The scores for both questions do not differ significantly from the respective overall average. They are both positioned well within the neutral band around the respective overall means. The agreement between the current and the 'should be' situation is slightly above average only. The score is 2.3784 in comparison to 2.4765 for the overall mean.

The score for the perceived efficiency is positioned slightly below average. The score is 2.4054 in comparison to 2.35 for the overall mean.

These two factors together lead to a rather ambiguous overall picture.

According to the empirical results, there is some agreement and some disagreement between the current and the 'should be' situation mixed with a relatively moderate perceived efficiency. Therefore, the results in this section do not contradict those gained in Chapter 7, but they do not clearly support them, either. Apparently, there are some significant similarities and some significant differences between the situation as it is and the one preferred by the members of this Professional Culture. As the leadership and organization structures are based on the preferred situation, it may be assumed that those structures also differ only marginally from those actually in use.

In connection with the only moderately efficient work environment for this Professional Culture, it is safe to assume that this situation could be improved. Unfortunately, considering only the results of the current section, it is not clear if that improvement could be carried out with the help of the leadership and organization structures proposed in Chapter 7, or by other structures. Nevertheless, following the clear and unambiguous results depicted in Chapter 7, it still seems to be advantageous to implement the structures developed there.

In summary, it should be noted that the results in this section for the Specially Qualified Production Experts' Professional Culture do not give any further indication concerning the possible superiority of the developed leadership and organizational structures. But neither do they contradict them. Hence, in connection with the high quality of the empirical results of Chapter 7, the suggestion will be upheld that these structures are actually superior to those in current use.

8.8   Innovation and Development

Members of the Innovation and Development Professional Culture rate both questions in the significantly positive area. The agreement scale is scored with a value of 2.3077, significantly higher than the overall mean of 2.4765. However, the significance level is lower than usual with a value of 0.041.

The perceived efficiency scale is statistically significantly above the overall mean with a score of 2.1154. The significance level here is slightly higher than for the agreement scale, approaching, with a value of 0.003, the optimum value of 0.000.

These two results clearly support the findings of Chapter 7.

Following again the above line of argument, it can be stated that the high degree of agreement between the situation as it is and as it should be according to the members of the Innovation and Development Professional Culture leads to the assumption that the prevailing leadership and organization structures are relatively close to those developed in Chapter 7.

Apparently, these structures lead to a high perceived efficiency, which indicates that they are appropriate to the current Professional Cultures. Therefore, the findings of this section clearly strengthen the results gained in Chapter 7 and support the developed leadership and organizational structures.

In summary, it can be retained that the current Professional Culture is another example of the clear and unambiguous support of the results of Chapter 7. In that sense, the Innovation and Development Professional culture is well in line with those cultures of the Pilots and the Flight Attendants.

8.9   The Project Leaders

The score on the agreement scale for the Project Leaders' Professional Culture is located in the neutral band. Its numerical value, of 2.5556, is slightly below the overall average of 2.4765. Therefore, no statistically significant deviation from the overall mean can be stated.

The score for the perceived efficiency scale is located in the negative area. The score of 2.7222 is significantly below the overall average of 2.35.

These values support the findings of Chapter 7, but unfortunately only to a rather limited degree. The neutral to slightly negative rating on the agreement scale shows that there are noticeable differences between the situation as it should be according to the Project Leaders and the situation as it is perceived in reality. Following the above-described line of argument, this indicates that there are indeed differences between the leadership and organizational structures developed in Chapter 7 and those in current use, if only to a limited degree.

Considering now the low perceived efficiency in this group, this indicates that the way this Professional Culture is led and organized has potential for improvement.

Under due consideration of the results gained in this chapter and in Chapter 7, this improvement can apparently be best achieved with the leadership and organization structures depicted in that chapter. The results of the current section are obviously not as unambiguous as those, for example, for the Pilots' Professional Culture, but they nevertheless point to the support of the above-developed leadership style and organizational design.

In summary, it can be retained that the members of the Project Leaders' Professional Culture do see the potential for improvement. Furthermore, they see disparities between the way they consider their professional environment to be optimally structured and the way it actually is structured.

Therefore, the results of the current section do strengthen the findings of Chapter 7 and support the leadership and organizational structures developed therein.

8.10   The Higher Administration

Both scales are rated in the negative area by the members of the Higher Administration Professional Culture. The agreement scale receives a score of 3.3913, which is not only positioned in the significantly negative area, but also the second lowest value of the whole sample in absolute terms.

The perceived effectiveness scale is also located in the negative area. Here again, the value of 3.3043 is not only significantly lower than the overall average of 2.35, but in addition it represents the lowest value of the whole sample in absolute terms.

These results clearly indicate that there are significant differences between the way the Higher Administration expects its professional environment to be structured and the way it actually is structured. In addition they show a significant lack of perceived efficiency.

Following the above-described line of argument, this combination strongly indicates a sub-optimal structure of leadership and organization in the professional environment of the Higher Administration. Joining these results with those of Chapter 7, there is also indication that the leadership and organizational structures developed in that chapter are indeed superior to those in current use.

In summary, it can be retained that the results of the current section clearly support the results of Chapter 7. The extremely negative ratings received by both scales strongly suggest that there is ample room for improvement in the professional environment of the Higher Administration.

Under due consideration of the results of Chapter 7 and the current section, the recommendation to implement these improvements with the use of the leadership and organizational structures developed above is clearly strengthened.

8.11   The Operational Management

The Operational Management Professional Culture rated both scales in the negative area.

The agreement scale was valued at 2.7619. This score is significantly lower than the overall average of 2.4765. Although the significance level itself is slightly lower than usual, it is still well within the significant area with a significance level of 0.001.

The perceived efficiency scale is also located in the negative area with a value of 2.8095. This represents a significant deviation from the overall average of 2.35 and clearly shows that the members of the Operational Management do not perceive their professional environment to be sufficiently efficient.

As before, these results indicate a clear discrepancy between the expectations of the current Professional Culture and the found reality, paired with a relatively low perceived efficiency. Following the usual line of argument, these results indicate that the leadership and organizational structures appear to be less than optimal, which infers significant potential for improvement.

Joining the results of the current section and those of Chapter 7 indicates that the improvements necessary can best be achieved with the leadership and organizational approach depicted in Chapter 7.

In summary, it can be retained that the current Professional Culture is another example for the indirect support of the results of Chapter 7. Despite the fact that a direct support, as depicted in the introduction with 'the first situation', would be preferable, the clarity of the results of the current section unambiguously supports those of Chapter 7. Therefore, the recommendation to implement the approach developed in Chapter 7 is strengthened and consequently upheld.

8.12   The Strategic Management

The picture that evolves when analyzing the data for the Strategic Management's Professional Culture is not as unambiguous as in previous sections. This is due to the fact that only the agreement scale is significantly different from the overall mean, whereas the perceived efficiency scale is located in the neutral area.

The score for the agreement scale is 2.8. This score is significantly lower than the overall mean of 2.4765, clearly indicating significant differences between the professional environment preferred by the members of the Strategic Management's Professional Culture and the one currently experienced by them.

The score for the perceived efficiency though is, with a value of 2.4, only marginally lower than the overall mean of 2.35. Therefore, some potential for improvement seems to exist, but not as unequivocally as in previous sections.

Hence, the results of this section are not as supportive of those of Chapter 7 as in previous sections. Nevertheless, the only moderate efficiency, paired with the clear discrepancy between the situation as it should be and the prevailing one according to the members of the Strategic Management's Professional Culture, indicates that the approach proposed in Chapter 7 is indeed advantageous.

In summary, it can be retained that the need for improvement for the current professional environment exists only to a limited degree. Nevertheless, this need does exist and should be taken care of, considering the extreme importance of the members of the current Professional Culture for their respective organizations. Therefore, the recommendation to implement the leadership and organizational structures developed in Chapter 7 is once again supported and strengthened, and will thus be upheld.

8.13   Closing Remarks

The results of the current chapter all support, to varying degrees, the results of the previous two chapters. Although some Professional Cultures did show a somewhat ambiguous picture, not a single one of them contradicted the different approaches proposed in Chapters 6 and 7.

As already implied, the data available for this chapter are not sufficient to actually prove the possible superiority of the leadership and organizational designs developed in Chapters 6 and 7. Nevertheless, the overall tendency to confirm the different results of Chapters 6 and 7 is definitely encouraging. Therefore, this current chapter is another strong sign for the soundness of the approach chosen in the previous two chapters and its results.

In summary, it can be said that by joining Chapters 6, 7 and the current chapter it is possible to strengthen significantly the results and statements of Chapters 6 and 7. Therefore, the various leadership and organizational approaches developed and depicted in the previous two chapters were all significantly strengthened by the results of the current chapter.

With that logic, this chapter can be seen as a first step in the actual confirmation of the possible superiority of the leadership styles and organizational designs developed in the previous chapters.

To close, an overview of the results of the current chapter will be given in Table 8.1.

Table 8.1   The Numerical Values Regarding Perceived Efficiency and Agreement in an Overview

	The Agreement Scale Mean = 2.4765	The Perceived Efficiency Scale Mean = 2.35
The Blue Collar Workers	2.4=*	2.72↓*
The Flight Attendants	1.6↑*	1.56↑
The IT-Experts	2.85↓	2.5=
The Pilots	1.4706↓**	1.5098↓
The Production Experts	2.3784=	2.4054=
The Project Leaders	2.5556=	2.7222↓
Innovation & Development	2.3077↑	2.1154↑
The Service Providers	4.6552↓**	3.0345↓
The Middle Administration	2.45=	2.55↓
The Higher Administration	3.3913↓	3.3043↓
The OP Management	2.7619↓	2.8095↓
The Strategic Management	2.8↓	2.4=

* (=,↑↓) indicate the respective value is *not* statistically significantly different from the indicated mean (=); statistically significantly *higher* (↑); statistically significantly *lower* (↓)

** values underlined are either the *highest* (**↑) or the *lowest* (**↓) of the respective question

PART 3
The Further Implications

Chapter 9

Summary and Prospects

In this chapter, a final evaluation of the results and their further implications will be given. In order to do that, the developed leadership and organizational structures will first be analysed to check in how far these structures are relevant beyond the boundaries of the current study. This is particularly important as preparation for the further analysis, to be undertaken subsequently, of the relevance of the results from both an academic and practical point of view.

The following two sections will give a joint comprehensive overview of the importance the current study has for academia and practice and will thus put it into a significantly broader context. In addition, indications as to the necessity of further research will be given in order to facilitate future access to the research topic treated in this survey. Hence the role of the current chapter is twofold. On the one hand, it will give final thoughts directly concerning the various insights gained in the course of this study. On the other, it will point out which aspects of the research topic raised need more in-depth research in the future, so as to broaden and deepen these very insights. Consequently, the current chapter is simultaneously closing the present study and creating a bridge to facilitate future research in the area of Professional Culture, in particular, and the concept of cultures in general, as defined previously.

9.1 The Developed Leadership and Organizational Structures: a General Solution? Some Concluding Thoughts

One of the most important questions arising out of this study is whether the leadership and organizational structures developed in the context of the current research project can be generalized beyond the boundaries of the present study. Although this topic could have been treated within the following section in the context of the general relevance of the current study, it was decided to treat this particular topic in a separate section. This decision is a consequence of the centrality of the topic of leadership and organization for both academia and practice.

The main question in this context is whether the characteristics of the aviation industry, on the one hand, and the characteristics of the employees sampled, on the other, are such that the results gathered in this survey are not just a product of these self-same particularities of the aviation industry. These questions have already been raised a number of times throughout the current work. Nevertheless, under due consideration of the results, a final examination will be undertaken, as these results facilitate a more detailed and sound analysis as to the possibility of generalizing the findings of this study.

Therefore, this section will generate some additional insights that are complementary to those already given in previous chapters. In consequence, the present section, in conjunction with previous chapters, will generate a broader picture of the relevance of the leadership and organizational structures developed. In order to facilitate this undertaking, a quick overview of the key results depicted in Chapters 6 and 7 will be given at this point.

- The Blue Collar Workers (see Section 6.1 for details) necessitate a leadership style, which can be subsumed under the term Patriarchal leadership; a leadership style that gives clear guidance and exhibits supportive and protective behaviour towards the employees.

  According to the results portrayed above, the appropriate organizational structure is based on a hierarchical solution in the sense of the Administrative Approach according to Fayol (1984), which supports the Patriarchal leaders in their leadership task and clearly puts them in charge of the decision-taking process within the group; a truly Team-Based organization is not advisable.

- Together with the Pilots, the Flight Attendants exhibit an idiosyncrasy that is a direct consequence of the specific work environment in which they live: the distinction between a micro- and a macro-level of leadership and organization. As can be seen in Section 6.2, the micro-level focuses on the individual cabin crew, whereas the macro-level focuses on the different divisions of a company in which the corps of Flight Attendants is organized. The appropriate leadership style on the micro-level is based on behaviour that emphasizes the following of published rules and procedures in order to provide a maximum level of protection for the individual cabin crew member by sticking to these published rules, so as to create a 'worry-free' work environment. Furthermore, it is necessary for the leader to exhibit a Participative and Human-Oriented leadership style, as a harmonious and conflict-free working environment is also highly important to the members of the current Professional Culture; where applicable Team-Oriented elements should be included.

  Due to the rather limited occasions on which direct leadership is necessary on the macro-level, it is sufficient for the leader to employ a 'Management by Exception Approach' in which the respective leader interacts with the subordinates only in case of arising problems.

  The appropriate organization design is based on Bureaucratic Rule according to Weber (1976), who postulates that the organization should be based on a detailed framework of pre-established written rules and procedures, which replaces direct leadership wherever possible. Only such parts of the work process of the Flight Attendants that are clearly inaccessible to prescribed rules and procedures should be left to direct leadership, such as for example certain parts of the interaction between passengers and crew.

- The Information Technology Experts (see Section 6.3 for details) favour a leadership approach that takes into account both their need for guidance and good interpersonal relationships on the one hand and a need of freedom on the other. Therefore, it is virtually equally based on the Charismatic and the Team-Oriented leadership style. This base should be enriched by a distinct

Human-Orientation of the leaders, in which they exhibit care and concern for their employees in order to create the above-mentioned good interpersonal relationships.

Following the results depicted in Chapter 6, the organizational design favoured has to support the leadership style described and be in line with the characteristics of this Professional Culture. Therefore, independently acting work teams should be created in which the respective leader can implement the above described leadership style; this approach is rooted in the theoretical framework depicted in the context of Complexity Theory.

• Regarding the Pilots (see Section 6.4 for details), an analogous distinction to that of the Flight Attendants, into a micro- and a macro-level, has to be made.

On the micro-level of leadership, which incorporates the Flight Crew, it is advisable for the leader (the Captain) to be focused on the creation of a positive work atmosphere. This relatively limited focus is based on the fact that most aspects of a Pilot's life are governed by pre-established rules and procedures, which renders most parts of direct leadership rather obsolete. Hence, the Captain should pursue a leadership style that is based on Team-Orientation and Participative decision taking. This should be rounded off by the leader's distinct Human-Orientation, in order to facilitate the implementation of the above-mentioned positive work atmosphere.

On the macro-level (higher Pilots' management), this picture changes dramatically. Here, direct leadership loses most of its importance. This is due to the fact that direct and regular interactions between the individual Pilots and their management will often be rather hard to realize, on the one hand, as a consequence of the size of the respective departments. On the other, the need for direct leadership is quite limited, as most parts of the Pilots' work environment can be organized more efficiently by indirect leadership with the help of rules and procedures. The role of the leader is centred mainly on the creation of a viable Vision, which takes the characteristics of this Professional Culture into account. Other aspects of direct leadership lose most of their importance, which is why indirect leadership through organization is of such importance in the current setting.

The appropriate organization design for the current Professional Culture should be based on the Bureaucratic Rule according to Weber (1976). The reason for this is the extremely high acceptance of prescribed rules and procedures within the Pilots' culture, this being a direct consequence of their specific work environment. Hence, maximum use should be made of this possibility in order to integrate efficiently the Pilots' Professional Culture into the organization.

• The Service Providers (see Section 6.5 for details) are governed by collective values and are, in addition, highly consensus driven. Therefore, the appropriate leadership style is centred on these values, relying heavily on Participative and Team-Oriented Leadership. In particular, Participation is of crucial importance, as only a Participative decision-taking process can ensure a maximum degree of acceptance of a decision taken. In addition, a Vision should be developed for the members of the current culture in order to strengthen and support this consensus-driven leadership relationship.

The appropriate organization design has to take these core values into consideration, which leads to Complexity Theory being the organizational approach of choice. The actual implementation should be undertaken with the help of work teams in the form of the Lateral Organization (e.g. Loosely Coupled Systems) or, if possible, even the so-called Virtual Organization, to facilitate a maximum degree of professional freedom and individual participation.

- The Middle Administration Culture (see Section 6.6 for details) represents an example of a culture that necessitates almost no direct leadership at all. Members of this culture rely heavily on indirect leadership. A direct intervention by the leader is only required in case of unsatisfactory results of the employees; 'Management by Exception' is the key approach in these situations.

  The appropriate organization design is based on Bureaucratic Organization according to Weber (1976). This is due to the high appreciation that members of the current culture have for a rules- and regulations-based work environment. Therefore, maximum use should be made of the possibilities of structuring this work environment along pre-established procedures.

- The Specially Qualified Production Experts (see Section 7.1 for details) require a rather demanding leadership style in order to match their expectations of guidance, freedom and perceived importance of themselves for the production process. Consequently, it is necessary for the leader to create a viable Vision, which should be implemented in a Team-Oriented and Participative atmosphere. Team-Orientation and Participation are important mainly in order to increase the acceptance of the Vision and to ensure that a free exchange of ideas and information can take place within the corps of Production Experts.

  The appropriate organization design is based on the theoretical framework of Complexity Theory. Therefore, a maximum degree of freedom should be given by the organization to the respective Production Experts, so as to permit them to lead their departments efficiently. Furthermore, this freedom should also include the possibility of directly tapping into the competencies of other entities; 'Integration through Lateral Organization' is a possible approach to these demands.

- The members of the Innovation and Development Culture (see Section 7.2 for details) favour a leadership style that is focused on the creation and implementation of a compelling Vision. The self-image of the members of the current culture in connection with their objective importance renders both Team-Orientation and Participation highly important for both the actual implementation of this Vision and subsequent day-to-day business. Finally, members of the Innovation and Development culture consider good interpersonal relationships to be highly advantageous. So the leaders have to make sure that they create a work environment that favours the development of such relationships; understanding, care and helpfulness are key words in this context. The appropriate organization design should be based on

Complexity Theory. Hence, independently acting teams that receive as much independency as possible should be created. This will result in a relatively flat hierarchy that values competencies and knowledge; a combination highly important in any innovative process.

- The appropriate leadership style for the Project Leaders (see Section 7.3 for details) revolves around a compelling Vision that clearly demonstrates the importance the Project has for the future success of the company. This Vision should then be implemented by transferring as much decision competency as possible to the respective Project Leaders. Finally, the leader has to strive for good interpersonal relationships with the individual Project Leaders.

  The organizational framework for the integration of the project should be as loose as possible. Once again the theoretical base can be found in Complexity Theory, whereas the actual implementation should be in the logic of 'Loosely Coupled Systems'. This means that the organizational guidance for the individual Project Leaders should be restricted to the setting of an overall goal for the project and subsequent occasional checks regarding the degree of achievement of this goal.

- The Higher Administration Culture (see Section 7.4 for details) is another example of a culture with a very low appreciation of direct leadership. The similarities to the members of the Middle Administration are striking in that aspect. A leader should develop a Vision that shows the importance of the task carried out by the members of the current culture, whilst sticking to a clear 'Management by Exception' approach for actual day-to-day business. Thanks to the high motivation of the Higher Administration to appropriately carry out their work though, such interventions will only rarely be necessary.

  The appropriate organizational design is analogous to that for the Middle Administration. The main difference is that the Bureaucratic Organization retained has to take into account the rather high qualification level of the members of the Higher Administration culture. Therefore, it is necessary to design the organization and its rules and regulations in such a way that enough room is left for the individual members of the Higher Administration culture actually to shape their own decisions without being overly restrained by the underlying Bureaucratic Organization.

- The Operational Management Culture (see Section 7.5 for details) requires a relatively complex leadership approach. On the one hand, members of the Operational Management culture express the need for guidance and 'reason why', which can best be matched with a Charismatic leader. On the other, they expect to be included in the decision-taking process as regards operational decisions, which necessitates Participative leadership elements. In addition, a Team-Oriented work environment is appreciated when the task structure makes it possible. The whole approach needs to be rounded off by a leader who is willing and able to protect the employees against externally induced fears and problems, which implies the need for some Human-Orientated leadership elements.

  The appropriate organizational design is a reflection of these rather complicated leadership requirements. Initially, it is necessary to come to a clear-cut distinction between operational and strategic decisions. On the operational level, the organization should be based on the theoretical framework provided by Complexity Theory, which leads to giving as much decision competency as possible into the hands of the individual Operational Manager. Strategically, however, the need for guidance and 'reason why' clearly supersedes any other aspect, which in turn leads to a clearly hierarchical solution in the sense of the Administrative Approach according to Fayol (1984). For those situations, finally, which are neither clearly operational nor strategic, the organization also has to cater for a joint approach of the leader and the employees.

- The Strategic Management Culture (see Section 7.6 for details), requires a relatively straightforward leadership style. Strategic Managers expect their leader to develop a captivating Vision. The development should be undertaken in a Participative environment, as its subsequent implementation should be, including the following day-to-day business. In addition to the Participative elements, the actual day-to-day business should be dealt with in a highly Team-Oriented atmosphere.

  The appropriate organization design is a reflection of the need expressed by the Strategic Managers for Participation and Team-Orientation. Therefore, Complexity Theory is once again the theoretical approach of choice, leading to an organizational design that shows a very flat hierarchy and strongly Team-Oriented work environment, which takes into consideration all competencies and opinions present in the team. In principle, a consensus driven decision-taking process should be pursued; only in exceptional circumstances should a decision governed by the prevailing opinion of the leader be considered. Therefore, the organizational design should provide for these exceptional circumstances only – the power base necessary for a leader unilaterally to push a decision through.

- The insights gained in the course of the evaluation undertaken of a cross-cultural leadership and organization design (see Section 7.7 for details) showed that every work group composed of more than one Professional Culture needs an individual and, most of the time, a rather demanding leadership style in order to cater for the different and sometimes contradicting demands of the various cultures present in the group.

  Organizationally, these demands imply that it is necessary to provide a structure that is as flexible as possible, and which permits the leader actually to live the appropriate leadership style. The only possible way to achieve that is the implementation of a Complexity Theory based approach, which is the best adapted approach to suit such a demanding environment.

  Finally, the results clearly show that it is not always possible to join two or more Professional Cultures into one integrated work team if the characteristics of these cultures are too different and/or contradictory. This final insight is of key importance, as it demonstrates once again that reorganizing work into Teams at all costs is not the solution of choice.

In the following, these results will be evaluated to determine in how far they may present a general solution beyond the boundaries of the current work.

As demonstrated in Section 1.1, the decision to choose the aviation industry was based on the specific characteristics this industry has to offer. As mentioned in that section, the demands on leadership and organization are rather significant. This in turn leads to problems within the leadership and organizational structures surfacing more clearly than in most other industries. This, again, is a highly advantageous trait for identifying and isolating these problems, and subsequently developing appropriate solutions. It does not, however, hinder the generalizability of the solutions found. This is due to the fact that, in a less demanding environment, the nature of the demands on leadership and organization does not change, but only loses some of the significant importance it exhibits in the current environment. Furthermore, the structure of the aviation industry allows a significant number of different business aspects to be included in this survey, while staying within the boundaries of the industry. As can be seen with reference to the appropriate chapters, these aspects include, for example, manufacturing on various levels, service tasks on both the business-to-business and the business-to-consumer levels, companies of various sizes, and so on.

Thus, the variety of occupations encountered within the aviation industry is such that it encompasses significant portions of any workforce within most other industries. This aspect also supports the generalizability of the results of this study.

Finally, owing to its global nature, the aviation industry also permitted the inclusion of a wide variety of geographically dispersed entities, which further increases the quality of the findings depicted above.

In conclusion, the aviation industry can be considered to be appropriate for achieving the different goals of the current study. In addition, the nature of the aviation industry as described throughout this work shows that it represents a kind of overarching model whose core elements, of which 'composition of work force', and 'appropriate leadership and organizational structures' are a part, is mirrored partially or even in its entirety in other industries. Considering the above-described diversity within the aviation industry, it will only in specific, unusual, situations that another industry will be faced with leadership and organizational demands that were not treated within the current environment.

Furthermore, national and organizational diversity and, consequently, the diversity within the workforce deemed necessary could, as shown throughout the current book, be easily achieved by focusing on the aviation industry. This statement is strengthened by the results as detailed in Chapters 6 and 7.

The diversity of the Professional Cultures observed could not have been achieved if the underlying population had represented only a relatively homogeneous minority of the workforce to be found in business environments in general, and the business environment of the aviation industry in particular. Therefore, this diversity is a clear indication for this study having incorporated significant parts of the professional environment created by the aviation industry.

The Professional Cultures themselves represent a large variety of functions to be found not only within the aviation industry, but in virtually any kind of organization in both the public and private sectors. This indicates, once again, that the results achieved are not restricted to the current industry, but should also be valid in other industries.

It must be left to future research to judge whether the variety of Professional Cultures isolated is indeed exhaustive. Nevertheless, it should be noted here that at least a large part of the Professional Cultures to be found in various business environments, their characteristics and their requirements regarding leadership and organization, is reflected within the current study.

In connection with the demonstrated satisfactory quality of the results gathered in Chapters 6 and 7, this points to the possibility of extending the validity of the developed leadership and organizational structures to other industries. Thus, the main task for future research is twofold.

On the one hand, it is necessary to check the actual superiority of the developed leadership and organizational structures, i.e. if they actually do function as intended. Such a survey would have to go significantly beyond the initial evaluation undertaken in Chapter 8. It would need to include a variety of aspects such as motivational factors on the side of the employees, possible efficiency gains due to the actual implementation of the various structures developed, etc. On the other hand, it is necessary to check whether the results gathered in the context of the aviation industry can be reproduced in other industries.

Despite the fact that it seems rather likely that the developed leadership and organizational structures can be transferred to other industries, it would nevertheless be helpful and highly instructive to base this statement on a broader and more in-depth empirical analysis. Therefore, future research would have to be broadened to include other industries, and deepened within the aviation industry to verify and extend the findings gathered in this work.

Nevertheless, to sum up, it can be retained that the leadership and organizational structures developed in the current study appear to be valid and advantageous in other industries as well. Hence, following the above question of whether the developed leadership and organizational structures may be considered to be a general solution will be answered positively. The main task of future research in the context of leadership and organization regarding Professional Cultures will therefore be the validation or non-validation of the above-given statement.

9.2   The Relevance of the Current Study Considering Academic and Practical Aspects

In the following, the general relevance of the research project undertaken and its results will be treated in more detail, starting with the academic relevance.

The current study is, in a number of ways, important for the academic world, ranging as it does from basic academic research into a new area of knowledge to more practical considerations in leadership and organization theory.

The basic research that was undertaken is of significant relevance, as it broadens and deepens the knowledge base regarding cultures in a professional environment. This is particularly important, as existing research is concentrated on single professions and their traits, without however providing any broader impression of Professional Cultures and their requirements in general. The main problem with this approach is the fact that it cannot cope with the phenomenon encountered here, that Professional Cultures structure themselves along functional lines and not 'job titles'.

Furthermore, it could be demonstrated that, after due adaptation, the research tools developed for the complex of Organizational Cultures can also be employed successfully in research into Professional Cultures. This is particularly important for future research as it demonstrates a relatively economic way of designing and implementing means for research into the complex of Professional Cultures. As previously mentioned, the existing literature already points to this possibility. Nevertheless, the extensive empirical base now existing clearly enhances the viability of this approach, which in turn appreciably facilitates future research.

Another rather important aspect is the introduction of a third cultural construct into the complex of cultures, in addition to those of National and Organizational Culture. This is highly advantageous, as it closes a significant gap in the knowledge base regarding cultures in the workplace. This, in turn, represents an important step forward for leadership and organizational theory and research. This is due to the relevance that cultural research has gained over the past years for the development of leadership and organizational structures. But focusing these cultural influences solely on National and Organizational Cultures leaves a significant number of influencing factors out of the respective research efforts.

As demonstrated, leadership and organizational structures that are not adjusted to the cultural background of the employees concerned are most likely to produce sub-optimal results (e.g. House *et al.* 2004). Hence, it is necessary for academia to develop appropriate leadership and organizational structures, in order fully to grasp the cultural environment to be encountered in the professional world.

To be able to develop these appropriate structures, however, it is equally necessary for academia to have a complete and sound theoretical knowledge base. Therefore, the basic research undertaken with the introduction of Professional Cultures will be highly beneficial for academia in various aspects in the future. It provides a significantly more holistic picture of the processes taking place in the workplace, permitting more appropriate and thus superior research approaches.

In this context, it would also prove to be useful for future research to examine the interrelationships that exist between the constructs of National, Organizational and Professional Culture. It would be highly beneficial to check for the influences that the different constructs have on one another. In particular, the different dynamics that may evolve if the cultural constructs are, for example, highly similar in their orientation and therefore supportive of each other, or highly dissimilar, which would imply conflicts in the individuals' cultural system, etc., would deserve further attention from the academic world.

Beyond these basic considerations, however, the present research project also provides a number of highly interesting insights into the more application-oriented research areas of leadership and organization. According to the empiricals of this study, it is not advisable to develop leadership and organizational structures without taking the respective Professional Cultures into consideration. Therefore an approach that postulates that certain leadership and organizational traits are always and in any setting appropriate cannot be upheld after due consideration of the above results.

One interesting aspect in this context is that the deviations from current mainstream convictions regarding leadership and organization become more pronounced when moving away from the population usually surveyed in leadership and organization research.

The population usually surveyed is located in the upper-middle to upper echelons of the organizations being surveyed. The results of these Professional Cultures are relatively close to those that can be found in existing literature. When moving away from these employees, though, this picture changes dramatically.

As can be seen in Chapters 6 and 7, some Professional Cultures prefer leadership and organizational structures that have not been deemed be appropriate to any professional group for quite some time.

The relatively strict focus on a rather limited portion of the workforce to be found in an organization seems to be at the source of certain convictions such as the quasi 'universally superior nature' of Team-Oriented leadership. From an academic point of view, the verdict that appropriate leadership and organizational structures are apparently highly varying across different professional functions indeed needs to be investigated further in future research.

To sum up, it should therefore be noted here that, as far as academia is concerned, the current research project is of significant importance for both basic research and application-oriented research.

For practitioners, the results themselves are of primary importance. This is because the results can be structured like a manual in order to help leaders in both leadership and organizational matters. As already mentioned, the results can be used in the context of a large variety of different professional decisions, such as personnel selection and training, organization development and change, project management, and so on. Thus, it is of the utmost importance that academia provides practitioners with appropriate solutions in order to permit them to lead and organize their respective entities successfully.

The important point of this aspect is that, despite the fact that the current research project focuses for a significant part on academic basic research, it also provides answers for very practical problems. Therefore, it clearly demonstrates that academia and practice can and should cooperate, as the insights gained are highly beneficial for both of them.

On the one hand, it would have been impossible to gather the data in the necessary quality and quantity without the cooperation of the industry. On the other, the industry will be able to take significant advantage of the various insights gained in the course of this work. Hence, the current study is of significant relevance for both academia and practice. It paves the way for a new and more appropriate approach to cultural research on the one hand and leadership and organization theory, research and practice on the other.

In summary, it can be said that the joining of the construct of Professional Culture with the constructs of National and Organizational Culture will have highly beneficial consequences for all parties concerned, from both academia and practice. Therefore, the relevance of the current study for both academia and practice cannot be overestimated and should lead to this study clearly helping future research in this highly interesting and important field.

9.3   Final Word and Prospects

The current work should have given the reader a multitude of new and, sometimes probably, surprising insights. Indeed, the introduction of a completely new field of knowledge into the academic world and the subsequent use of these results are sometimes of necessity surprising.

Future research in this newly created field of knowledge will be highly beneficial for all parties concerned, due to area's novelty and importance. This is true for both academia and practice. In particular, the complex of cultural research in a business context should gain great benefits from the various insights described above. This is due to the fact that, apparently for the first time, all relevant culturally influencing factors in the work field are being identified. This should in turn lead to sometimes radically different and, in any case, superior results than was possible in the past. The same is true for practitioners. The very specific answers given in this work regarding different Professional Cultures and how to lead and organize them will be of tremendous use when applied to practical challenges.

It is therefore of the utmost importance that future research picks up the work presented here. In particular, the verification of the actual appropriateness of the leadership styles and organization structures developed and the potential to generalize these findings will be highly important for practitioners.

For academia, the pursuit of the topic of Professional Cultures and the possible identification of other Professional Cultures and their characteristics should be a priority. This is especially true, as this basic research will be extremely beneficial to areas such as leadership and organization theory and research in particular, and application-oriented areas of academia in general.

Therefore, the current book depicts highly interesting and important results for the whole academic 'value creation chain', beginning with basic research, including application-oriented research, and reaching as far as the direct application of these results by practitioners. Furthermore, it has opened the door to a highly beneficial new perspective for academia and practitioners, which should provide both with radically new and enhanced perspectives and solutions regarding the complexes treated in this work.

Appendices

Appendix 1. The Link between Leadership and Organization

In the following, a description of the relationship between leadership and organization will be given. In order to reach this goal, a number of aspects have to be considered (Weibler 2001, pp.103ff.).

First, both leadership and organization can be seen as aiming to influence the individual's behaviour in some intended sense. The way this goal is to be reached varies, however, as organizations and their rules are not bound to specific persons, whereas leadership is. This evidently has consequences for the way the influence is exercised.

- Organizations influence individuals prior to a specific situation, whereas leadership is usually exercised in response to a specific situation.
- Organizational influence is targeted not explicitly at persons, but at posts; leadership, on the contrary, is targeted at specific persons and their actions.
- Organizations influence people in a non-personal way through rules and regulations, whereas leadership is, by definition, a personal act.

The main question now is why there is a need for leadership at all, i.e. why a focus on leading individuals solely through the organization is apparently insufficient. The following reasons offer a feasible answer to this question.

An organization coordinates the actions of people without explicitly knowing these people. Therefore, it is not always assured that the place the organization reserves for the individual really suits this individual. Furthermore, it is possible that, at least temporarily, the individual's goals are not in accordance with the organization's goals. Both of these possibilities lead to the need for corrective action of some sort, which is dependent on the situation and the people concerned. Finally, organizations are social entities, which leads to the need to integrate these entities beyond mere technical integration, to give the people a 'reason why' of the organization and for being part of this entire organization.

The relationship between organization and leadership can therefore be seen as follows. On the one hand, organization defines a structured leadership space. This is due to the fact that without at least some sort of organization there is no one to lead and thus no leader. On the other hand, however, organization needs to be explained, put into reality, and changed. Rules and regulations are not always comprehensible per se. Furthermore, the realization of the theoretical construct 'organization' is the task of individuals leading other individuals not only to understand, but also to internalize and live this organization. Depending on the type of organization, as seen above, this also implies that change has to be initiated and implemented by specific people, which is another reason for leadership to be present.

In conclusion, it can be said that leadership and organization are mutually dependent, but are also able to substitute each other to a certain degree. These degrees vary, of course, depending on the organization type present; for example, a hierarchical organization will have a genuinely different distribution of leadership and organization in compared with an organization that resembles the model of Complexity Theory. Nevertheless, it can be stated that leadership without organization is as impossible as organization without leadership.

Appendix 2. Excerpt of the Standardized Questionnaire

Part A (The Core Cultural Dimensions):

1. In order to reach appropriate professional behaviour, orderliness and consistency *should* be stressed, even at the expense of experimentation and innovation.

Strongly agree			Neither agree nor disagree			Strongly disagree
1	2	3	4	5	6	7

2. Members of your profession *should* be encouraged to be:

Aggressive						Non- aggressive
1	2	3	4	5	6	7

3. Members of your profession who are to be successful *should:*

Plan ahead						Take life events as they occur
1	2	3	4	5	6	7

4. In your professional group, a person's influence *should* be based primarily on:

One's ability and contribution to the organization						The authority of one's position
1	2	3	4	5	6	7

Part B (The Demographical Questions):

In the following, 8 general questions are asked. These are used to render the answers of Part A accessible to a useful interpretation. There will be *no* further use to this data

1.   Which part of the industry are you in?

Supplier of components   Producer of 'final'
to the aviation industry   products   Low-cost Airline   Network Airline

2.   Please indicate your ***main*** professional/occupational background (e.g. marketing, technician, buyer). Please avoid general designations such as administration, management, worker and alike. Choose for your statement the occupation you carried out the longest including times spend for education/training. Please be as precise as possible.

3.   How many years did your professional training/education take? If more than one profession acquired please indicate for the one marked in question two.

☐   ☐   ☐   ☐   ☐   ☐

1 year and less 2 years and less 3 years and less 4 years and less 5 years and less more than 5 years

4.   For how many years have you been working in your profession?
         If you worked in more than one profession throughout your
         career please mark the one you indicated in question two.

☐   ☐   ☐   ☐   ☐   ☐

2 years and less 5 years and less 10 years and less 15 years and less 20 years and less more than 20 years

5.   Do you have to fulfil any significant tasks that are beyond the
         boundaries of your profession (e.g. administration, management)?

☐   ☐
Yes   which?   No

6.   In summary, I consider my professional peer group (e.g. my fellow
         engineers in a development department) to be rather efficient.

Strongly   Neither agree nor   Strongly
agree   disagree   disagree

    1   2   3   4   5   6   7

Appendix 3. All the Numerical Results in an Overview

In the following an overview of the numerical values and their relative position towards each other will be given. The superscripts denote:

* Value is located within the 'High' area of that Cultural Dimension
** Value is located in the 'Medium' area of that Cultural Dimension
*** Value is located in the 'Low' area of that Cultural Dimension

	Uncertainty Avoidance 6.45≥High ≥ 4.77 4.77>Medium≥3.11 3.11>Low≥1.43	Assertiveness 5.87≥High≥4.46 4.46>Medium≥3.05 3.05>Low≥1.64	Future Orientation 6.23≥High≥4.67 4.67>Medium≥3.1 3.1>Low≥1.53	Power Distance 4.67≥High≥3.4 3.4>Medium≥2.14 2.14>Low≥0.87	Collectivism 1 6.24≥High≥5.16 5.16>Medium≥4.08 4.08>Low≥3.0
Blue Collar Workers	5.23*	2.07***	4.76*	3.6*	4.27**
Flight Attendants	5.39*	1.99***	1.66***	1.86***	5.82*
IT-Specialists	5.72*	3.98**	5.82*	3.9*	4.62**
Pilots	6.45*	2.14***	4.88*	2.63**	6.24*
Service Providers	2.3***	4.39**	4.6**	4.38*	6.21*
Middle Administration	4.0**	4.17**	4.43**	3.7*	4.43**
Production Experts	4.54**	4.12**	4.92*	3.97*	5.46*
Innovation & Development	3.53**	4.79*	6.22*	4.17*	6.08*
Project Leaders	3.57**	4.5*	5.35*	4.67*	5.5*
Higher Administration	4.32**	4.48*	6.03*	4.35*	5.08**
Operational Management	4.06**	5.87*	4.84*	4.27*	5.56*
Strategic Management	3.63**	4.73*	6.23*	4.02*	5.3*

	Performance Orientation 6.75≥High ≥ 5.5 5.5>Medium≥4.26 4.26>Low≥3.01	Gender Egalitarianism 6.52≥High≥5.45 5.45>Medium≥4.39 4.39>Low≥3.33	Human Orientation 5.59≥High≥4.42 4.42>Medium≥3.25 3.25>Low≥2.08	Collectivism II 6.6≥High≥5.57 5.57>Medium≥4.54 4.54>Low≥3.51
Blue Collar Workers	4.45**	4.72**	4.21**	4.85**
Flight Attendants	3.75***	6.19*	5.5*	4.02***
IT-Specialists	6.0*	5.72*	4.23**	6.0*
Pilots	5.77*	4.14***	2.5***	6.16*
Service Providers	6.32*	6.02*	3.95**	6.23*
Middle Administration	5.12**	5.22**	4.55*	5.34**
Production Experts	6.14*	6.04*	4.03**	6.04*
Innovation & Development	6.41*	6.24*	5.29*	5.46**
Project Leaders	6.39*	5.81*	5.59*	6.06*
Higher Administration	5.03**	6.52*	4.06**	6.2*
Operational Management	6.57*	5.71*	3.78**	5.56**
Strategic Management	6.75*	6.05*	4.07**	6.6*

List of References

Abbott, A. (1991) The order of professionalization. An empirical analysis. *Work and Occupations*, 18(4), pp. 355–384.

Alioth, A. (1995) Selbststeuerungskonzepte. In: A. Kieser, G. Reber and R. Wunderer (Eds), *Handwörterbuch der Führung*, 2nd edn (Stuttgart: Schäffer-Poeschel), column 1894–1902.

American Educational Research Association/American Psychological Association/National Council on Measurement in Education (1999) *Standards for Educational and Psychological Testing* (Washington, DC: American Educational Research Association).

Argyris, C. (1960) *Understanding Organizational Behavior* (London: Tavistock Publications).

Argyris, C. (1964) *Integrating the Individual and the Organization* (New York: Wiley).

Argyris, C. (1976) Single-loop and double-loop models in research on decision making. *Administrative Science Quarterly*, 21(3), pp. 363–377.

Argyris, C. and Schön, D.A. (1978) *Organizational Learning: A Theory of Action Perspective* (Reading, MA: Addison–Wesley).

Ashkanasy, N.M., *et al.* (2002) The anglo cluster: legacy of the British empire. *Journal of World Business*, 37(1), pp. 28–39.

Ashkanasy, N.M., *et al.* (2004) Future orientation. In: R.J. House *et al.* (Eds) *Culture, Leadership, and Organizations. The GLOBE-Study of 62 Societies*, pp. 282–342 (Thousand Oaks: Sage Publications).

Bacher, J. (2002) *Clusteranalyse. Anwendungsorientierte Einführung*, 2nd edn (München, Wien: R. Oldenbourg Verlag).

Bandura, A. (1986) *Social Foundations of Thought and Action: A Social Cognitive Theory* (Englewood Cliffs, NJ: Prentice-Hall).

Barnard, C.I. (1971) *The Functions of the Executive. 30th Anniversary Edition* (Cambridge, MA: Harvard University Press).

Bass, B.M. (1985) *Leadership and Performance Beyond Expectations.* (New York: The Free Press). London: Collier Macmillan Publishers).

Bass, B.M. (1990) *Bass & Stogdill's Handbook of Leadership: Theory, Research, and Managerial Applications*, 3rd edn (New York: The Free Press; London: Collier Macmillan Publishers).

Bass, B.M. and Avolio, B.J. (1993) Transformational leadership: a response to critiques. In: M.M. Chemers and R. Ayman (Eds) *Leadership Theory and Research: Perspectives and Directions*, pp. 49–80 (San Diego: Academic Press).

Bass, B.M., and Steyrer, J. (1995) Transaktionale und transformationale Führung. In: A. Kieser, G. Reber, and R. Wunderer (Eds), *Handwörterbuch der Führung*, 2nd edn (Stuttgart: Schäffer-Poeschel), column 2053–2062.

Berger, U. and Bernhard-Mehlich, I. (1995) Die verhaltenswissenschaftliche

Entscheidungstheorie. In: A. Kieser (Ed.) *Organisationstheorien*, 3rd edn (Stuttgart: Verlag W. Kohlhammer).

Black, T.R. (1999) *Doing Quantitative Research in the Social Sciences. An Integrated Approach to Research Design, Measurement and Statistics* (London : Sage Publications).

Blake, R.R. and Mouton, J.S. (1985) *The Managerial GRID III. The Key to Leadership Excellence* (Houston, Texas: Gulf Publishing Company).

Blank, W., Weitzel, J.R. and Green, S.G. (1990) A test of the situational leadership theory. *Personnel Psychology*, 43(3), pp. 579 – 597.

Bloor, G. and Dawson, P. (1994) Understanding professional culture in organizational context. *Organization Studies*, 15(2), pp. 275–295.

Böhnisch, W. (1991) *Führung und Führungskräftetraining nach dem Vroom/Yetton–Modell* (Stuttgart: C.E. Poeschel Verlag).

Brien, A. (1998) Professional ethics and the culture of trust. *Journal of Business Ethics*, 17(4), pp. 391–409.

Brislin, R.W. (1976) *Translation: Applications and Research* (New York: Wiley).

Brockhoff, K. (1989) *Schnittstellenmanagement, Abstimmungsprobleme zwischen Marketing und Forschung und Entwicklung* (Stuttgart: C.E. Poeschel Verlag).

Bühl, A. and Zöfel, P. (2002) *SPSS 11: Einführung in die moderne Datenanalyse unter Windows*, 8th edn (München: Pearson Studium).

Burns, J.M. (1978) *Leadership* (New York: Harper Colophon Books, Harper & Row).

Carayannis, E.G. and Sagi, J. (2001) Dissecting the professional culture: insights from inside the IT 'black box'. *Technovation*, 21(2), pp. 91–98.

Carl, D., *et al.* (2004) Power distance. In: R.J. House *et al.* (Eds), *Culture, Leadership, and Organizations. The GLOBE-Study of 62 Societies*, pp. 513–563 (Thousand Oaks: Sage Publications).

Cascio, W.F., *et al.* (1991) Statistical implications of six methods of test score use in personnel selection. *Human Performance*, 4(4), pp. 233–264.

Cronbach, L.J. (1990) *Essentials of Psychological Testing*, 5th edn (New York: Harper Collins).

Czarniawska-Joerges, B. (1997) Symbolism and organization studies. In: G. Ortmann *et al.* (Eds), *Theorien der Organisation: die Rückkehr der Gesellschaft*, pp. 360–384 (Opladen: Westdeutscher Verlag).

Daft, R.L. (1989) *Organization Theory and Design* (St. Paul: West Publishing).

Davidson, A.L., *et al.* (2001) Professional cultures and collaborative efforts: a case study of technologists and educators working for change. *The Information Society*, 17, pp. 21–32.

Davis, S.M. and Lawrence, P.R. (1977) *Matrix* (Reading, MA: Addison-Wesley).

Deal, T.E. and Kennedy, A.A. (1982) *Corporate Cultures: The Rites and Rituals of Corporate Life*. (Reading, MA: Addison-Wesley).

den Hartog, D.N. (2004) Assertiveness. In: R.J. House *et al.* (Eds), *Culture, Leadership, and Organizations. The GLOBE-Study of 62 Societies*, pp. 395–436 (Thousand Oaks: Sage Publications).

Deci, E.L. (1975) *Intrinsic Motivation* (New York, London: Plenum Press).

Dingwall, R. (1999) Professions and social order in a global society. *International*

Review of Sociology, 9(1), pp. 131–140.

Dorfman, P.W. *et al.* (2004) Leadership and cultural variation. The identification of culturally endorsed leadership profiles. In: R.J. House *et al.* (Eds), *Culture, Leadership, and Organizations. The GLOBE-Study of 62 Societies*, pp. 669–719 (Thousand Oaks: Sage Publications).

Douglas, M. (1982) *Essays in the Sociology of Perception*. Edited by M. Douglas (London: Routledge & Kegan Paul).

Douglas Caulkins, D. (1999) Is Mary Douglas's grid/group analysis useful for cross–cultural research? *Cross-Cultural Research*, 33(1), pp. 108–128.

Dülfer, E. (1992) Kultur und Organisationskultur. In: E. Frese (Ed.) *Handwörterbuch der Organisation*, 3rd edn (Stuttgart: Poeschel), column 1201–1214.

Emrich, C.G., Denmark, F.L. and den Hartog, D.N. (2004) Cross cultural differences in gender egalitarianism. In: R.J. House *et al.* (Eds), *Culture, Leadership, and Organizations. The GLOBE-Study of 62 Societies*, pp. 343–394 (Thousand Oaks: Sage Publications).

Everitt, B.S. (1993) *Cluster Analysis*, 3rd edn (London: Edward Arnold/Halsted Press).

Facheux, C. (1997) How virtual organizing is transforming management science. *Communication of the ACM*, 40(9), pp. 50–55.

Fahrmeir, L. (1996) *Multivariate statistische Verfahren* (Berlin: de Gruyter).

Fayol, H. (1984) *General and Industrial Management* (New York: IEEE Press).

Fenton-O'Creevy, M. (1995) Empowerment. In: N. Nicholson (Ed.), *The Blackwell Encyclopedia of Management Volume VI: Organizational Behavior*, p. 155 (Blackwell Business).

Fiedler, F.E. (1967) *A Theory of Leadership Effectiveness* (New York: McGraw-Hill).

Field, R.H.G. and House, R.J. (1990) A test of the Vroom–Yetton model using manager and subordinate reports. *Journal of Applied Psychology*, 75(3), pp. 362–366.

Fleishman, E.A. and Quaintance, M.K. (1984) *Taxonomies of Human Performance: The Description of Human Tasks* (Orlando: Academic Press).

Forsyth, P.B. and Daniesiewicz, T.J. (1985) Toward a theory of professionalization. *Work and Occupations*, 12(1), pp. 59–76.

Freeman, J. (1995) Contingency theory. In: N. Nicholson (Ed.), *The Blackwell Encyclopedia of Management Volume VI: Organizational Behavior*, pp. 105–106 (Blackwell Business).

Freidson, E. (1986) *Professional Powers: A Study of the Institutionalization of Formal Knowledge* (Chicago, London: The University of Chicago Press).

Frese, E. (1992) Organisationstheorie. In: E. Frese (Ed.), *Handwörterbuch der Organisation*, 3rd edn (Stuttgart: Poeschel), column 1706–1732.

Gagné, R.M. and Fleishman, E.A. (1959) *Psychology and Human Performance: An Introduction to Psychology* (New York: Holt, Rinehart & Winston).

Gelfand, M.J., *et al.* (2004) Individualism and collectivism. In: R.J. House *et al.* (Eds), *Culture, Leadership, and Organizations. The GLOBE-Study of 62 Societies*, pp. 437–512 (Thousand Oaks: Sage Publications).

Georg, W. (1993) *Von der Berufskultur zur Unternehmenskultur. Arbeitspapiere aus der Berufs- und Wirtschaftspädagogik* (Hagen: Fernuniversität Hagen).

Goldman, S.L., *et al.* (1995) *Agile Competitors and Virtual Organizations: Strategies for Enriching the Customer* (New York: Van Nostrand Reinhold).

Gottschalch, W. (1999) Sozialisation. In: R. Asanger and G. Wenninger (Eds), *Handwörterbuch Psychologie*, pp. 703–707 (Weinheim: Psychologische Verlags Union).

Gulliksen, H. (1987) *Theory of Mental Tests* (Hillsdale, NJ; London: Lawrence Erlbaum Associates).

Gussmann, B. (1988) *Innovationsfördernde Unternehmenskultur: Die Steigerung der Innovationsbereitschaft als Aufgabe der Organisationsentwicklung* (Berlin: Erich Schmidt Verlag & Co.).

Hackman, J.R. and Oldham, G.R. (1975) Development of the job diagnostic survey. *Journal of Applied Psychology*, 60(2), pp. 159–170.

Hackman, J.R. and Oldham, G.R. (1980) *Work Redesign* (Reading, MA: Addison–Wesley).

Hanges, P.J. and Dickson, M.W. (2004) The DEVELOPMENT AND VALIDATION of the GLOBE culture and leadership scales. In: R.J. House *et al.* (Eds), *Culture, Leadership, and Organizations. The GLOBE-Study of 62 Societies*, pp. 122–151 (Thousand Oaks: Sage Publications).

Hanges, P.J., Dickson, M.W. and Sipe, M.T. (2004) Rationale for globe statistical analysis. Societal rankings and test of hypothesis. In: R.J. House *et al.* (Eds), *Culture, Leadership, and Organizations. The GLOBE-Study of 62 Societies*, pp. 219–233 (Thousand Oaks: Sage Publications).

Hardwick, M. and Bolton, R. (1997) The industrial virtual enterprise. *Communication of the ACM*, 40(9), pp. 59–60.

Hartung, J. (2002) *Statistik: Lehr– und Handbuch der angewandten Statistik* (München/Wien: R. Oldenbourg Verlag).

Hersey, P. and Blanchard, K.H. (1977) *Management of Organizational Behavior: Utilizing Human Resources*. 3rd edn (Englewood Cliffs, NJ: Prentice-Hall).

Herzberg, F., *et al.* (1959) *The Motivation to Work* (New York: Wiley).

Hofstede, G. (1980) *Cultures Consequences: International Differences in Work-related Values* (Beverly Hills, CA: Sage Publications).

Hofstede, G. (2001) *Cultures Consequences : Comparing Values, Behaviors, Institutions, and Organizations Across Nations*, 2nd edn (Thousand Oaks: Sage Publications).

Hofstede, G. and Bond, M.H. (1988) The confucius connection: from cultural roots to economic growth. *Organizational Dynamics*, 16(4), pp. 4–21.

Hofstede, G., *et al.* (1990) Measuring organizational cultures: a qualitative and quantitative study across twenty cases. *Administrative Science Quarterly*, 35, pp. 286–316.

House, R.J. and Javidan, M. (2004) Overview of GLOBE. In: R.J. House *et al.* (Eds), *Culture, Leadership, and Organizations. The GLOBE-Study of 62 Societies*, pp. 9–28 (Thousand Oaks: Sage Publications).

House, R.J. and Shamir, B. (1993) Toward the integration of transformational, charismatic, and visionary theories. In: M.M. Chemers and R. Ayman (Eds) *Leadership Theory and Research: Perspectives and Directions*, pp. 81–107 (San

Diego: Academic Press).

House, R.J. and Shamir, B. (1995) Führungstheorien-Charismatische Führung. In: Edited by A. Kieser, G. Reber and R. Wunderer (Eds) *Handwörterbuch der Führung*, 2nd edn (Stuttgart: Schäffer-Poeschel), column 878–897.

House, R.J. *et al.* (1999) Cultural influences on leadership and organizations: Project GLOBE. In: W.H. Mobley *et al.* (Eds), *Advances in Global Leadership*. Volume 1, pp. 171–233 (Stanford, CN: JAI Press).

House, R.J. *et al.* (2004) *Culture, Leadership, and Organizations. The GLOBE-Study of 62 Societies* (Thousand Oaks: Sage Publications).

Hyland, P.W., *et al.* (2001) Occupational clusters as determinants of organisational learning in the product innovation process. *Journal of Workplace Learning*, 13(5), pp. 198–208.

Jago, A.G. (1995a) Führungsforschung/Führung in Nordamerika. In: A. Kieser, G. Reber and R. Wunderer (Eds) *Handwörterbuch der Führung*, 2nd edn (Stuttgart: Schäffer-Poeschel), column 619–637.

Jago, A.G. (1995b) Führungstheorien-Vroom/Yetton-Modell. In: A. Kieser, G. Reber and R. Wunderer (Eds) *Handwörterbuch der Führung*, 2nd edn (Stuttgart: Schäffer-Poeschel), column 1058–1075.

Javidan, M. (2004) Performance orientation In: R.J. House *et al.* (Eds), *Culture, Leadership, and Organizations. The GLOBE-Study of 62 Societies*, pp. 239–281 (Thousand Oaks: Sage Publications).

Jesuino, J.C., *et al.* (2002) Latin Europe cluster: from South to North. *Journal of World Business*, 37(1), pp. 81–89.

Kabasakal, H. and Bodur, M. (2004) Humane orientation in societies, organizations, and leader attributes. In: R.J. House *et al.* (Eds), *Culture, Leadership, and Organizations. The GLOBE-Study of 62 Societies*, pp. 564–601 (Thousand Oaks: Sage Publications).

Keller, E.v. (1989) Comparative management. In: K. Macharzina and M.K. Welge (Eds), *Enzyklopädie der Betriebswirtschaftlehre Volume XII, Handwörterbuch Export und Internationale Unternehmung* (Stuttgart: Schäffer-Poeschel), column 231–241.

Keller, E.v. (1995) Kulturabhängigkeit der Führung. In: A. Kieser, G. Reber and R. Wunderer (Eds) *Handwörterbuch der Führung*, 2nd edn (Stuttgart: Schäffer-Poeschel), column 1397–1406.

Kelly, J. (1995) Scientific management. In: N. Nicholson (Ed.), *The Blackwell Encyclopedia of Management Volume VI: Organizational Behavior*, pp. 505–506 (Blackwell Business).

Kieser, A. (1992) Organisationsstrukturen, historische Entwicklung von. In: E. Frese (Ed.), *Handwörterbuch der Organisation*, 3rd edn (Stuttgart: Poeschel), column 1648–1666.

Kieser, A. (1995a) Managementlehre und Taylorismus. In: A. Kieser (Ed.), *Organisationstheorien*, 2nd edn (Stuttgart: Verlag W. Kohlhammer).

Kieser, A. (1995b) Max Webers Analyse der Bürokratie. In: A. Kieser (Ed.), *Organisationstheorien*, 2nd edn (Stuttgart: Verlag W. Kohlhammer).

Kieser, A. (1995c) Der Situative Ansatz. In: A. Kieser (Ed.), *Organisationstheorien*,

2nd edn (Stuttgart: Verlag W. Kohlhammer).

Kluckhohn, F.R. and Strotbeck, F.L. (1961) *Variations in Value Orientations* (Evanston, IL: Row, Peterson).

Kopalle, P.K. and Lehmann, D.R. (1997) Alpha inflation? The impact of eliminating scale items on Cronbach's alpha. *Organizational Behavior and Human Decision Processes*, 70(3), pp. 189–197.

Kossbiel, H. (1988) Kulturabhängigkeit der Führung. In: H. Jacob (Ed.), *Allgemeine Betriebswirtschaftslehre: Handbuch für Studium und Prüfung*, 5th edn, pp. 1045–1253 (Wiesbaden: Gabler).

Kühnel, S.M. and Krebs, D. (2001) *Statistik für die Sozialwissenschaften: Grundlagen, Methoden, Anwendungen* (Reinbek: Rowohlt Taschenbuch Verlag).

Küpper, W. and Ortmann, G. (1986) Mikropolitik in Organisationen. *Die Betriebswirtschaft*, 46(5), pp. 590–602.

Lamnek, S. (1995a) *Qualitative Sozialforschung, Volume 1, Methodologie*, 3rd edn (Weinheim: Beltz, Psychologische Verlagsunion).

Lamnek, S. (1995b) *Qualitative Sozialforschung, Volume 2, Methoden und Techniken*, 3rd edn (Weinheim: Beltz, Psychologische Verlagsunion).

Larson, M. (1977) *The Rise of Professionalism. A Sociological Analysis* (Berkeley, CA: University of California Press).

Lewin, K. (1948) *Resolving Social Conflicts* (New York: Harper & Row).

Lewin, K., Lippit, R. and White, R.K. (1939) Patterns of aggressive behavior in experimentally created social climates. *Journal of Social Psychology*, 10(2), pp. 271–299.

Lewin, R. and Regine, B. (2000) *Weaving Complexity and Business: Engaging the Soul at Work* (New York, London: Texerre LLC).

Likert, R. (1932) A technique for the measurement of attitudes. *Archives of Psychology*, 140, pp. 1–55.

Likert, R. (1967) *The Human Organization: Its Management Value* (New York: McGraw-Hill).

Lord, R.G. and Maher, K.J. (1991) *Leadership and Information Processing: Linking Perceptions and Performance* (London : Unwin Hyman).

Lowe, S. (2002) The cultural shadows of cross cultural research: images of culture. *Culture and Organization*, 8(1), pp. 21–34.

Luhmann, N. (1973) *Zweckbegriff und Systemrationalität: Über die Funktion von Zwecken in sozialen Systemen* (Tübingen: Suhrkamp).

Lux, E. (1995) Verhaltensgitter der Führung. In: A. Kieser, G. Reber and R. Wunderer (Eds), *Handwörterbuch der Führung*, 2nd edn (Stuttgart: Schäffer-Poeschel), column 2126–2139.

Mann, L. (1969) *Social Psychology* (Sydney: John Wiley & Sons Australasia Ltd).

Manz, C.C. and Sims, H.P. (1995) Selbststeuernde Gruppen, Führung in. In: A. Kieser, G. Reber and R. Wunderer (Eds), *Handwörterbuch der Führung*, 2nd edn (Stuttgart: Schäffer-Poeschel), column 1873–1894.

Manz, C.C. and Sims, H.P. (2001) *The New SuperLeadership. Leading Others to*

Lead Themselves (San Francisco: Berret-Koehler).

March, J.G. and Simon, H.A. (1958) *Organizations* (New York: Wiley).

Mardia, K.V., *et al.* (2003) *Multivariate Analysis* (Amsterdam: Academic Press).

Marr, R. and Hofmann, K. (1992) Rationalisierung. In: E. Frese (Ed.), *Handwörterbuch der Organisation*, 3ʳᵈ edition (Stuttgart: Poeschel), column 2141–2150.

Martin, J. (1995) Organizational culture. In: N. Nicholson (Ed.), *The Blackwell Encyclopedia of Management Volume VI: Organizational Behavior*, pp. 376–382 (Blackwell Business).

Maslow, A.H. (1970) *Motivation and Personality*, 2nd edn (New York: Harper & Row).

Maynard Smith, J. (1976) Evolution and the theory of games. *American Scientist*, 664, pp. 41–45.

McClelland, D.C. (1985) *Human Motivation* (Glenview, IL: Scott, Foresman).

McGregor, D. (1960) *The Human Side of Enterprise* (New York: McGraw-Hill).

Meffert, H. (2000) Marketing. *Grundlagen marktorientierter Unternehmensführung. Konzepte – Instrumente – Praxisbeispiele*, 9th edition (Wiesbaden: Gabler).

Mitchell, T.R. (1982) *People in Organizations: An introduction to Organizational Behavior* (New York: McGraw-Hill).

Morgan, G, *et al.* (1983) Organizational symbolism. In: L.R. Pondy *et al.* (Eds), *Monographs in Organizational Behaviour and Industrial Relations*, pp. 3–35 (Greenwich, CN: JAI Press).

Mowshowitz, A. (1997) Virtual organization. *Communication of the ACM*, 40(9), pp. 30–37.

Murphy, K.R. (1994) Potential effects of banding as a function of test reliability. *Personnel Psychology*, 47, pp. 477–495.

Nachreiner, F. and Müller, G.F. (1995) Verhaltensdimensionen der Führung. In: A. Kieser, G. Reber and R. Wunderer (Eds), *Handwörterbuch der Führung*, 2nd edn (Stuttgart: Schäffer-Poeschel), column 2113–2126.

Nash, J.F. Jr. (1996) *Essays on Game Theory* (Cheltenham, Brookfield: Edgar Elgar)

Neuberger, O. (1995) *Führen und geführt werden, Basistexte Personalwesen*, Volume 3, 5th edn (Stuttgart: Ferdinand Enke Verlag).

Ortmann, G. (1976) *Unternehmensziele als Ideologie. Zur Kritik betriebswirtschaftlicher und organisationstheoretischer Entwürfe einer Theorie der Unternehmungsziele* (Köln: Kiepenheuer und Witsch).

Orton, J.D. and Weick, K.E. (1990) Loosely coupled systems: a reconceptualization. *Academy of Management Review*, 15(2), pp. 203–223.

Ott, W. (1972) *Handbuch der praktischen Marktforschung* (München: Verlag Moderne Industrie Wolfgang Dummer & Co.).

Ouchi, W.G. (1980) Markets, bureaucracies, and clans. *Administrative Science Quarterly*, 25(1), pp. 129–141.

Ouchi, W.G. (1981) *Theory Z: How American Business can meet the Japanese Challenge* (Reading, MA: Addison-Wesley).

Ouchi, W.G. and Jaeger, A.M. (1978) Type Z organization: stability in the midst of mobility. *Academy of Management Review*, 3(2), pp. 305–314.

Peters, T.J. (1993) *Liberation Management. Necessary Disorganization for the*

Nanosecond Nineties (London: Pan Books in association with Macmillan).

Peters, T.J. and Waterman, R.H. (1982) *In Search of Excellence. Lessons from America's Best-Run Companies* (New York: Harper & Row).

Perrow, C. (1984) *Normal Accidents. Living with High-Risk Technologies* (Princeton, NJ: Princeton University Press).

Pfeffer, J. (1981) Management as symbolic action: the action and maintenance of organizational paradigms. In: L.L. Cummings and B.M. Staw (Eds), *Research on Organizational Behavior*, volume 3, pp. 1–52 (Greenwich, CT: JAI-Press).

Preißner, A. and Engel, S. (1997) *Marketing*, 3rd edn (München, Wien: R. Oldenbourg Verlag).

Pugh, D.S. and Hickson, D.J. (1976) *Organizational Structure in its Context: The Ashton Programme I* (Westmead: Saxon House, D.C. Heath Ltd./Lexington Books, D.C. Heath & Co).

Quinn, R.E. (1988) *Beyond Rational Management: Mastering the Paradoxes and Competing Demands of High Performance* (San Francisco: Jossey-Bass).

Raelin, J.A. (1985) *The Clash of Cultures: Managers Managing Professionals* (Boston, MA: Harvard Business School Press).

Reber, G. (1995) Führungsforschung, Inhalte und Methoden. In: A. Kieser, G. Reber and R. Wunderer (Eds), *Handwörterbuch der Führung*, 2nd edn (Stuttgart: Schäffer-Poeschel), column 652–666.

Redding, G. (1995) Culture, national. In: N. Nicholson (Ed.), *The Blackwell Encyclopedia of Management Volume VI: Organizational Behavior*, pp. 125–126 (Blackwell Business).

Reihlen, M. (1999) Moderne, Postmoderne und heterarchische Organisation. In: G. Schreyögg (Ed.), *Organisation und Postmoderne: Grundfragen – Analyse – Perspektiven*, pp. 265–303 (Wiesbaden: Gabler).

Ridder, H.G. (1999) *Personalwirtschaftslehre* (Stuttgart: Kohlhammer).

Robbins, S.P. (1990) *Organization Theory : Structure, Design, and Applications*, 3rd edn (Englewood Cliffs, NJ: Prentice-Hall International).

Roethlisberger, F.J. and Dickson, W.J. (1947) *Management and the Worker. An Account of a Research Program Conducted by the Western Electric Company, Hawthorne Works, Chicago* (Cambridge, MA: Harvard University Press).

Saabeel. W., *et al.* (2002) A model of virtual organisation: a structure and process perspective. *Electronic Journal of Organizational Virtualness*, 4, pp. 1–16.

Saffold, G.S. (1988) Culture traits, strength, and organizational performance: moving beyond 'strong' culture. *Academy of Management Review*, 13(4), pp. 546–558.

Saltstone, R., Skinner, C. and Tremblay, P. (2001) Conditional standard error of measurement and personality scale scores: an investigation of classical test theory estimates with four MMPI scales. *Personality and Individual Differences*, 30(4), pp. 691–698.

Scharf, A. and Schubert, B. (2001) *Marketing: Einführung in Theorie und Praxis*, 3rd edn (Stuttgart: Schäffer-Poeschel Verlag für Wirtschaft, Steuern, Recht GmbH & Co. KG,).

Schein, E.H. (1996) Three cultures of management: the key to organizational learning. *MIT Sloan Management Review*, 38(1), pp. 9–20.

Schein, E.H. (1984) Coming to a new awareness of organizational culture. *Sloan Management Review*, 25(2), pp. 3–16.

Schein, E.H. (1991) The role of the founder in the creation of organizational culture. In: P.J. Frost *et al.* (Eds), *Reframing Organizational Culture*, pp. 14–25 (Newbury Park, CA: Sage Publications).

Schein, E.H. (1992) *Organization Culture and Leadership. A Dynamic View*, 2nd edn (San Francisco, Oxford: Jossey-Bass).

Scherm, E. and Süß, S. (2001) *Internationales Management. Eine funktionale Perspektive* (München: Vahlen).

Schlittgen, R. (2000) *Einführung in die Statistik: Analyse und Modellierung von Daten*, 9th edn (München, Wien: R. Oldenbourg Wissenschaftsverlag GmbH).

Schoonhoven, C.B. (1981) Problems with contingency theory: testing assumptions hidden within the language of contingency 'theory'. *Administrative Science Quarterly*, 26(3), pp. 349–377.

Schreyögg, G. (1992) Organisationskultur. In: E. Frese (Ed.), *Handwörterbuch der Organisation*, 3rd edn (Stuttgart: Poeschel), column 1525–1537.

Schreyögg, G. (1995) Führungstheorien-Situationstheorie. In: A. Kieser, G. Reber and R. Wunderer (Eds), *Handwörterbuch der Führung*, 2nd edn (Stuttgart: Schäffer-Poeschel), column 993–1005.

Schreyögg, G. (1999) *Organisation: Grundlagen moderner Organisationsgestaltung*, 3rd edn (Wiesbaden: Gabler).

Schütz, P. (2003) *Grabenkriege im Management. Wie man Bruchstellen kittet und Abteilungsdenken überwindet* (Frankfurt/Wien: Redline Wirtschaft).

Scott, W.R. (1998) *Organizations: Rational, Natural and Open Systems* (Upper Saddle River, NJ: Prentice-Hall International).

Scott, W.G. and Mitchell, T.R. (1972) *Organization Theory: A Structural and Behavioral Analysis* (Georgetown, Ontario; London: Richard D. Irwin, Inc. and The Dorsey Press).

Seidel, F., Jung, R.H. and Redel, W. (1988) *Führungsstil und Führungsorganisation. Volume 1. Führung, Führungsstil, Erträge der Forschung. Volume 254* (Darmstadt: Wissenschaftliche Buchgesellschaft).

Shao, Y.P., *et al.* (1998) A model of virtual organizations. *Journal of Information Sciences*, 24(5), pp. 305–312.

Sheer, V.C. and Chen, L. (2003) Successful Sino-Western business negotiation: participants' accounts of national and professional cultures. *The Journal of Business Communication*, 40(1), pp. 50–85.

Sonnenstuhl, W.J. and Trice, H.M. (1991) Organizations and types of occupational communities: grid-group analysis in the linkage of organizational and occupational theory. *Research in the Sociology of Organizations*, 9, pp. 295–318.

Sully de Luque, M. and Javidan, M. (2004) *Culture, Leadership, and Organizations. The GLOBE-Study of 62 Societies*. Edited by House, R.J. *et al.*, pp. 602–653 (Thousand Oaks: Sage Publications).

Stacey, R.D. *et al.* (2000) *Complexity and Management: Fad or Radical Challenge to System Thinking?* (London, New York: Routledge).

Szabo, E., *et al.* (2002) The Germanic Europe cluster: where employees have a voice. *Journal of World Business*, 37(1), pp. 55–68.

Taylor, F.W. (1967) *The Principles of Scientific Management* (New York: The Norton Library).

Tannenbaum, R. and Schmidt, W.H. (1958) How to choose a leadership pattern. *Harvard Business Review*, 36(2), pp. 95–101.

Thom, N. (1992) Organisationsentwicklung. In: E. Frese (Ed.), *Handwörterbuch der Organisation*, 3rd edn (Stuttgart: Poeschel), column 1477–1491.

Thomae, H. (1999) Motivation. In: R. Asanger and G. Wenninger (Eds), *Handwörterbuch Psychologie*, pp. 463–497 (Weinheim: Psychologische Verlags Union).

Trice, H.M. (1993) *Occupational Subcultures in the Workplace*. Cornell Studies in Industrial and Labor Relations (Ithaca, NY: ILR Press).

Trice, H.M. and Beyer, J.M. (1984) Studying organizational cultures through rites and ceremonials. *Academy of Management Review*, 9(4), pp. 653–669.

Ulijn, J., *et al.* (2001) The impact of national, corporate and professional cultures on innovation: German and Dutch firms compared. *Journal of Enterprising Culture*, 9(1), pp. 21–52.

Ulrich, P. (1984) Systemsteuerung und Kulturentwicklung. Auf der Suche nach dem ganzheitlichen Paradigma der Managementlehre. *Die Unternehmung*, 38(4), pp. 303–325.

Vahs, D. (2001) *Organisation: Einführung in die Organisationstheorie und -praxis*, 3rd edn (Stuttgart: Schäffer-Poeschel Verlag).Van Maanen, J. and Barley, S.R. (1984) Occupational communities: culture and control in organizations. *Research in Organizational Behavior*, 6, pp. 287–365.

van Maanen, J. and Barley, S.R. (1984) Occupational communities: culture and control in organizations. *Research in Organizational Behavior*, 6, pp. 287–365.

van Teijlingen, E.R. and Hundley, V. (2001) The importance of pilot studies. *Social Research Update*, 35 (Winter).

Venkatraman, N. and Henderson, J.C. (1998) Real strategies for virtual organizing. *Sloan Management Review*, 40(1), pp. 33–48.

Vroom, V.H. and Jago, A.G. (1988) *The New Leadership: Managing Participation in Organizations* (Englewood Cliffs, NJ: Prentice-Hall).

Vroom, V.H. and Yetton, P.W. (1973) *Leadership and Decision-Making* (Pittsburgh: University of Pittsburgh Press).

Völker, U. (1980) Grundlagen der humanistischen Psychologie. In: U. Völker (Eds), *Humanistische Psychologie: Ansätze einer lebensnahen Wissenschaft vom Menschen*, pp. 13–37 (Weinheim, Basel: Beltz Verlag).

Walter-Busch, E. (1991) Entwicklung von Leitmotiven verhaltensorientierten Managementwissens. *Managementforschung*, 1, pp. 347–399.

Weber, M. (1976) *Wirtschaft und Gesellschaft: Grundriß der verstehenden Soziologie*, 5th rev. edn (Tübingen: J.C.B. Mohr (Paul Siebeck)).

Weibler, J. (2001) *Personalführung* (München: Verlag Franz Vahlen).

Weibler, J. (1997a) Unternehmenssteuerung durch charismatische Führungspersönlichkeiten? Anmerkungen zur gegenwärtigen Transformationsdebatte. *Zeitschrift Führung + Organisation*, 66(1), pp. 27–32.

Weibler, J. (1997b) *Vertrauen und Führung. In: Personal als Strategie: Mit flexiblen und lernbereiten Human-Ressourcen Kernkompetenzen aufbauen.* Edited by R. Klimecki and A. Remer, pp. 185–214 (Neuwied: Hermann Luchterhand Verlag GmbH).

Weik, E. and Lang, R. (1999) Postmoderne Organisationen oder 'The Trouble with Harry'. In: G. Schreyögg (Ed.), *Organisation und Postmoderne. Grundfragen-Analysen-Perspektiven*, pp. 305–331 (Wiesbaden: Gabler).

Wiener, Y. (1988) Forms of value systems: a focus on organizational effectiveness and cultural change and maintenance. *Academy of Management Review*, 13(4), pp. 534–545.

Wright, S. (1940) Breeding strucuture of populations in relation to speciation. *The American Naturalist*, 74, pp. 232–248.

Wunderer, R. (1992) Vom Autor zum Herausgeber? – Vom Dirigenten zum Impresario – Unternehmensführung und Unternehmenskultur im Wandel. In: F.P. Ingold and W. Wunderlich (Eds), *Fragen nach dem Autor. Positionen und Perspektiven*, pp. 223–236 (Konstanz: Universitätsverlag Konstanz).

Wunderer, R. (2001) *Führung und Zusammenarbeit: eine unternehmerische Führungslehre*, 4th edn (Neuwied-Kriftel: Hermann Luchterhand Verlag).

Yukl, G. (2002) *Leadership in Organizations*, 5th edn (Upper Saddle River, NJ: Prentice-Hall).

Index

Note: Bold page numbers indicate tables & figures; Numbers in brackets preceded by *n* refer to footnotes.